Land, Credit and Crisis

Agrarian Finance in the Hebrew Bible

Philippe Guillaume

Routledge
Taylor & Francis Group
LONDON AND NEW YORK

First Published 2012 by Equinox Publishing Ltd, an imprint of Acumen

Published 2014 by Routledge
2 Park Square, Milton Park, Abingdon, Oxon OX14 4RN
711 Third Avenue, New York, NY 10017, USA

Routledge is an imprint of the Taylor & Francis Group, an informa business

ISBN: 978-1-84553-927-6 (hardcover)
ISBN: 978-1-84553-928-3 (paperback)

British Library Cataloguing-in-Publication Data

A catalogue record for this book is available from the British Library

Library of Congress Cataloging-in-Publication Data

Guillaume, Philippe.
Land, credit and crisis: agrarian finance in the Hebrew Bible/
Philippe Guillaume.
p. cm.—(BibleWorld)
Includes bibliographical references and index.
ISBN 978-1-84553-927-6 (hb)
1. Economics in the Bible. 2. Finance—Biblical teaching. 3. Sabbatical year (Judaism) 4. Jubilee (Judaism) 5. Money—Biblical teaching. 6. Interest rates—Biblical teaching. 7. Land tenure—Biblical teaching. 8. Bible. O.T.—Criticism, interpretation, etc. I. Title. BS1199.E35G85 2011
221.8'33813—dc22

2010042254

Typeset by S.J.I. Services, New Delhi

Land, Credit and Crisis

BibleWorld

Series Editors: Philip R. Davies and James G. Crossley, University of Sheffield

BibleWorld shares the fruits of modern (and postmodern) biblical scholarship not only among practitioners and students, but also with anyone interested in what academic study of the Bible means in the twenty-first century. It explores our ever-increasing knowledge and understanding of the social world that produced the biblical texts, but also analyses aspects of the Bible's role in the history of our civilization and the many perspectives—not just religious and theological, but also cultural, political and aesthetic—which drive modern biblical scholarship.

Contents

Part III – No Crisis in Yehud

Illustrations

Figures

Tables

Acknowledgements

This book develops ideas that came to light while working on a volume on the Priestly Document published as *Land and Calendar* (Guillaume 2009). The present project has benefited from the generous support of a visiting fellowship at the Department of Biblical Studies of the University of Sheffield granted by the British Academy (VF 2008/49088). I thank these institutions as well as Professor Diana Edelman at Sheffield and Professor Ernst Axel Knauf in Berne for sharing their expertise in the biblical, archaeological and historical fields. I also owe a debt of gratitude to Georges Mills. The credit simulation in Chapter 5 is based on his long experience in investment and development in the Third World. He has also polished and tightened my style. Thanks are also due to the Equinox team, Philip Davies, Valerie Hall, the copyeditors and the other persons who produced this volume.

Introduction

This volume seeks to render biblical exegetes more familiar with ancient farming and its techniques by integrating some of the growing body of knowledge derived from economic studies of ancient Mesopotamia and Egypt. As a body of literature written by scribes who grew most of the food they ate, the Hebrew Bible presupposes a world that is beyond the immediate reach of academics who live in affluent post-industrial urban settings where hunger is absent and the relation between work and food is entirely mediated through money.

For the last few decades, social-scientist exegetes have led the way in reaching behind the biblical text and the results are impressive. Combining insights from archaeology, sociology and anthropology has greatly sharpened our figuration of actual conditions in ancient Canaan and provided a wider perspective against which the biblical texts can be read. Yet, social-scientific exegesis seems to me bogged down by the repetition of a number of slogans. Ingrained ideological reflexes elevate untested assumptions to the rank of evidence. Particularly problematic is land ownership, often considered as the prerequisite to freedom, freedom as the prerequisite to abundance, abundance as the proof that the 'rich' are oppressing the 'poor', and loans as the first step towards slavery (see §4.5 for other slogans). The present study challenges some slogans in the hope to give a new impulse to the study of farming in ancient Palestine. Read in light of what we know about ancient land tenure and credit systems, famous stories such as Ahab's grab of Nabal's vineyard, Ruth's securing of Elimelech's 'field', Job's dealings with his business partners and the practical measures imposed by Nehemiah take on quite another meaning. Unfortunately, it was too late to benefit from the input of Michael Jursa (ed.), *Aspects of the Economic History of Babylonia in the First Millennium* BC (Münster: Ugarit Verlag, 2010).

Why Land and Credit?

Having land without the farmers to work it is useless. Holding the right to raise tribute without the army to enforce it is fictitious (Briant 1978: 7). As long as there is no massive introduction of machinery in agriculture, manpower is more important than land (Boserup 1970). Upon the ability to mobilize manpower (men, women and children) hung the survival of the elite as much as that of the rank and file. The troop was the prerequisite for ruling but the ability to rule also required an army of farmers to feed the troops. In many ways, the Bible deals more with farmers than with soldiers, thus reflecting the fundament of any economy: the means of production. Hence, biblical exegetes correctly infer that arable land constituted the primary means of production in ancient Israel, but they tend to take manpower for granted.

Land was plentiful, especially in the province of Yehud which had lost over half of the population it had in previous centuries. It is farmers that were in scarce supply since there were no machines to replace manpower. Hence, power did not derive from land ownership but from the ability to mobilize farmers and to extract agricultural surplus. To this aim, credit was and still is crucial as a means of financing investment to raise production levels as well as consumption smoothing to keep the farmers alive in times of famine. In the Bible, however, credit is encountered mostly in prophetic accusations of the merchant's false scales and of his rapacity. Usury is considered the source of economic evils, with disastrous consequences for the understanding of many biblical texts.

Why Crisis?

The notion of crisis is popular among exegetes who find it hard to resist the prophetic tone of many biblical texts relative to economic relations. Biblical texts are often understood as written in reaction to particular crises. The mother of all crises is the destruction of Jerusalem in 586 BCE, a crisis that would have spurred the first version of the so-called Deuteronomistic History. Paradoxically, the rise of a new elite is seen as a crisis as much as its deportation. The consolidation of the monarchy in the eighth century BCE is viewed as a critical development that set off prophetic reactions denouncing the abuses of the elite, especially in Samaria. A similar process is postulated in the Persian period when Nehemiah is presented as dealing with a major economic crisis. Hence, a central tenet of social-scientific exegesis is that the rise of the Israelite and Judean kingdoms and their replacement by the Assyrian, Babylonian and Persian empires imposed an unbearable burden of taxes, corvée and loans against high interest that led to debt slavery and the consolidation of latifundia. In turn, the economic hardship would have fed a literary reaction in the form of calls for justice. This volume challenges the use of the concept of crisis in biblical exegesis.

The Structure of the Book

Land, Credit and Crisis is made up of three parts, dealing with each term of the title in order. Part I discusses the distortions deriving from the application of modern concepts of land ownership. Informed by Islamic and Ottoman land categories, biblical evidence for communal land tenure is recovered from Micah, Jeremiah, the Psalms, Ruth and Joshua. Then, a number of slogans relative to land and credit are debunked and the results applied to relevant biblical texts.

Part II challenges the notion of usury and reveals the importance of credit and patronage. Relevant biblical passages are revisited and new insights gained in particular from the books of Ruth and Job.

Part III sets the main biblical regulations relative to credit (*šemiṭṭah,* jubilee and the ban on charging interest) in the context of the history of Persian Yehud. These measures reflect common economic sense rather than the existence of an economic crisis.

A glossary of unfamiliar technical terms is compiled at the end.

Method

Biblical studies suffer from a lack of new data. To avoid repeating *ad nauseam* the same ideas, archaeological excavations of biblical lands, one of the most intensively dug areas of the world, bring some fresh grist to the academic mill. Another source of data is the historical sources of more recent periods. The Palestinian highlands belong to a coherent ecological ensemble exhibiting striking similarities across the 7,000 km of highlands between 500 and 1,000 metres that form a belt around the Mediterranean Sea with similar climates and soils (Braudel 1972). Since this belt constitutes one of the best known areas of the ancient world, there is no dearth of sources. The abundance of sources poses the problem of their relevance.

Are Ottoman practices relevant to the study of Persian Yehud? Twentieth-century historiography was based on two basic postulates:

the uniqueness of each nation and the radical otherness of the past (Baldwin 2004: 6–7). In biblical historiography, the uniqueness of the nation translated into isolating Israel from its Canaanite environment. In spite of multifarious connections revealed by archaeological and historical discoveries, popular histories of Israel of the twentieth century uncritically adopted the ideologies of the biblical writers and presupposed 'at the very centre of the history of Israel phenomena for which there is no parallel at all elsewhere' (Noth 1958: 2–3). The radical otherness of Israel resulted in the failure to access Ottoman and Islamic records that provide a wealth of relevant data because they come from similar regions to the Bible and from economies that experienced similar climatic conditions.

The standard work on ancient Israelite agriculture assumes that things did not change much since the Iron Age (Borowski 2002: xxi). True enough in regard to climatic conditions, this assumption becomes problematic when it is used to ignore Islamic sources completely and to envisage modern Israeli conditions as more relevant to the study of Iron Age agriculture than those from the Ottoman period.

Although Islamic sources pertain to later periods, they are more relevant to biblical Israel than modern comparisons because they reflect pre-industrial revolution conditions. Roman, Byzantine and Islamic authors wrote agricultural treatises, and Ottoman sources provide a wealth of information relevant to the study of biblical agriculture. Because the reforms of the Tanzimat era were inspired by European models (Hanioğlu 2008: 72–108), pre-Tanzimat land tenure systems are bound to be more relevant to the study of agriculture in ancient Israel than post-feudal European conditions.

The introduction of machinery and the demographic explosion of the last centuries have totally altered rural life and farming conditions. This does not imply an acceptance of the Orientalist dogma of the passive and immutable Orient. Changes did take place in Palestine between the Persian and the Ottoman eras. Yet, the sum of the changes that took place during these two millennia is no greater than that of the last two centuries. Agriculture, more than any other human activity, is subject to geographic and climatic conditions, the two pillars of the *longue durée*. The arrival of the diesel engine greatly reduced the influence of climate and allowed major modifications to topography. Dams and pumps irrigate areas that depended solely on rain. Roads are cut and trucks carry tons of goods over great distances. Within a century, the almost static *longue durée* has experienced changes as never before. Therefore, the tendency to ignore Islamic and Ottoman sources must be overcome to gain fresh insights into biblical farming. The *longue durée* rather than any Oriental sloth justifies the claim that the world of Islam, including the pre-Tanzimat Ottoman Empire, are more relevant to the study of ancient Israel than modern agriculture.

I purposely use the term 'Levant' to describe a coherent climatic and cultural entity bordering the eastern shores of the Mediterranean. Despite the imperialist connotations of Orientalism and the rightful denunciations it has attracted, the Levant has the advantage of being broad enough to set the narrow compass of Palestine in its larger context that precludes attributing to Israel any inherent specificity. Islam used the same category, *al-Mashreq*, for centuries before European Orientalists did. Therefore, I see no need to coin a new word. The Mashreq serves as a self-definition as much as a convenient differentiation from the other side of the Mediterranean (Foucault 1972).

Readers will rightly object to the heterogeneity of the chosen universe. Surely the *longue durée* is not enough to establish the validity of comparisons drawn from Assyrian, Hellenistic and Islamic sources. The Ottoman Empire itself presents a great variation of conditions relative to state control, commerce and agriculture, in particular in a fringe area such as Palestine. Hence, this book is more a compote than a careful composition where every feature is positively correlated. I leave this task to better qualified others. At this time, the situation calls for radical thought. In the face of the tremendous levels of wealth generated by the global economy and of the undernourished billion of our contemporaries, the details into which scholarly discussions get bogged down are unable to challenge the social-scientific slogans that prevail in the exegesis of the Hebrew Scriptures.

Part I

Land

Chapter 1

LAND TENURE

1.1 Vines, Figs Trees and Their Possessors

In Zech. 3:10, the angel of the Lord assures Joshua that the guilt of the land will be removed in a single day. As a consequence, the inhabitants will invite each other under 'your vine and fig tree' as the NRSV translates it. In fact, the Hebrew has no possessive pronouns (אל תחת גפן ואל תחת תאנה) but translators add them because relaxing under any old fig tree does not seem good enough a blessing. The idea that the return of divine favour entails the restoration of private property is supported by the bucolic description of life on the farm during the golden age of Solomon's reign where the same expression is used (איש תחת גפנו ותחת תאנתו) with the possessive pronouns (1 Kgs 5:5 [Eng. 4:25]; Mic. 4:4). Yet, the absence of these pronouns in Zechariah suggests that the focus is more on the act of enjoying the shade of the trees than on owning them. Ownership implies property, but what is property?

1.1.1 Property

Everyday speech uses the term 'property' to designate the object that is owned. Most commentaries of Zech. 3:10 infer that the people will invite each other under their *own* trees (Sweeney 2000: 603-604; Smith 1984: 202; Redditt 1995: 66). Yet, correctly speaking, property denotes a *relationship*, not an object. The term 'property' is an 'abbreviated reference to a quantum of socially permissible power exercised in respect of a socially valued resource' (Gray and Gray 1998: 15). The confusion between the right of ownership and its object is already found in Islamic legal tradition which states that ownership is not a right (*ḥaqq*) but a piece of property (*māl*). The identification of a property with a material thing brought the question whether land tenure could be considered as property owned (Delcambre 1993: 60). This question never arises in the Bible. There, landholding, land tenure and right of use are clearly distinguished from land ownership. In Deuteronomistic texts, landholding is based on the notion of grant predicated upon the strict observation of the terms of the grant. The notion of grant excludes 'private' property in the modern sense of the term. Land is possessed conditionally but never owned. As long as they observe the commandments, the children of Israel enjoy vines and olive trees they did not plant (Deut. 6:11; Josh. 24:13). Conversely, the punishment for the non-observance of the commands is to build a house and plant a vineyard that others will enjoy (Amos 5.11; Zeph. 1:13).

In Priestly texts, the sole owner of the land of Canaan is God. The children of Israel are tenants (Lev. 25). The common designation of the land of Canaan as *Eretz-Israel* has no backing in the Torah. The formula does not appear before 1 Sam. 13:9 (Leibowitz 1995: 161). Canaan is indeed designated as 'your land' in Exod. 23:10; 23:26, 33, but possessive pronouns express one's hold and cannot dismiss the conditionality of that hold. Drinking the wine from the vines one has planted is presented in Isa. 65:21-22 and Amos 9:14 as a promise to be fulfilled in eschatological times. Such a promise would make no sense if the norm were ownership rights sanctioned by the full legal apparatus of a modern state.

Even in modern parlance, the notion of ownership is too narrow to cover the entire gamut of rights over land. While a host retains full control of his property, his guest is not a trespasser as long as he respects the courtesies of social intercourse. Lodgers, tenants, leaseholders and freeholders enjoy increasing levels of property. A neighbour may have a claim over someone's property in the form of a right of way. After a number of years, even squatters gain some rights over a property. Property confers a bundle of rights and obligations where the domain of the state and the domain of the individual are in tension. Private property never remains entirely private and property in land is infected with extensive public law significance (Gray and Gray 1998: 51). The distinction between possession and ownership is therefore crucial.

1.1.2 Ownership and Possession

In the Bible in general, one of the dangers facing the children of Israel is to behave as the owners of the land of Canaan once they reside in it. Israel's relation to Canaan is expressed in terms of possession rather than in terms of ownership. In fact, yearnings of ownership threaten possession. Notions of land allocation or possession are preferable (Boer 2007: 40).

Yet, because in the modern world land ownership is a source of power, biblical exegetes tend to miss the distinction between ownership and possession. When applied to ancient economies, the notion of private ownership of land is 'useless, confusing and harmful' (Steinkeller 2004: 93) because, unlike the modern situation, land in the ancient world had little or no value, because it was over-plentiful. This is true for ancient Sumer as much as for medieval Europe (Bloch 1961: 115; Cripps 2007: 5-6). Yet, one should not fall into the opposite pitfall and deny the existence of private property in the so-called Asiatic Mode of production (Mandel 1971: 116-39). The study of ancient economics, and by consequence the exegesis of many biblical texts, has been vitiated by the debate between Marxist and liberal models. Neither model is relevant to the ancient world. Both reflect the difficulty for Europeans to understand a world that did not fit European models ('Abbas Hamid 2002: 37-49).

Although possessors of assets tend to behave as owners, possession is not ownership. Buyers of real estate may be surprised to discover that in fact they do not own land. Only holders of allodial titles own land absolutely. In common law lands such as England and Wales, no subject can own the land upon which he lives or runs his business. The crown grants the use of the land (MacKenzie and Phillips 2006: 4; Baker 1990). But even under civil law that seems to grant a firmer hold, ownership is limited by governmental powers of taxation, eminent domain, police power and escheat. A number of encumbrances restrict the freedom of owners: aviation and mining easements, right-of-way, gleaning and hunting rights and municipal regulations concerning the height and the distance of buildings relative to other properties. These limitations affect ownership under common law as much as under civil, customary and religious systems of law.

Whereas possession involves physical occupation and requires no title, ownership may be asserted without possession. Ownership is best regulated by titles based on topographical surveys, mapping, and cadastral registers. These complicated operations did not exist before the end of the nineteenth century CE (Pottage 1998). Even in the modern world, ownership is a legal right on which the practical applications are not always clear (Baker 1990: 255). When discussing ancient farming, it is crucial not to confuse ownership and possession. Someone may hold rights of disposition over some land or land-shares without ever setting foot in it or contributing any work to make it fructify. On the other hand, possession entails the right of disposition of the fruit or benefits of a particular parcel, building or tree. Hence, the presence or absence of a possessive pronoun is irrelevant to possession. It does not matter who is the legal owner of the fig tree or the land in which it is planted. What matters is to enjoy its shade and its fruit.

Many rights of use can be superposed or juxtaposed over the track of land where a fig tree is planted. Next to the farmer who, for all practical purposes, behaves as the owner of land around the fig tree because he has often ploughed it and because his son is likely to continue to do so, the local community may consider itself as the trustee of the same land. Should the farmer mortgage his land to secure a loan, the creditor acquires a hold over the mortgaged land. The king may grant the entire region to one of his officers and that officeholder will claim some of the figs as taxes. Bedouin may raid the area and steal the figs or they may demand something to 'protect' the figs from the exactions of other tribes. Or the fig tree was planted on someone else's land with a contract stipulating that the one who planted it only owned a share of the figs. In that case, neither the tree not the land on which it is planted belongs to the planter. Or the owner of the tree may hire someone to pick or transport the figs to his farm. In this case, wages lay an indirect claim to the value of the figs by someone who owns neither the land, the tree nor the figs. Had the fig picker himself been bought, his master may lay claims over the slave's revenues. Eventually, one's hold over anything is only temporary since another owns the breath of life and will claim it back without fail (Qoh. 8:8). The superposition of levels of hold over a particular piece of land was and remains the norm. Nowhere is this clearer than in the modern state of Israel that appropriated 93% of the land it controls by buying or extinguishing the communal rights of the Palestinians and of the Bedouin (Home 2003).

In the ancient Orient, as in most places today, farmers cultivate land they mostly do not own. Transfers pertaining to land concern rights derived from use rather than from the ownership (Menu 1998b). In the operative section of Aramaic conveyance documents, the part of the document that describes the legal change that takes place as a consequence of the transaction, the transfer is expressed with a variety of verbs: רשי, שלט or חסן all conveying notions of authority, power, control or claim over something (Cussini 1992: 46).[1] The expression 'it is yours' (זילך הו) and the Akkadian expression *amtum amassu*, 'she is her own slave woman', next to the object of sale do convey some sense of ownership (Gross 2008: 92-99). The distinction between ownership and use, however, was not clearly stated. Akkadian *šalāṭu* is always used negatively to sever ownership, usually of pledges, while Aramaic שליט is used in both positive and negative phrases (Muffs 1969: 41; Gropp 1993: 31-36; Dušek 2007: 76; Gross 2008: 110-12; Seow 2008: 189-217). Very much like their modern counterparts, sellers transferred whatever rights they held to buyers, but no transaction ever transfers universal rights of ownership (Botta 2006; 2008).

More surprising, alienation of land did not deprive sellers of some residual claims of ownership. The permanent alienation of land is a recent phenomenon that was achieved after several centuries of struggle between modern states and very ancient customary practices to individualize tenure and to clarify tax liability. Ancient tenure systems are still alive in Africa and they are well documented in the Ottoman Empire and in eighteenth century CE China. Transactions in land were characterized by unlimited redemption rights, conditional sales that enabled sellers to keep claiming extra payments whenever the value of land increased, multiple ownerships, and the differentiation between topsoil rights rented to tenants and subsoil rights retained by the owners (Macauley 2001). This cursory reminder of legal categories suggests that much of exegetical literature relative to land is inadequate because it assumes ownership from possession and confuses property with an object.

1.2 When Theologians Write about Biblical Farmers

Although the English-speaking world is the domain of common law, Anglo-Saxon biblical exegesis is deeply marked by the Roman notion of ownership. Roman *dominium* entails less relativity of title than does common law. It grants a firmer hold to owners over their property. The jural aspect of classical *dominium* took political connotations during the Renaissance when it evolved into a mystical idea connoting complete and unchallenged domination and control of the land as a polemic against feudal systems.

> An allodial ownership system was propounded in order to cut the link between wealth and socio-political power; allodial ownership requires that owners buy the labour power of workers in labour markets, rather than command the workforce to farm the landlords' demesne as an incident of tenure. Thus Roman ownership ideas were claimed as a liberating ideology favourable to capitalism and hostile to feudalism. (Getzler 1998: 82-83)

In their struggle against feudalism, the rising nation states crafted the fiction of an absolute *dominium* remotely linked to the Roman notion. Civil law sought to render the relation between owners horizontal by reducing the significance of the feudal overlord that rendered vertical the relation between owners under common law. Then, classical liberalism regarded private property in land as an essential instrument for promoting political freedom, turning the fiction of absolute *dominium* into the dogma of private property. Private ownership was presented as the solution to overcome economic stagnation attributed to the stifling of individual initiative in economic activity subsumed under the vague notion of Oriental Despotism (İslamoğlu 2001: 370).

Yet, the notion of absolute *dominium* permeates biblical exegesis. The liberal ideology of private property is unconsciously applied to the ancient Levant where, despite centuries of European influences, the rule of common and religious law remains in force. Private property is considered as the norm even by exegetes who do not see themselves as hard-core liberals. A recent monograph dedicated to the study of land and economy in ancient Israel is a case in point. As most previous studies on the subject, it views tenancy as an unfortunate deviation from the normal status of free farming and the cause of major disturbances. Land ownership is defined as 'a special sort of property, having attributes not shared by any other types of property, e.g. it is permanent and it is the major source of livelihood' (Pastor 1997: 1).

Biblical prophets have long been imagined as critics of latifundia during the eighth century BCE (Fager 1993; Coote 1991; Chaney 1993; Cook 2004: 149-51). The standard view on the evolution of land ownership in ancient Israel is that land was owned by an increasingly small aristocracy or became crown-land. The concentration of land ownership in the hands of the elite is thought to have continued in Judah until the Babylonian era when the landowning aristocracy was deported. At that point, landless farmers took possession of the land left behind by the landlords until, with the backing of the Persian authorities, the returnees were re-established as large landowners at the expense of those who were already in the country (Pastor 1997: 14). Having repossessed 'their' patrimonies, the landlords forced the non-exiled residents to either pay rent as tenants, or move to marginal land. This new situation is said to have created a tenant-farmer class and the conflict between the exiles and the people of the land. The books of Ezra and Nehemiah would present as a religious issue what was in fact a clash over land ownership.

Forced to meet their debts by extra labour on their creditors' behalf, tenants and their family members ended up being sold into slavery to pay their debts (Pastor 1997: 169). Thus continues the litany of smallholders' woes that became a literary motif in Old Testament studies. Although its main proponents consider themselves as liberation theologians of sorts, they unconsciously reproduce the classical liberal dogma of private property. The norm of a healthy economy is viewed as land-ownership and the absence of debts. As every narrative needs a crisis, landlords and moneylenders are the villains who pervert the system and remove the farmer from *his* vine and *his* fig tree. Israelite prophets, the heroes of the tale, stand up fearlessly for the rights of helpless farmers in the (lost) fight against the combined forces of greed and of idolatry. Identifying themselves with the biblical model, the prophets of the social critique feel confident enough to offer advice pertaining to the economic problems of the modern world (Albertz 1990; Milgrom 1997). The motif is now spilling over into the domain of practical theology.

A recent monograph draws up a biblical agrarian perspective to read modern ecological concerns as a spiritual crisis. Ellen Davis's version of ancient Israelite agriculture is yet another Western theological artefact that attempts no dialogue with ancient reality (Davis 2009; Fick 2008; Evans, Vos and Wright 2003). She postulates that biblical farmers were similar enough to modern agrarians to justify the claim that North American agrarian writings can make us better readers of Scripture (Davis 2009: 22). Davis's ethical burden is praiseworthy in its particular context. As is the case with most biblical ethics, however, biblical texts are mere proof-texts evoked in support of ecological concerns without engaging the reality of real life in Canaan. A romantic depiction of land emerges. Under the influence of Earth theology (Habel and Trudinger 2008), the land is said to have a capacity to enjoy itself, and the practical intelligence to figure out the necessary economic conditions for it to have joy (Davis 2009: 110). As prototypes of modern agrarians, Israelite prophets are recruited to defend the old rural economy against latifundia and specialized agriculture (Davis 2009: 122-24).

These readings are variations on Rousseau's theme of the Noble Savage, free, healthy, honest and happy in the pure state of nature.[2] Whereas Rousseau identified civilization as the scourge of humanity, blaming cities, agriculture and metallurgy for the rise of private property that caused inequality, envy and unceasing warfare, for agrarian theologians the 'fall' and the source of all evil in Israel was the monarchy. The ideology of the Book of Samuel is taken over wholesale.

The aim of the present chapter is not to contest the validity of modern ecological and economic concerns. Theologians may have a contribution to offer in these crucial issues, but the validity of their contribution hinges upon the ability to get in touch with reality, ancient and modern. To this aim, integrating the results of social sciences is essential. My critique of liberation-minded interpretations of the Hebrew Scriptures is not motivated by any animosity to things Marxist, Socialist or Communist, as were some of the critiques levelled against Gottwald's work (Gottwald 1993: xvii). In the same way that social-critical studies uncovered the bourgeois outlook of previous scholarship, isolated from the brunt of prophetic critiques by setting them within the framework of revelation, it is time to submit the social critique to a critical evaluation and winnow some ideological chaff to get a more accurate view of the economic conditions that prevailed in the society that produced the Bible. Norman Gottwald envisioned pre-monarchic Israel as the result of a social revolution that replaced a tributary mode of appropriation to a communitarian society, in which there was no place for taxes, rents or interest-laden loans (Gottwald 1993: xvi-xxviii). Did such a counter-culture ever exist beyond exegetical writings?

In a recent article that starts with an overview of the use of the social sciences in biblical exegesis where he deems Gottwald's Marxist model for the development of society a kind of tragedy, Rainer Albertz (2007) continues with a naïve paraphrase of pet biblical texts passed as a social historical perspective on the early monarchy. Despite a vibrant call for the integration of social sciences, Albertz has little to offer besides repeating the standard scenario of economic prosperity resulting in the impoverishment of traditional smallholders. Thanks to economic developments during the ninth century BCE, prophets such as Elijah and Elisha were able to free themselves from the tutelage of the royal court and take up the cause of the impoverished. Albertz admits that Elisha himself had been a prosperous farmer and that he had good contacts with members of the upper class, but the group around him suffered great poverty. Albertz needs rich enough prophets to enable them to be economically independent while they should also be poor enough to gather a group of disgruntled outsiders around them. Increasing prosperity may indeed provoke discontent because the gap between the rich and the poor increases. The social sciences, however, contribute little to Albertz's argument that is based on an uncritical reading of biblical propaganda, in particular the story of Naboth's vineyard (see below, §4.1).

Baruch Levine's approach is more elaborate than Albertz's, but it also opposes private farms in Israel to royal lands, temple estates and other forms of ownership classified as public (Levine 1996). Particularly misleading is the notion of land ownership since it impinges on any reconstruction of the situation of farmers.

1.3 The Ambiguity of Terminology

Since Biblical terminology is notoriously imprecise and the translation of biblical terms is a source of confusion, the first task is to sharpen the vocabulary relative to land.

1.3.1 Divine Land Ownership

Ownership of land is a tricky concept, more so in the ancient world where vocabulary did not differentiate between 'ownership' and 'possession'. For instance, the Greek ἀπεδοντο means both 'sold' and 'leased' (Lewis 1973: 190). It is hard to imagine a world where the difference between buying and renting, selling and leasing were not clearly differentiated (Bingen 1973: 219; Manning 2003: 195; Tabuteau 1988: 95-112). The Semitic terms for 'lord' (אדון, בעל) do not distinguish between possession and ownership (Simkins 1999: 131). Real estate property, modern as much as ancient, is not so much property in land as property in the usufruct or 'a place within a complex gradation of use-rights' (Thompson 1978: 328). In the ancient world, true individualized private property applied mainly to weapons, tools and honour. Family or clan collective ownership applied to houses, animals, gardens and trees in which individuals held shares (Manning 2003: 199). Neither the Demotic *nb* nor the Greek *georgos* distinguish between a man who farms his own land and an agricultural labourer. Land ownership went unrecognized and unprotected because land tenure was not based on ownership but on rights of use. As actual plots of land were regularly redistributed (§2.1), the correlation of an individual with a particular lot was loose. As a result, cartography and registers of cadastre were absent. Access to land was not mediated through land title but through one's relations to a social group or to a sovereign who had the ability to grant land.

Rooted as it is in earlier Oriental systems, the Islamic tradition focuses more on the techniques of production (trees, animals, tools, seeds) than on the land itself. As a means of production, the land comes from God and cannot be owned, contrary to the fruits of people's labour (Lancaster and Lancaster 1995: 106). The biblical notion of landhold is similar. In Lev. 25:23, YHWH claims the land for himself (הארץ לי). The lack of verb could be used to argue that the phrase does not imply divine ownership as such. In fact, 'the land is mine', literally 'the land is for me', means that YHWH is the overlord. In this case, we are close to an English common-law concept. YHWH holds the allodial title to the land of Canaan as does the British sovereign in the name of God. Any human holder in Canaan is therefore a possessor, not an owner. This negates Pastor's claim that 'the land was rooted in cultural traditions regarding the land as a patrimony belonging ultimately to the family in the widest sense' (1997: 169). However wide one may stretch the notion of family, the divine overlord limits patrimony and excludes civil law and liberal notions of private property. Divine ownership did not prevent landholders from mortgaging, conveying and transmitting the land to their heirs, all without titles of ownership. It is confusing to claim that YHWH transferred ownership to humans but retained residual control (Kitz 2000: 605).

On the opposite side of the theological spectrum, the legal fiction of Joshua's conquest vests the control of the land in the hands of the tribe, a rather vague entity which, if nothing else, excludes individual control. It is no accident that the Book of Joshua presents the allotment of entire regions to individual tribes but stops short before the next logical step, the narration of the allotment to individual farmers. Hence, neither Leviticus nor Joshua place land in the hands of individuals. Farmers hold land as God's tenants or as members of a social group. When land has no value, as was the case in the ancient world, there was no need to buy it. When land has become a precious commodity as it is today, it is too expensive for farmers to buy it. In both cases, farmers do not own much of the land they cultivate.

1.3.2 Land Tenure (aḥuzzah)

In the Bible, land tenure is expressed by the word *aḥuzzah* (אחוזה) derived from a root with the same meaning as tenure, 'to seize, hold' (HALOT I, 32). Yet, the influence of modern concepts of ownership produces much confusion in the understanding of tenure. Referring to its use at the end of the episode of the rape of Dinah in Genesis 34, Levine equates the right to exercise *aḥuzzah* as the right to buy land in Canaan from its legal owners (Levine 1996: 239). The context is a matrimonial alliance between the sons of Hamor and the sons of Jacob, but it has nothing to do with buying land:

> והארץ תהיה לפניכם שבו וסחרוה והאחזו בה (Gen. 34:10b)
>
> ...and the land is in front of you, settle and travel it/trade it and have *tenure* in it.

Although the feminine pronoun appended to the verb 'travel' (סחרוה) could suggest that the land is the object rather than the locale of the trading or travelling, the opposite is the case (Westermann 1985: 534; Wenham 1994: 312). Tenure does not refer to ownership but to possession. After having sold a land-share (ויקן את חלקת השדה) to Jacob (Gen. 33:19-20), Hamor goes one step further in the integration of the sons of Israel by granting them rights to roam the land around Shechem free of charge. The aim is not to set the Israelites up as estate agents to buy and sell that land as Levine's interpretation suggests, but to have them graze and cultivate it themselves. Strictly speaking, the sons of Jacob do not become owners. In the same way, Abraham did not buy the field and the cave of Machpelah from Ephron but acquired a burial tenure (Gen. 23:20, ויקן אחזת קבר השדה). Through the transaction, Abraham gained the right to use the cave and the land in front of it for funerary purposes without dispossessing the landlord (Bauks 2004; Gerleman 1977; Fager 1993: 89).

Misleading as it is, the confusion between private property and tenure is hardly surprising since ancient farmers transmitted the land they worked to their heirs. The theoretical distinction between ownership and use of agricultural land must, however, be retained since the failure to do so is the source of many errors when discussing biblical farming (§§2.3, 4.1-5). The same applies today in the Third World where providing individual land titles is not necessarily the most appropriate or practical option to help the poor and where other types of tenure better meet their needs. From the least secure to the most secure type of tenure, the range covers pavement dwellers, squatter tenants, squatter owners, tenants in unauthorized subdivision, owners in unauthorized subdivision, legal owners in unauthorized construction, tenants with contract, lease holders and, finally, freeholders (Payne 2004). Hence, land ownership was and remains irrelevant to farming. What is crucial to farmers is access to land, land use, landhold and land tenure.

1.3.3 Naḥalah*?*

Another crucial term in discussion of ancient farming is *naḥalah* (נחלה). Oded Borowski considers *aḥuzzah* and *naḥalah* as synonyms and classifies them under the category of private property (Borowski

1987: 22; 2003: 26). This is surely incorrect for *aḥuzzah* and there is no indication that it is correct for *naḥalah* either. *Naḥalah* is often translated as 'inheritance' although it derives from a root 'to bestow, to grant, to present' (HALOT II, 686). The objection of Habel (1995: 34) to the translation as inheritance, because the land is the Lord's, is invalid since a right of use can be inherited. Yet, *naḥalah* has indeed a broader sense than something received as an heirloom. The etymology refers to the mode of acquisition rather than to the type of hold. In that sense, *naḥalah* would designate any kind of grant, fief, gift, donation or heirloom. The *naḥalah* may or may not be transmittable to one's heirs. The etymology of the word *naḥalah* designates something received or granted rather than bought or acquired. Therefore, the sense of 'hereditary property' supplied in HALOT (II, 687-88) has the support of etymology but should be broadened to include land grants. Another sense commonly given to the *naḥalah* is 'inalienable property' (HALOT 1995: 687). This notion is heavily influenced by interpretations of the story of Naboth's vineyard that are refuted below (§4.1). For the present purpose, it is enough to insist that *naḥalah* is in no way synonymous with *aḥuzzah*. When ancient farmers farmed the same land as their fathers, their *aḥuzzah* happened to be equivalent to their *naḥalah* in the narrow sense of heirloom. But there were other ways than inheritance to gain a hold over land and one should not fall into the trap of an overly static view of ancient farming. The Bible retained two different terms because the situations it referred to were fluid. Hence, tenure (*aḥuzzah*) focuses on the actual hold over land while *naḥalah* designates the way one acquired a hold: inheritance, gift or grant. Since it is difficult to find an English equivalent that would include all three senses of inheritance, gift and grant, I leave the word *naḥalah* untranslated.

1.3.4 Land Shares (ḥeleq haśadeh)

Although it is moving at an impressive speed around the planet's axis, land tends to be classified as immovable property. Except in cases of major cataclysms such as flood and earthquake that alter the landscape, land remains placed irrevocably at one particular point on the earth's surface in relation to its neighbours (Sparkes 2007: 97-103). Yet, a field share (חלק השׂדה) is not equivalent to a particular plot of land or a field. A field is a parcel of land clearly distinguished from neighbouring properties by fixed boundaries. Land shares correspond to stakes in a larger pool of land controlled by an authority above individual farmers.

Hence, possession is often expressed in terms of shares. As seen above, the one share of the field Jacob acquired from Hamor locates the altar Jacob built near Shechem but it does not imply that Jacob's tent had to remain planted at that site. In the same way, in Ruth 4:3, Naomi is not selling a field but her late husband's land share. Naboth's field share where Jehu met Joram (2 Kgs 9) is more specific than a field. These texts are discussed below. At this point, it is enough to distinguish a share of a field from a field. The share or portion is obviously smaller than the field which is allotted between different people (2 Sam. 14:30-31) or different crops (2 Sam. 23:11-12; 1 Chron. 11:13-14). When it is associated to a named individual, the 'field' element drops and the share on its own indicates that person's holding, insisting on the fact that individuals do not hold fields but divisions of larger units (2 Sam. 14:30-31; 2 Kgs 9:21, 25; Jer. 12:10; Amos 4:7). The different methods used to allocate strips to shareholders is discussed below (§2.1).

The definitions given here are admittedly stricter than the way they are used in the Bible. As is often the case, there is some overlap and some loose usage of these words. Because the reality presupposed by biblical writers is not obvious to us, our use of words should be stricter if we want to avoid imposing our conceptions. Yet, the hope that neat categories may be drawn from the Bible is illusory since the semantic field of terms is likely to have fluctuated across the centuries during which the texts were produced. If vocabulary is too ambiguous to serve as a firm basis of analysis, some help can be gained from Islamic land categories as they were used in the Ottoman tenure system.

1.4 Ottoman Land Categories

Stated in no ambiguous words in Lev. 25:23 as 'the land is mine', divine ownership of the land is much more than a theological nicety. It is the fundamental notion of the biblical and the Islamic approach to land (Sūrah 7:138; 'Abd al-Kader 1959). Islam transmits a variegated system based on principles that, in spite of the time gap, is more relevant to the biblical situation than modern categories can be. The Islamic system of land tenure presents a range of access to land from occupation, possession, usufruct and full ownership that correspond to the Roman distinction between *dominium* (ownership proper), *possessio* (restricted power granted by the owner to another person over a leased, tenured or hired object) and *detentio* (the right to lay claim to an object at some time in the future in the case of a mortgage).

The Islamic system is best documented in its Ottoman version that recognizes the following categories (Fisher 1919; Tute 1927; Lewis 1979; Sait and Lim 2006; İslamoğlu 2001).

1.4.1 Mulk

Mulk, a word derived from the Semitic root meaning 'king', denotes freehold and is equivalent to *dominium* or full ownership. As is the case with 'real estate' (freehold land) or its American equivalent 'realty' where the word 'real' is derived from the word 'royal', viz. Spanish 'real', the owner has 'kingly' power over his property, including the right to alienate it or transfer full title of ownership to someone who is not his heir. *Mulk* land is the category closest to private property. This category, however, was restricted to small surfaces: houses, gardens, terraces, and the belt of gardens, fenced or walled, intensively cultivated, thanks to its proximity to residential areas and usually irrigated (Schaebler 2001: 257; Rafeq 1984: 374).

1.4.2 Mīrī

Mīrī land represented most of the arable land beyond the belt of gardens and orchards around villages and cities. *Mīrī* land is state-owned land, the state being represented by the Emir. Here, the notion of ownership is irrelevant (Menu 1971). The farmer cultivating *mīrī* land owns the right to use land that belongs to another. This is the definition of usufruct. Usufruct is the right of enjoying all the benefits derived from a good that belongs to another, provided the good in question is not altered in its substance (Wåhlin 1994: 61). Usufruct entails the right to cultivate, rent or mortgage the land and to transmit its use to one's legal heirs. In a similar way, Plato insisted that the allotment of land should be made so that the recipients should still consider their lot as common property of the state (*Laws* 740a). Through the cultivation of arable land, every farmer was a tenant of the king and the political power enjoyed the theoretical ownership of most of the arable land of the realm. Since kingly power over the land derived its legitimacy from God, the ultimate divine ownership of the land placed the king himself in the position of a tenant. Hence, divine land ownership functioned as theological justification for the inalienability of *mīrī* land and for the right of the ruler to tax the produce of the land (Eyre 2000: 187).

1.4.3 Maṭrūqa

Maṭrūqa ("withdrawn") land is required for public purposes and therefore withdrawn from cultivation. It includes military bases, roads, forest land, public buildings (markets, sanctuaries), installations (threshing floors, clay pits, middens), open spaces in villages and towns, passageways between houses and areas reserved for special purposes such as pastures and woodlands. It cannot be appropriated for private use.

1.4.4 Maḥlūl

Maḥlūl is *mīrī* land left uncultivated because of persistent neglect or absence of heirs. After a number of seasons exceeding the ordinary fallowing rhythm, usually three years, the hold of the previous possessor has lapsed. The state may decide to auction the use of the abandoned land to anyone prepared to cultivate it and pay taxes on its produce since *maḥlūl* land represents a shortfall in fiscal revenues. This category parallels klasmic land in Byzantium (Dölger 1960: Fiscal Treatise 116, 119). What is auctioned is the usufruct, not the land that remains *mīrī*.

1.4.5 Mawāt

Mawāt (dead) land is waste-land at a certain distance from inhabited land, about a mile and a half, or where a human voice could not be heard or areas improper for any kind of cultivation. Aristotle mentions something similar when he refers to ancient laws prohibiting the acquisition of land above a certain amount unless it is beyond a certain distance from the central citadel and city (*Pol.* 1319A8). Waste-land could be put under cultivation by anyone with no need to secure any kind of legal ownership thanks to *ihya al-mawāt*, 'revival of dead land', or *wad' yad*, 'placing of the hand', the right of use of waste-land to whoever cultivates it (Doumani 1995: 164; Altorki and Cole 2006: 641; Velud 2000). Cultivation turned *mawāt* land into *mīrī* land. The cultivator held the usufruct to the land he put under the plough but the owner remained the state.

Waste-land was a pool of land to keep apace with demography without reducing the size of individual holdings. Any increase of mouths to feed led to an increase of hands to clear waste-land and to terrace slopes. Even during the demographic peak of the late Roman era, waste-land was appropriated in a free-for-all process encouraged by the authorities that were interested in having the largest number of producers to tax (Bar 2004: 86). Many passages in Roman legislation concern taxation of waste-land. Although *agri deserti* is usually described as marginal abandoned land, in part these rulings addressed land never previously cultivated that was claimed by new settlers (Whittaker 1976; Whittaker and Garnsey 1998).

1.4.6 Mubah

Mubah ('open, licit') or *khalya* ('empty') is uncultivated *mīrī* land. It is not *mawāt* because it has been cultivated previously. It is not yet *maḥlūl* because it has not been abandoned long enough. An official authorization and the payment of a fee may be required before putting it under the plough. Like *maḥlūl* and *mawāt* land, ploughed *mubah* land remains *mīrī*. After ten years or so of continuous cultivation, the usufruct is transferable to the heirs of the possessor.

1.4.7 Waqf

Waqf land (mortmain) is held in trust for religious and charitable purposes. In theory, only *mulk* property can be endowed, but there were ways to endow *mīrī* land as well. The endowment is irreversible, in theory. Offering some security from the exaction of political powers, huge amounts of land were converted into *waqf*, dedicated to the support of families rather than charitable institutions, and functioned as credit institutions.

1.5 Pre-Islamic Land Categories

1.5.1 Mulk *before Islam*

A notion similar to mulk is found in Lev. 25:29-30, which draws a distinction between houses in rural and in walled settlements (Paulus 2009). Biblical cities (עיר) were primarily storage places the walls of which had a significance that extended beyond considerations of safety.[3] It was probably the administrative function of the city rather than its size or a wall around it that differentiated cities from their 'daughters'. Villages as much as cities were often walled (Faust 2009) and the difference is not visible archaeologically.

Mulk corresponds to the Greek term κυριεία used in the so-called *kyrieia* clause on Greek papyri for the transfer/investiture clause (Gross 2008: 92). In the LXX, this term is only used in Isa. 40:10 and in Dan. 11:3, 4 to translate משל. Theodotion uses it in Dan. 4:22(19); 6:27 as well (Lust Eynikel and Hauspie 2003: 361). Hence the Arabic *mulk* probably derives from Greek legal practice.[4] Another possibility for the origin of the word *mulk* is a derivation from the Sumerian *lugal* found on ritual stones (kuddurru) with a possible meaning of 'owner' (Powell 1994: 101).

In ancient Babylonia, land categories are not so clear and they are disputed (Cardascia 1959). The concept of full ownership was rendered as *makkūr* but contrary to *mulk*, it was restricted to gods (Van der Spek 1995: 190-92). *Detentio* was rendered with *šalāṭu,* to have power over a pledge' (Greek *kratein*), while *possessio* as usufruct was expressed with the verb *akālu*, 'to eat' (Van der Spek 1995: 184). When temples ceded rights of use, the beneficiary never became owner.

1.5.2 The Mulk/Mīrī *Interplay*

The farmer reigned over his house, gardens and orchards, his *mulk* property but not over his fields that were *mīrī* land, which he received, in theory, from the crown (Maon 1972). The Emir reigned over his kingdom, but only as God's deputy. The interplay between *mulk* and of *mīrī* land functioned as a double check that prevented either party from appropriating the means of production. The crown had no hold over *mulk* land, not because it was inalienable, but, on the contrary, because it was freehold property that the farmer had full liberty to alienate. The *mīrī* category functioned in the opposite direction. Farmers were encouraged to cultivate as much of it as they could since it increased the revenues of the crown, but they could privatize it and turn it into *mulk* land. The same applied to land granted by the sovereign to elite members. It was not taken from *mulk* land but from *mawāt, maḥlūl* or *mubah* land and it remained of *mīrī* land as long as it was cultivated, even if the grandee who used it transferred its use to his heirs.

The fundamental dualism *mulk/mīrī* land disavows the claim that agricultural intensification led to 'an increase in *mulk*-like over *mīrī*-like holdings for a few' (Coote and Whitelam 1986: 134). Intensification resulted in putting more *mawāt, maḥlūl* and *mubah* land under the plough, a process that increased the surface of *mīrī* land without altering the amount of *mulk* land. The official attribution of arable land to private individuals is not attested before the Tanzimat reforms. In 1858, the Ottoman land code granted cultivators full possessory rights to individual farmers on the condition that land titles were drawn up and registered. The land transfer laws of the Mandate continued in the same direction, seeking to reinforce the private rights of farmers in order to phase out communal tenure systems (Home 2003: 301). Communal tenure is discussed in Chapter 2. What matters at this point is to note that the Tanzimat reforms were inspired by European notions of land ownership. The aim of the land reform was to reassert state control over land by reducing the acreage controlled by *waqfs* and by attributing deeds to individual farmers. Contrary to the standard model that imagines that 'the state establishes the great economic advantage of a small class of urban elite officers, warriors, and land owners' (Coote and Whitelam 1986: 142), state building entails reducing the privileges of the elites that stand between the state and its subjects. Hence, instead of expropriating freeholders, the Ottoman state forbade communal hold in order to simplify taxation liability and allocate uncultivated land to individuals. Land registration and consolidation continued under the Mandates, while cadastral mapping provided a bird's eye view of individual ownership that cut across 'the maze of property relations and established administrative controls over the land, its resources and population' (İslamoğlu 2001: 383).

The opposite situation prevailed after the creation of the modern State of Israel. Although the State of Israel retained the Ottoman land code and assumed the traditional role of the state as the protector of tenants, it is the rights of imported tenants that the State of Israel protects (Kedar 2001). Hence, the State of Israel appropriated 93% of its territory, establishing it as public domain. This record high was achieved by declaring the Negeb *mawāt* land (against the Bedouin), by appropriating land forfeited by Palestinian refugees in 1948 and preventing their return, and by confiscating *waqf* land, a sixth of the country at the time (Dumper 1994). Through the strict application of the three-year rule, the State of Israel continues to appropriate land from Palestinian farmers by using aerial photography to identify uncultivated land (*maḥlūl*). This unprecedented level of appropriation of land does not apply to earlier periods. Because the Ottoman Empire sought to extract taxes rather than land, it rarely applied the three-year rule and did not consider an absentee dead until 90 years after his birth date, thus protecting his rights and those of his heirs should he ever return home. It is crucial, however, to note that the Israeli appropriations do not result in the transformation of *mīrī* land into *mulk* land. This modern example is a warning against the dangers of reading biblical texts in light of simplistic notions of land ownership.

The aim of this cursory presentation of Ottoman land categories is to avert biblical scholars from polarizing on modern European concepts of land tenure, rather than suggesting that the Islamic concepts are directly relevant to Persian-era Palestine. Ottoman concepts were the result of centuries of debate and interaction between Islamic notions, imperial policies and custom, since, in spite of the sophistication of the legal schools of Islam, the validity of common law (Ar. *'urf*, was recognized and common law sometimes got precedence over Islamic law (Wåhlin 1994: 60; Jackson 2006). As practice that was not regulated by laws, communal regimes of land tenure are highly relevant to biblical agriculture.

Notes

1. Greenfield (1992: 309-14) considers שליט and רשי as synonyms since P. Yadin 7 (Babathra archive) uses them together. At line 24, a husband empowers his wife over a house should she become a widow (ושליטה רשיה). Yet, he adds (ll. 39-40) that she is not empowered to bring a husband into that house (שלטיה תהוא למנאלו לביתא הו ולא רשיה ולא).
2. 'Le premier qui ayant enclos un terrain s'avisa de dire, *Ceci est à moi*, et trouva des gens assez simples pour le croire, fut le vrai fondateur de la société civile' (Vaughan 1915: 11).
3. Assyrian sources distinguish URU.É 'cities of houses' (*ālu* + *bītu*), URU.BÀD 'cities of walls' (*ālu* + *dūru*) and URU.ŠE 'cities of grain' (*ālu* + *še'u*; Fales 1984).
4. Another likely Hellenistic influence on Islam is the Quranic word *dayn* 'loan', probably derived from da&neion with a metathesis of the *yod* (Thür 1997).

Chapter 2

Communal Land

2.1 Musha‘

Beside the neat categories of Islamic law existed a type of customary tenure that Ottoman and Mandatory authorities sought to abolish by compulsory land registration and consolidation. In Syria, villagers used the term *musha‘* to refer to waste-land shared by several villages for grazing (Aswad 1971: 43). The term was first used in reference to a specific type of arable land tenure in the Hauran by the Swiss traveller Johann Ludwig Burckhard (1819: 97-100). Although Elihu Grant (1976: 132) described *musha‘* tenure in Palestine without mentioning the name, academic writings now use the term *musha‘* to designate communal land allotted temporarily by lottery between shareholders.

The term *musha‘* also applies to trees that are held in share ownership, but at this point I focus on the *musha‘* that concerns the communal exploitation of arable *mīrī* land at the village level. The particularity of *musha‘* tenure was the attribution of shares of arable land to individual farmers according to two main systems: 'open-ended' and 'quantified-share' (Nadan 2003; 2006: 261-98; Adams 1982; Wåhlin 1988; Weulersee 1946: 99-109; Firestone 1990: 92-94; Schaebler 2001; Schloen 2001; Canaan 1916; Klat 1958; Jaussen 1948; Warriner 1975). In the open-ended *musha‘*, the amount of land received by each unit varied according to non-land factors: the number of males—adult males or married males (*dhukūr*)—or the number of ploughing teams owned (*feddān*). In the quantified-share *musha‘*, only the amount of land was counted, irrespective to changes in the shareholding households.

Shares of *musha‘* lands were subject to periodic redistribution, so that a shareholder cultivated plots he had not cultivated in the previous distribution. The periodicity of distribution was variable but the holding of plots was temporary. Between harvest and ploughing, as well as during fallows, plots were turned over to grazing by the village flocks for the purpose of weeding and manuring. *Musha'* land was usually organized in several quarters (*wajahāt*)[1] representing the different types of soil available. Each unit received narrow non-contiguous strips or *sahm*, 'portion, share, lot', or *mārethlmāreś*, 'rope' or 'inheritance' (Bergheim 1895: 194-5), from the different quarters. The strips were a few furrows (*tilm*) wide; about the width a sower could cover in a single throw (Sonnen 1927: 77). Strips in fairly flat country could reach a kilometre in length, cutting across any obstacle.

The long strips saved on hedges and fences and on reversals of direction for the ploughing team. Each *mareth* was marked out by a double furrow (*taḥm*) visible in the background in Figure 1 (below). Stone heaps (*ḥadd*) or other signs (*rasm*) could be added in the corners and in the middle to mark out different strips.

Rather than a fixed legal and economic category, *musha'* was a flexible system reflecting status, power relations and a notion of the common good between geography and institution (Mundy 1996; Schaebler 2001: 244-48). The aim of the distribution and of the re-allotment was the attribution to each shareholder of manageable holdings, adjusted according to the ability of each production unit, which itself depended mostly on the size of the household and of the family stock. The political situation within the village and the balance of power between the different lineages, however, played a role in the allocation of shares. For this reason, actual practice varied greatly from one village to another. Some groups, not necessarily linked by ties of kinship and marriage, managed better than others in pooling resources. The idiom of such collaborative groups was not owning so much land, but sharing common resources and common needs according to the labour (animal and human) each member commanded (Mundy and Saumarez Smith 2007: 145-49). *Musha'* tenure was an individual type of cultivation of common land (mostly *mīrī* land) that required communal organization. Often, tasks began on the same day from the same side by every one to avoid mistakes and cheating (Grant 1976: 135). Assembled in the evening in the Sheikh's guest room, the farmers decided which zone would be worked the next day. Crop rotation and fallow, grazing and watering rights, as well as the acceptance of newcomers were decided together and imposed upon everyone. Planting the same crop in each sector enabled turning the entire quarter to grazing after the harvest or during fallows.

Risk spreading between the different families was a crucial factor. When one area suffered from excessive moisture or drought, other strips benefiting from different soil, sun, exposure and gradient would fare better (Kramer 1982: 35; Atran 1986: 275). The impact of localized adverse factors such as pests, hail, fire and raids was reduced by the scattering of plots attributed to each shareholder across the entire arable domain of the village. Plot scattering was also a major strategy to spread the work over time as identical crops did not ripen simultaneously in the different quarters of the village (Sarpaki 1992: 62).

The method for the actual distribution of shares of *musha‘* tenure varied. As observed in Aleppo, each applicant brought a personal object (knife, nail...) which was drawn out of the pile by someone who did not know to whom the objects belonged. In Palestine, Bergheim (1895: 194) reports the use of inscribed pebbles (*grl* = גרל) placed in a bag and drawn by a child less than five years old. The land to be shared out had been divided into strips each measuring about 15 to 18 furrows (*jwz*). The owner of the first object to be drawn received the first strip, the owner of the second object got the second strip and so on. Each farmer owned a number of *feddān* corresponding to his ploughing and seeding power. Hence, between three farmers worth ¼, ¾ and 1½ *feddān* each, the weakest one received 15 strips and the others 45 and 90 strips each. To ensure a fair distribution of the various land types and for optimal risk spreading, the strips each farmer received were not contiguous. Strips were redistributed whenever modifications in the value in *feddān* required it (Dalman 1964: 39-40). Yearly redistributions were reported in certain places in Palestine and Transjordan (Nadan 2003; Bergheim 1895: 191-99).

As the relation of a shareholder to a particular plot changed according to the season and after each new distribution, there was no need to register individual claims to own land. Individuals owned shares, not particular plots. In an attempt to reassert direct control over the provinces, the Ottomans sought to abrogate *musha‘* land by compulsory land registration and consolidation to improve tax collection. Shifting the fiscal liability from the village community to the individual was meant to eliminate intermediaries. All *musha‘* lands were classified as *mīrī* and a slow process of registration began. In ‘Ajlun, olive trees were sometimes also owned in shares. In this case, olive tenure was *mulk* (Mundy 1986: 84). But in Greece, individual trees planted on ‘private’ estates were designated as ‘sacred’ or ‘public’. The landholder cultivated the trees but their fruit went for the sanctuary or the community that owned them

Figure 1: Two furrows separating strips are visible behind the ploughing team (Dalman 1964: Bild 25; reproduced with permission of Manfred Olms Verlag AG).

(Burford 1993: 24). The Mandate authorities that succeeded the Ottoman continued in the same direction, targeting *musha'* as a major obstacle to development (Granott 1952: 202-12; Stein 1984: 15; Latron 1936: 192-94; Dowson 1930: 4-5). In Syria, where the issue was not complicated by Zionist colonization, some Mandate officials realized that in fact *musha'* constituted an extremely robust, healthy and balanced system (Weulersse 1946: 99-108). Aware that it had a real basis in the social life of the country, they suggested that it should not be abolished (Schaebler 2001: 283). The *musha'* was particularly well adapted to conditions of loose central control in fringe areas such as the flats of Jordan and Syria and the moderately steep highland of Palestine. The dispersion of plots and their fragmentation into strips were the fruit of a long experience of adaptation to the climate by spreading the risk borne by each unit of production over a wide range of soil types. As demographic pressure and mechanization made it less and less practical, the *musha'* was already on the wane when Ottoman and Mandate authorities began to abrogate it, and the evolution towards individual tenure would have taken place with or without state intervention. Although tractors and motor pumps dealt a blow to the *musha'* in most parts of Syria (Métral 1984: 471), land consolidation did not lead to the total disappearance of the *musha'*. To this day, some farmers continue to rotate plots and cultivate collectively (Schaebler 2001: 282; Seeden and Kaddour 1984). The *musha'* remains pertinent in certain situations and the United Nations are discussing *musha'* as a strategy to secure land tenure for vulnerable social groups

(United Nations 2005). Because *musha'* is as much a reflection of social as agricultural imperatives, the distribution of lots was preceded by intense negotiations that involved an intricate combination of clanic principles with the basic division according to the number of ploughing teams each unit owned or the number of adult males it represented (*dhukūr*). Hence, quarters would sometimes be first divided into *tubna*s reflecting the bargaining power of each clan and then subdivided according to the economic (*dhukūr*) and human (*feddān*) resources of the village (Schaebler 2001: 283). Communal land tenure was not restricted to the Islamic world.

2.1.1 Open-field Regimes in Asia, Europe and America

Open-field systems prevailed across medieval Europe with the 'champion' that shared many features with the *musha'* (Blum 1978: 120-25). The land controlled by the village was divided into grazing and arable. When used for cropping, the arable was privately controlled and exploited. The non-arable land was controlled by the village community which protected it from the encroachment of outsiders. The arable was grazed collectively during fallow and between harvest and sowing (Dahlman 1980: 25; Friedmann 1984; Ault 1973; Duby 1968). In the Russian *rase campagne,* the open-field system was combined with periodic redistribution and continued in modern-era Russian peasant communes, the *mir* and the *obshchina* (Confino 1969: 99-115; Bartlett 1990; Atkinson 1983).

Communal land regimes were also the rule in the initial phases of European settlements in the New World, for instance the Jamestown settlement (1607), the Plymouth settlement (1620) and the Mormon settlement at Salt Lake (1847). The choice was dictated by the need to share risk as famine, disease and raids reached their highest levels during the first generation of settlers. Under these harsh conditions, a communal land regime was deemed the most efficient strategy for risk management:

> The efficiency thesis predicts that group land ownership will be more prevalent in situations in which risks are high and a group cannot employ a superior insurance mechanism. The settlers of the three pioneer communities initially faced conditions of precisely this sort. That the risks were acute cannot be doubted. All three pioneer settlements were remote outposts, located weeks or months away from civilization. The first parties of settlers faced lethal dangers, including raids by Indians, infections from exotic diseases, and difficulties in learning how to farm in their strange environments. Remoteness precluded risk-spreading

> through multi-generational kinship networks, insurance markets, or government welfare programs. The settlers could spread risks only among themselves, and one option was to have a collective economy that guaranteed each member some share of total group output. (Ellickson 1993: 1342)

As soon as conditions improved and mortality decreased significantly, within a dozen years at most, all surviving settlements had shared out the common land into private lots and production increased dramatically. Risk was the determinant factor in the choice between collective and individual tenure. As they gradually learned how to prevent Indian raids, avoid disease, and grow crops, the pioneers shifted their attention from risk-spreading to increased production. The settlers began parcelling their land when the risk-spreading benefits of group land ownership would no longer outweigh its shortcomings, such as the shirking that notably afflicted Jamestown and Plymouth (Ellickson 1993: 1342). The development of more efficient social insurance mechanisms, such as informal mutual-aid relationships, tithe-supported churches and tax-supported governments accelerated the shift towards privatization.

By comparison, a similar colony in Bermuda established in 1609 parcellized its land within the first five years because the settlers enjoyed a safer environment, free from Indian attacks and from most diseases that affected their counterparts in Jamestown. 'In short, the unusually deadly environment at Jamestown not only decimated the labour force, but also helped perpetuate institutions that spread risks but put less food on the table' (Ellickson 1993: 1344).

The same correlation between risk and communal tenure applies to the Israeli *kibbutzim*. Although Mandate authorities claimed that *musha'* tenure was inefficient and that land consolidation and settlement should break collective ownership to improve efficiency, many early Zionist settlements worked land along communal lines because they were established in dangerous border areas or at strategic points within dense Arab areas. The German economist Franz Oppenheimer predicted the demise of the communal model of the *kibbutzim* by arguing that its fatal weakness was its muzzling-of-incentive equality. Hence, Oppenheimer imposed wage differentials as an incentive for the settlers and an externally appointed manager at Merhavia, a Zionist agricultural settlement that failed because its Russian settlers resisted Oppenheimer's ideas and wanted equal wages and self-government (Near 1992: 30). The voluntary aspect of the *kibbutz*, in opposition to the *kolkhoz*, contributed to disprove Oppenheimer's predictions (Barkai 1996: 52).

But the voluntarism of the *kibbutznikim* was strongly supplemented by the historical context of war where ideological concerns spelled out by Zionism maintained a high level of motivation until the 1980s. At that point, the political context changed and confirmed Oppenheimer's argument. Hence, Oppenheimer had been right too early because he had not taken into account the particular Israeli political context. Changes in the level of risk appear as the main reason for the initial success and subsequent demise of the *kibbutzim*. A similar influence is visible at Degania, an agricultural settlement that succeeded and symbolically became the mother of all communal settlements in Israel and the nucleus of a Hebrew Defence organization, Hashomer (Gorni 1989; 1998: 250). After a generation or two, the level of risk decreased significantly thanks to improved machinery, irrigation, military victories over neighbouring countries and the policing of the local Arab population. At this point, the *kibbutznikim* started to clamour for private property. The dramatic evolution of Israeli and Russian societies from collectivist to ultra-liberal models also reflects the stark reduction of risk in the last decades of the twentieth century. The level of security has improved so much that it is social cohesion that is now at risk (Del Sarto 2006: 87-105).

2.1.2 The Efficiency Cost of Communal Tenure

Risk spreading has a cost since communal land tenure regimes entail a loss in efficiency. How much produce is lost when land is worked communally rather than individually has been hotly debated in relation to the English open-field system. McCloskey claimed that open fields implied a loss of 10% of the yield, which he explained was an insurance premium farmers accepted to pay in exchange for the greater security provided by the reduction of risk on scattered plots. It has been suggested that, by identifying difference in soil and conditions, open-field systems help farmers select optimal seeding rates (on the recognition of the efficiency of the system in Europe, see McCloskey 1975: 73-119; 1976: 124-70; 1991; Dahlman 1980: 58-64). Recent studies confirm the benefits of open fields in risk spreading while rejecting the notion that it was less efficient than consolidated systems. Although it was a low benefit method of spreading risk, scattering was also low-cost. Its main advantages appear when it is considered in relation to other communal strategies. Low levels of capital forced farmers to plough and harvest cooperatively. Intermingling fields facilitated the mutual monitoring of crucial tasks such as weeding and saved on the prohibitive cost of fencing and enclosing small-holdings (Richardson 2003; Bekar and Reed 2003).

Scattered plots also had a number of 'hidden' advantages. Spreading the risk between the entire village's tenants fostered solidarity in disaster situations that affected all, who thus stood united when they pressed for tax and rent reduction.

Hence, the risk spreading aspect has held its ground in academic studies as much as on the ground. Farm fragmentation did not disappear from the European landscape before fertilizers, transport and farm machinery significantly increased yields and reduced risks. Lowered risk levels also explain the evolution of land tenure in late Ottoman Palestine and Greece (Thompson 1963; Du Boulay 1994: 265-73). The highlands, less exposed to raids, tended towards individuated plots without redistribution while the more recent and less stable settlements of the coastal plain tended towards shareholding and periodic redistribution (Gerber 1985: 208-209). The same pattern was observed in late nineteenth century 'Ajlun where *musha'* predominated in plains and in open country whereas individuated plots were the rule in mountainous areas.

Musha' tenure was the Levantine version of a very widespread strategy of risk spreading inherent to farming in fringe areas when the technical solutions available to modern farmers did not exist. Every group had to make some trade-off between individual liberty and privacy on the one hand and community and equality on the other (Ellickson 1993: 1345). In agricultural societies, land tenure is the major battleground on which this conflict is resolved. This does not exclude other types of risk-reducing strategies such as patronage, storage, crop diversification and animal husbandry, but when it comes to the production of grain, *musha'* tenure offered a viable compromise between communal and individuated tenure in an environment which for millennia offered conditions that were not quite safe enough for private holdings but too developed for purely collective solutions. Major oscillations in yields and in levels of risk from natural and security factors prevented a complete shift towards individual tenure and contributed to the survival of communal systems across centuries.

2.1.3 Sharing the Tax Burden in Communal Tenure Regimes

Besides spreading production risks, communal land tenure ensured the fair distribution of the tax burden. Ya'akov Firestone has demonstrated the fiscal aspect of land redistributions in *musha'* tenure that appears as 'a rather sophisticated set of adjustments evolved by peasant communities in response to the heavy exactions of fiscal feudalism' (Firestone 1981: 833). The same reason is evoked to explain why in many

Japanese provinces before the Meiji land tax reforms (1873 CE), villagers redistributed land among themselves to ensure a fair distribution of the collective tax burden that was assessed at the village levels (Brown 1985). Firestone seems to limit the tax burden that spurred the development of the *musha'* to the late Ottoman era, although it is obvious that taxes were levied upon farmers at all times and that the burden was always felt as crushing, whatever its actual weight. Hence, the tax burden is yet another aspect of risk to which communal tenure systems responded by equating the tax burden of the village as closely as possible to the ability of each productive unit through regular redistributions of arable land. The notion of risk accounts for the great variety of actual patterns of laying out land, crop rotation, and collective discipline in production observed in the Levant and elsewhere (Mundy 1986: 84-87). Risk spreading and the efficiency thesis provide a general principle applicable to different times and places.

2.1.4 Land Scarcity Phases out Communal Tenure

Finally, land scarcity plays a crucial role in speeding up the evolution of communal land systems into individuated tenure. Abundance of land fosters inalienability (Ellickson 1993: 1376). In Ghana, Kenya and Rwanda, as population increased and land became scarcer, groups relaxed many restraints on alienation (Migot-Adholla, Hazell, Barel and Place 1991: 161-64). Abundance of land also discourages the parcelling of commons (Ellickson 1993: 1330) and offsets the negative effects related to the lack of land stewardship in systems based on usufruct (Ellickson 1993: 1367). Land scarcity fostered economic development in Northern Europe and in Japan (Powelson 1994: 73-74). When land is in greater supply than the demand, as was the case across the ancient world (Van Driel 1998), there is no pressure to share it out between individuals. Hence, the three factors of risk spreading, production efficiency and land availability determine land regimes.

2.1.5 A Theoretical Model for the Evolution of Land Tenure

Since changing levels of risk, production and land availability dictated changes in land regimes in recent centuries across a wide range of climatic and political contexts, these factors can be integrated into a simple theoretical model plotting the likely occurrence of types of land regimes on a continuum between common and individual tenure. The aim is to determine the likelihood of the practice of *musha'* tenure in ancient Palestine through the estimation of probable variations in risk, production requirements and land availability.

Risk is determined by natural and human factors. A majority of farmers from every age can be credited with a reasonable ability to cope with most natural and political risks or humanity would not have survived. Since crises tend to be recurrent and to have similar causes, farmers developed the ability to measure risk and to cope with crisis. Overall, political risks posed a greater challenge to Mediterranean farmers than natural risks, but because wars leave more trace in the historical record, they are easier to correlate with economic crises. Military operations and periods of political instability increase risk and foster communal tenure. Conversely, periods of relative political stability decrease risk, encourage individual initiative and the privatization of tenure. Stable political conditions are also likely to raise tax pressure, which in turn forces farmers to produce more, and more efficiently, further bolstering the trend towards privatization. Under unstable political conditions, the collection of taxes is disrupted but this does not mean that farmers are better off. They have to switch to survival strategies that involve producing smaller amounts and hiding them from foraging armies and raids from neighbouring tribes. Stable political conditions tend to reduce land availability through the effects of rising demography resulting from natural growth and sometimes through the introduction of settlers from abroad. Hence, under the combined effects of better tax collection and better policing, tax pressure increases while risk declines, leading to more privatization. The effects of the three factors can be summarized graphically (Figure 2).

The validity of this theoretic model for the ancient Levant should be tested against evidence from ancient sources. If evidence of communal tenure and periodical land redistribution is found in the pre-Ottoman Levant, the existence of communal tenure such as the *musha'* can be postulated in ancient Israel and traces of it can be sought in biblical texts.

<table>
<tr><td rowspan="3">Communal
land regimes</td><td>abundance</td><td>LAND</td><td>scarcity</td><td rowspan="3">Individual
land regimes</td></tr>
<tr><td>subsistence</td><td>PRODUCTION</td><td>surplus</td></tr>
<tr><td>high</td><td>RISK</td><td>low</td></tr>
</table>

Figure 2: Modelling land regimes

2.2 Pre-Ottoman Musha' *Tenure*

As much as commons such as pastures and forests in Byzantine law, *musha'* land was not registered and the fiscal administration did not know how to handle it (Kaplan 1992: 189). Unrecorded land by definition falls through the written record and yet these lands existed and provided important resources. *Musha'* tenure was an informal practice, not a land category. The practice gave rise to innumerable local variations as to the method of division, the types of shareholders, crop rotation and cycles of redistributions. *Musha'* tenure worked because it was flexible and adaptable to local variations, but its extent is disputed.

2.2.1 Haim Gerber

On the one hand, Abraham Granott estimated that in 1858 practically all the arable land in Palestine was cultivated under the *musha'* system (Granott 1952: 174; Kamen 1991: 136-43). The proportion of *musha'* tenure was estimated at 70% in 1917 (Patai 1949: 441). These estimates are based on unknown sources and cannot be given too much weight (Nadan 2003: 332). On the other hand, Haim Gerber opposes the notion that *musha'* tenure was an important practice in the Palestinian central range (Gerber 1985: 77-78, 147-48). Gerber based his claim on Ottoman sources that cannot be easily dismissed and appear much more systematic and reliable than Mandate estimates. The strength of Gerber's studies are their ability to reveal that the disintegration of *musha'* began long before the First World War, and that villagers were discontinuing land redistribution on their own accord before the reforms of the 1860s. At the close of the Ottoman period, *musha'* tenure 'by and large no longer existed in the mountains of Jerusalem' (Gerber 1985: 207). This is hardly surprising since the nineteenth century was a period of growing population in the highlands. According to the model delineated above, land scarcity and the need to intensify production would have gradually phased out *musha'* without state intervention (Bosrup 1970: 70-76). Gerber, however, overstates his case when he extends the validity of his finds to earlier periods to suggest that 'the documents of the Council of Jerusalem include proofs that at least in part of the countryside of Jerusalem there was no collective ownership of land, even before the beginning of land registration in the 1860s' (Gerber 1985: 207). Fast disappearing in the mountains, the *musha'* was still common in the plains because, as the domain of the Bedouin, the lowlands experienced higher risk and low demography, bereft as they were of settlements and under the constant menace of the nomads (Gerber 1985: 201, 217). Gerber admits that the sources do not 'permit even a rough evaluation as to what proportion of the land in the Jerusalem area was in fact registered' at the end of the nineteenth century CE (Gerber 1985: 203). Therefore, the lack of sources does not help to decide whether Gerber's claim that *musha'* tenure was never prevalent in the Palestinian highlands is acceptable or not.

Since Gerber shows that *musha'* tenure was prevalent in the lowland before the nineteenth century CE as it was widespread elsewhere, for instance in the Maghrib (Pellat 1993), one needs a solid reason to explain why the highlands of Palestine were exceptional and did not practice *musha'* tenure on a large scale. Gerber (1985: 29) introduces a topographical argument into the discussion. As over half of the agricultural lands in the Judean mountains were made up of terraces (Ron 1966), Gerber argues that *musha'* tenure was not suited for the highlands. This figure, however, is based exclusively on the Israeli side of the area, west of the Ramallah-Hebron line, indeed the most rugged part of the country and the least favourable for dry cereal farming and *musha'* (Ron 1966: 33). By contrast, the eastern side of the Ramallah-Hebron line forms a wide plateau where the proportion of cereal to olive is much higher than on the western slopes (Finkelstein 1997a: 112). It is significant that Ron's maps indicate the border between the Israeli and the Arab sides only for the area around Jerusalem (Fig. 2). The border is not indicated for the northern part, precisely where the slopes turn into a plateau. It is there, between Jerusalem and Ramallah, that the plateau is widest and most suited for dry cereal farming (Fig. 5). In this area, non-terraced arable land is abundant (Finkelstein 1989: 54), but since it is not on the Israeli side, it is not reflected in Ron's 56.4% ratio of agricultural terraces to the total surface. Ron (1966: 121) presumes that this figure is similar in the other parts of the Central Range, but were the plateau on the Palestinian side with its intermontane valleys included, the proportion of terraced land would diminish sharply and the likelihood of *musha'* tenure would rise proportionally to the amount of flatter tracts conducive to dry grain cultivation. Gerber's topographic argument is flawed by its exclusive focus on the sharp slopes that separate the coastal plain and the plateau, the area that was the least conducive to *musha'* tenure. Although the few existing figures are imprecise, there is reason to suppose that *musha'* tenure was practiced in the highlands before the nineteenth century on a larger scale than Gerber admits.

A political argument can also be adduced in favour of a widespread practice of *musha'* tenure from Gerber's work itself. Gerber attributes the successes of the Ottoman Empire to its ability to support village communities against the rise of elites that would have endangered both the farmers and the Sultan (Gerber 1987: 14). *Musha'* tenure is the hallmark of village communities and reflects their dynamism based on local solidarity and limited urbanite encroachments on land tenure. One could even argue that, in trying to phase out *musha'* tenure, the 1858 land reforms contributed to rather than prevented the rise of a landed elite as some farmers preferred to have their land registered in bulk under the name of a local dignitary (*mukhtar*) to avoid conscription. Downplaying the prevalence of *musha'* while insisting on the vitality of village community, Gerber's argumentation is somewhat paradoxical. If the *musha'* was one of the pillars of village cohesion, forcing the men to work together, the *musha'* contributed to the success of the Ottoman Empire. To save Gerber's point, one would have to show that the level of risk rose suddenly during the nineteenth century CE, causing a short spell of *musha'* tenure that ended soon after.

2.2.2 Ancient Near Eastern Musha'

However solid the Anatolian archival evidence at seventeenth-century Bursa is (Gerber 1987: 8, 19), it is not sufficient to counter the number of attestations of tenure systems that favoured the fragmentation of land and the scattering of strips in medieval Europe, seventeenth-century America, nineteenth-century Japan, Russia and the Maghrib, as well as twentieth-century Greater Syria and Greece (Forbes 1976; Foxhall 2002: 213; Burford 1993: 119). If so many farmers in so many different times and places worked under common land regimes because they faced similar risks (raids, crickets, mildew, draught, hail and taxes), there is good reason to consider that the geographical extent of the *musha'* was less restricted than Gerber (1987: 77) claimed. Ideological reasons may have motivated Gerber's position since the Zionists were most vocal against *musha'* tenure because it hindered the acquisition of land by the Zionist Agency (Abcarius 1946: 128-29). Gerber is surely correct when he affirms that 'the *musha* system was, in fact, never universal in the central mountainous area of Palestine' (Gerber 1987: 78). That it was not universal and that it was in decline at the beginning of the twentieth century does not exclude the possibility that it was common earlier, much earlier.

There are clues of similar practices in Assyrian texts back during the second millennium BCE. Middle Assyrian Law B§8 refers to encroachment upon the 'great boundary of companions' (*taḫūmu rabi'u ša tappā'ī*). Then, B§9 deals with encroachment upon the small boundary between the lots (*taḫūmu ṣiḫru ša pūrânī*; Driver and Miles 1935: 433; Postgate 1982: 309). The best explanation for the difference between great and small boundaries is the presence of an open-field system where sectors of village land were subdivided into strips attributed to different families (Driver and Miles 1935: 304). The great boundaries separated the different quarters of village land. The small boundaries separated individual strips within each quarter. These strips were subject to periodical redistribution (Jankowska 1991: 253) and a text from Ashur (KAV 125-29) confirms that the *pūru* (lots) were distributed by lots (Schroeder 1920). Encroaching upon either boundary was detrimental to other farmers but the Middle Assyrian Law stipulates a lighter punishment for encroaching upon the small boundaries since the separation between individual strips within the same quarter was marked out by a mere furrow, a few stones or sticks that could be trespassed inadvertently whereas the separation between quarters was more obvious. The division between quarters was permanent because it was not subject to periodic redistribution and it followed obvious topographical features, contrary to the strips that were regularly reshuffled to reflect demographic variations.

The Byzantine Farmer's Law deals with the same problem when it enjoins farmers not to encroach upon their neighbour's furrow.[2] This problem is less acute in consolidated field configurations where the limits between adjacent plots are marked by more stable and visible signs (trees, hedges, ditches, stones walls) because they do not keep changing. But when furlongs are shared out between the different members of the community, it is impossible to decide from a distance whether someone is encroaching or if he is working in one of his own strips. For this reason, farmers tended to operate in the same zone at the same time to foster mutual monitoring (Grant 1976: 135).

Without jumping to the conclusion that the Islamic *musha'* was already practised in Late Bronze Age Assyria, the similarity of risks faced by Assyrian and Ottoman farmers indicates that the periodical redistribution of scattered strips was a strategy imposed by geography, climate and security conditions, structural factors that hardly change over the *longue durée*. Land systems similar in principle to *musha'* tenure were particularly well adapted to frontier areas characterized by scarce population, abundant land and high risk (Schaebler 2001: 288).

Before the industrial revolution with the sharp rise in population and the deep transformations that ensued, scarce population, abundant land and high risk were prevalent for millennia in the Orient and beyond, which explains the similarity of approaches to land tenure across a wide range of climatic zones.

Around the Mediterranean, periodic land redistribution is reflected in the use of the word 'lot' (Greek κλῆρος and Hebrew גורל) to designate both a plot of land and the procedure to share it out. The vocabulary reveals how closely arable plots were associated with drawing lots.

Principles similar to *musha'* tenure can be recognized in Classical Greece in the insistence that colonists should receive plots of equal size from each zone separately and that the fairness of the original distribution should be preserved at all costs (Isager and Skydsgaard 1992: 124-26). To this aim, Aristotle envisaged legal limitations of the number of children the citizens of the ideal city would be allowed to engender (*Pol.* 1365a39-b14, 1335b20-27). Such measures were obviously impracticable. In real life, the periodic redistribution of plots sustained social justice by correcting demographic fluctuations. Diodorus 5.9.4-5, referring to the Lipari Islands, mentions redistribution every twenty years (Burford 1993: 24-25). Demands for redistributions (*Anadasmos tes ges*) were often made in classical Greece (Davies 1977: 105-21).

2.3 Musha' *in the Hebrew Bible?*

There are good reasons to suspect that arable land was cultivated on a communal basis in Ancient Israel through a kind of tenure similar to the *musha'*. When the factors of land, production and risk are applied to ancient Palestine, the province of Yehud during the Babylonian and the Persian eras displays all the conditions required for the practice of *musha'* tenure. The population in Yehud decreased sharply after the destruction of Jerusalem and remained below seventh century BCE levels at the end of the Persian era (see Chapter 4). Low demography implies plenty of land for ploughing and grazing, small villages, great distances between settlements, and reforestation. Natural risks remained constant while the absence of a strong central government increased the danger of raids against isolated settlements.

Biblical evidence for the redistribution of land is scarce but it has long been recognized (Buhl 1899: 57-59; Von Rad 1943; Kohler 1959; Neufeld 1960: 32; Elliger 1962; Kaufman 1984: 280; Lemche 1985: 196-98; Bendor 1996: 141-60). In a study of Israelite land tenure, Henrey (1954: 9) described something very similar to *musha'* tenure without naming it as such. He referred to communal land of which each family was allotted a section although it would remain 'common' property. Others mentioned *musha'* by name and suggested that it was practised in biblical times (Alt 1959; Chaney 1983: 64-65; De Geus 1983). Wright (1990: 70) accepts biblical *musha'* although he restricts episodic redistributions to tribal territory which he opposes to family patrimony. Levine admits that *musha'* tenure displays similarity to the allocation of the land of Canaan but adds that more study would be required to ascertain in what sense *musha'* land can be classified as private (Levine 1996: 226).

Wright's distinction between tribal territory and family patrimony reflects a common confusion between the actual allocation of arable land at the village level and the ideal division of tribal territories that have little or no practical implications. It will be seen below (§2.3.7) that the Book of Joshua presupposes *musha'* tenure.

The distinction between *mulk* and *mīrī* land (§1.4.2) answers Levine's question about how far *musha'* land could be classified as private. Although some farmers continue to rotate plots and cultivate privatized land collectively (Schaebler 2001: 282; Seeden and Kaddour 1984), *musha'* tenure presupposes the existence of 'public' or *mīrī* land, land that was susceptible to periodic redistribution because farmers held usufruct rather than ownership. The continuation of collective cultivation after land consolidation is a token to the beneficial aspects of *musha'* tenure and of the limited usefulness of the notion of ownership to farmers.

The recognition of the relevance of the *musha'* in biblical studies has been impaired when *musha'* tenure got embroiled in ideological debates over the existence or not of some kind of primitive communism derived from Karl Marx's model of the Asiatic Mode of Production (Marx 2003: 229-46; Boer 2007: 31-34; Houston 2008: 35-43). Communal tribal tenure was deemed a feature of the nomadic ideal of ancient Israel destroyed by the rise of the kingdoms of Israel and Judah. Evidence for the existence of such communism was traced in prophetic reminiscence of a golden age of communal property marred by the ills of capitalism and privatization. The ideological presuppositions of such ancient and modern 'prophetic' views were easily debunked as confusing family ownership with national communism (Wright 1990: 66-70). The evidence for a *musha'*-like tenure in the Hebrew Bible is indeed discreet, but it is there.

2.3.1 Musha' *in Micah 2:5*

The clearest attestation of a periodical measuring out of land lots is found in Mic. 2:5:

> לכן לא יהיה לך משליך חבל בגורל בקהל יהוה
>
> Therefore, there will be no one extending the measuring rope for you in the lot in the assembly of YHWH.

If any connection between verse 5 and verses 1-2 is intended (Wagenaar 2001: 73-75, 208-20), the addressee is excluded from the distribution of land lots in retaliation for the seizure of fields and houses (v. 2). Since Albrecht Alt, the passage is cited as evidence for the formation of latifundia during the eighth century BCE (Alt 1959). Latifundia were large estates in Italy denounced by Pliny (*Nat. Hist.* XVIII.7) as the cause of many evils (see §4.5.2). For the present purpose, it is enough to heed Ehud Ben Zvi's warning that the writer was not interested in what actually happened in Israel during the monarchic period. He depicted a sinful Israel to explain Judah's calamity during his time. The land grabbers are a literary and theological foil to address the fall of the monarchy and evoke a brilliant future (Ben Zvi 1999: 96). If this text is not a reliable source for the study of the social history of eighth-century BCE Palestine, the punishment envisaged does reveal something of the reality in which the writers lived. They considered the exclusion from the distribution of land a fitting punishment for the land grabbers. The writers could not conceive a more serious punishment, although its actual effect would have been nil on *latifundisti*. Had they amassed a large estate for themselves, their exclusion from the distribution of communal land would have been of no consequence. Either there would have been no more land to share out or the land grabbers could have managed without their share of communal land. No, latifundia were not part of the world of those who penned Mic. 2:5. For these people, the practice of parcelling out land lots with a measuring rope was the only method they knew to secure some arable land and they could not imagine a more dreadful punishment than being excluded from the distribution of strips of common land. In Amos 7:17, the measuring rope is applied to Amaziah's soil (אדמתך בחבל תחלק) before he is sent to exile. Amos probably presupposes the intervention of foreign invaders who would dispossess Amaziah and share out his family and land. In Mic. 2:5., however, the mention of the local assembly (קהל) disproves the notion of a foreign invader punishing the land grabbers by confiscating their estate. Micah refers to the routine of land redistribution in peaceful times. Hence, Bendor's claim that Mic. 2:5

refers to periodic land redistribution within the village community should be maintained as the best option (Bendor 1996: 148-52 against Wagenaar 2001: 217).

2.3.2 Musha' *in Jeremiah 37*

Another clue for an open-field system in ancient Judah is found in Jeremiah's departure from Jerusalem for Benjamin 'to apportion' as soon as the Babylonians lifted the siege of the city:

> ויצא ירמיהו מירושלם ללכת ארץ בנימן לחלק משם בתוך העם (Jer. 37:12)
>
> Jeremiah came out of Jerusalem to go to the land of Benjamin to apportion from there among the people.

The expression 'to apportion' (לחלק) has given trouble to early translators and modern commentators alike. Holladay (1989: 288) proposes the loss of לקחת through haplography. The Septuagint translated it as ἀγοράσαι, 'to buy', in an attempt to connect this episode with Jeremiah's buying of a field from his uncle in Jer. 32:6-15, a suggestion followed by many commentators (Freedman 1977: 250; Nicholson 1975: 116; Boadt 1982: 94-95; Carroll: 1986: 675; Holladay 1989: 288; Jones 1992: 457). The connection, though, is doubtful (Feinberg 1982: 256; Thompson 1980: 633-34). Matters arising from an uncle's estate could have waited until better times and hardly explain Jeremiah's decision to risk further accusations of disloyalty by leaving the city at such short notice. The notion of buying land is contradicted by Aquila, Theodotion and Symmachus (α', σ', θ') who stay close to the MT with the notion of division (μερίσασθαι) that makes sense in the context of land allotment (Graupner 1991: 113-14). In an attempt to prove the pre-exilic origin of the jubilee, this distribution of land has been presented as a measure required by the laws of the jubilee (Fried and Freedman 2001: 2261). The calculations to obtain a jubilee precisely on that year are highly speculative and even if Zedekiah's ninth year happened to be the year of the jubilee, the 'law' of the jubilee does not entail any redistribution of land (§7.4).

Jeremiah's haste finds a more straightforward explanation as the consequence of an impending redistribution of *musha'* tenure. Rather than going to Benjamin to divide the property of a deceased family member between his heirs for which Jeremiah would be acting as estate executor (Carroll 1986: 674), Jeremiah, as every courtier at Jerusalem, drew most of his revenues from his own tenure that he cultivated himself or through some sort of arrangement with a relative. Hence, Jeremiah was anxious to reach Anathoth to be present 'among the people' (העם בתוך), the holders of shares of arable land around Anathoth, to claim his share of arable land during the re-allotment that was to take place that year. Whether or not Jeremiah was conscious that his departure might be interpreted as desertion, he left in earnest because individual strips had already been measured out with ropes and marked out while the elders of Anathoth were waiting for the arrival of the last shareholders to throw lots and allocate the strips. The elders of Anathoth may have delayed the allotment to give Jeremiah and any other son of the village held back in Jerusalem a chance to be present, but the allotment could not be held off much longer since it was high time to start ploughing. According to Jer. 39:1, Jeremiah's attempted departure took place before the return of the Babylonians in the tenth month of Zedekiah's ninth year, that is January 588 BCE, which dates the lifting of the siege on 29 December, 588 BCE (Fried and Freedman 2001: 2260). This is at most a few weeks late for the normal start of the winter ploughing (Sonnen 1927: 66; Dalman 1964: 216, 261), but the siege had prevented Jeremiah from leaving earlier. Had rain started a little late that year, Jeremiah would have just made it for the allotment at his home village.

The text supplies no hint as to whether the distribution about to take place was a yearly procedure or if it was prompted by the exceptional political circumstances that the kingdom was experiencing. If the Babylonians were already reorganizing the provincial administration at the time, a general redistribution of land there and then would make plenty of sense (Lipschits 1999). Jeremiah's haste suggests that he had to be physically present to place his personal token among the others or he would not receive his lot that year. In any case, communal tenure offers a likely explanation for Jer. 37:12, which can be added to the list of clues for the practice of periodical redistribution of land strips in a system similar to *musha*ʿ tenure. Additional evidence can be gleaned from the Psalms.

2.3.3 Musha*ʿ in the Psalms*

Three verses from the Psalms place the terms נחלה and חבל in parallel:

> חבלים נפלו לי בנעמים אף נחלת שפרה עלי
>
> The ropes fell for me in a good [place] indeed a fair portion for me. (Ps. 16:6, literal)
>
> The boundary lines have fallen for me in pleasant places; I have a goodly heritage. (NRSV)

ויגרש מפניהם גוים ויפילם בחבל נחלה וישכן באהליהם שבטי ישראל

He chased peoples in front of them. He cast [for] them by a rope a portion.

He settled according to their tents the tribes of Israel. (Ps. 78:55, literal)

He drove out nations before them; he apportioned them for a possession and settled the tribes of Israel in their tents. (NRSV)

He drove out the nations before them, and felled them on their upland patrimony. (Dahood)

On the basis of Ugaritic *ḥbl,* Dahood (1981: 237, 245) renders חבל as 'hill' instead of 'rope' and the casting of the rope becomes the felling of the Canaanites. An agricultural context is more likely. The tribes are not settled in tents as the NRSV suggests. The tents provide the number of units into which the fields are divided, as is the case in Psalm 105:

לך אתן את ארץ כנען חבל נחלתכם

To you I will give the land of Canaan, the rope of your *naḥalah.* (Ps. 105:11)

To you I will give the land of Canaan as your portion for an inheritance. (NRSV)

To you I will give the land, Canaan will be your upland patrimony. (Dahood)

Here again, Dahood (1981: 49) renders the rope as upland. Yet, the 'rope' is simply the measure of the strips of arable land distributed to each shareholder. The 'rope of your *naḥalah*' is the size of the land grant. Because arable land was regularly redistributed, the measuring rope used to share out the strips came to designate the land itself (Fig. 3). This meaning of the word 'rope' is lost in translation when it is rendered directly as 'land', 'portion' or 'lot' (Weiser 1962: 536; Hossfeld and Zenger 2005: 284).

2.3.4 Musha' *in Deuteronomy 32*

The loss of the primary meaning of the measuring rope becomes acute in Deut. 32:9 where the rope is used in parallelism with a share (חלק):

כי חלק יהוה עמו יעקב חבל נחלתו

For YHWH's share is his people; Jacob is the rope of his *naḥalah.* (Deut. 32:9)

[T]he Lord's own portion was his people, Jacob his allotted share. (NRSV)

Figure 3: Measuring out strips with a rope (Aswad 1971: Plate XII, reproduced with permission of Museum of Anthropology Publications of the University of Michigan).

This time, it is חלק that the NRSV renders as 'portion' and חבל dissolves into the 'allotted share'. Through the abuse of synonymy, the measuring rope vanishes and the metaphor negates its referent. As translators have to use concepts that modern readers can grasp and as the measuring rope is a metaphor of arable land, the shift from the literal 'rope' to the figurative 'land' is legitimate. Yet, rendering land instead of rope obscures the evidence for the periodic redistribution of land strips and leads readers in thinking that Joshua's original distribution was a once-for-all procedure and that it fixed each family to a particular plot.

2.3.5 Musha' *in Ruth and Elsewhere*

Boaz's recommendation that Ruth should carefully check which field his working team is harvesting (עיניך בשׂדה; Ruth 2:9) is superfluous in an enclosed-field regime, but makes much sense if the 'field' is made of a number of non-contiguous strips separated by the strips allotted to the other landholders of Bethlehem. In that case, the risk that Ruth may glean someone else's strips would be far greater than if each field was a larger parcel of land delimited by permanent boundaries. That in Ruth 4:3 Naomi trades Elimelech's share of land (חלק בשׂדה) rather than a particular field is another clue that the Book of Ruth presupposes an open-field system. The implications of this crucial point are discussed above (§1.3.4).

Once the measuring rope is rescued from the translations that erase it, *musha'* tenure becomes a common feature in the world of the biblical writers. Measuring ropes (חבל מדה, Akk. *ašlu*; Powell 1990: 459) are also mentioned in Zech. 1:16; 2:5 and the measuring rod (קנה המדה) in Ezek. 40:3. Because strips were regularly redistributed with the measuring rope, the two different roots *ḥbl* and *ḫbl* cover actions of 'twisting, writhing, binding and destroying' as well as 'borrowing, owing', and by derivation 'obligation, debt, interest, pledge, region, territory, draught animals, terraced land, pregnant or fertile women' (HALOT I: 285-86; Mankowski 2000: 55-56; Denizeau 1960: 98; Barthélemy 1935: 144).

The lack of more direct evidence for periodical redistribution derives from the nature of the phenomenon, which was done at the local level and was governed entirely by tradition at the discretion of the elders of each village. It left no physical traces on the ground precisely because boundaries kept shifting regularly to keep up with demography and tax-burden. Records of sale do not mention it because they concern freehold property such as houses, threshing floors, tombs, gardens, vineyards and orchards, arable land being mentioned in passing but never the main object of the sale as such.

2.3.6 Moving Boundary Markers

The importance of boundary markers and the prohibitions to move them (Deut. 19:14; 27:17; Hos. 5:10) is taken as indicative of land settlement. Boundary markers supposedly show that arable land in Israel was divided into separate fields (Wright 1990: 70) and that communal tenure was not practiced in ancient Israel (Deist 2002). Deist insists that the lot (גרל) was the piece of land allotted once for all to a family. As the property allotted to each household was determined by chance, some lots would have been better than others (Deist 2002: 144).

It is precisely this kind of injustice that *musha'* tenure seeks to correct through the periodical redistribution of furlongs that were carefully measured with a rod or a rope and marked out to prevent encroachment and cheating. Yet, periodic redistribution prevented setting up firm and permanent boundaries between strips. These were delimitated by flimsy markers such as sticks or stones that were easily moved.[3] The stone heaps over the furrows of fields mentioned in Hos. 12:12b could be just this type of marker. They were placed only or mainly at the head of the strip as the word ראשנים in Deut. 19:14 indicates.

The common translation of these 'heads' in Deut. 19:14 as 'ancestors, former generations', reinforces the impression of immovable boundaries when in fact it is their periodic reshuffling that ensured fairness in land allotment. It is only when, due to increasing population, the communal land of neighbouring villages came into contact and provoked bitter disputes between villages that permanent boundary markers were set up to mark out the territory controlled by each village. The setting of corner irons by British Mandate surveyors was the aspect of land surveys most welcomed by Palestinian farmers, contrary to the settlement of land within villages (Wåhlin 1994: 59). Given the low demography in Judah and even more so in Yehud, no such measures were necessary as the arable land of any village would be separated from the fields of the neighbouring villages by large tracts of waste-land. Within the village's fields, however, the prohibition of moving boundaries reflects the flimsy markers between strips rather than hedges, ditches, walls and large trees that mark permanent limits. The existence of boundary stones that are liable to be moved supports the existence of open fields rather than a definitive consolidation where the limits between plots are not so easily altered (see §2.2.2).

2.3.7 Musha' *as Paradigm in Numbers and Joshua*

Joshua's division of the land of Canaan into tribal territories is often used as a grid to interpret biblical texts relative to land. For instance, Marvin Sweeney (2007: 249) applies it to the Naboth story and Ziony Zevit (2005: 595) to Ruth. Exegetes imagine Joshua's initial allotment as a once for all procedure that was never repeated (Goldingay 2006: 230-31; Vesco 2006: 184). Because it was never repeated, it is then argued that the borders established by Joshua were intangible and that that land was inalienable. In that case, the Book of Joshua would contradict the notion that communal tenure was practised in ancient Israel.

The actual allotment is only reported in the briefest terms in Josh. 14:1-2; 18:2, merely stating that 'their *naḥalah* (was) by lots' (בגורל נחלתם). The narration stops short of a description of the procedure for the actual allotment family by family. Yet, Num. 26:56 and 33:54 insist that land is to be allocated in proportion to the size of each tribal unit. Hence, Canaan is not simply divided into twelve lots. Units smaller than the tribe have to be considered. The two censuses of Numbers 1 and 26 reveal that it is not the number of *mishpahot* that determines the number of lots but the number of individual adult males, which implies the *dhukūr* type of *musha'* tenure. Off-putting as they are, the lists transmit the prerequisites for the allotment of particular strips to individual adult males to equate the available resources as closely as possible to the actual needs. After 40 years and a plague (Num. 26:1), the data from the first census is useless and the number of adult males must be updated thanks to a second census (Num. 26:4-51). The second census stresses the importance of correcting the inevitable demographic fluctuations (shown by large differences in the numbers recorded in the two censuses) through periodic re-allotment. The same insistence on the need to keep abreast with demographic changes by regular updates of the available resources is found in Josh. 18:2-10. The delay encountered in the allotment of land for seven tribes rendered the previous land survey obsolete. A new survey had to be organized before lots could be cast.

Obviously, the casting of the measuring rope over plots for individual farmers cannot be narrated and the final step, without which the allotment is incomplete, is never told. It is presupposed but exegetes unfamiliar with ancient tenure systems conclude that the allotment by Joshua and Eleazar is a once for all procedure marking out immutable tribal territories. In fact, tribal territories with fixed borders are as much a fiction as the notion of a unified conquest (Knauf 2008: 150). Joshua's answer to the sons of Joseph who complain that their single lot is too small for their numbers (Josh. 17:14-15) shows that tribal territories have no hard and fast boundaries and that demography is always well below the supporting capacity of the available land.

The impossibility of equating tribal territories with individual tenure claims is made plain by the painfully inadequate solution delineated in the two episodes of the daughters of Zelophehad who are requested to refrain from marrying outside their father's tribe (Num. 27:1-11; 36:1-12). In practice, women do marry outside their father's tribe whether their brothers like it or not. Moreover, villages do incorporate strangers into the community whenever an extra pair of hands is seen as an asset. The tribe is an identity marker which states preferences for spouse selection. Tribal affinities, however, stand in tension with claims to arable land that are governed by membership in the village. The local community manipulates tribal genealogies to correlate tribal purity with the constant flux of manpower. The hostility towards a foreigner wanes as soon as he shoulders the village tax-burden or the burden of feeding local widows and orphans through marriage. At that point, tribe and clan adapt to the exigencies of land tenure (Conte 2003). The outsider is co-opted into the tribe and integrated in the genealogy because land tenure overrides blood considerations. As people must produce enough food to survive before they can take considerations of identity into account, a foreigner useful to the group soon loses his or her foreignness.

The tribal territories in Joshua are ideal constructs since the cornerstone of tribal links is kin, not land (Van den Berghe 1981; Sparks 1998b). The Transjordan tribes are a case in point. Two-and-a-half tribes spill over the ideal map of Canaan in Numbers 32 and insist that kin is beyond geography. These tribes provide their shares of fighters for the wars of an Israel they are supposed to belong to, but when they return home, they run their fields according to the decisions of the village community. The concept of tribe is important on the level of ideology, but it has little economic relevance (Lemche 1999: 94). On the agricultural level, *'ir* is more significant than *mišpaḥah* (Bendor 1996: 98-107). Therefore, nothing in the Book of Joshua can be adduced against the practice of communal tenure similar to the *musha'* in ancient Israel. Rather than proving the absence of periodical redistribution of land, the allotment of entire regions to 'tribes' transposes the practical procedure of *musha'* tenure at the village level onto an ideal regional level. It is against this background that the notion of an original distribution tribe by tribe in Joshua makes sense (Kitz 2000).

The conclusion of this section on traces of *musha'* tenure in the Bible is that Gerber's doubts over the ancient origins of the *musha'* are as unjustified as the claim that 'there is little likelihood that village arable was periodically redistributed' (Coote and Whitelam 1986: 362). Periodical redistribution does not fit the agenda of social-scientific exegesis that needs a crisis to justify prophetic fulminations. Yet, the books of Numbers and Joshua delineate the principle that governs a communal tenure subject to regular re-allocation. The measuring rope in Mic. 2:5 is the clearest attestation of redistribution of land strips by the local assembly, the most obvious explanation for the exclusion of the land grabbers denounced in the previous verses. Redistribution of strips explains Jeremiah's hasty departure from Jerusalem better than any other explanation offered so far. Ignorance of the practice of periodical redistribution of arable land brought much confusion in the translation of technical terms in the Psalms and in Deuteronomy 32. Finally, the prohibition of moving boundary markers at the head of fields makes better sense in the framework of strips that are reshuffled periodically and are thus delimited with flimsy marks. There is thus enough evidence to consider that the open-field system and the periodical redistribution of strips was an integral feature of the life of the people who wrote the Bible. The concept of inalienability of land often encountered in exegetical literature only makes sense in the context of communal tenure. Applying inalienability to privately owned land (*mulk*) is a contradiction in terms since the foundational aspect of ownership is the ability to alienate. By contrast, inalienability applies to land that is used but not owned (*mīrī*). Land is inalienable because its possessor does not own it and is therefore deprived of the ability to alienate it.

The relevance of the Islamic and Ottoman land tenure systems to biblical studies is clear. Given the insuperable difficulties in dating biblical texts, it is not possible at this stage to narrow the time range and assert that *musha'* tenure was practised in Persian Yehud. Before attempting a reconstruction of the rural conditions during this particular period in Part III, the next section offers a reminder of other methods used by ancient farmers to cope with the challenges of growing one's own food.

2.4 Other Aspects of Ancient Palestinian Farming

2.4.1 Mughārasa

Besides *musha'* tenure, Ottoman farmers had the possibility of getting hold of land through the institution of *mughārasa.* A sharecropper makes a contract with a landholder stipulating that the sharecropper ploughs some of the holder's land and plants it with specified perennial species (vine, olive, almonds and fruit trees). Several years later, when the plantation bears fruit, the produce and the land are shared out between the partners according to the input of each (Weulersse 1946: 130; Issawi 1982: 149; Wåhlin 1998: 66). The sharecropper who provided all the work, the young plants and the water they needed during the first summers, may get half of the land besides half of the trees. If he gets no land, he may be able to grow crops between the trees. Contrary to *musha'* shares, the duration of the hold of the sharecropper is limited to the life of the plants. The contract is automatically extinguished upon their disappearance. In 1930, 4% of the Palestinian families in the villages investigated by the Johnson-Crosbie Committee owned trees but no land (Granott 1952: 183). In the seventeenth century CE, 50% of the peasants in the Bursa region were landless. Yet, this does not indicate that all were poor since some of these landless farmers specialized in non-agricultural activities and owned large houses (Gerber 1987: 27-29).

2.4.2 Staggered Harvests and Wage Labour

Such is the steepness of the Palestinian ground that major climatic changes due to altitude occur within short distances. With a time lag of four to six weeks between the coast and the central range (Granott

1952: 173), farmers of the highland found extra resources as day workers within walking distance. The Judeans involved in the confiscation of a garment during the harvest near Minet Rubin, at a site since re-named Meṣad Ḥashavyahu, were either serving their term of corvée work or taking waged employment in the coastal plain (Naveh 1960). In either case, the highland provided a reservoir of manpower for the coastal settlements, which offered opportunities for highland farmers who had few other ways to reduce the months of inactivity between ploughing and harvest. When economic activity was particularly depressed on the coast, highland farmers could themselves seed some lowland fields to benefit from the difference in altitude. These fields were organized as *khirbe,* satellite settlements rather than 'ruins' where farmers lived in shacks during times of intense activity.

2.4.3 Other Survival Techniques

Farmers had a range of other strategies at their disposal to cope with the challenges of farming. Constant sky scrutiny helped forecast the weather and adapt seeding strategies. When autumn rains were insufficient, farmers decided not to sow or to sow little to avoid wasting seed. In modern Syria, when spring rains are insufficient, farmers rent their sown fields to herders to graze the grain on the blade and recoup some of their loss (Métral 2000: 131). Gathering and preserving wild flora, hunting and mercenary work provided non-negligible resources, in particular in times of low demography when game, berries, mushrooms, herbs were plentiful. Various methods of family limitation such as the sale of children, abortion, infanticide and exposure helped adapt the number of mouths to available resources (Brunt 1987: 131-55; Bar Ilan 1990: 3-25). In times of famine, the youngest and the oldest members of the family were left to starve to preserve the health of the active adults upon whose survival the future of the group depended. Occasional banditry (not the exclusive privilege of the Bedouin) would supply additional resources (Gallant 1991: 113-69). Pooling resources was another successful strategy to achieve effective exploitation for small subsistence farmers. Sharing rights over such a minimal pool of property as a slave, a donkey or a mule reduced wasteful underemployment and avoided the cost of the occasional hire of animals and workers. Hence, small holders benefited from the service of draught animals without shouldering all the feeding and maintenance costs.

Someone who holds no share of an animal may always borrow it and ancient legal collections commonly refer to the borrowing of animals and to the legal intricacies resulting from the death or injury of a borrowed beast (Lirb 1993: 263-95). In fact, draught animals were not always economically viable. The comparative merit of the hoe versus the plough cultivation is now recognized. The absence of a ploughing team, usually interpreted as a sign of poverty, in fact enabled small farmers to save on the high feeding costs of draught animals and to produce higher yields than farmers who cultivated greater surfaces. Roman studies indicate that two hectares were sufficient to feed a family if they were worked by spade and hoe, while five hectares were needed if work animals were kept. Another factor in favour of the competitiveness of small units of production was sowing by dribbling rather than by broadcasting that was more wasteful in seeds and provided lower seed-to-yield ratios (Halstead 2002: 65-66). In light of the various strategies to cope with adverse conditions, ancient farmers were not helpless victims of intractable higher powers. Small units were often in a better position to cope than larger ones.

Notes

1. Hebrew גויה (Gen. 47:18; Zeph. 2:14) designates the different sectors of village land and corresponds to Arabic *wajahāt* (وجهات).
2. §1: 'The farmer who is working his own field must be just and must not encroach on his neighbour's furrows (αὔλακας). If a farmer persists in encroaching and docks a neighbouring lot—if he did this in ploughing-time, he loses his ploughing; if it was in sowing-time that he made this encroachment, he loses his seed and his husbandry and his crop—the farmer who encroached' (105.§60). 'Let those who in harvest-time come into another man's furrow and cut bundles or ears of corn or pulse be whipped and stripped of their shirts' (Ashburner 1912: 87).
3. Slanski (2003) shows that the Babylonian *kudurrus* were no boundary stones but *narûs*, entitlement monuments often placed in temples to commemorate royal and non-royal land grants, grants of sinecures, tax exemptions, adjudication of lawsuits, and affirmation of land titles or land purchase. It is not certain that the *horoi* Solon is said to have removed from Athenian land marked the hypothecation of land. Ober (2006) argues that they established facts on the ground.

Chapter 3

The Myth of the Helpless Peasant

Peasant helplessness is a recurring cliché in biblical exegesis. Ancient farmers are regularly depicted as the hapless victims of state taxation, conscription, natural disasters and greedy moneylenders. For instance, Fred Gottheil (1986) and Gabriel Baer (1983) quote catastrophic reports from Western observers who exaggerated or misunderstood the evidence. Exegetical literature is full of broad depictions of biblical farmers losing their land, their families and their freedom, as suggested by readings of Nehemiah 5 (§7.2).

The same notion is found in studies of the ancient Levant. In an impressive synthesis of Mesopotamian land regimes before the turn of the era, Johannes Renger (1995: 308) explains the rise of large manorial estates held by grandees of the Neo-Assyrian empire as 'of course the result of the gradual impoverishment of small landowners or landholders'. The huge temple estates are also understood as the result of the enslavement of impoverished persons who became oblates or bondsmen of the temple. 'They had lost their personal freedom short of becoming slaves in the narrow sense' (Renger 1995: 312). As these oblates were not able to plough all the temple estates, land was leased to agricultural entrepreneurs who contracted landless individuals to do the job (Renger 1995: 313).

The template of the 'the gradual impoverishment of the lower echelons of society' functions particularly well whenever a concentration of wealth is identified (Renger 1995: 319). As the theory goes, any accumulation of wealth must result from the deprivation of others. Yet, the question of how the rich can get richer by fleecing the poor remains. The oblates whom Renger considers as impoverished landowners may have felt privileged in being dependants of the temple as much as modern tenured professors and civil servants derive job security from belonging to large governmental or non-governmental structures, a security that free-lancers lack cruelly in times of crisis. People of all times are ready to go a long way in trading freedom for security (Gelb 1965; Jursa 2008). For this reason, ancient farmers may have willingly endowed part or all of their land to a temple in exchange for access to the system of redistribution and this may have contributed to situations where temples 'owned' large tracts of land. As for the people who provided work on temple land to supplement the oblates, nothing indicates that they were landless. The same applies to corvée teams who received rations while they were press-ganged for state projects. These rations functioned as wages of sorts and supplemented their own production, which suggests that impressments in teams of forced labour linked farmers to the redistribution system and provided them with a welcome source of extra revenues if the work was required outside peaks of farm activity. Notions of freedom and ownership were vastly irrelevant to cultivators who were more concerned with the amount of produce they managed to secure to feed their families.

Since the supposedly relentless process of dispossession is dated from the rise of the monarchy to the Roman era, it is a miracle that enough peasants survived to feed the scribes who penned the Bible and the rich corpus of ancient literature. The simple fact that the Bible was written at all demonstrates the existence of efficient strategies to cope with famine and the most severe disasters. Given the inadequacy of sources, it is impossible to produce statistical studies, but the Wrigley and Schofield (1981) paradox is likely to have some validity for periods earlier than the early modern period in England upon which it was based. Although long-distance grain trade was insignificant in biblical times compared to England, biblical people compensated this lack by higher mobility and moved where the grain was (Gen. 12:10; 26; Ruth 1:1, but see Ezek. 27:17) rather than waiting for the grain to come to them. The Wrigley and Schofield paradox is based on the observation that crisis years in grain production are poorly correlated with crisis years in mortality, which indicates the existence of effective methods of smoothing consumption. Hence, one must be careful in equating too closely food shortage with mortality among the poor. Epidemics and war struck the rich as much as the poor, while the rich had a vested interest in the survival of their poorer fellows. The survival of the medieval poor remains something of a mystery because informal solidarity networks are invisible (Van Leewen 2000: 17; Geremek 1997: 71). Despite the drama of academic depictions, biblical farmers never were passive victims, neither to natural, economic or political factors. Therefore, Walter Houston (2009) suggests that the victims of the social injustices mentioned in prophetic accusations resided mostly in Samaria and Jerusalem, and that they were not peasants. The existence of an urban proletariat in agricultural societies such as ancient Israel and Judah is unlikely since urbanites were involved in food production, if in lesser degrees than inhabitants of villages. Yet, Houston's suggestion is a welcome move away from the standard portrait of the victimized farmer.

3.1 Collective Exclusivity and Bargaining Power

Farmers did not live alone. Members of open-field villages assumed corporate responsibility and acted as a juridical person (Dahlman 1980: 209-10). Having relinquished some of their individual rights over the land to the village commune, farmers entered into contractual agreements as one body. Within a body of several dozen families, the 'powerless' farmer was in a better position to negotiate matters of taxation, conscription, criminal and financial liabilities than if he had been alone. Hence, the ancient farmer was not a lone prey at the mercy of vastly superior commercial and political powers. The financial and judicial authorities had much to gain in dealing with a village as a whole. The efficiency of village communities was maintained by their relatively small membership. They were of an optimal size beyond which pressure on land combined with increasing transaction costs arising from the growing anonymity of greater settlements made communal tenure inefficient (Dahlman 1980: 136). Hence, smallish village communities were economically viable units that gave small farmers a political leverage well beyond the apparent misery they lived in.

Another factor in favour of small farming communities is the transformation of an individual's hold over resources into a bundle of property rights that could be traded and transmitted but not withdrawn. The individual freedom that fostered credit operations through the use of land as security was counter-balanced by the impossibility for shareholders to threaten the system by withdrawing their shares from the common pool. Hence, scattering and common tenure were economically viable and consistent with risk aversion (Dahlman 1980: 139). Moreover, *musha'* tenure combined private property rights in the arable with large-scale grazing in the open fields during fallow and between harvest and ploughing, at precisely the time when grazing was in short supply in the common pastures and on waste-land. The advantageous negotiating position with external agents and the stability of the system go a long way in explaining the resilience of open-field systems. The notion of the helpless farmer is thus the direct consequence of the failure to integrate communal tenure in ancient agriculture. Given the Marxian interest in the 'use and abuse of power as a means of attaining skewed distributions of economic influence and income' (Dahlman 1980: 219), it is no surprise that the main institution that checked these abuses, the village commune, was left aside until recently (Gottwald 1999: 11).

The bargaining power of peasants was also bolstered by the simple fact that, in the ancient world, land was plentiful while farmers were in chronic shortage (Van Driel 1998: 190-98). Hence, the notion that ancient the Oriental ruling elite were 'for the most part dismissive of the interests of the populace at large in spite of the political rhetoric trumpeting their just and peaceful rule' carries its own fair share of rhetorical trumpeting (Gottwald 2003: 198). It is very much in the interest of every monarch, ancient or modern, to make the majority of the ruled feel that the ruler cares about their interests because claiming that rebellion against the representative of the highest authority is rebellion against God (Exod. 22:27 [Eng. 28]) only works up to a point (Sneed 1996: 303). The bargaining power of the producers and workers was far from nil because they were always in short supply. Hired workers refused to work when pay and rations were late or low and threats of violence made employers anxious to satisfy the demands of workers because they could not be replaced with slaves (Dandamayev 1987: 278). Even the poorest elements of society had a political significance that exceeded their economic power since, as recipients of concrete shows of redistributive justice, they bolstered the legitimacy of the ruler. Social peace rested in the authority of the ruler, which rested with his ability to negotiate settlements with the different components of society. These settlements reflected the actual balance of power at any particular point of time. When communal strategies failed, moving was a viable option.

3.2 Peasant Mobility

Records from ancient Egypt reveal a constant difficulty in forcing farmers to sow the land. Tenants and sharecroppers often fled the land by the customary practice of *anachōrēsis*, withdrawing their labour after having sown royal land and leaving the standing crop unharvested (Rowlandson 1985: 338; Rostovtzeff 1941: II, 898-99; Manning 2003: 115-16). In principle, farmers of the Ottoman Empire could not leave the land and had to pay a special tax, the *čift bozan resmi*, if they did (Lewis 1979). The need to impose a tax as a deterrent shows that farmers did abandon their land when they considered it profitable so to do. As late as the mid-nineteenth century CE, despite a sharp increase in the population that would have put some pressure on land availability, the Egyptian government had to offer special incentives to have peasants farm vacant land (Ghalwash 1998: 126-27).

At roughly the same period, Burckardt noted during his extensive travels across Syria and Palestine that in fringe areas few individuals, Druzes or Christians, died in their native village. Families were continually on the move, a situation that explained the absence of orchards in the Hauran (Burckhardt 1819: 299). In fringe areas (Palestine often was one) peasant mobility caused major fluctuation of settlement levels that cannot be taken as indications of changes in prosperity and birthrate. The five population estimates for Qanawat in the Hauran cover two centuries:

1596: 85 inhabitants, some Bedouin among them
1805: 0?
1812: 5-6 families in the ruins
1821: 300 inhabitants
1822: 600 inhabitants (Schaebler 2001: 251)

However imprecise the figures are, the variations show that fringe localities could fill in or empty out within a decade, depending on the political situation. Therefore, migration and squatting must be integrated as viable options for the survival of biblical farmers whose numbers were low enough to leave large tracts of fertile land uncultivated.

Although far from a fringe area, the kingdom of Ugarit had problems with peasant defection (Liverani 1965; Heltzer 1976: 58-62). The archives document the special case of the *nayyālu*, 'idler or lazy' individuals who defaulted on their obligations and whose land was transferred to others (PRU III, nos 15:114, 112; 16:238, 107; 16:132, 140). The root of the problem was more probably peasant mobility than laziness. Michael Heltzer refers to the transfer of the *nayyālu*'s property as confiscation, a means to enrich the crown and the treasury (Heltzer 1976: 51-57). Confiscation is surely not the correct description. The *nayyālu*'s estate was transferred to someone else in order to limit the crown's loss of revenue on land left uncultivated. The crown was not enriching itself by confiscating estates. It was limiting its losses by seeking a holder for derelict holdings. That the previous holder did not cultivate it does not necessarily entail duress.

As a consequence of his understanding of the transfer of the *nayyālu*'s property as confiscation, Heltzer claims that the only way for a *nayyālu* to survive was to enter into royal service and to become a *bnš mlk*, a royal dependent (Heltzer 1976: 57). Instead of clarifying the status of the *nayyālu*, this suggestion adds to the problem of how the crown fed these royal dependents. It cannot be assumed that the king fed them since the king himself was deeply involved in food production to feed his own house. Who fed the large crowd of royal dependents that is said to make up a third of the population of the kingdom of Ugarit (Heltzer 1987: 244)? The answer is that the king's men fed themselves by working on royal estates rather than on their own land, a distinction that implies no superiority of a class of freemen over other kinds of tenants (Heltzer 1996; Liverani 1975). Hence, some cases of *nayyālu* should be viewed in the context of peasant mobility. For whatever reason, some people left some of their holding uncultivated. In Ottoman terms, the abandoned estate fell under the category of *maḥlūl* land. The confiscation of abandoned holdings is a contradiction in terms and does not have the same implications as the confiscation of productive units. The aim was not to take away land from someone who needed it to enrich someone else, but to ensure that as little land as possible remained uncultivated. A similar preoccupation is attested in Athens (Plutarch, *Solon* 31:5) where a law against *argia* (laziness) seems to stipulate that it was everyone's duty to cultivate land (Isager and Skydsgaard 1992: 145).

Peasant migration was also a problem for the Abbassids and later for the Ottomans who produced laws stipulating that farmers who had moved away from their village could be forced to move back within a ten-year period after which they had to be registered in their new village. Cahen (1954) mentions the use of indelible marks and collars with the name and the origin of non-Muslims (Michel 2001; 2002). Village elders tended to welcome newcomers since the *mīrī* tax was levied upon a village for as long as it was at all inhabited, however few its inhabitants. Hence, besides deterrent measures that never completely curbed migration (Schaebler 2001: 252-53), the authorities sought to identify the reasons that caused farmers to move away from their villages. Action was taken against oppressive Ottoman officials who were recognized as the main cause of the abandonment of land. Peasant migration remained a problem in Palestine as late as the nineteenth century CE in spite of a fast growing population (Gottheil 1986: 220-22). Peasant migration was of a piece with blunt refusals to pay taxes, assaults on tax collectors, hiding of harvests and cultivation of hidden plots: the peasants' everyday resistance to taxation (Singer 1992).

The fixed capital stock of farmers was sufficiently light in value and in actual weight not to deter mobility (Gottheil 1986: 220). By contrast, trees and other perennial plantations constituted a form of durable attachment. Their care after the initial years, however, was minimal and they could survive several years without much tending while they could be harvested by populations living at a distance or hiding in caves to evade taxation and conscription. Egyptian peasants in arrears of taxation were said to be moving from one village to another in a process of musical chairs (Lancaster and Lancaster 1995: 120). When the standard coping strategies failed, as soon as impositions began to eat into the peasant's subsistence and threatened their livelihood, peasant revolts erupted. Despite the superiority of regular armies, no central power could afford to ignore the threat of social unrest since loss of lives and disruption of the economy hurt the over-taxing authority as much as the farmers. When Prov. 3:30 claims that people do not despise a thief who steals to satisfy his hunger, it is clear that the elite who penned these words recognized the validity of hunger riots (Houston 2003: 230). For lack of vision and organization, peasant revolts rarely lead to significant political change, but they put a price tag to over-taxation. Therefore, whoever wanted to extract revenue from farmers had to find a *modus vivendi* with the *fellahin*. The amount of taxes levied on farmers and the amount of privileges and exemptions granted are always a function of the relative strength and bargaining power of a given community (Schaebler 2001: 243). This point is worth emphasizing as scholars often hold together gross over-taxation and crass enrichment of the taxing authority without realizing that they are mutually exclusive.

Niels Peter Lemche, for instance, reports a catastrophic reduction of village settlements in Greater Syria between 1525 and 1865 that he explains as the consequence of Turkish neglect in the area. Following the tradition of the former Greek, Roman and Arab imperial masters, the Ottoman sold the taxation rights to local officers without ever controlling their activity through the presence of an imperial army. Hence, explains Lemche, tax farmers were absolutely free to hire a private police force to extract as much revenue as they wished from the local population as long as they delivered the budgeted amount to the Porte (Lemche 1997: 325). As the peasants are said to abandon their villages and to revert to a nomadic lifestyle in order to escape the bullies of the tax collectors, one is left wondering how much revenue was left to collect by the tax farmers who would have found themselves unable to pay their dues to the Sultan. One may also ask whether tax farmers had not as much to gain from the absence of an imperial army as the tax collectors did. However much taxes they wished to collect—no doubt a very high amount—the prospect of peasant unrest acted as a limiting factor on the amount of revenue that the tax collectors actually collected since peasant riots resulted in the arrival of an imperial force.

Hence, the notion of tax collectors free to extract as much as they wished is a fallacy. Neither the ancient states nor the Bedouin could afford the costs of tight supervision required to curb tax evasion effectively while avoiding peasant revolts and the resulting losses in lives and revenues. In fact, the simultaneous presence of competing sources of taxation tended to improve the peasants' bargaining power as tax farmers played the state and the Bedouin against each other. The state itself was not a unified front. Officials competed with each other for revenues as much as tribes, farming families and villages competed with each other for lesser shares of the tax burden. Around the sixteenth century, a period of Turkish neglect of Palestine, according to Lemche, the court records of Jerusalem are strewn with the complaints and petitions of villagers that show that peasants turned to the qadi for redress against Ottoman officials. The greater number of suits against peasants by officials reveals that peasants had numerous strategies at their disposal for getting the better of local officials. The qadi's records reveal the constant give-and-take between peasants and officials and the range of acts each committed against the other. Singer (1994: 99-118) lists various peasant strategies: cultivation of unregistered fields while leaving registered ones fallow, beginning the harvest before the authorized date and then complaining that the product was about to spoil, making sure the supervisors were too busy to control all the operations, intentional use of small and large measures (*mudd*), moving to another village to complicate registration, diversion of water, peddling produce on the streets rather than in the market place, outright refusal or consistent delay in paying taxes and arrears, stoning and knifing of officials, sending off complaints directly to Istanbul to gain the support of the Sultan against his own officials. Peasant accusations of officials could be used by other officials against rivals. Punitive actions against rebellious villages had to be authorized by the qadi and the Sultan protected the villages against collective punishments. The arsenal of everyday peasant resistance included foot-dragging, dissimulation, false compliance, pilfering, feigned ignorance, slander, sabotage and so forth (Scott 1987). A list of conscripted workers reveals a high rate of absenteeism (20%) aggravated by the fact that most of those who did turn up were elderly men and children (McGinnis 2003)! The sheer number of peasants and their superior knowledge of local conditions ensured that their position was not that of an abject agrarian mass (Singer 1994: 130). The aim of the state was primarily to keep the peace at the lowest cost possible since it was unwilling to devote all its resources to the thorough extraction of taxes. The only way to increase revenues substantially was for the state to bring in settlers from outside and for the Bedouin to take up cultivation by themselves or by buying slaves to do it for them. Slaves were rarely economically viable options. As for the first solution, bringing in people from elsewhere, most empires practised it but it also required a major mobilization of resources.

Therefore, moving was always an option for farmers, in the enclosed habitat of Egypt and all the more so in Syria-Palestine. Clearing some of the vast tracts of fertile *terra rossa* lying fallow for years was not as unattractive as it seems. Ploughing them for a few seasons before moving to the next synclinal when the natural fertility decreased and when tax collectors became more daring or foragers of passing armies more greedy remained an option until modern states were able to effectively police the population. Beyond the neat Islamic categories, a mobile population lived on the fringes, evading taxation and making the most of empty areas where ready supplies of pasture, wood, game and other spontaneous resources compensated for the effort of clearing land for ploughing and living in ruins or shacks. Quantitative tests have shown that it takes between fifty to one-hundred years of continuous cropping of wheat and barley to exhaust the soil since drought contributes to preservation of soil fertility by inhibiting plant capacity to take up chemicals from the soil (Sallares 1991: 373-76). Clearing new land every so often was well worth the effort, in particular if the cleared land was not totally new but had remained abandoned for some decades. With more surface available, farmers could also reduce seeding rates and rely on tillering, a practice that improved the seed-to-yield ratio through the multiplication of stems from each plant. The sudden introduction of a new workforce in a demographically depleted area would produce high yields in the first decade. In the absence of an empire to import settlers, some groups spontaneously took advantage of the profitability of fringe farming. This explains the presence of settlements on fringe areas such as the Negev that are characterized by the distance that separates each residential unit from the other, and the small number of units. In contrast to villages that huddle together for security reasons, these settlements do not feel threatened because they belong to Bedouin themselves, whom the villagers fear (Safrai and Sion 2007).

Living on the geographical and social fringe of society, such mobile groups were nevertheless an important economic factor.

3.3 Squatters

The importance of peripheral social groups should be integrated into the discussion of farming. Squatter occupation is identified in most archaeological digs by the poor quality of the remains. Squatters obviously belonged to the lowest rungs of society. But did they lead miserable lives? Were they landless? An example from Kenya sheds some light on the matter. The British 1918 Resident Native Labourer Ordinance stipulated that squatters had to provide no less than 180 working days per year for the settler on whose farm they lived in return for the right to live there and to cultivate a parcel to feed themselves and their families. A minimal wage was paid for the work done and the squatters' wives and children were also expected to come and work in the settler's fields during peak labour periods (Banaji 1997: 97). Compared with the settler who controlled the land by right of conquest guaranteed by a colonial power, the squatters seem powerless. Yet, the settler was desperate for manpower to work 'his' land. Hence, he gave up some of it in exchange for labour provided by squatters who grew their own food and even received some cash for their work and that of their families. Without investing funds, without sharing risks except those incurred by the cultivation of their plots, the squatters controlled an amount of land and funds that they considered sufficient for their livelihood and that made moving away or making the most of their numerical superiority and of the vulnerability of the settler's position unattractive. However ruthless the empire, however acquisitive the settler (they undoubtedly were and remain so), the landlord had every interest in striking a reasonable agreement with his squatters, keeping them healthy and numerous enough to get the job done and making working conditions attractive enough to prevent squatters leaving for another estate, settling on empty land or slaughtering his family. The bargaining power of 'landless' farmers remained significant as long as overpopulation did not render land inaccessible and labour over-plentiful. The owners of large estates in Roman Egypt had to revert to various methods of inducement to keep a ready pool of workers at hand. Rathbone (1991: 182-83, 404-406) mentions the leasing of accommodation, gardens, mills, bathhouses, fishing rights, the opportunity to raise pigs, to rent flocks of 'immortals', and tax collectives. The greater the estate, the more it was at the mercy of the availability of causal labour at seasonal peaks of agricultural activity. A dozen centuries later, the remarkable floruit of Andalousian agriculture occurred in a period of high demography (Bolens 1974).

These lines are not meant to present colonialism as a benevolent phenomenon. The object at hand is to let go some of the ideological baggage that hinders biblical scholars from moving beyond the crude opposition between the all-powerful 'rich' and the miserable 'poor', the parasitic urbanites living off the countryside, skimming off a substantial portion of the proceeds of agricultural production hardly leaving the pauperized *fellahin* sufficient means for their bare existence. The more careful writers would sometimes admit that they are 'going slightly beyond the information given in the biblical sources' while claiming that 'in the light of anthropology, the scattered bits of economic and social information fit into a definite and clear picture known as rent capitalism' (Lang 1982: 52). In fact, such descriptions are faithful reflections of prophetic propaganda, but they have little contact with the growing body of knowledge of the ancient Orient.

Therefore, peasants are never helpless victims. By their sheer number they hold a significant bargaining power that neither the crown nor the local elite can afford to ignore. The constraints imposed by constant rivalry and conflict of interests between the crown, the elite and the producers are basic to changes in any society (Malina 1982: 235). No one party can dispense with the others, and the most exposed party in the triad was not necessarily the peasants.

Chapter 4

New Perspectives on Land Passages

Thanks to the recovery of the importance of communal tenure systems and of strategies farmers used to cope with natural and social risks, a fresh look can be cast at a selection of biblical passages relative to land.

4.1 Poor Naboth (1 Kgs 21)

The story of the appropriation of Naboth's vineyard by criminal means is one of the pillars of biblical latifundialism (1 Kgs 21:1-19). Albrecht Alt (1959) saw Ahab's offer as evidence for the rise of a 'Canaanite' commodification/mercantilization of land tenure that was at loggerheads with the 'Israelite' *Bodenrecht.* Alt took Shemer's sale of the Samaria hill to Omri (1 Kgs 16:24) as an illustration of Canaanite land laws that allowed the sale of land, whereas Naboth's refusal to sell his vineyard to Ahab proved that in the Israelite conception land was inalienable. The Canaanite right was later considered as proto-capitalist in opposition to the Israelite concept that then could legitimize any anti-capitalist ideology (Bohlen 1978: 349).

David's purchase of a threshing floor from Araunah (2 Sam. 24:24) challenges the notion of an Israelite land law distinct from its Canaanite counterpart and exegetes spent treasures of ingenuity in exonerating David from his Canaanite behaviour (Ben-Barak 1981). The Islamic tenure system shows that inalienable tenure and alienable freehold property can co-exist within one system and that the Canaanite versus Israelite opposition reflects the ideology of prophetic texts rather than ancient reality.

Nevertheless, the story of Naboth's vineyard is presented as evidence for the existence of a land market in Israel and of prophetic resistance to it (Silver 1983: 74; Brueggemann 1993: 209). Land transactions supposedly reveal the transformation of the egalitarian Israelite society along Canaanite lines during the eighth century BCE. The fashion having shifted away from the early monarchic to the Persian era, the point of departure for the Naboth story plot is slowly shifting to Second Temple exegesis of the Torah (Rofé 1988; Blum 2000; Knauf 2010). On the basis of analogies found in Nehemiah, Cronauer (2005: 185-88) dates the vineyard story between the sixth and the fourth centuries BCE. If, however, the Book of Nehemiah happened to be a Hellenistic creation, as is sometimes argued today, the production of 1 Kings 21 would be dated at the end of the fourth century if not later (Finkelstein 2008b). As for the actual situation in Persian Yehud, reflected by the expropriation of Naboth, Cronauer remains very vague, merely repeating the usual slogans: 'The suffering of the people under the burden of reconstruction was exacerbated by crooked, cruel, and wicked leaders and rulers, both Jewish and non-Jewish' (Cronauer 2005: 194) and by 'the abuses of the poor by the rulers and wealth classes' (Cronauer 2005: 198). Before suggesting a date for the story, it is essential to understand the text. An evaluation of the architecture at Jezreel sets the enclosure phase (Phase III) in the eighth century BCE, during the last phase of revival of the Israelite kingdom around the reigns of Joash and Jeroboam II. Phase II, the pre-enclosure phase, is Omride. It is dominated by an ashlar-built monumental building, the construction of which could well reflect the land swap related in the Naboth story. It is impossible to know how big Jezreel was before the enclosure. If the cisterns were all inside the earlier complex then it was larger than the enclosure. Moreover, it is not certain that Naboth the Jezreelite had the disputed vineyard in Jezreel (Williamson 1991: 88). He was from/born in Jezreel but he may well have been living in Samaria—hence his name 'the Jezreelite' (Franklin 2008).

The story begins as an ordinary offer of exchange by a landowner who wants to consolidate his estate by buying out an adjacent plot. The text carefully locates the vineyard close or contiguous to Ahab's house (1 Kgs 21:2). As Ahab explains that he wants to convert the vineyard into a garden, in Islamic parlance, the plot would be classified as *mulk*. *Mulk* is the only freehold category of land that could be traded freely between private individuals. If one doubts the relevance of Islamic categories, Lev. 25:29-31 can be evoked to confirm that Naboth's vineyard, an urban plot situated within a walled settlement, was a freehold property that could be alienated forever. Hurowitz (1992: 73-74) puts the Naboth story in parallel with Sargon's Cylinder Inscription that describes Sargon's acquisition of fields for silver or against other fields to build a temple. The difference is that Ahab wants a garden rather than a temple. In support of the freehold category, there is no mention of tenure (*aḥuzzah*) in the Naboth story, while Prov. 19:14 classifies vineyards in the same category as houses and wealth in the paternal *naḥalah* (בית והון נחלת אבות). Houses and vineyards were far more likely objects of sales than shares of land tenure (§2.2.2). In this case, Ahab's guilt is not in his offer to buy Naboth's vineyard but in the murder of Naboth. No one doubts that killing one's neighbour to get hold of his property is unacceptable. Yet, this solution does not satisfy modern exegetes because they consider it crucial to hold on to Alt's Israelite *Bodenrecht*. Although biblical and Islamic categories suggest that Naboth's vineyard could be traded, although the murder is more than enough to confirm Ahab's guilt, modern exegesis clings to the notion of a land law invented in the twentieth century CE. Against all odds, Naboth's vineyard must be inalienable and Ahab's offer to buy it must be wrong in itself.

To prove that Ahab's offer was wrong from the start, exegetes focus on the paternal *naḥalah* (נחלת אבות) that Naboth evokes to justify his refusal to cede the vineyard. Naboth's refusal is seen as the proof that in Israel the paternal *naḥalah* was inalienable. The Bible is then sifted for confirmation of the inalienability of *naḥalah*. On the basis of Shemer's tribal affiliation in 1 Kgs 16:24, Sweeney claims that Ahab's offer threatens the tribal structure that constituted ancient Israel, because Ahab, like Shemer from whom Omri bought the hill of Samaria, probably belonged to the tribe of Manasseh, while Naboth must be from the tribe of Issachar because Jezreel is recorded under this tribe in Josh. 19:18. Sweeney (2007: 249) adds that even if Ahab gave Naboth a better vineyard 'there is no guarantee that it will be in the territory of Issachar'. That is a lot of suppositions that assume the relevance of intangible tribal territories in Joshua (see §2.3.7) to impose on a story that functions perfectly well without them. Moreover, it is not clear whether the vineyard was in Samaria or in Jezreel since the LXX lacks the MT's location 'in Jezreel' and deems Naboth an Israelite rather than a Jezreelite. Schenker (2004: 104-105) considers that the MT has been reworked. If the MT transmits an alteration of the earlier version preserved in the LXX, Sweeney's argument may well reflect the line of thought that governed the alteration. In this case, we have a perfectly circular inner-biblical reasoning, a midrash that makes no claim about the historicity of the inalienability of the paternal *naḥalah* at any point in Israel's past. In reverse, if the LXX transmits a revision of an older story found in the MT, the notion of tribal territories was not part of the translators' world. For the present purpose, there is no need to decide which of the MT and of the LXX reflects the older tradition. Neither textual tradition supports the notion that the inalienability of Naboth's vineyard was as rooted in an ancient Israelite land law as it is in the modern exegetical imagination.

Considering the vineyard as a metaphor for Israel and how Naboth becomes the victim of Ahab's battle for the control of Israel, as does Nielsen (2007: 221), hardly helps deciding whether the *naḥalah* was alienable or not. The LXX's repetition of the paternal lot (κληρονομίαν πατέρων μου) in verse 6 certainly contributed to the notion that the paternal *naḥalah* was by definition sacred and inalienable. By also adding εἶς in verse 1, the LXX dramatized the episode and built a parallel between Naboth's (only) vineyard and the poor man's only ewe in Nathan's accusatory fable in the David–Bathsheba affair (2 Sam. 12:3; Avioz 2006: 123; Turkanik 2008: 181).

The uncertainty of the status of Naboth's *naḥalah* is complicated by the fact that it is mentioned in the context of an oath (חלילה לי מיהוה). Is the oath motivated by the sacredness of the paternal *naḥalah* or is it the other way round? Is it the oath that renders the *naḥalah* inalienable (Cronauer 2005: 211-18)? Considering the conciseness of the text, it is impossible to decide whether Naboth could swap his vineyard or if he simply did not wish to do so (Whitelam 1979: 173). Cronauer (2005: 127-28) argues that Ahab's immediate return to his house after Naboth's refusal shows that the king had no other options and that Naboth's oath shows that he believed he could not sell his inheritance. This line of argument requires postulating Ahab's original ignorance that the vineyard was part of the patrimonial *naḥalah*, although it was next to his house. The very conciseness of the relevant verse (1 Kgs 21:3) compared to the elaborate description of the machinations that led to Naboth's murder (1 Kgs 21:4-15) argues against the relevance of the discussion over Naboth's motives. For the writers of the story, it was Ahab and Jezebel's rejection of Naboth's refusal to sell that mattered. It is simply impossible to infer from 1 Kings 21 whether or not an Israelite could sell part of his paternal *naḥalah*. Therefore, exegetes turn to legal texts.

Adducing 'legal' texts to claim that Naboth could not exchange the vineyard because it belonged to his paternal *naḥalah* is precarious since it (wrongly) presupposes that ancient legal collections reflect actual practice (Westbrook 1989). Limiting the scope of the Naboth story to an inner-biblical discussion that reflects a Persian situation rather than the eighth century BCE, Cronauer (2005: 127) refers to Gen. 12:7;

Lev. 25:23-24; and Josh. 21:43-45; 24:12-13, none of which, however, mentions any *naḥalah*. In Num. 27:4, the daughters of Zelophehad ask for a אחוזה, but Moses is instructed to give them a אחזת נחלה among the brothers of their father, which is rephrased in the same verse as the *naḥalah* of their father (נחלת אביהן, Num. 27:7; see 36:2-12), the only exact parallel to Naboth's paternal *naḥalah*. Such fluctuation in the use of the terms נחלה and אחוזה precludes drawing any precise legal conclusion from this episode.

The relevance of the inalienability of the paternal *naḥalah* loses yet more credibility in light of the fact that the references to the Naboth story in the narrative of Joram's demise in 2 Kings 9 mention neither vineyard nor paternal *naḥalah*. Although the burden of 2 Kings 9 is to prove that Elijah's oracle concerning Ahab was fully accomplished at Jezreel (2 Kgs 9:17), Jehu meets Joram at a place called Naboth's share (חלק) and Joram's body is cast upon Naboth's 'share of field' (חלק שדה). Stating the obvious, Cronauer (2005: 24) writes that the share of Naboth's field does not equate the whole of the owner's property in 2 Kings 9, but he still understands the 'share' as property in general. Beyond the vagueness of the terms, it is surprising that Joram's murder is not connected more precisely with the vineyard and the *naḥalah* that exegetes deem so fundamental to Naboth's refusal to part with his vineyard. In 2 Kings 9, it is the murder of Naboth that leads to Joram's assassination. In 1 Kings 21, it is Naboth's refusal to cede the vineyard that causes his murder. In both cases, the inalienability of the paternal *naḥalah* is irrelevant. The assassination of the murderer's son provides the resolution of the plot without any reference to the fate of the famous vineyard. The inalienability of land plays no role in the narrative. The reasons for Naboth's refusal to part with that particular plot are not supplied and Ahab does not further discuss the matter with Naboth.

From an entirely different vantage point, Axel Knauf (2010) also holds on to the inalienability of Naboth's *naḥalah*. Dating the Naboth story in the Persian era, Knauf abandons the notion of an ancient Israelite *Bodenrecht*. Reversing the traditional order, Knauf sees the inalienability of the vineyard as an innovation rather than the ancestral norm. The innovation was brought about by the Torah presented as an 'intellectual revolution towards the liberty of men'. In the Torah, land was suddenly deemed inalienable whereas it had always been transferable. The revolution, according to Knauf, consisted in replacing the ancient Near Eastern king with YHWH in Israel's laws on landed property (Lev. 25:23). As a 'fief' of ancient Near Eastern feudalism, the *naḥalah* was land granted by the king in exchange for services to the state. The fief is inalienable on the side of the fief-holder (possessor), because it remains the property of the fief-giver who may dispose of it otherwise if the fief-holder neglects his duties. Stating that it is YHWH rather than an earthly king who granted the land 'was a way, for the Second Temple, to save a piece from the estate of the late Israelite and Judean kingdoms for its own coffers', and to 'prevent the emergence of a competing landed aristocracy' (Knauf 2011). Before the 'revolution', Ahab in his position of suzerain would have been free to withdraw the vineyard from Naboth and grant him another fief. After the revolution, however, Naboth's suzerain would have been YHWH and Ahab would not have been able to dispose of the vineyard.

The advantage of Knauf's approach is that it removes the discussion from the realm of actual practice. The Torah is an intellectual framework that advances revolutionary notions that would eventually have real consequences, but not as a legal body regulating a particular society. The problem with Knauf's argumentation is the weakness of its textual base. To claim that the Torah establishes the inalienability of the *naḥalah*, Knauf cites Lev. 25:23 and Deut. 19:14. In fact, Lev. 25:23 mentions the land (הארץ) but no *naḥalah*. The *naḥalah* appears in Deut. 19:14, but in the context of the prohibition to move boundaries (§2.3.6) that has little to do with the sale of land. Forbidding the encroachment on neighbouring plots has no bearings on the inalienability of land. Ezekiel 46:16-18 (not in the Torah!) presents the only clear prohibition relative to *naḥalah* but what it opposes is its being taken away (לקח), violent dispossession (ינה) and expulsion (פוץ), not the regular sale or exchange offered by Ahab. Hence, it is doubtful that a serious case for the inalienability of the *naḥalah* can be built from the Bible. The stress should rather be shifted from the *naḥalah* itself to its paternal aspect. That the vineyard was a *paternal naḥalah* indicates that Naboth's abhorrence in giving up his vineyard was rooted in filial devotion, not in Torah observance.

Another approach to indict Ahab is to state that his offer violated a sacred Israelite law or usage and that Naboth's refusal was based on a pious observance of his ancestral religious obligation (Hens-Piazza 2006: 206). On the basis of the (fifth) commandment to honour one's parents, a case it made that Naboth's attitude 'epitomizes the sense of responsibility to one's ancestors that shaped an Israelite's use of land' (Wright 1990: 152). Confirmation is then sought in notions of responsibility towards one's ancestors. Because what was supposed to be a typical Israelite trait soon borders on typical Canaanite ancestor worship, it is deemed safer to subsume parents and ancestors in one's responsibility towards God and claim that Naboth's refusal to part with a portion of his ancestral patrimony was as much a duty to God as to his ancestors (Wright 1990: 159). This retreat to safer ground leaves Naboth's refusal unexplained. Are we to believe that Naboth was afraid of his ancestors' wrath if he swapped a vineyard for another? The Argonauts are said to have taken care of pacifying the ancestors of previous landowners by pouring libations 'to Earth, to the gods of the land and to the souls of its dead heroes' when they arrived on the banks of the Phasis (Malkin 2005: 247). To a similar aim, the new settlers in Samerina are said to have hired a priest, but to pacify YHWH rather than the ancestors of previous landholders (2 Kgs 17:28), because devotion to the ancestors is rejected (Edelman forthcoming). Were impious Ahab seeking to impose a Canaanite *Bodenrecht*, there is no reason to believe that he would not have pacified Naboth's ancestors with the libations required by Canaanite religion.

From a legal point of view, the proposed deal is regular and there is nothing in the text itself to suggest that Naboth's refusal is based on anything other than his personal abhorrence to swap grandad's vineyard. The narrator has no law, tradition or practice to quote because there was none to quote (Dearman 1988: 67; Cronauer 2005: 211-18). The text loses none of its bite when Jezebel gets Naboth killed for refusing to sell for personal rather than legal reasons. The rigorous legality of the proposed deal is part and parcel of the narrative strategy.

From an economic point of view, Ahab's generous offer to exchange the vineyard against a better one voids the claim that the vineyard could not be alienated because it was essential to feed Naboth's family, as Mette (2006: 144) claims. Ahab's offer of an unspecified equivalent in silver supports its soundness from a commercial point of view. Nothing in the story supports the presentation of King Ahab's proposed deal as the crooked manoeuvre of a wicked ruler abusing the poor. It is Naboth's murder that the story uses to depict the northern kingdom as the worse kind of dictatorship where the actual tyrant is not even the king but a woman, a foreign one at that, who manipulates a ridiculously weak ruler. Ben Zvi (2007: 45) notes that, although Ahab figures more prominently in Chronicles than other Israelite kings and that his house is a paradigmatic case of a sinful royal house, Chronicles make no mention of Naboth. This, surely, is significant.

It is extremely difficult to decide which element of the infernal cocktail (xenophobia, misogyny and Zionism, since the text is found in a Judean book) may reflect real conditions. The only thing that can be advanced with a reasonable degree of confidence is that the text is strikingly domestic in tone. The episode presents how a man and wife deal with a difficult next-door neighbour. There is a house instead of a palace, a vegetable garden rather than a hacienda. Even the seal used to stamp the fateful letter (1 Kgs 21:8) does not necessarily evoke a king. It is only the speedy effect it produces that evokes the imagery of state apparatus. Hence, the story can be taken as reflecting the classical distinction between *imperium* and *dominium*, whereas the sovereign's *imperium* over the realm was not equivalent to the *dominium* wielded over his own possessions (see §1.3). Ahab's status relative to land is that of a private individual, as was the case in Mesopotamia where kings managed their own estates to sustain their family (Van der Spek 1993; 1995: 196).

Islamic land categories should be integrated into the discussion of the inalienability of the ancient Israelite *naḥalah* to avoid the blunt conclusion that it is a figment of the modern exegetical imagination. As mentioned at the beginning of this section, 1 Kgs 21:2 provides clear indications about the land in question. It was a vineyard and it was to be turned into a garden. Therefore it was *mulk* land, freehold property that could be alienated, as was the case for the fields of Magganubba that Sargon bought to set up his new capital (Na'aman 2008: 211). For this reason, a sham legal procedure was the only resort to override Naboth's refusal, which was final because Naboth held it as freehold. Naboth's kingly position over the vineyard could not be overwhelmed by Ahab although he was king of the realm. It is only through a gross abuse of kingly powers that Ahab took hold of the vineyard. Jezebel's understanding of kingship (1 Kgs 21:7) was no more Israelite than Canaanite.

Hence, the Naboth story confirms the validity of the Islamic category of *mulk* land for biblical exegesis. In terms of value, *mulk* land was the most precious. In terms of surface it was the smallest. Most of the land was made up of ploughed fields in dry cereal cultivation (arable) land, common pastures and woods, and areas unfit for agriculture, that is *mīrī* and *mawāt* lands. Dead (*mawāt*) land was no one's concern, but inalienability was fundamental to *mīrī* land. As Knauf (2011) notes, the grantee of a fief did not have the liberty to alienate it, even if he was able to transmit it to his heirs and if it became part of their paternal estate. From the perspective of the grantor, however, the fief was alienable. It was the privilege of the sovereign to dispose of crown land as he wished, in the limits of political considerations that dictated the attributions and the reshuffling of land grants. Hence, the notion of inalienability is correct but it must be qualified. Inalienability applies to crown/*mīrī* land and from the point of view of the grantee only. The grantor retained the ability to grant an estate to another grantee or to himself. That grantees always sought to secure their holding is a well-attested phenomenon, but it is far from established that the Torah sought to curtail the sovereign's right to withdraw a land grant.

As Ahlström warned, the Naboth story cannot be taken as evidence of a monarchic programme of land expropriation (Ahlström 1993: 587; Cogan 2001: 486). What the story does evidence is the importance of the spiritualization of poverty that led to the elevation of Naboth as the archetypical poor, a process that academic readings perpetuate in the name of social criticism (Ambrose of Milan, *De Nabuthae*). Naboth is the ideal victim, a sheep led to slaughter without resistance. To academics working in rich societies, Naboth the landowner becomes the hapless poor whose cause they take up to indulge in the easy denunciation of the rich and powerful because the Bible generously endows its readers with the legitimacy they seek. Hence, 'academic' pamphlets take prophetic slur as a description of actual economic conditions (Dietrich 2005: 55-58). In its present location in the canon, the Naboth story elaborates upon Samuel's oracle on royal taxation (1 Sam. 8:10-18) to demonstrate that the prophecy has been accomplished and that Samuel was a true prophet.

4.2 Were Estates Established on Patrimonial Land (1 Sam. 8:14)?

Another chapter of the biblical litany of political abuses is found in 1 Sam. 8:10-18 where Samuel warns the Israelites of the cost their demand for a king implies. Samuel's description of kingship is in tension with other biblical passages, particularly Deuteronomy 17, which allows what 1 Samuel 8 deems an apostasy. Serge Frolov (2004: 201) notes that the tension between Deuteronomy 17 and 1 Samuel 8 is a thorn in the flesh for the notion of a Deuteronomistic History (already Edelman 1991: 41). Moreover, the rule of priests described in the Torah is also a costly affair for the average sinner. Observant farmers would have had to sacrifice most of their products to atone for their sins and would have ended up feeding the priests rather than their own families. Nowhere does the Bible promise a tax haven. Hence, the anti-monarchic charge of the passage seems directed at a particular king, Saul, rather than against kingship in general (Launderville 2001: 119-28). The litany of kingly evils anticipates Samuel's negative confession where he claims that he never took anything from the people (1 Sam. 12:3), creating a stark contrast between Samuel and Saul (Heller 2006: 113). The description of tyranny in 1 Sam. 8:11-17 is a ritualized critique comparable to reminders of the dangers of political power during New Year ceremonies (Hamilton 2006). The aim was to warn all foreign conquerors to protect the city and the rights of its elite (Smith 1982; but Sommer 2000: 81-95).

Despite these qualifications, 1 Samuel 8 is a favourite of social scientific readings. Samuel lists sons, daughters, tithes, slaves, cattle and donkeys that the king will demand from them. The list includes fields in verse 14:

> ואת שׂדותיכם ואת כרמיכם וזיתיכם הטובים יקח ונתן לעבדיו
>
> Your good fields, your good vineyards and your good olive trees he will take and give to his servants.

Taken at face value, this verse is often presented as evidence for the expropriation of small farmers to set up royal estates (Levine 1996: 231-32). With the verbs לקח ונתן, the text unambiguously states that the king took the best land away from the Israelites and transferred it to the recipients of royal favours. Yet, despite the polemical tone, the text is strikingly more measured than its interpretations. Instead of describing a catastrophic despoliation, 1 Sam. 8:14 indicates that the fields, orchards and vineyards given to the king's servants are distinct from the king's ploughing and harvesting mentioned in verse 12. Since only the best fields are taken, it is clear that the text does not suggest that farmers became landless. It merely describes the basic principle of taxation. The placement of sons and daughters in various palace occupations entails career opportunities. No shrewd farmer would resent sending some of his offspring close to the centre of power even for menial tasks. The benefits somewhat compensated the tax burden. It is significant that corvée is mentioned on the king's field only and not on the courtiers' estates, although this is attested at some periods.

Nevertheless, Samuel's claim that the king would take fields away to grant them to his servants does not square up with what is known about land grants. As far as we can tell from later examples, estates were not granted as a result of expropriation. Monarchs granted estates either as part of a strategy of land reclamation or where the grant only concerned tax collection.

When the state was eager to increase its own tax revenues, it gave incentives to enterprising individuals who hoped to recoup funds they had to invest to bring unproductive land under the plough. In the early

Islamic era, agricultural estates (*qaṭā'i'*) were usually emphyteutic grants, that is, made so that holders would improve the grant by putting unused land into production. A clause often stipulated that the grant would be revoked if the land was not cultivated within two years. When the estate included villages, the rights of existing property holders had to be respected, which did not prevent these investments from being very profitable. During the first century of Islamic domination, these estates were a major source of income for the elite. In the next century, presumably when the amount of waste-land that could be brought under the plough with minimal investment decreased sharply, tax-farming became more profitable than farming. These changing circumstances are relevant for the evolution of elite revenues during the Persian and early Hellenistic era in Yehud (Kennedy 2004: 19). This means that when an entire region was granted, the status of land already under production was not changed. The local farmers continued to work their land as before. Apart from cases of treason when a productive estate would be confiscated and granted to someone else (Saul's land granted in turn to Meribaal and to Ziba, 2 Sam. 9:7; 16:1-4; 19:25-31), it made no sense to take productive land away from those who already worked it and paid taxes from its produce. Estates were units of production from which the royal administration derived revenues in the form of taxes and services (Briant 1978).

Alternatively, the land was granted in exchange for military duties such as those David performed for Akish (1 Sam. 27:6-12). The Ugaritic tablets relative to the transfer of the land of *nayyālu* simply name the new beneficiary (§3.2). No transfer of population took place. On the strength of the document, the new grantee went about collecting the revenues of the specified fiscal unit. The grant was merely a fiscal rather than an agricultural transaction. The land was already cultivated and the grantee was given the right to collect the taxes. David did not take the land of the inhabitants of Ziklag to give it to his own retainers. Therefore, neither the agricultural nor the fiscal land grants affected the status of farmers who cultivated the granted lands. Land grants were not land consolidations. Hence, the presence of estates does not imply expropriation, as Samuel would imply.

Contrary to the accepted wisdom, the formation of estates was generally more beneficial than detrimental to the local farmers, offering venues for labour contracts besides the required corvée duties imposed by the state. Because sharecropping is a convenient way to share the risk between the landlord and the tenant, estate holders would lease out some of their cultivable surfaces to neighbouring farmers, especially when their duties called them away from the estate and reduced their ability to supervise production. For this reason, Levantine estates were fragile entities against which the state and the peasants maintained a strong position. The recent break-up of governmental estates in the Syrian Jezira shows that large estates remain a short-term reality, in spite of the availability of machinery (Ababsa al-Husseini 2007). It is difficult for modern readers to realize that estates did not turn freeholders into tenants or slaves (Inalcik 1991), not even during the Byzantine Empire when the direct exploitation of arable land on estates was generally marginal (Lefort 2002: 243). Despite the overall demographic increase in the Levant between the Persian period and the Byzantine Empire, the bargaining power of farmers was far stronger than is generally thought, because, in the absence of machinery, hands remained in shorter supply than land (Kaplan 1992: 164). The number of farmsteads seems to increase sharply in the Greek world in the fourth century CE. They are characterized by the presence of towers and their often relatively isolated locations (Pečíka 1973). Here a popular fallacy that goes back at least to Max Weber must be exposed. It is simply untrue that 'Large estates can be exploited more easily than individual household plots on which the survival of the smallest kinship units depended' (Blenkinsopp 1995: 4). Even if estates had encroached on communal land, estates offered extra day labour and sharecropping opportunities, increasing the economic security of smallholders through the shortening of idle periods, with a positive effect on the overall economic climate. In fact, estates could not afford encroaching on communal land and developing at the expense of small farmers because estates survived in intimate symbiosis with the small farmers around it. Symbiosis was essential because individual farmers were more efficient than large farms until modern machinery rendered small farms expandable.

Coincidently, the issue of the concentration of land into the hands of a few is also found in classical studies in reference to Aristotle's discussion of Solon's *seisachtheia* in the early sixth century BCE. Written more than two centuries after the fact, Aristotle's report is the earliest mention of some kind of enslavement of the poor by the rich:

> For the Athenian constitution was in all respects oligarchic, and in fact the poor themselves and also their wives and children were actually in slavery to the rich; and they were called Clients, and Sixth-part-tenants (for that was the rent they paid for the rich men's land which they farmed, and the whole country was in few hands), and if they ever

> failed to pay their rents, they themselves and their children were liable to arrest; all borrowing was on the security of the debtor's persons down to the time of Solon. (Aristotle *Ath. Pol.* 2:2)

It is not clear how sharecroppers could not pay their rents since even in case of a complete harvest failure, when the fields produced absolutely nothing, the sharecroppers would still be able to pay a sixth of zero and avoid slavery. Nor is it clear why paying a sixth is considered bad. In comparison with other data, it appears to be a rather advantageous term, even if the sharecroppers supplied the seeds as well as the traction. For instance, on the shores of the Sea of Galilee, sharecroppers who only provided their work received a fourth of the harvest (Sonnen 1927: 70-71). Hence, some suggest that the *hektemoroi* actually paid five-sixths of the produce and that the sixth in question was what the *hektemoroi* kept for themselves (Van Wees 2006: 379). In that case, the deal is clearly oppressive, but too much so to be convincing. Hence, the current view is that the *hektemoroi* were bound to surrender a sixth of their produce (almost a double tithe) to an overlord and could be enslaved if they failed to do so (Rhodes 2006: 252-53).

At this point, it may be useful to recall William Woodhouse (1938: 150-60) who suggested that the *hektemoroi* lost the ownership of their land to lenders but retained its possession as tenants and paid an interest-rent of a sixth of the yearly production, whatever the size of their debt. Much decried by subsequent research (Roubineau 2007), Woodhouse's thesis has the great advantage of avoiding discussing the reasons for the destitution of the farmers, reasons that Aristotle ignored, and to postulate a system of rural dependency placed within a wider network of patronage. This point is discussed below but I can already state here that one sixth of the produce is a common proportion farmers paid to service their debt (§6.5).

In conclusion, 1 Samuel 8 does not support the notion of large-scale expropriations of communal or freehold land by kings and governors at any period of Israel's past. Samuel merely describes the general principle of taxation by corvée. Absence of taxes only exists in dreamed up peaceful egalitarian tribal societies characterized by barter and solidarity which gave way to taxes, money and social stratification by a bellicose monarchy. The notion of a primitive egalitarian Israelite society goes back to Antonin Causse (1937). According to Causse, the original pastoral nomadic community lost its organic solidarity as it settled down. The original bond between society and religion was severed, collective responsibility dissolved into private interests (Frick 1999: 237).

Sir Arthur Evans projected similar values on Minoan archaeology (Gere 2009). In fact, taxes are a mode of wealth redistribution that preserve rather than reduce equality within a society. Kings and taxes of one kind or another were a given at any period, a fact that leaves few clues for dating the production of 1 Samuel 12. The king 1 Samuel 8 denounces could be a Persian king who seizes estates not for himself but to assign them to his men (Müller 2004: 144). In 1 Sam. 12:12, the Israelites' desire to have a king is clearly motivated by military threats against which it would be preferable to pay taxes in exchange for protection. Bullying neighbours are another universal phenomenon and becoming like the other people (1 Sam. 8:5) is a survival technique. One agrees to turn over a percentage of one's resources to fund self-defence unless immediate submission to superior forces is considered preferable. In either case, taxes are due. The type of political structure that draws them, kingdom, empire or tribe, makes little difference. Tribal societies are no less violent than empires; the difference is one of scale. Let us now consider another prophetic passage relative to the recovery of an estate.

4.3 The Shunamite's Usufruct (2 Kgs 8:1-6)

Elisha's dealings with a rich woman at Shunem illustrate Israelite patronage. In return for her favours, Elisha asks YHWH to give her a son whom he later raises from the dead (2 Kgs 4). The same woman reappears four chapters later, as Gehazi is entertaining the king of Israel with reminiscences of Elisha's great deeds. Having returned from the land of the Philistines to escape a seven-year long drought, as Elisha had advised her to do, the Shunamite appeals (צעקה) to the king concerning her house and her field (בית ושׂדה), the use of which she was unable to retrieve. In 2 Kgs 8:6b, the king orders a eunuch saying:

> השיב את כל אשר לה ואת כל תבואת השדה מיום עזבה את הארץ ועד עתה
>
> Restore everything that belongs to her and all the income from her field from the day she abandoned the land until now!

The gist of the passage is to exhibit Elisha's foreknowledge of future events and how the man of God continues to support his patroness (Cogan and Tadmor 1988: 87). The scene, however, takes place in the absence of the prophet and the vignette leaves much unexplained. First of all, the mention of the house beside the field poses the problem of the use of vocabulary. 'House and field' is probably a *merismus* (like 'heaven and earth') to denote the woman's entire estate. It would be over-interpreting the evidence to conclude that no distinction existed between built and arable land and that ancient Israel did not distinguish between *mulk* and *mīrī* categories. Leviticus 25:29-31 shows otherwise, but since the story does not reveal whether it considers Shunem as a walled settlement or as a rural settlement, nothing can be said about the Shunamite's house. In fact, the vagueness of the terms reveals the relative unimportance of actual houses compared with land tenure. Sun-dried brick houses were made at little cost and would hardly exist after seven years of neglect. During the dry season, a woman could settle in a shack or in a single room in the compound of relatives or in the guestroom of the village chief. The Book of Ruth confirms that food was the main problem. A house is never mentioned. Finding lodgings was not the main concern.

A second problem is that the king's reaction appears surprisingly positive considering the portrayal of Israelite kings in the Elijah–Elisha cycles. The king's motivations are left unexplained and there is no way to know whether his favourable answer to the woman's plea reflects normal practice or if he does her a favour. If the king simply enforces the normal procedure, Borowski is correct in using this passage as a clue that plots were maintained in the family even under harsh conditions (Borowski 2003: 26). If, however, moved by the extraordinary stories Gehazi is telling him, the king does Elisha's patroness a favour, nothing can be deduced as far as ordinary conditions went. The fact that the king provides an officer to enforce the order shows that resistance was expected from the present possessors of the house and field and that the king's order was not a normal procedure. It is therefore doubtful that the Shunamite's domain had reverted to the crown during her absence (Ben-Barak 1981: 82). Rather, the appeal suggests that the Shunamite had to turn to the king because her claim lacked the support of common practice. If the house and field belonged to her husband's patrimonial estate, the village elders had attributed the abandoned estate to someone else. The prolonged absence of the woman placed it in the *maḥlūl* category. Representing a higher authority, the king was the only one who could overrule the decision of the village elders who refused to return the house and the land after seven years. These seven years are meaningful since, in Ottoman practice, it falls halfway between the customary three years to classify the abandoned estate as *maḥlūl* and the ten years of continuous cultivation necessary before the new possessor secured inalienable rights to the usufruct of the estate. These figures cannot be considered valid for ancient Israel, but they suggest that, having cultivated the land for some years, the present possessors were not prone to relinquish it as they would have gained a permanent holding over it within a few more seasons of continuous cultivation.

It is also possible that the Shunamite was a widow with an under-aged son. The root of her problem then was that her son was too young to claim a share of the village tenure. In any case, the 'prophet' has nothing to say regarding the land in question (Bergen 1999: 151). The reason for the silence is that in doing Elisha's patroness a favour, the king was forcing an unfair settlement on the inhabitants of Shunem who had shouldered the tax burden during the time of hardship (Bergen 1999: 154). Asking the new possessor or the village as a whole to pay the revenues drawn from the land on top of returning the usufruct was sure to cause an outcry in Shunem (2 Kgs 8:6). In the wake of the Naboth story (§4.1), the king's insistence that the full income be returned along with the use of the house and of the field belongs to the redactor's aim to throw a negative light over an Israelite king. As an indirect beneficiary of a favour demonstrating the abuse of power by Israel's kings, Elisha keeps a low profile.

As with the seizure of Naboth's vineyard, the story of the Shunamite's recovery of her possessions illustrates Samuel's oracle about the ways of Israelite kings and supports the legitimacy of the ideology prevailing in the books of Samuel–Kings. It is legitimate to seek clues about actual practices relative to land tenure in these episodes, but the extraction of information is wrought with problems. There is definitely the matter of the extinction of holding over derelict possessions, but the Shunamite's 'house and field' are too vague to ascertain whether the *maḥlūl* category applied only to arable land or if houses suffered the same fate. Seven years was probably a significant length of time after which custom was not enough to reclaim one's possession. Beyond that, it would be necessary to know the exact composition of the Shunamite's estate, whether or not she was a widow and the age of her son to gain a closer understanding of customary practices. The Book of Ruth makes up for this lack of crucial data as it paints a more precise picture of the options a woman had when she returned home after ten years.

4.4 Ruth, Naomi and Elimelech's Land Share

The Book of Ruth presents a more complicated case of *two* childless widows. Ruth had not borne any sons while Naomi survived her sons. Ruth was still young enough to marry again but she was Moabite, she had probably never been in Bethlehem before and was apparently sterile.

Naomi, Ruth's deceased husband's mother, had more connections with Bethlehem but was past childbearing (Ruth 1:11). The return of these two destitute women constitutes a peculiar economic challenge to the people of Bethlehem. Studies of the Book of Ruth have focused much upon the theological and legal aspects of the tale, but it is the practical solutions to the plight of the two women that are of particular interest here.

4.4.1 Tricksters at Work

A methodological caveat is in order before trying to unravel the nature and the consequences of the transaction between Naomi and Boaz. The Book of Ruth is a tale. As such, the story follows narrative rules. Ruth's marriage to Boaz is but one step towards the denouement which, as in every good narrative, is supplied at the end of the story. As the women of Bethlehem proclaimed, Naomi's adoption of Ruth's newborn son is the key. The aim is to supply worthy ancestors to King David. This is done in two ways: trickery and hints to mythological motifs of divine adoption. Naomi's adoption of Obed in the final scene alludes to Near-Eastern parallels that legitimize the king by having a goddess suckle him (Sasson 1995: 233-40). It is thus precarious to use this last scene to infer actual practices.

Besides mythological motifs, trickery enhances the presentation of three resourceful and daring individuals in David's ancestry. In league with each other, they play a trick that comes to full fruition when Boaz plays his trump card and bypasses the relative who holds the right of pre-emption over Elimelech's land share. The trickster's motif is crucial (Sasson 1995: 230-32; Nielsen 1985: 203; Kerény 1972). Stratagem rather than legality is the guiding principle. Naomi, Ruth and Boaz are presented as tricksters worthy of a long chain that runs from Abraham to Tamar, who is duly mentioned in Ruth 4:12. Through pluck and daring acts, the trickster renders possible, within the fixed bounds of what is permissible, an experience of what is not permitted. Hence, Ruth's decision to return with Naomi, Naomi and Ruth's ploys to secure a good marriage and Boaz's act at the city gate do not quite reflect normal procedures. They constantly toe the fine line that demarcates what is just about acceptable from what is definitely unacceptable. The daring acts of the protagonists regale the audience with the heroes' ability to circumvent the strictures of common practice (Sasson 1995: 229). Yet, everything must remain within the limits of acceptable practice or the heroes would become villains in the eyes of the audience. Therefore, if the story does not reflect common practice, it nevertheless provides some hints as to what was possible, which in turn sustains the relevance of the Book of Ruth for the study of land tenure in ancient Palestine.

Following Sasson's analysis, a number of elements commonly used to interpret Ruth can be eliminated (Sasson 1995: 229). Levirate marriage does not apply since Ruth is free to marry anyone as Boaz himself states (Ruth 3:10). Apart from this moral vignette by which the narrator stresses that marrying a rich man is preferable to marrying a young one (Artus 2009: 12-14), Ruth transmits little regarding the legal position of widows and the redemption of land. Agnethe Siquans (2009: 450), who develops a legal interpretation, has to admit that the laws on redemption and levirate marriage do not correspond to Ruth's situation. In fact, the book imagines a rather complicated case-study that enables the protagonists and the narrator behind them to reveal their mettle.

4.4.2 Trading the Usufruct of a Share of Communal Land

In light of ancient tenure systems, I postulate that upon her return, Naomi holds the usufruct of Elimelech's share of village land as stated in Ruth 4:3 (Gray 1967: 420; Lacocque 2004: 126). The share of land (חלק השׂדה) is commonly rendered as a 'parcel' or 'piece' of land, which leads interpreters to come up with complicated scenarios. Taking the share of land for an actual field, and village land for a vague category of clan ownership, Ziony Zevit infers that the redemption of Elimelech's share was the consequence of a debt contracted by Naomi. He then states that the closer kinsman (Polony Almony 'so-and-so') was not investing anything other than a symbolic sense to keep it in the clan (Zevit 2005: 595). Yitzhak Berger (2009: 448) imagines that Naomi had previously sold Elimelech's field which now had to be redeemed. There is no support for these suggestions in the text and Kirsten Nielsen (1997: 83) states that the discussion over the previous fate of the field is superfluous. The text focuses upon a share of land that Elimelech held. Hence, Naomi did not sell any field near Bethlehem.

In the context of a village practising *musha' dhukūr* (§2.1), Elimelech owned a share of communal land allocated annually as long as he resided in Bethlehem. Elimelech's land share could only be transmitted to another male while widows held the usufruct of their husband's share, a practice well attested in Neo-Babylonian times. The wife had neither disposition of nor usufruct in the dowry, but acquired the usufruct as a widow (Wunsch 2005). The claim that at Elephantine 'daughters inherit even when there is a son' (Eskenazi 1992: 31) does not alter this view. The

Elephantine contracts deal with real estate, houses and urban land that were subject to different regulations from arable land, which is never mentioned in the transactions in Elephantine.[1] As Elimelech's widow, Naomi is entitled to the use of her late husband's share when she returns to Bethlehem. Elimelech's share had reverted to the common pool of village land during his absence. Practically, this simply means that he was not included in the redistribution of strips of communal land following the departure of Elimelech's family from Bethlehem. Either the other shareholders were allowed more strips or more quarters were left fallow. Contrary to the extinction of the Shunamite's estate after seven years, no one contested the validity of Naomi's claim when she came back, in spite of the fact that her absence lasted some ten years (כעשר שנים, Ruth 1:4). This is another reflection of the absence of any pressure on land at the time the story was written.

Naomi came back to Bethlehem to find food, rather than to 'obtain some legal redress for her husband's nearly extinct household' (against Matthews 2009: 18). Her return at harvest time rendered a redistribution of land necessary before the next ploughing season when, as the usufructuary of her husband's share, a number of strips of common land would have to be allocated to Naomi. In the meantime and until the next harvest, Naomi would have to survive on charity as she came back empty-handed (Ruth 1:21).

To make things worse, Naomi did not return alone. In the context of the *musha' dhukūr*, Ruth may have been entitled to the usufruct of her own husband's share of arable land at Bethlehem. Because her Moabite origins are repeated seven times, it is likely that they impinged upon that claim.[2] Ruth's Moabite stock complicates the plot and heightens the tension. The people of Bethlehem could legitimately ask why Ruth did not go back to her *mother's* house to find another husband in Moab as Orpah did (Ruth 1:8-9). Even if the village elders accepted her claim as valid and granted Ruth the usufruct of Mahlon's share (Ruth 4:10), a further two-hundred kilos or so of grain in addition to those necessary to feed Naomi would have to be set aside from the present harvest to feed Ruth until the next harvest.[3] The equivalent of four-hundred kilos of wheat was a large amount for someone who had not sown the required surface in advance. Moreover, neither Naomi nor Ruth had the means to cultivate the strips of arable land they would receive. No wonder their arrival in Bethlehem caused an uproar against them (עליהן, Ruth 1:19). Therefore, Naomi devised a scheme the full implications of which only become clear when Naomi adopts Obed.

The scheme is played out as a triple act. First, Boaz informs Polony that Naomi is willing to trade the usufruct of her late husband's share. Then, Boaz convinces Polony to abandon his right of pre-emption. At last, Boaz changes the conditions relative to his own acquisition of Elimelech's share. The notion of the sale of usufruct has to be clarified. Each of Boaz' words spoken in front of the village council is important:

> חלקת השדה אשר לאחינו לאלימלך מכרה נעמי
>
> the share of field that was for our brother, for Elimelech, Naomi traded. (Ruth 4:3)

Despite the terms 'to sell, trade' (מכר) and 'to buy' (קנה) in Ruth 4:3-4, the purchase involves a transfer of responsibilities rather than the disbursement of money. At least this is how the Greek translators understood the deal when they rendered מכר as δέδοται, 'to give'. I understand the problem of the accomplished form מכר as indicating that since her return Naomi had put Elimelech's share up for sale but nobody had shown any interest. On that fateful morning, Boaz refers to the trading in the past although it has not been completed (Sasson 1995: 108-15).

Had he been alive, Elimelech would have been free to exchange part of his share of communal land with another shareholder. As a widow, however, Naomi can trade her right of use of Elimelech's share, but not the share itself which can only be traded between 'brothers', that is, between shareholders in the communal land of Bethlehem. Practically, Naomi needs someone to work the strips corresponding to Elimelech's share against a fraction of the produce so that she will not rely on charity from the next harvest on. No money is involved. If Elimelech's share was sufficient to feed his family, Naomi should be able to feed herself with a fraction of its produce since all the production costs would be shouldered by the sharecropper who 'bought' her usufruct. It would have been very informative to know the exact proportion of produce a widow could have expected from the produce of her husband's share, but that was obviously not the narrator's concern. It is likely, however, that upon Naomi's death, Elimelech's share would revert back to the common pool as it had when Elimelech had left Bethlehem.

Having reminded the representatives of the village council that no one had shown any interest in Naomi's offer, Boaz informs publicly the next of kin that he is willing to acquire Elimelech's share because there are some unexpected implications to the deal (Ruth 4:5). Again, the formulation of the statement is crucial:

ביום קנותך השדה מיד נעמי ומאת רות המואביה אשת המת קניתי להקים
שם המת על נחלתו

The day you acquire the field from Naomi, I have already acquired from Ruth the Moabite the wife of the dead (the right) to raise the name of the dead over his *naḥalah*. (Ruth 4:5)

By these words, Boaz warns Polony, who has just stated that he is willing to acquire Elimelech's share, that Ruth has accepted him as the prospective father of a child to raise the name of the dead man over his inheritance. This could be a marital union conditioned by the birth of a male. It nevertheless involves the immediate transfer of Ruth's upkeep from the village to Boaz's sole shoulders. The crux of the matter is: why does Polony decide to withdraw from the deal as soon as he hears that Boaz is taking Ruth?

4.4.3 Ketib *or* Qere*?*

The ambiguity over Polony's reasons to let Boaz acquire Elimelech's share has given rise to the *ketib-qere* at verse 5. According to the *ketib*, Boaz warns that the day Polony acquires Elimelech's share from Naomi, 'I (Boaz) have already acquired (יקנית)' from Ruth the right to raise the name of the dead on his *naḥalah*. The case of Ruth is thus separated from Elimelech's share. The versions follow the *qere*, 'you (Polony) have also acquired' (קניתה) the duty to raise the name of the dead. In this case, Ruth is packaged with Elimelech's share.

The *ketib* has the support of grammar and of the logic of the previous chapter (Sasson 1995: 119-36). The accomplished form (קניתי) indicates that whenever Polony decides to acquire Elimelech's share, Boaz has already purchased something from Ruth. There is no mystery over the purchase. The audience knows that Ruth went home that very morning with six measures of barley taken directly from Boaz's heap so Boaz's statement is straightforward. Boaz's praise of Ruth's choice not to go after younger men whether poor or rich (Ruth 3:10) prepared the audience in considering Polony as younger and thus inferior to Boaz in the village. The difference implied by the *ketib* is that even if Polony had greater means, Boaz's purchase has already so depreciated Elimelech's share that Boaz has effectively deprived Polony of the choice of buying it.

If the result is the same, the whole interest of the story lies in its presuppositions. How did Boaz convince Polony to drop his claim? The *qere* suggests that Polony baulked at the expense involved in marrying Ruth and producing an offspring for Elimelech. The *qere* is, I suggest, the result of an inner-biblical reading of Ruth in light of the law of levirate marriage in Deut. 25:5-10. This exegetical approach introduced a number of interesting legal intricacies that have kept exegetes busy ever since. Yet, food and land, not levirate marriage, are the main issues of the Book of Ruth. I follow Sasson (1995: 229) who prefers the *ketib* and I want to show that it makes even more sense than Sasson suggests when it is read in light of the survival strategies at the level of a *musha'*-practising village.

Whether one prefers the *ketib* or the *qere*, it is clear that ploughing, seeding, weeding and harvesting the extra strips of Elimelech's share was no problem to Polony since he was ready to acquire Elimelech's share until Boaz made his public announcement. Until then, Polony was totally unaware that the presence of Ruth produced a complication.

At this point, the interpretation runs the risk of reaching beyond the text and coming up with all sorts of hypotheses as to why Polony desisted. Since the narrator left Polony's reasons unexplained, apart that it would endanger his *naḥalah*, it is wise not to press the point. All that can be said is that Boaz put the matter forcefully enough for Polony to back out immediately. The narrator only conveys what Polony sensed: that Boaz would take umbrage if he exercised his right. Therefore, Polony chose not to aggravate a stronger man even though he was perfectly entitled to take Elimelech's share. It was a matter of diplomacy, not of legality. If Polony yielded to Boaz's stronger political position in the village, it is vain to reconstruct laws and custom from this passage. I conclude that the *qere* is a red herring.

Polony's problem stems from Boaz's involvement in raising the name of the dead. The narrator's refusal to name that dead man, Elimelech or Mahlon, is part of the trick. From a genealogical point of view, a new son would continue the line of both men since they were father and son. Yet, the identity of the man whose name Ruth's son would raise has direct economic implications for Ruth's husband.

4.4.4 The Trick

Having announced his marriage to Ruth *before* Polony could acquire Elimelech's share, Boaz cut short any hopes Polony could have entertained in securing a permanent hold over Mahlon's share by engendering a male for Elimelech's line. When Ruth gives birth to Obed, Boaz secures Mahlon's share of communal land for his own *naḥalah*. Then, the final adoption scene confirms that Ruth's son is also Naomi's son, which means that Boaz secures Elimelech's share as well as Mahlon's. That is not all.

There is another part in the conspiracy, a part that is missed by most exegetes. Theoretically, Chilion's share of communal land is excluded from the discussion since Ophrah, Chilion's widow, did not follow Naomi and Ruth to Bethlehem. Yet, Boaz states as a matter of fact that he has acquired everything that belonged to Elimelech and everything that belonged to Chilion and to Mahlon (Ruth 4:9). By publicly naming Chilion before Mahlon, whereas in Ruth 1:2 and 1:5 he stands in second position, Boaz sandwiches Chilion's share between Elimelech's and Mahlon's and thus 'frames' the other shareholders by integrating Chilion's share in the deal. The inversion of the order of the names of Elimelech's sons is significant (against Bush 1996: 238). Through this rhetorical feat, Boaz secures Chilion's share besides Elimelech's and Mahlon's.

Boaz's acquisition of Chilion's share is totally unjustified and it is little commented upon, other than by Robert Hubbard (1988: 255) who notes that 'the extent of the purchase probably took the reader by surprise'. Hubbard wonders if 'Boaz has tricked the naïve kinsman' but leaves it at that. In fact, Boaz's self-attribution of three shares crowns the plot.[4] Had Boaz not held a dominant position, the elders would have protested unless Boaz offered a trade-off that convinced them that it was better to bow down to the sheer mastery of the trick and applaud without grumbling. The trade-off is that by taking the two widows home immediately, Boaz relieved the elders of their collective responsibility to feed two extra mouths until the next harvest. By granting Chilion's share to Boaz in the next distribution of strips, the elders also placed the burden of Orphah's potential usufruct upon Boaz's shoulder. Should Orphah ever change her mind and follow Ruth's steps, the village community was in a position to force Boaz to deal with her without further ado.

Identifying Boaz's trump card as the acquisition of three shares instead of the one offered to Polony shifts the focus away from the inheritance of Ruth's prospective son towards the more immediate concern of the number of shares of *musha'* tenure to be granted to each shareholder in the impending land redistribution. The use of the verb 'to buy' (קנה) instead of the usual 'to take' (לקח) for Boaz's marriage in Ruth 4:5, 10 underlines the economic aspects of the tale (Hubbard 1988: 243-44). The question of the attribution of land to Ruth's sons would not arise before they reached maturity twenty years thence, when both Naomi and Boaz would be dead.

The manipulation of the rules governing the distribution of shares of *musha‘* land by Boaz illustrates how local politics in *musha‘*-practicing villages were played out in the context of the long negotiations leading to the next redistribution of strips.

A side issue that may be added to the credit of the trickster is found in the six measures of barley taken directly from the heap to secure the marriage promise (Ruth 3:15). This disbursement was done at night with the recommendation that it remained unknown (Ruth 3:14), although Boaz announced his decision to marry Ruth the next morning. Besides dubious considerations of morality (virginity was no issue in this case), the secrecy could be motivated by the fact that the six measures were taken before the heap was measured and the taxes assessed. In that case, as owner of the grain, Boaz short-changed the tax collector and any shareholder for whom Boaz acted as sharecropper. Boaz granted himself a tax rebate to offset the cost of his generosity towards the maintenance of the two widows. The swindle was better left unpublicized, except to the audience in whose eyes a successful case of tax evasion further endeared the tricksters.

The moral evaluation of Naomi and Boaz's dealings is a question of personal appreciation. The narrator presents a case of clever manipulation of custom that enables Boaz to secure a long-term hold over the shares of communal land of three dead men. Hence, Boaz's generosity should be qualified. Roland Boer terms it pure exploitation (Boer 2003: 83), but exploitation may be preferable to charity. Is it fair to state that Boaz nowhere engages 'in any work as such, nowhere is he involved in the production of the necessary items for human existence' (Boer 2003: 83)? The Book of Ruth lauds enterprise, mutual exploitation of the sexes and the generations under the form of marital partnership and patronage. Each party makes the most of the limited assets at hand by putting them on the marriage market, trading them with those who need those assets and are able to exchange them against needed resources.

4.5 Latifundia, Absentee Landlords and Landless Farmers

Discussions of ancient economics by biblical scholars follow a rather rigid pattern. Whatever the epoch under discussion, farmers (the poor) are presented as oppressed by landlords (the rich) who mostly live in cities, although they control most of the land. The urban-propertied class is said to skim off the largest possible portion of the agricultural produce as a regular income or rent claimed on the basis of liabilities or full urban ownership of land. To live a life of luxury and idleness in the cities, the rich must lord it over the farmers ruthlessly or their kindness would be interpreted as signs of weakness (Lang 1982: 50; Coulange 2007; Houston 2003). The creation of large estates is thus deemed inevitable. It split society between absentee landlords in luxurious cities and miserable landless farmers who worked the estates. Armed with this basic framework, Premnath (1988: 49) renders Isa. 5:8 as follows:

> Woe to those who accumulate house to house,
> And add field to field
> Until there is no small landholding;
> And you have become possessors of land
> All by yourselves in the midst of the land.

Biblical latifundialism is rooted in Marxist notions of the reduction of the workforce into proletarians, leading to the expropriation of agricultural labourers that, on the basis of English economic history, Karl Marx identified as the social process that led from the feudal to the capitalist mode of production (Macfarlane 1978: 37-38). Although Marx himself excluded the Levant from this model by crafting the controversial Asiatic Mode of Production, the proponents of biblical latifundialism consider first-millennium BCE Palestine from the angle of feudalism (O'Leary 1989).

Latifundialism is defined as the accumulation of land in the hands of a few wealthy landowners. Premnath (1988: 302-305) presents the case for 'biblical latifundialism' in a most convenient synthetic fashion:

1. The formation of large estates entails the deprivation of the peasantry.
2. The growth of large estates is inversely proportional to the size of the landowning class.
3. Crop failures force small farmers into debt and finally lead to foreclosures, which in turn afford further means of land accumulation.
4. Commercial crops require extensive plantations that adversely affect the production of staple crops.
5. The shift from local exchange to a wider market leads to the distribution of goods according to power rather than to need.
6. The opulence of the rich is achieved at the expense of the poor.
7. Disdaining physical labour, the elite extract surplus from the producers to afford a life of luxury and leisure.

Premnath considers latifundialism as concomitant with the rise of monarchy against those who set the process during the reign of Hezekiah. He rightly insists on the necessity to integrate comparative evidence from agrarian societies. Evidence from agrarian societies, however, suggests that the process of latifundialism in ancient Palestine is unlikely before the Roman era. Premnath's points are discussed as listed above.

4.5.1 Did the Formation of Large Estates Entail the Deprivation of the Peasantry?

Latifundialism is unlikely at any time in ancient Palestine since the land was characterized by low demography, in particular during the reigns of David and Solomon envisaged by Premnath. Establishing large estates on village land would be a sure recipe for failure since large estates can only be productive if they can tap into an abundant supply of local manpower (see §4.2). Estates were necessarily established on waste-land. They would not encroach on land already tilled by local farmers. Studies of early Greek cemeteries show that the elite lived and died in close proximity to the remainder of the community, contrary to the medieval model of European nobility that lived in isolated manors (Galant 1982: 118). Hence, instead of the zero-sum approach that understands land as a fixed quantity and estates developed at the expense of freeholders, one has to understand that estates stimulated activity in the area where they were set up because the amount of land available was flexible. Labour was the critical factor. The ability to mobilize labour determined the extent of surface cultivated and consequently the amount of surplus produced (Gilsenan 1984: 456). Through the corvée, local farmers provided the manpower required to clear land and build what was necessary to make the estate viable. Once the estate was functional, local farmers and their families continued to supply manpower during peaks of agricultural work, both as corvée duties and as paid day work. The estate holder also found it convenient to lease some of the estate's land to local farmers in a range of tenancy contracts, in particular when military duties to distant war theatres kept the holder away from his estate for extended periods. The estate holder had every interest in sharing risk with sharecroppers and in reducing the need for supervision and wage labour. Métayage or sharecropping offered owners maximum yield but at the cost of shouldering most of the risk plus the costs of tight supervision to control the amount produced. Under fermage (fixed-rent leases), the owner received a fixed amount but shared the risk with the tenant and saved on supervision.

In spite of the lacunose evidence and in spite of the complexity of the actual situations, the development of estates fostered a vigorous independent peasantry in Egypt at the height of the Roman Empire, precisely when latifundia are supposed to have liquidated it (Rathbone 1991: 393). Evidence to the contrary would need to be brought forward before Premnath's claim that the formation of estates entails the deprivation of the peasantry could be accepted. In fact, the Bible itself undercuts the notion of the concentration of land in a few hands. According to 2 Kgs 15:19-20, King Menahem was able to gather a tribute of a thousand talents of silver by taxing all the wealthy in Israel at 50 shekels a head. At the standard rate of 3,000 shekels per talent, 60,000 Israelites were capable of paying 50 shekels. With dependants, this amounted to a total of 300–400,000 people, the maximum population of eighth-century BCE Israel according to current estimates. If evidence of land concentration in 737 BCE is lacking, it is hardly forthcoming for the following centuries.

Estates did at times grow from the consolidation of small farms. In this case, however, the process was voluntary. Under certain conditions, small farmers offered their land to bigger landlords in a process known as *talji'a* in Islamic sources and *patrocinium fundorum* in the Byzantine Empire. Small free-holders chose to become tenants and sharecroppers on large estates to gain protection against tax-farmers, marauders and bandits (Haque 1977: 243). Of course, this choice was dictated by hardships, but these kinds of hardships were common to most eras. Marauding tribes, foraging troops and greedy tax collectors were rather common fixtures. The decisive factor was not the greed of landlords. They suffered from the same ills, but, being larger, they were in a better position to resist them. Under these conditions, the formation of large estates was one strategy among others to improve the lot of small farmers. In every case, the very existence of agricultural estates presupposes the presence of a surplus of manpower nearby, a surplus to which the estate offered fresh avenues of employment. Because they were fragile economic entities, estates had to function in symbiotic rather than in parasitic relation with their social surrounding.

4.5.2 Was the Growth of Estates Inversely Proportional to the Size of the Landowning Class?

In Pharaonic Egypt, as in Byzantine Egypt, the large estates of aristocrats were neither contiguous nor consolidated holdings of arable land cultivated by permanently employed labourers. Large estates were conglomerations of small plots worked as small farms on a variety of tenures from more than one flood basin in order to spread risk (Eyre 2004: 184; Hickey 2007: 295). The same applies to southern Italy where the latifundia relied on the presence of smallholders who lived nearby as a source of seasonal labour (Rosafio 1993: 169; Fales 1984: 9).

Although a common claim, it is not at all certain that the Ptolemies treated most of Palestine as royal land. John Kloppenborg's study of the parable of the tenants (Mk 12:1-12; Gospel of Thomas 65) marks a major advance in our understanding of Hellenistic viticulture. Kloppenborg recovers the realism of the story's details, large-scale landholding and tenancy, wine and wealth, labour conflict, and inheritance. For instance, a dispute with tenants of an estate at Batanaia reveals that some tenants owned vineyards of their own besides leasing extra vineyards from a large estate owner (Kloppenborg 2006: 359-64). Rather than losing their land to the estate, these farmers diversified their portfolio. One mistake of Kloppenborg's otherwise impressive study is to postulate, against the evidence that he himself advances, the displacement of smallholders from their land and the shift from freehold poly-cropping to large-scale monoculture which forced smallholders to marginal land and created a mass of landless peasants (Kloppenborg 2006: 287-308). In fact, the entire gamut of landholding and labour contracts co-existed on estates (Banaji 1997: 95). A small freeholder could be leasing some land from other smallholders and from the estate while at the same time providing members of his family occasional labour on the estate. This does not imply dispossession and distress. It merely shows that large estates were integrated into the local economy (Foxhall 1990; 2002). In a more recent article, Kloppenborg mistakenly claims that the unavailability of land was one of the factors that hamstrung small cultivators (Kloppenborg 2008: 52) and that 'The growth of large estates of course also had the corollary of enlarging the pool of unlanded laborers that existed alongside underemployed peasant proprietors' (Kloppenborg 2008: 54). These claims have been found unsubstantiated by the study of Byzantine farming, a period characterized by a larger population and larger estates than was the case before the turn of the era. Lefort lists the definition of a village as a collection of free smallholders, smallholdings viewed as factors of prosperity and large estates as implying the reduction of smallholders to serf status as some of the popular notions that have to be abandoned (Lefort 2002). Even in Roman southern Italy and Sicily, where they were the most widespread, latifundia left room for a large number of smallholders (White 1970: 76). Instead of depopulating an area or turning locals into landless farmers, the extension of latifundia meant more work for the mass of the population (White 1970: 70).

In a world of chronic under-employment, more work meant increased total production for small farmers who could supplement their own holding with sharecropping contracts on nearby estates. Estates also offered additional opportunities of employment for local families. Hence, the British 1918 Resident Native Labourer Ordinance in Kenya expected squatters' wives and children to come and work in the settlers' fields during peak labour periods (Banaji 1997: 97). When the estates were tied to military duties, the entire area gained in security, a crucial condition for agriculture. Estates with a tower offered refuge to the surrounding population during raids. The crucial matter was not the land but the ability to mobilize corvée gangs to clear waste-land and build the necessary installations. In exchange, holders of large surfaces found it more profitable to lease some land rather than to pay year-round employees or slaves who need constant supervision and cannot be occupied profitably round the year.

Despite the symbiotic relation between small farms and large estates, Pliny's dictum, *latifundia perdire Italiam* (*Nat. Hist.* XVIII.7), remains very influential because it came to denote the plight of Irish immigrants in New York when they were chased from their land by British landlords. Emile de Laveleye presented Pliny's slogan as the denunciation of the replacement of the varied cultivation carried on by small proprietors by a few sumptuous villas and immense pastures. Many doubts have been raised concerning the reliability of classical sources relative to latifundia. Like Pliny, Plutarch denounced the rapacity of the rich that emptied the countryside of free citizens and filled Italy with gangs of foreign slaves cultivating the estates of the rich (*Ti.Gracch.* 8:1). This has long been recognized as an extreme propagandist picture (Frederiksen 1971; Capogrossi Colognesi 1979: 331; Rosafio 1993: 173).

Even if, for argument's sake, one accepts Plutarch's claim at face value, it does not entail that it is relevant to Palestine or Greece. In fifth-century BCE Sparta and Athens, the proportion of land controlled by the rich is estimated at between a quarter and a third of the total cultivated land (Osborne 1992: 24; Foxhall 2002: 211). This proportion reflects a constant level imposed by the structural requirement of the availability of tenants to work the land of those who had more land than they could work by themselves. The economic viability of large estates is directly affected by the number of farmers living nearby who could rent estate land besides their own land. To make the latifundia productive, manpower was the crucial factor.

In Scotland and later in Ireland, the system of enclosures did starve the local population because it took away existing land instead of developing new tracts. However, the same effect cannot be inferred from the ancient Orient characterized by a much lower demography and large surfaces of waste-land. Free peasants always outnumbered agricultural slaves, even in Italy of the late Republic when slave numbers were at their highest (Kloppenborg 2006: 305). With little or no supervision, tenants were always more profitable than slaves because they had a direct interest in the yield, especially when they were sharecroppers. Due to the close supervision necessary to prevent idleness, Columella I.7 considered tenants as the best method to run a farm when the landlord is unable to till the land himself (Martin 1971: 343-74). Even on the large latifundia of nineteenth-century CE Southern Italy, latifundisti granted some land to the inhabitants of their social territory as a means to improve under-developed areas, to keep wages low by providing land as the major source of subsistence, and to maintain traditions and loyalty to the master (Petrusewicz 1996: 188). The latifundia of southern Italy and Sicily were an exception and are not attested elsewhere.

A widely attested form of estates across the Eastern Mediterranean world, from Egypt as far as Sassanid Iran and until modern times, is 'village estates' (Banaji 2001: 172). Ownership of a village estate implied the integration of tenancy and wage labour in many combinations of sharecropping, labour paid in kind, casual or day labour, permanent labourers who might be tenants as well but who at least were not necessarily a landless labour force. The origin of these village estates is not clear, but they did not imply a degradation of the living conditions of farmers.

Silver (1983: 76) rightly states that it is not obvious that land consolidation must be accompanied by the impoverishment of the former free landowners. But he adduces this for the wrong reason. Silver evokes Adam Smith's claim that uncoerced exchange benefits both parties, with the seller better off than if he had not sold. Trade is a positive-sum game and the small farmer does not sell his land if he knows he will be worse off (Silver 1983: 75). The question is what he would do with the money, how long would he survive without the means of production which was his land. These questions are intractable and lead nowhere because they are based on false premises: estates were not always the result of the consolidation of small farms. The transformation of waste-land into *mīrī* land was an important factor in the formation of estates, a phenomenon that could only develop because it benefited all parties concerned. The state as much as the elite to whom the estates were granted, as well as the local farmers who worked on the estates, gained from it. Tenants, sharecroppers, employees and day workers were often better off from the presence of an agricultural estate; whether or not they lost possession of 'their' land in the process, since becoming a wage labourer on one's land often entails higher levels of security. Leigh Shaw-Taylor (2001: 641) notes that it is possible at certain times that farmers may become both more proletarian, that is more dependent on wage labour, and materially better off. Hence there can be no *a priori* assumption that estates implied poverty or that wage-workers were necessarily worse off than free farmers or tenants. When good land is freely available, the growth of large estates did not encroach on subsistence farms since the estate needed an abundant supply of self-supported local farmers to provide corvée duties and wage-workers to survive. In the absence of machinery, the extraction of revenues from the land is tied to the availability of man- and beast-power.

4.5.3 Did Crop Failures Force Small Farmers into Debt and Lead to Foreclosures and Land Accumulation?

The standard understanding of a landlord is a rich urban individual extracting maximum profit from helpless tenants while using foreclosure on the land of the last freeholders. The scenario runs as follows: 'Absentee landlordism proliferated. Many peasants were left no alternative to survival other than through loans at *de facto* interest rates usurious by any standards. Foreclosure upon family land and family members pledged as collateral was often at the discretion of the creditor' (Chaney 1999: 107). The syndrome of the hapless farmer has struck again (§3). Small farmers are depicted as caught in the vortex of a vast conspiracy to despoil them. 'The vast majority were the victims of a process they hated...the workings of political economy rendered them helpless' (Chaney 1999: 109). Considering the amount of prophetic denunciations that vindicated the cause of the poor who made up the 'vast majority' of the kingdom, social rebellions are surprisingly few in Israel's recorded past. Were the dispossessed too hungry to rebel or were they somehow collaborating with the land-grabbers? This is indeed what Isaiah 5 suggests when it condemns the entire people for sins which they were told to believe were committed by a small minority (Chaney 1999: 111). But Marvin Chaney (1999: 109) himself holds the solution: 'The injustice of their loss of hereditary lands and livelihood was aggravated by a cruel irony—many now worked land that had been in their families for generations, but they worked it as landless day-laborers.' If landless farmers continued cultivating their hereditary lands, the irony is cruel indeed!

More seriously, one wonders how large estates prospered as the result of crop failures. Crop failures led all farmers into debts since there is no evidence that owners of large estates manipulated rainfall and produced surplus when small farmers did not. Crop failures and debts affected large estates as much as small farms. The greater the sown surface, the greater the risk involved and the greater the loss in the event of crop failure. Size never guarantees profit. Before the motor pump, everyone was subject to the vagaries of rainfall. In Roman and later in European agriculture, small family holdings were more productive than large estates:

> Despite the resounding success of peasant agriculture in the Low Countries, eighteenth- and nineteenth-century economists and agricultural writers produced a flood of propaganda decrying the ignorance, lack of innovation, traditionalism, and inefficiency of the peasantry. Arguing that only tenant farmers with considerable capital were prepared to utilize the most advanced agricultural techniques, this concerted campaign did a great deal to salve the consciences of the English landed classes as they completed the dispossession of what remained of the English peasantry. Anglo-Irish, Scottish, Prussian, and southern Italian landowners also fastened eagerly onto this literature as a justification for brutally exploiting and ultimately driving off the land millions of nineteenth- and early twentieth-century peasants and rural labourers. (Kron 2008: 99)

Foreclosures, when they occurred, did not lead to land accumulation since loans were not extended in order to gain more land. Land could be bought cheaply if one wanted to increase landed property to enhance one's social status (Renger 1994: 203).

Although large estates were neither more productive than small-holdings nor immune from the problems inherent to farming, their size did put them in a better position to face problems relative to tax collection. For this reason, working as a tenant on a large estate was at times preferable to being a freeholder. Contrary to the modern scholarly fixation upon the ideal of freehold, to the person who actually does the work, paying land taxes as a proprietor was not necessarily more desirable than paying rent as a tenant. 'The freer the ancient peasant, in the political sense, the more precarious his position… The genuinely free peasant had no protection against a run of bad harvests, against compulsory army service, against the endless depredations in civil and foreign wars' (Finley 1981: 108). The ancient peasant's dilemma is encapsulated in Phaedrus' fable of the Dog and the Wolf (Williamson 1996: 63-64). One is free and hungry while the other is fat but bears the marks of a collar by which he is chained. An extreme illustration of the value of the dog's chain is found in Libanius (*Orationes* XLVII 1-16) who describes a strategy used by Syrian farmers of the fourth century CE to protect themselves from over-taxation. They paid a regular bribe to the *dux* of the province to station troops in their village, apparently a self-defeating strategy, until the well-entertained soldiers were used to eject the tax collector or the agents of the landlord. If the government or the landlord sought legal redress, the case would be brought to the *dux*'s court since soldiers were among the defendants, and the *dux* would judge in favour of the villagers (Jones 1964: 775).

Salvian (*De gubernatione dei* v.38), on the contrary, describes patrons who seem to support Premnath and Chaney's point. These estate holders offered protection to individual farmers against the tax collector in exchange for the reversion of the farmer's land on his death. The sons of the clients, according to Salvian, were expelled from their fields but nonetheless bore the tax burden of the property they had lost. If Salvian was correct in claiming that the land-grabbers invaded the property and the poor farmers paid the taxes for the land-grabbers, at the very least it proves that the sons were not physically expelled from the land but carried on working their fathers' land. Jones (1964: 777-79), however, warns that the tragic tone of the text is rather overdrawn since the tenants must have gained from the deal. They would pay the regular taxes but were spared many additional exactions. The depiction of generation after generation of peasants losing their holdings through foreclosure is evidence of the survival of smallholders in spite of the literary reports of their fast disappearance (Postgate 1987: 263).

4.5.4 Did Commercial Crops Adversely Affect the Production of Staple Crops?

Plantation of olive trees for the production of oil, the main export good in Palestine, did not adversely affect the production of staple food because olive groves offer plenty of space for the growth of staple crops between and under the trees (Stolper 2001: 101). Any of these crops mature well before the olive harvest in the autumn (Mundy 1986: 83). Moreover, extensive plantations produced fuel and food from the pruning and from olive pressings. Local farmers with their families and beasts gained fresh employment opportunities for ploughing the groves, pruning, harvesting, transporting and pressing the olives. Local potters produced containers that others had to transport. Because planting large numbers of trees is a long-term investment, the estate holder and the central administration that taxed him were bound to invest resources to protect the assets permanently against raiders. Hence, extensive plantations had various positive spin-off effects on small farmers that gravitated around the estate, one of them being stability and long-term security. Security and stability are as essential as rain to successful farming since assets are spread across open fields for months and years at a time. Stability offsets duties extracted in the form of corvée and shares of the produce. In the absence of a central government, the small farmer has to forfeit a portion of his produce to the tribes who fill in the power vacuum and whose methods to extract produce from farmers are less predictable but no less violent than those of regular tax collectors.

The opposition between commercial and staple crops is thus largely fictitious. Domeris (2007: 139) states that large estates required new crops and mentions a Late Bronze shipwreck off the Turkish coast. The ship transported materials used for perfume manufacture, as well as figs, olives, grapes and cereals. He concludes (2007: 141-42) from such a list of staple goods that the rise of trade and of large estates sounded the death knell for subsistence agriculture, although he notes that wine and olive by-products were Israel and Judah's main products for export. Commercial crops were but staple crops produced in higher quantities by putting more land under cultivation. Terracing hillside pastures to plant vines and olives did *not* abrogate anyone's grazing rights as long as land was freely available (Hopkins 1996: 134). And even then, the loss of grazing rights was amply compensated by the economic opportunities offered by the plantations. The status and welfare of 'free agrarians' compared with that of peasants is an inflated commodity.

4.5.5 Did the Market Lead to the Distribution of Goods according to Power Rather Than to Need?

Behind this claim stands the illusion of an original egalitarian tribal society, a category also used to over-interpret archaeological data by Faust (2007: 31-32) who establishes a typology of villages:

1. Villages owned by the palace or by an absentee landlord characterized by a bare subsistence level because the profits went to the city.

2. Villages owned by a present landlord who lived in the single-stone house surrounded by many mud huts.
3. Communal villages whose inhabitants enjoyed a higher standard of living.

Predictably, Faust discovers that Israelite villages of the Iron II fit the third category of villages. They were corporate and egalitarian, *kibbutzim* before their time. Besides the difficulties in measuring levels of wealth from meagre remains of rural settlements, the basic question is whether variations in wealth are the consequence of particular types of socio-economic organization or whether they reflect different economic contexts. That Iron II villages are comparably wealthy is hardly surprising given the overall economic development of the period. Yet, favourable economic circumstances produce social stratification and increase the gap between rich and poor, while poverty and underdevelopment fosters equalization and forces greater levels of egalitarianism. The fate of the *kibbutzim* is a glaring demonstration of that principle (§2.1.2). When resources are scarce, the survival of the group depends on the ability to share out whatever produce is available. Yet, power struggle is at work in every group and the presence of a defensive wall that Faust uses as an indicator of cooperative organization can be given other interpretations. Hierarchies develop even among the poorest groups. The difference between the extremes is less because there are fewer resources, not because there is less coercion and extortion. At the individual level, control is tighter in simpler societies than in great imperial networks because there are fewer mediating agencies between the ruler and the ruled. This leads to the next point.

4.5.6 *Was the Opulence of the Rich Achieved at the Expense of the Poor?*

It is very difficult to become rich by extracting revenue from people who have none unless the accumulation of wealth is considered a zero-sum process which postulates that 'Since it was virtually impossible to increase one's wealth without taking the possessions of someone else, the rich turned to oppression in order to increase their wealth' (Pleins 2001: 173; Rose 1968). The pervasiveness of the zero-sum approach may be attributed to the once popular American activist Henry George (2005: 14) who wrote in his most famous book, 'to seek the law which associates poverty with progress, and increases want with advancing wealth.'

As a matter of fact, the rich only get richer when the majority of the poor gets richer too, or hungry mobs will make sure the rich get poorer (Quataert 1991). The economic crisis that began in 2008 demonstrates that the poor do not get richer when the rich get poorer, far from it. The widening of the gulf between rich and poor in no way proves that the poor are getting poorer. The opposite is the case. The increase of wealth is by necessity a shared process since the poor are always more numerous than the rich. In Greece, 70 popular uprisings are recorded between 370 and 170 BCE, an average of more than one uprising every three years, a rhythm that exceeds the expected frequency of harvest failure (Fuks 1984: 17; Gehrke 1985; Garnsey 1988: 8-16). Hence, Xenophon, *Oeconomicus* ii.6, has Socrates feel deeply sorry for his rich friend Critobulus as he lists the heavy financial burden his position requires him to shoulder. The burden, warns Socrates, will nearly crush Cristobulus who has no way of avoiding it since 'Whenever you seem to fall short of what is expected of you, the Athenians will certainly punish you as though they had caught you robbing them.' In times of severe food crisis, it was and still often is a question of life or death for the rich to remit debts and to finance relief operations, unless the famine is so severe that a significant number of people emigrate, leaving behind those who are too starved to react (Garnsey 1998; Quass 1993: 230-50; Liverani 1975: 154). Most states run mechanisms of food distribution, either in the form of taxation of the rich or as voluntary liturgies, *eisphorai, sitonia*, and debt release edicts. It is war rather than crop failure that provokes famine through the disruption of trade routes.

Therefore, Premnath's point can be turned on its head. The opulence of the rich is maintained if not achieved at the benefit of the poor. The reputation and at times the salvation of the rich is tied to their ability to maintain the poor alive, either directly as patron or indirectly as providers of funds for the various consumption-smoothing devices that exist in every society. The destiny of the rich is tied to that of the poor. The rich must feed the poor as much as they exploit them. Keeping the poor alive is indeed a form of exploitation that perpetuates poverty rather than eradicates it. This is another matter. What must be emphasized here is that the rich need the poor as much as the poor need the rich and that the relation between them is a two-way process. The rich cannot be the only exploitative party. Societies collapse when the poor are unable to exploit the rich to the benefit of both rich and poor.

4.5.7 Did the Elite Disdain Physical Labour and Extract Surplus from the Producers to Afford a Leisurely Life?

The notion of elite idleness echoes Max Weber's formulation of the consumer city as centre of an economy of rentiers where the urban elite lived off the surpluses extracted from the countryside. Cities are viewed as the locale where absolute surpluses are converted into extra people freed from the drudgery of farming (Weber 1976: 170-84; Foxhall 2002: 216; Veblen 1899; Childe 1954). Lenski defines the elite as 'those within an agrarian economy who, without themselves engaging in agricultural labour, live off the land by controlling the peasants so as to be able to take from them part of their products' (1984: 220). Cities are imagined as centres of culture where powerful members of the provincial elite sought to base themselves for a better standard of living (Houston 2008: 43). Lack of sanitation and crowded conditions throw doubts on the urban advantage relative to the standard of living. Yet, in light of the 'evidence' from Amos, the all-time favourite of the champions of social justice, the elite becomes a leisure class living parasitically at the expense of the working class. The rich do nothing but feast (Isa. 5:11-12; 56:12; Amos 2:7-8; 3:9), lolling in beds inlaid with ivory (Amos 6:4) where father and son use the same girl (Amos 2:7). The cliché was applied to Amos' description of Samarian women as cows of Bashan in ivory palaces, although Amos does not tell where the men found the wine their 'cows' were clamouring for (Amos 3:15–4:1).

The image of the bed reappears in Mic. 2:1-2 as the place where wickedness and evil deeds are devised, in particular the seizing of fields and houses (§2.3.1). Yet, Micah has his evildoers out of bed at the crack of dawn. Getting rich was hard work, even for the wicked. Accumulation does not happen on its own. The elite whose voice is heard in the Book of Proverbs is well aware of it. The book is full of warnings against idleness presented as a sure path to poverty. Proverbs closes with a poem of the ideal woman (Prov. 31), a workaholic who stresses that prosperity is not the daughter of idleness, even for the elite (Houston 2003: 232). It is hard to reconcile this celebration of hard manual work with the notion that the elite valued nothing above idleness especially since many biblical figures are presented as actively engaged in farming (Houston 2006: 24-25). Elite idleness comes rather from the writings of the spokesmen of wealthy Athenians who disdained what 'deteriorates the condition of the body' as well as 'the industries that earn wages'. Liberal sciences were sometimes considered equally vulgar occupations, a sort of limited slavery (Kyrtatas 2002: 144). The Bible is exempt from this kind of class prejudice, or it reflects the prejudices of the lower class.

Admitting, for argument's sake, that disdain of manual labour would be a distinctive trait of the elite rather than a tendency found at every level of society, not being directly involved in manual work does not mean that one does nothing. The 'absentee landlord' who leads a life of pleasure while wealth just keeps pouring into his coffers is an enduring fallacy rooted in a long literary tradition.

Accumulating wealth from agriculture requires careful management of one's estate. Farming is subject to many small changes which entail spatial, seasonal, mechanical and biological subtleties that cannot be routinized. Farmers great and small need constantly updated knowledge of precise conditions to take crucial decisions that cannot be obtained at a distance (Schulz 1965: 119). For this reason, absentee landlords are not in the best position to run profitable estates. They have to delegate the daily running of their farm to managers who also require close supervision if the lord is to collect any surplus. Landlords could not enrich themselves if they were only to enjoy a life dedicated to leisure without being actively involved in the running of their estate, whether or not they lived permanently on the farm. Landlords who showed little interest in their land were prone to see their possession contested whenever population pressure induced boundary disputes and conflicts with new settlers who claimed *maḥlūl* land for themselves, as happened in Anatolia at the end of the nineteenth century CE (Terzibaşoğlu 2005).

If the position of rich landlords in society depended on surpluses extracted from their estates, the good management of the estate was a constant concern. 'The idea that rich landowners were not involved or interested in the profits from the produce of their land—or that we should be surprised when they were involved—is quite simply absurd' (Whittaker 1983: 173). Columella (I.4.7) was of the opinion that the worst system of farm organization is that of the landlord who lives in town and prefers to till his land with slaves rather than with his own hands.

Without taking Charmides in Xenophon's *Banquet* (iv.31) at face value, his claim that since the loss of his wealth he stretches out and enjoys a sound sleep points out that being wealthy involved some work. It would be ridiculous to infer from Charmides' words that the rich actually had all the hassle while the poor were kings (Gauthier 1973: 166), but the poor did not have all the hassle while the rich did nothing. Charmides' aristocratic point of view is as partial as Premnath's.

The notion of urban landlords is misleading since the urban-rural divide was less marked than is the case today. Contrary to their modern counterparts, city dwellers were farmers like village dwellers (Grabbe 2001: 96). Ancient urbanites had their own gardens within or just outside the city wall where they grew most of the food they ate. Hence, digs in the city centre of Ugarit yielded 400 flint pieces with clear marks of wear, showing that these wealthy dwellers were engaged in agriculture as much as their rural counterparts (Yon 2006: 162-63). Persian Jerusalem, as much as Omayyad Cairo and Istanbul, had plenty of space for gardens inside the city (Ussishkin 2006; Courby and Picard 1924: 89-100; Gayraud 2003; İslamoğlu-İnan 1994; Stoianovitch 1976: 68; Braudel 1973: 376-80). Ancient urban elites, kings included, grew their own food. Joab is said to have barley growing in a strip next to Absalom's (2 Sam. 14:30-31). This does not imply that Joab and Absalom did all the work themselves, but it is probably not before the intensification of the Hellenistic era that the elite could devote itself entirely to non-agricultural activities. Therefore, a landlord residing in the city did not necessarily qualify as absentee (Pečíka 1973: 118).

The rural/urban divide is not marked by production. Food was produced by both sectors. The difference between urban and rural was located in the greater involvement of city dwellers in interregional trade. The rise of the urban elite is not the consequence of a parasitic class of consumers squeezing out more than the surpluses produced by farmers. City economies were distinct from rural economies in the sense that they specialized in interregional exchange (Blanton 2000: 74). Urban wealth results from the transformation of perishable agricultural surpluses into more permanent assets. Except under extreme conditions, surpluses are available since farmers make sure they produce more than enough to be on the safe side.

Agricultural surpluses, however, are perishable; they arrive on the market all at the same time and in quantities that cannot be foreseen months ahead. Trade manipulates time and geography by mobilizing perishable surpluses during their limited lifetime, extending their lifetime through storage and enhancing their value through transport to areas where a difference in value may offset the expenses of storage and transport to produce a net profit. Individual producers do store their products and sell their own surpluses on local markets but in a modest way compared with institutions and private specialists who are in a better position to collect small amounts of domestic surpluses, build storage facilities and mobilize transport to trade significant amounts of surplus instead of letting it go to waste in the granaries of individual farms. For this reason, the rise of elites is linked to the ability to trade domestic surplus (Pearson 1957; Sahlins 1974: 140; Gamble 1982). The point is not to eat what others have produced in order to keep one's hands clean, but to generate greater revenues on distant markets than is possible through agriculture alone. Adding value to agricultural surpluses through trade benefits the producers as well as the traders, albeit to a lesser degree. Hence, Judg. 5:6 rightly equates the cessation of trade with times of dearth.

To be sure, producers resent those who buy their surpluses as they feel that the trader lives off the producer. In the absence of trade, however, producers are not better off since their surpluses go to waste, unless the producers risk themselves at trading them, but they soon realize that trade entails as much work and worries as production. Trade affords as much or as little leisure as production does to farmers who, under Mediterranean conditions, experienced long spells of near-idleness between peaks of intense activity. Occupational specialization brings about a differentiation in luxury and life-style, but no idleness. The emergence of the idle aristocrat and of the dandy was but a fleeting moment in the history of Europe. The common fate of idle people is bankruptcy, for rich and poor alike.

Premnath's portrayal of latifundisti enjoying a life of leisure and luxury while the small farmers they enslaved enable them to control the market *and* produce surpluses in order to buy out more small peasants has little grounding in the ancient reality as it can be reconstituted at the moment. There is no such thing as soil without toil. The lazy rich is as much a stereotype as the lazy poor of the books of Proverbs and Sira (Domeris 2007: 123-24).

A less ideological translation of Isa. 5:8 would run like this:

> Woe to those who cause a house to touch a house
> They make a field approach a field until there is no space
> As if you resided by yourselves in the midst of the land.

In this sense, consolidation rather than latifundialization is at stake, since cuneiform evidence suggests that sales of real estate were often motivated by practical rather than economic reasons leading to the consolidation of one's resources after inheritance had fragmented plots into shares too small to be practical (Wunsch 1999: 401). Or, what is condemned is the encroachment on public space through buildings and ploughing. Encroachment and the moving of boundary markers are common occurrences in scattered strip regimes. Public space can also be encroached upon, as happened in classical cities where shops established along colonnaded streets gradually narrowed them (Kennedy 1985). The process described in Isa. 5:8 suggests a thriving urban life rather than the expulsion of farmers and the desertification of the countryside.

4.6 Chapter Summary

At the close of this chapter, a number of points can be listed as guidelines for further studies attempting to recover the actual situation of biblical farmers.

Possession and tenure should be preferred to ownership when dealing with land in the ancient Orient, in particular, arable land that should be distinguished from gardens and terraces. The recovery of the importance of the Hebrew *aḥuzzah* is crucial but it requires a better appreciation of the concept of *naḥalah*, something that has not been possible here. These terms are clearly not equivalent, but as they do not necessarily have the same meaning in every biblical text; much work remains to be done on this subject.

Lumping land into a single entity is the source of much confusion. In practice, land, which the biblical writers rarely bother to qualify, was probably differentiated into different categories each with its own particular status. A full recovery of these categories of land is probably impossible, but the Ottoman differentiation between *mulk, mīrī, maḥlūl, mawāt* and *waqf* offers a grid that can serve to interpret biblical texts relative to land. The texts discussed above in light of Ottoman categories are but a sample of the potential of this approach.

Given the quasi universality of open-field systems before the industrial revolution, a system similar to the *musha'* is presupposed by most biblical texts. Hence, exegetes must be aware of the outworking of open-field systems and of their possible implications for the interpretation of biblical material.

Finally, exegetes ought to shed the common patronizing stance by which they set themselves as the champions of the cause of hapless peasants. The struggle for justice is too important a cause to benefit from the repetition of slogans. Contending for justice requires a less ideological understanding of economic realities than the greedy rich versus the holy poor dichotomy. To this aim, the next part focuses upon credit.

Notes

1. In light of the suspicions surrounding items from the Moussaïeff collection, I refrain from citing the inscription called the 'widow's plea' (Bordreuil, Israel and Pardee 1998: 12).
2. Ruth 1:4, 22; 2:2, 6, 21; 4:5, 10. Ruth designates herself once as a foreigner as a social convention that the narrator deconstructs with a clever play on the

words 'foreigner' (נכריה) and recognize (נהכירי, Ruth 2.10). Siquans (2009: 448-49) has different views.

3. Modern fieldwork estimates a minimal intake of 250 kg of wheat equivalent per year per adult (Hopkins 2002: 197). Meat would have been less of a problem since an ox can feed roughly 600 people and a sheep 60 people (Allred 2006: 65). See also the comparison between the monthly 45-50 litres of barley equivalent for a hardworking man established on the basis of FAO figures and the standard of 90 litres per month current in Mesopotamia in Jursa (2008: 390-417) and the standard monthly ration of 30 litres of barley for adult male *kurtaš* in Persepolis (Aperghis 2000: 131). The ephah Ruth gleans (Ruth 2.17) is estimated at between 22 to 45 litres (Schottroff 1999: 149 n. 47).
4. Targum Ms Sassoon 282 (twelfth century CE) omits Mahlon (Beattie 1994: 31) and thus avoids the issue of the third share.

Part II

Credit

Chapter 5

Agricultural Credit

Because farming entails a time gap of several months between the investment in seeds and work before the harvest, a gap that swells into years when animals and trees are involved, credit is essential to farmers. Credit is also necessary to smooth climatic shocks, the risk involved in growing plants and raising animals and the mortality of breadwinners. Hence, lending and borrowing are often mentioned in the Bible, but there is a long history of misunderstanding of the effects of credit.

5.1 When Theologians Write about Ancient Credit

Prophetic invectives read in light of Marxian categories serve both as the primary source of the narratives and the interpretative method to reconstruct the plight of biblical peasants. In short, the good prophets of social justice fought the exploitation of the poor by the rich. It is crucial for self-proclaimed 'social-science' readings to date prophetic social critiques early to avoid the disturbing suggestion that they were penned to explain major political downturns after the fact. Were Amos' critiques of social oppression 'more closely connected with Jewish and Christian idealization of the godliness of the poor' (Levin 2003: 327), an entirely different light would be cast upon these texts and the class-struggle romanticism of the exegetical defenders of the poor would appear as a theodicy à la Job's friends. Since the poor are always and everywhere to be found (Deut. 15:11; Mk 14:7) and since dating oracles is well nigh impossible, exegetes are free to create prophets in their own image and see themselves as modern prophets. At least the identification is correct on one point: they belong to the elite of their own society as their ancient model did. One is necessarily poor when addressing God in prayer—so much so that Num. 12:3 calls rich kid Moses poor (Levin 2003: 333). Talking about the defence of the poor is a must for the biblically minded rich.

Yet, biblical depictions of economic relations are about as historical as any casual discussion of the contemporary world economy in a local pub where patrons who invariably see themselves as poor as the psalmist complain that they work too much, that they pay far too many taxes, that the price of food (and beer) is too high, that the rich are far too rich, that society is not doing enough for the poor, and that most politicians, judges and priests are corrupt. The list of perceived abuses includes the oppression of women and children in Isa. 3:12, the taking of widows and orphans as spoil in Isa. 10:2, the use of pledged cloaks as picnic blankets on which to drink the wine of fines in Amos 2:8, or the levies of grain in Amos 5:11. Yet, the economic welfare of anyone living in the twenty-first century CE is beyond any comparison with that of Levantine farmers of the first millennium BCE, as mortality rates and demography demonstrate. Poverty is relative. It cannot be measured from the harangues of trade unionists and biblical prophets. Demonstrating the existence of structural extortion and of the systematic fleecing of the farmers by the rich would require more solid evidence, unless extortion and fleecing are simply used as synonyms for regular economic relations. Or one should also accuse the elite of cannibalism, since Mic. 3:1-3 states that the heads of Jacob tore the skin off the people and ate them while Prov. 30:14 confirms that its generation devoured the poor off the earth.

If one baulks at too literal readings, the use of dishonest scales (Ezek. 45:9-10; Hos. 12:7; Amos 8:5) should also be read as hyperbole. No doubt some merchants were dishonest, but this does not establish the existence of a structurally corrupt economic system. Farmers had their own ways to cheat the tax collector and the merchant but the Bible was obviously not written by merchants. The present chapter seeks to introduce a measure of realism in the exegesis of biblical texts relative to economic life in ancient Israel. The aim is not to deny the existence of exploitation. Exploitation is always resented as extortion and injustice by the exploited, but exploitation and taxation are signs of economic health that benefit everyone, albeit in different proportions.

The results of the previous chapter on land tenure can be integrated to draw a more subtle description of economic life in ancient Palestine that may in turn benefit the use of the Bible for today's social critique. Social justice is hardly promoted by the repetition of slogans, however passionate and biblical they may appear. In the long run, the champions of social justice run the risk of appearing as naïve armchair idealists with little grip on reality. That the biblical writers formulated no economic theory is no excuse for merely repeating their slogans. Economic relations cannot be reduced to the 'exploitation of the poor' (Grabbe 2008: 208).

It is necessary to get beyond the customary depiction of credit in entirely negative terms. Credit was essential for the economy as a whole, for agriculture as much as for commerce and it consolidated social relations among peers and between clients and patrons (Van de Mieroop 2002a). Walter Houston's work marks a watershed in the study of social justice in the Old Testament. Houston rejects several of the academic shibboleths that Premnath synthesized in such a vivid way (§4.5). Houston states that traditional society never was egalitarian, that there was no drastic deterioration in the standard of living during the monarchic period, and no latifundia (Houston 2004; 2008: 48; Bloch-Smith and Nakhai 1999: 76). Houston devotes a large place to patronage, a crucial structure regulating social and economic relations between unequals. The following builds upon Houston's work and offers some correctives, for instance, on his presentation of Boaz's relation to Ruth as patronage (Houston: 2008: 46). Before discussing patronage, a reminder of the common understanding of the ancient credit system is in order.

5.2 Joseph and the Hungry Egyptians: Taxes as Rent

The story of how Joseph completely dispossessed the Egyptians during the seven years of lean cows (Gen. 47:13-26) provides the classical model for understanding the effects of debt. Although the narrative is clearly aetiological, attributing to Joseph the origin of the Pharaonic concept of land tenure by which the crown owned the entire realm except temple land (vv. 22 and 26), many exegetical studies apply the principle of dispossession through debt as a valid economic process.

The point of the story is clear. The Egyptians pay a rent equivalent to the fifth of their crop to Pharaoh to whom they had sold their land for food. The sale of the land occurred as the last resort. The first year, the Egyptians bought food with the silver and the animals they brought to Joseph, nicely illustrating the hoarding function of animals. Their fat and milk stored the ephemeral surplus of winter grass into resources that could be used later. The story is not interested in the technical practicalities involved with the fate of the thousands of horses, flocks, herds and donkeys the Egyptians brought to Joseph (Gen. 47:17). They are only there to signify the total dispossession of the Egyptians, but in reality Joseph would have needed some huge deep-freeze facilities to turn these millions of animals into valuable assets.

Then, the destitute Egyptians exchange their land and their bodies (גוי) against food and seed. It is significant that the term for 'land' is the soil (אדמה). Hence, despite Pharaoh's acquisition of the entire Egyptian territory including all its inhabitants, the text indicates that the status of Egyptian farmers was not fundamentally altered. They lost neither their tenure (אחוזה) nor their *naḥalah*. Although the versions claim at verse 21 that they became Pharaoh's slaves, the conclusion shows that they became Pharaoh's sharecroppers. The storyteller is playing with numbers and sets the final dispossession in year two so that the five remaining years explain the fifth due to Pharaoh.

Centuries later, Flavius Josephus retold the story according to the institutions of his time. In his *Jewish Antiquities* 2:189-93, Josephus has Joseph return the land in perpetuity to the farmers. For Josephus, the fifth owed by the farmers to the crown was a tax as the use of the verb *telein* makes clear (Martinez-Sève 2007: 407). Fiction is not reality, although the importance of the legal fiction transmitted by Genesis 47 is demonstrated by another legal fiction relative to Egyptian land tenure produced a millennium and a half after the writing of the Joseph story.

Ibn Humam (d. 1457 CE) first articulated the Hanafi doctrine concerning land ownership as vested in the treasury and delegated to intermediaries and cultivators contrary to the original Islamic notion of individual possession. To explain the transition during the Mamluk era, Ibn Humam argued that as a result of the death of the individual landowners the entire land of Egypt had passed to the state treasury (Johansen 1988). In practice, the rent/tax debate is more relevant to the continuous struggle between the state/crown/Sultan and local elites vying with the state for the control of agricultural surplus than to the farmers themselves (Mundy and Saumarez Smith 2007: 11-39; Cuno 1995; Jackson 1956; Haque 1977: 194-218).

The purpose of Gen. 47:13-26 and of Ibn Humam is the justification of the ruler's right to raise taxes by presenting them as a rent for the use of state land. The fifth due to the ruler is passed as rent rather than a tax, illustrating continued resistance to taxation across the millennia. The story of Joseph's acquisition of the entire Egyptian realm for Pharaoh explains why farmers have to give away a share of the fruit of their labour, but it cannot be taken as an illustration of the consequences of debt.

Nevertheless, the textual problem at verse 21 reflects two ways to understand the effect of drought. Modern translations tend to follow the Samaritan, LXX and Vulgate that read 'enslavement' instead of 'transfer'. Joseph either enslaved the Egyptians or he removed them to cities

(KJV following the MT). Both happened in the past at different times. The most famous case of displacement is the thousands of slaves sold to Egypt to build Alexandria. This dramatic case, however, was not the most common practice. As the Letter of Aristeas (III,§12-14) indicates, once the job was accomplished, slaves were very expensive and Ptolemy was looking for a way to free them so they would feed themselves. The other option, the enslavement of the entire population, does not imply any displacement. The slavery presented here does not correspond to debt-bondage since debt slaves would be released once they paid back their debt. Not so here. As the aim is to justify a permanent state of tenancy towards the crown and pass taxation as rent, the slavery entails the loss of ownership rather than the loss of freedom. Hence, Egyptian farmers are presented as tenants, very much like the children of Israel who, according to Lev. 25:23 work the land of Canaan owned by YHWH. The fundamental principle is that arable land does not belong to the farmers. They are tenants who pay rent to the landlord, Pharaoh or YHWH.

To justify the common understanding of Genesis 47 as a demonstration of the relentless cycle of debt, one needs to compound the two different readings of verse 21. Having lost their possessions and their freedom, farmers were then taken away from their land and sold as slaves. The text only offers one option at a time. According to the versions, the slaves were in fact sharecroppers owing only a fifth, which entails that they supplied all the work as well as all the seeds and draught animals. Hence the 'slaves' functioned as independent farmers paying taxes to the state in the form of produce and they were even exempt from corvée. According to the MT, the farmers were taken away from their land but not as slaves! The text need not consider the practicalities of feeding cities when the countryside had been emptied because until very recently city-dwellers engaged in farming as much as dwellers of rural settlements. What is at stake is fiscal status. That farmers lived in cities means that land within walled settlements had a different status from the arable land around the villages. The farmers did not own the land they ploughed and for this reason they paid a rent for its use as stated in Lev. 25:29-31 and by the distinction between *mulk* and *mīrī* land (§1.4). Moreover, the MT's notion that debt turned farmers into town-dwellers rather than into slaves reflects the observation of the economic consequences of the flow of revenues from the periphery towards urban storage centres. Cities, however, did more than store agricultural surpluses. They housed a complex network of converters who transformed raw products into cash. Towns and cities were essential relays for the flow of wealth which was far more complex than a one-way drain of riches towards the centre. The conversion function of urban centres grows proportionally to the geographic distance between where taxes and rents are raised and where they are spent. Through its tax collectors, moneylenders, store-managers, merchants, transporters, artisans and administrators, the town reflects the specialization of labour that the double flow of wealth induces (Hopkins 2002: 209).[1] Employed primarily in administrative tasks, the scribes who penned the Bible were in an ideal position to grasp the complementarity of taxes and trade.

Neither reading of verse 21 supports the notion that debt led to the dispossession of farmers and their removal from their land. If indebted farmers did become slaves, they continued functioning as ordinary farmers or they were displaced and became city-dwellers, but not slaves. How did debt affect ancient farmers?

5.3 Debt, Interest and Usury

Besides taking Genesis 47 as an economic model, discussions of the ancient economy tend to reproduce the medieval understanding of debt as part of a trinity of evils: debt, usury and foreclosure. The church regarded interest and commercial profits as a danger to salvation since charging interest was viewed as the exploitation of needs that necessarily entailed the further pauperization of the debtor. Another fundamental notion was that money cannot yield fruit.[2] This is the zero-sum concept encountered in the previous chapter concerning land, applied this time to money. For instance, scholars find in the Hebrew Bible a clear consciousness that the material gain of a certain group signifies a bigger loss for the whole of society (Fischer 2003: 20). The prohibition of interest was always circumscribed because it was obvious that money is not sterile and that lending against interest tended to enrich the borrower as well as the lender and that the stimulation of economic activity through lending was more beneficial to society at large than prohibitions of interest.

5.3.1 Interest

Interest rates are discussed in general ways in Mesopotamian legal codes.[3] In Egypt, the first mention of the mortgaging of the entire patrimony of a borrower appears during the reign of Apries (589–570 BCE). Before Apries, the practice that prevailed during the Ramesside era was the solemn oath of the debtor to refund the borrowed amount failing which he would be submitted to a penalty of a hundred strikes, on top of or instead of a doubling of the debt (Menu 1998a: 390). Oath and guarantee were, however, not always recorded and creditors were satisfied with the written promise to reimburse the capital with a 100% interest after one year. Kushite-era contracts mark a transition where, instead of promising to repay the loan, the debtor promises not to contest the document recording the debt.

From Darius I on, Egyptian contracts integrate clauses typical of Aramaic contracts. It is stated that the contract is handed over to the creditor and that the heirs of the debtor will compensate their father's debt with a certain number of workdays. The reign of Darius also saw the rise of compound interest (anatocism) in Egypt. Stein (1953: 165) claims, without quoting supporting evidence, that compound interest occurred as early as Old Babylonian times. Some sort of compound interest is attested in Babylon in 544 BCE (Wunsch 2002: 237). The notion of interest evolved from the original sanction of the doubling of the debt imposed when a debtor did not fulfil his obligations at the term of the contract. From this starting point grew the automatic accruing of the debt, whether the term had been respected or not, until the interest equalled the capital (Menu 1998a: 392). Never is the debtor's person put at the disposal of the creditor (Menu 1998a: 390). This challenges the notion that indebted farmers were automatically enslaved. Another clue in the same direction is the many loan contracts from ancient Babylonia that were preserved in archives when the tablets that documented them were supposedly broken or dissolved when the loan was paid back. Postulating that these loans must have been reimbursed or most Babylonian moneylenders would have been bankrupted, scholars suggest that archives were not meticulously sorted out (de Graef 2008), or that *mīšarum* edicts rendered the contracts invalid (Charpin 2000). A more straightforward explanation, apparently not yet considered, is that at least some of the unbroken tablets recovered in excavations were loans that were never reimbursed precisely because the creditor and the debtor were interested in keeping the debt alive. Moneylenders sought to secure the labour services of their debtors rather than drawing interest on the loans (Steinkeller 2002). For this reason, many contracts either omit interest, specify their absence or, when interest is mentioned, the term of the loan is often missing, suggesting that the loan was meant to live on.

As a very general rule of thumb, it might be argued that the Achaemenid era saw the generalization of the practice of combining the remuneration added to loans of grains (the additional 50%) and the sanction for not paying silver loans in time to all loans (Menu 1998a: 393). The novelty of the Ptolemaic period probably resided on the level of taxation with the generalization of poll taxes, first for males and then to the entire population, humans and animals (Muhs 2005). Therefore, despite the general claim that the Neo-Babylonian interest rate was normally 20% per annum with a trend towards higher rates at around 25-40% p.a. in the fourth and third centuries BCE (Jursa 2005: 198-202; 2006), credit practices were varied and are not easily ordered into neat categories. Despite biblical 'laws', Jews charged interest to other Jews while evidence of non-Jewish interest-free loans can be found in every period.[4]

To take one example, between 509–504 BCE (during the reign of Darius I), a selection of 144 texts with an institutional background from a total of approximately 1,700 recovered texts from the Egibi business family archives records five promissory notes concerning debts with interest while 13 promissory notes mention no interest and three explicitly state the absence of interest.[5]

#	*Date*	*Debt silver*	*Interest*
14		? m	To be paid on month VI
32	5 VII	50 š	To be paid by 20 VII
63		?	To be paid in month XI
73		16 m 44 š	1 š / month
78	3 XIIa	23 m	To be paid without interest in month II in Babylon
83		3 5/6 m 7½ š	
95	1 V	½ m	To be paid in month II
96	? V	50 š	To be paid in month II
105	26 VII	½ m	To be paid a year later
108	16 I	½ m	To be paid in one instalment at Til-Gula
109	15 VIII	15 š	To be paid without interest in month I
112	2 I	1 m	1 š / month from month III on
119	22 VIII	2 m	To be paid in month XII
122		2 ⅔ m	1 š / month in case of default after month III
125	24 X 17 10½ m	5 š	1 š / month from month XII on
131	3 III	10 š	To be paid at the end of month III
133	12 IV	9 š	To be paid on 12 XII
141	10 XIIb	45 m	To be paid in month III without interest in Babylon

Interest is charged only on debts of silver, never on foodstuffs. The longest loan duration (tenor) is one year (no. 105), but loan duration is usually a few months or even within the same month (no. 32). Given the metrological equivalence of one *biltu*/talent (30 kgs) = 60 minas = 3600 shekel (c. 8.3 grams), the interest rate seems fixed at one shekel per mina (one mina = 0.5 kg = 60 shekels) per month (Jursa 2005: 41). A loan of one mina to be repaid after 12 months and bearing interest at the rate of one shekel per mina per month would be serviced as follows:

1. If interest is paid monthly: the borrower pays the lender the sum of 1/60th of the principal at the end of each month (i.e. one shekel) and the principal, one mina, at the end of the 12 months.
2. If interest is capitalized at the end of each month and only paid at the end of the loan period, together with the principal, then the total balloon (i.e. total single) payment would amount to one mina and 13.16 shekels calculated according to the following formula:

   BP = $p \times (1+mr)^n$ where:

   BP = Balloon Payment (i.e. principal and capitalized interest paid at the end of the loan period)

   p = Principal (i.e. loan = initial amount lent/borrowed)

   mr = Monthly interest rate (expressed a fraction or decimal: e.g. 1/60 or 0.01666666)

   n = Tenor (duration) of the loan (expressed in number of months, e.g. 12 for a 12-month loan)

In the case of the above-mentioned loan of one mina at a compound interest rate of one shekel per month, the monthly interest rate is $1/60^{th}$ = 1.66667% or (if compounded) 21.93894% per annum. The balloon payment due at the end of the year is the principal (one mina) plus accrued monthly compound interest, which amounts to 0.2193894 mina or 13.163 shekels. There are other factors that might come into play.

A flat fee, regardless of the tenor of the loan, for example 10%, payable either at the start of the loan (i.e. deducted from the principle disbursed by the lender to the borrower) or at the end of the loan (i.e. added to the amount the borrower has to repay the lender).

Monthly instalments for the repayment of the loan: for example, at the end of every month, the borrower repays the lender 1/12 of the principal borrowed. These are called equal instalment repayments of principal. The interest is then calculated only on the principal outstanding. But there is also the notion of a grace period (or moratorium) during which interest is capitalized. For example, a grace period of three months means that the borrower only starts repaying the principal to the lender at the end of the fourth month. Interest is calculated accordingly.

Finally, the borrower can service the debt through fixed monthly instalments that include both capital/principal and interest as is the normal case with mortgage repayments on modern house-purchasing loans.

There is no correlation between the size of loans and the presence or absence of interest. Only one contract (#73) includes immediate interest, the other three are default penalties charging interest only after a period of two months (#112, 125). Several documents specify the location where the goods are to be delivered, indicating that transport costs were as significant as interest. Tellingly, there is only one true loan with interest (#73) and no tenor is mentioned for it, an important indication that making money through the interest charged to borrowers was not always the prime objective of lenders. As became common practice in Egypt from the reign of Darius I (Menu 1998a), the debt was secured by a lien on the land tenure of the borrower or by the services of a dependent of the borrower. Ever since the early second millennium BCE, a major motivation for agricultural lending was to secure a source of labour from the borrower rather than making money through the charging of interest (Steinkeller 2002). When grain or silver is paid back under the same species, one needs to take into account the seasonal and economic fluctuations of the price of commodities in order to reach a realistic appreciation of the actual interest paid. This is no easy task for loans contracted over two-thousand years ago, but when the borrowed grain or silver is reimbursed in the form of work, it becomes impossible to estimate the interest rate. The commercial risk taken by the lender was not negligible either. Credit has to be placed in the context of a complex web of financial entanglements where most merchant borrowers were also lenders and thus benefited from high credit costs. As much in medieval England as in Ottoman Damascus, creditors came from all walks of life. Borrowing did not imply destitution, but access to credit proves that the lenders considered his debtors creditworthy or that he expected some other kind of return from the loan in case of default. As many loans were concluded on the grounds of mutual confidence, without any record, and as interest was often concealed, it is impossible to gain a realistic estimate of the rate of interest from the remaining documentation. It is so for loans issued by moneylenders at the end of the British Mandate and it is more so for any older period (Nadan 2005: 29-31). As ancient economies were devoid of institutional banking, credit was a complex chain that facilitated production by getting everyone involved to pay for inputs after receiving payment for outputs (Richardson 2003: 317). Hence, claiming that interest rates were high by modern standards contributes nothing to the understanding of the economy (Williams 2009: 127). For this reason, the notion of usury should be discussed.

5.3.2 Usury?

Although in its original sense usury referred to any lending at interest, in modern parlance, usury is restricted to exorbitant interest (Millett 1991: 180). The narrowing of the definition of usury occurred in the late Middle Ages when, despite biblical prohibitions, the wholesale condemnation of charging interest was challenged and moderate rates became morally acceptable. Given the modern focus on the level of the interest rate as determining the presence or absence of usury, the frequent mentions of usury in exegetical literature is surprising. One would need precise data to identify usurious practices, but the state of the existing documentation and the complexity of credit practices rarely allow the evaluation of actual rates.

Interest rates between 33% and 50% can only be considered usurious in isolation of economic realities. Among socially integrated peasant societies, such rates were acceptable (Renger 1994: 195; Vargyas 2000: 1102). Today, interest rates currently applied by micro-finance systems, for instance the Grameen Bank in India and Pakistan, are usurious by any standard. Yet, the founder of the Grameen Bank was awarded the 2006 Nobel Prize because micro-finance systems are seen by development agencies as an effective way of empowering small and micro-enterprises or sole-market traders (Sider 1997: 120). Despite their clearly usurious rates, these systems are very effective, as their development shows, and demonstrate the invalidity of placing limits on interest rates. High interest rates, in actual practice, are necessary to cover the high transaction costs of small-size loans. Transaction costs are the costs of specifying and enforcing contracts and other relations upon which exchange and other forms of economic organization are based. They include resources used for obtaining and disseminating information, measuring of goods and staples, and the conclusion as well as the enforcement of contracts and the specification and guaranteeing of property rights (Renger 1994: 159-60). Hence, the rough principle that interest rates are in inverse correlation to the size of the loan (Duncan-Jones 1982: 134). Biblical exegetes would gain much insight from considering the world around them. Instead of imagining the state of economic equilibrium in farming as an absence of loans or the ability to reimburse them, they might come to realize that 'permanent over-indebtedness' (Kessler 2006: 120) seen as characteristic of the situation of biblical farmers from the eighth century

BCE until Nehemiah has in fact always been the norm, even more so today, and that it constitutes the mark of a healthy economy rather than the sign of a structural crisis. Obviously, permanent over-indebtedness is a contradiction in terms. If over-indebtedness is permanent, it cannot be considered excessive by the simple fact that both parties are able to survive it. Permanent indebtedness is the regular dependence of farming on rural credit.

At the standard rate for silver of one shekel per mina per month (Wunsch 2002: 230), the actual cost of credit was lower than it appears when it is presented in percentages and in annual rates that amount to between 20% and 33%. The small amounts borrowed and the shortness of the terms rendered the actual amounts paid more bearable than it seems (Van de Mieroop 2002b: 85). Yet, because they are supposed to have borrowed in order to survive instead of borrowing to invest in profitable ventures, the poor are presented as sinking ever deeper into debt until their few assets, their land, their children and their own persons were seized by their rapacious creditors who charged usurious interest rates to multiply the debt and hasten the forfeiture (Lang 1982; Gottwald 1999: 2). As the story goes, 'Many peasants were left no alternative to survival loans at de facto interest rates usurious by any standards. Foreclosure upon family land and family members pledged as collateral' enabled the rich to extend their own land and build latifundia for themselves (Chaney 1999: 107).

Declaring interest rates usurious by any standards is a good way to dodge a discussion of usury since biblical mentions of usury are hard to find, except in the rather biased translations of a few key verses. Consider Prov. 28:8:

> מרבה הונו בנשך ובתרבית לחונן דלים יקבצנו
>
> One who augments wealth by exorbitant interest gathers it for another who is kind to the poor. (NRSV)
>
> He who grows wealthy through usury and rents accumulates to benefit a patron of the poor. (Scott 1965: 164)
>
> He who increases his riches with usury and interest gathers it for him who is gracious to the poor. (Rosenberg 2001: 175)
>
> One who increases his wealth by charging interest, advance or accrued, amasses it for one who is generous to the poor. (Houston 2008: 121)

The last translation is one of the few that avoids the negative characterization of interest. The claim that poverty is preferable to wrongly acquired riches in verse 6 certainly casts a negative light upon the interest mentioned in verse 8, which is taken as the proof that usury was regularly practised (Tavares 2007: 70-71). Hence, Prov. 28:8 is taken as a proof of the collapse of reciprocity (Domeris 2007: 109). Yet, the mention of the relief of the poor provided by the wealth accumulated by the 'usurer' somewhat softens the accusation because the conciseness of the proverbial genre leaves it to the reader to decide whether the usurer is the same person as the reliever of the poor or whether providence despoils the usurer to enrich the philanthropist. For this reason, the NRSV improves the text with the addition of 'another' which makes the verse a clearer warning to the usurer that his fortune will pass into the hands of the poor (Gilbert 2007: 319) or of a generous person (Murphy 1998: 215).

As it stands, the condemnation of the usurer in Prov. 28:8 is less blunt than the one found in Ezek. 18:9, 19. Taken as an alternative to the gluttons of Prov. 28:7b, the accusation becomes even less biting (Tavares 2007: 70-71). Besides its clever play on words between הונו and חונן, Prov. 28:8 actually justifies lending against interest by claiming that the profits will eventually be used to alleviate the suffering of the unfortunate. Hence the translation, 'He who amasses his wealth by interest and usury—is (actually) gathering it for him who is kind to the poor' (Fox 2009: 823). Unless one insists that the sages who penned these verses were not wise enough to realize that society is not sharply divided into rich and poor (Scott 1965: 166), and that if all were poor no one could be charitable to the poor, the moralistic platitudes in the surrounding verses act as a sugar-coat for the core of economic realism in verse 8. Either as a patron who willingly grants favours or, through forceful taxation, wealth somehow ends up being redistributed. Was it beyond the capacity of the wise teacher of Proverbs to understand that there is no way to be generous if one does not first produce wealth? Were they better equipped than their modern counterparts to transcend the no-sum mentality which can only explain the increase of the fortune of the rich as the result of siphoning off the means of the poor? The usurer is not necessarily a different person than the alms-giver who redistributes profits as charitable gifts. The proverbial rich are as much a stereotype as the evil rich.

That lending at interest may be justified does not imply that all usurers were rich. In ancient Athens, usurers were not rich. As their name indicates, the *obolostatēs* lent very small sums at a high interest rate for a day or so to costermongers who purchased fruit and other perishables in the morning and returned the loan at the end of the day when sales were over (Millett 1991: 181-84). Risk was minimal, interest rates were high, but because the amounts were small and the term very short, the condition of usurers remained as modest as that of their customers.

The notion that the rich made fortunes on the backs of the poor through usury is devoid of economic foundations. The pledged cloaks (בגדים חבלים) used by the lenders as picnic blankets (Amos 2:8) betray the modest amount of loan which a cloak sufficed to secure, or if the loan was much larger than the actual value of the cloak, one can hardly talk of security. It is the limited means of the borrower that are underlined. The same can be said about the pair of sandals mentioned in relation to the poor in Amos 2:6 (Paul 1991: 77-79) and the pledged garments to be returned in the evening (Exod. 22:25-26; Deut. 24:12-13). These sandals and cloaks depict a situation similar to that of the Athenian *obolostatēs.* Short term and small amounts secured by modest pledges were returned in the evening of the same day, as the borrowed amount was paid back. The same applies if the objects in question are distraint rather than pledges (Paul 1991: 83-85). Neither the lender nor the borrower became rich, but neither was destitute. The forfeiture of the pledges would not make the lender much richer. The distraint of the borrower or of one of his dependants was a costly affair unless some wealthy relative redeemed the debtor before the costs of keeping the seized person alive added to the debt. The distraint person was usually put to work for the creditor, thus rendering the distinction between distraint and debt 'slavery' vastly irrelevant. There is thus a clear distinction between retail operators on local markets, designated with the paraphrase 'him of such and such product', of modest condition who borrowed modest smalls, and long distance wholesale traders, the *tamkāru,* who dealt with large sums borrowed over longer terms (Radner 1999a).

The highest returns on investment came from long-distance trade. The so-called *ḫarrānu* (caravan) partnerships in Mesopotamia and the Greek maritime loans offered the greatest opportunities for profit, but they involved large sums and high risk (Wunsch 2002: 237-38). Maritime loans may be mentioned in Qoh. 11:2 (Scott 1965: 252; but Seow 1997: 335). Because profits expected from investment in agriculture were much lower than those from trade, the Mediterranean countryside was and remains cash-starved (Faroqhi 2005: 203). Commercial loans fetched high interest but they cannot be considered usurious either. They were partnerships as the borrower was liberated from all obligations to reimburse the loan if the cargo was lost to pirates or by shipwreck, while the lender often travelled on the ship to supervise the operations and to make sure that he was not cheated (Millett 1991: 188-97). In any case, no poor were involved in this type of usury reserved for the rich. Despite the low returns offered by agricultural credit, credit was essential to farmers and traders of agricultural surplus.

5.4 A Simulation of Farm Credit

In support of the vulnerability of ancient farmers, it is commonly stated that two bad years in a row were enough to push farmers down into a spiral of debt. Or more than one bad harvest in four is said to have forced Iraqi farmers of the twentieth century CE into debt (Lang 1983: 55). The Mediterranean climate prevailing in the Palestine highlands would have made the financial status of biblical farmers even more precarious. Yet, there is a possibility that these figures reflect an ideal of autarkia more than any economic reality where credit and debt function as essential lubricants in the process of production and trade. Therefore, this section seeks to estimate the financial situation of a farmer over a sequence of years with arbitrarily set yields and determine how many bad harvests in a row could an average farmer weather (see Table 1, below).

5.4.1 Setting Carry-over and Yields

The farmer's main insurance against a harvest failure is his carry-over, the amount of grain that survived a year of eating and replanting. We postulate that the average ancient farmer was wise enough to do what was in his power to make sure that his family did not starve to death. Hence, he made sure to plough the surface, to scatter the amount of seed and spend the effort necessary to grow, weed and harvest enough to feed all his dependants, pay all his taxes, reimburse his debtors and have enough seed for the following year plus some extra for unexpected events. This postulate avoids the impossible task of evaluating ancient yields. Instead, one can use as reference the carry-over in late seventeenth-century England that is estimated at not more than four months (Thirsk and Cooper 1972: 814). Since this level was reached after a century or so of agricultural progress, we halve the English carry-over and consider it a reasonable working hypothesis for ancient Palestinian farmers. In reality, it may well have been higher, but for argument's sake it is cautious to retain a lower figure. The question, then, is: how long could a typical Palestinian farmer with a two-month carry-over cope with disaster?

The various options are worked out with an average lag between sowing and harvesting of barley and wheat of six months, ignoring the other cereals and pulses that farmers grew. In actual practice, the six months could be reduced by one month since in times of famine new grain could start being consumed before reaching complete maturity as parched grain (קלוי, Josh. 5:11). Carefully done, this practice reduces the final yield by less than the amount eaten early since the thinning process enhances the maturation of the rest of the crop.

Drought itself favours the survival of the small farmer since it has a positive effect on the storage of grain by dramatically reducing loss of germination power, estimated at 10 to 20 per cent per annum in more moderate climates. Ancient farmers needed but very basic storage facilities to store the modest amounts of surpluses produced in good years over a decade at little loss and cost. Hence, zero-cost self-storage can be integrated into the farmer's coping strategy. Military risks that depleted stocks and disease that depleted man- and beast-power were very real and we can safely postulate that the average farmer was well aware of them and took them into consideration by producing a little extra to cover expected or unforeseen losses and by hiding grain from foraging troops. Hence, we need not take them into account here. Bumper harvests (with yields up to 1:100) also occur once or twice per decade, but they need not be integrated into the model since their economic effect is negligible for the farmer. The commercial value of surplus decreases proportionally with the quantities available. Only the grain merchant has the means to capitalize surpluses in a series of operations that involve their own specific risks and costs. A long-distance grain market became very profitable only in the Roman period when great needs in Rome were supplied through maritime transport (Crone 2003: 14; Hopkins 2002: 222). Moving it from Alexandria to Rome became cheaper than carrying it from Beer-sheba to Jerusalem. Before the Hellenistic era when Palestinian grain surpluses were exported through Mediterranean ports (Jaffa, Dor and Strato's Tower) in significant amounts, local surpluses were only economically viable when consumed on the spot, mainly by armies along the routes to Egypt.

Taking as an average yield 14 months (one year plus two months of carry-over) of consumption for all the mouths he had to feed and the amount of seed required for the next season in order to meet the expected burden, levels of disaster oscillate between one-third and two-thirds of a normal yield, making one-half plausible (McCloskey 1976: 141). Gottlieb Schumacher (1889: 23) states that in Hauran, a 60- to 80-

fold yield for barley and wheat was not exaggerated. The Hauran yields were higher than those of Palestine, except for Gaza. The agricultural productivity of Gaza, Lajjun, Nablus and Aʿjlun during the fifteenth and sixteenth centuries CE was among the highest in the Ottoman Empire and stood above the productivity observed in Northern European countries at the same period. By contrast, the yields of the Jerusalem region were much lower (Coşgel 2006).

Based on these figures, we set a 'passable' yield at a seed to harvest ratio between 1:13 and 1:15. This yield is one that provides for the farmer's household consumption and all other charges such as taxes and rent and leaves him enough grain for the next sowing plus up to two months' carry-over, that is, grain surplus to the year's needs.

5.4.2 Illustrating Borrowing Needs

Table 1 below is intended to serve as a hypothetical illustration of the borrowing needs of a farmer over a seven-year period, according to varying yield levels obtained from the grain he sows from year to year.

Yield levels (shown at line E) have been selected at random and simply serve to demonstrate the way in which poor yields can lead to shortfalls in the supply of grain needed to feed a household or to allow for adequate sowing in the coming year (line H). A farmer would compensate for such shortfalls by borrowing grain, say from a merchant (line B), who would charge interest at an agreed rate (line G). The farmer would pay the lender both the principal borrowed and the accrued interest immediately after the following harvest, assuming he had reaped sufficient grain to allow him to do so (lines F and G).

In the event of a second poor harvest that does not allow him to honour his commitments, the farmer may need to borrow a further quantity of grain from the merchant, thus in effect capitalizing the accrued interest and increasing the amount of principal borrowed (an example of this appears at line B in year 6). In the example given, year 7 happens to produce a bumper crop (a yield of 50, which means that each ear of grain planted produces on average 50 grains, net), which allows the farmer to service his debt to the lender through a balloon payment (i.e. a single 'balloon' payment for both the accrued interest for that year plus the outstanding principal borrowed in years 5 and 6 as well as the capitalized interest). To simplify calculations, the units of value shown in the table are expressed in months of consumption (see definition under note 2, above).

Table 1. Projected Borrowing Needs Depending On Crop Yield Levels

		Year 1	*Year 2*	*Year 3*	*Year 4*	*Year 5*	*Year 6*	*Year 7*
All values represent months of consumption	*Notes*	*Jun-May*	*Jun-May*	*Jun-May*	*Jun-May*	*Jun-May*	*Jun-May*	*Jun-May*
A. Opening grain stock/shortfall	1	13.00	13.00	1.00	15.37	3.37	-10.75	21.04
B. Grain borrowed at start of June	2	0.00	0.00	12.00	0.00	9.63	23.75	0.00
C. Grain sowed at start of December	3	-1.00	-1.00	-1.00	-1.00	-1.00	-1.00	-1.00
D. Household grain consumption	4	-12.00	-12.00	-12.00	-12.00	-12.00	-12.00	-12.00
E. Grain reaped at end of May (i.e. yield level)	5	13.00	1.00	30.00	1.00	1.00	50.00	5.00
F. Borrowed grain due at end of May	6	0.00	0.00	-12.00	0.00	-9.63	-23.75	0.00
G. Grain due as interest at end of May	7	0.00	0.00	-2.63	0.00	-2.11	-5.21	0.00
H. Grain surplus/ shortfall (sum A:F)	8	13.00	1.00	15.37	3.37	-10.75	21.04	13.04

Notes

1. A minimum stock of grain of 12-month's consumption is assumed for the opening year of these projections.
2. Borrowing needs are calculated on the basis of total annual requirements of 12-months' consumption. A unit of *consumption* is defined as the total monthly needs of a given household, including grain paid out as dues for rent and tax but excluding grain kept for sowing in December (this is shown as item C). It is assumed that a farming household will always prefer to borrow at the start of June the whole of its total forecast needs for the coming 12 months (see rationale below).
3. One month's consumption of grain is sown each year at the beginning of December. This quantity is an arbitrary assumption, based on the expectation of an average net yield after harvesting that will provide adequate grain for one-year's household consumption (including rent and taxes due) while leaving a carry-over or surplus. Surpluses may serve to service (i.e. refund principal and pay interest on) any outstanding debt, as the case may be, or constitute a reserve for future years, or sold/bartered for essential goods.
4. The unit of measure used is the monthly consumption of grain of the farmer's household plus dependents.
5. Assumptions: Year 1: passable; year 2: very poor; year 3: very good; years 4 and 5: very poor; year 6: very good; year 7: poor.
6. It is assumed that all grain borrowed falls due immediately following harvesting at the end of May.
7. It is assumed that the annual interest rate is 22.94% (i.e. one-sixtieth per month, compounded) and interest falls due at the same time as repayment of borrowings.
8. Grain surplus or shortfall is the sum of items A to F and represents the farmer's position as at the end of May, just after harvesting.

For the purposes of the illustration, it is assumed that the first year and its preceding year were 'passable' years, that is, the yields for each were just sufficient to cover the farmer's needs for his household and dependants (those for whom he is responsible). Included in the calculations is any tax or rent he might have to pay in the form of a fixed contribution of his annual grain harvest. This is done by working in units each representing a quantity of grain equal to one month's total consumption (but excluding grain used as seed). For example, for a farmer whose total monthly grain-consumption requirements (including fixed tax/rent) amount to one tonne, the unit of measure used in the table would have a value of one tonne of grain.

When the yield levels are 'very poor' to 'poor' (1:1 to 1:12), the farmer might choose to tide over shortages by first consuming any surplus stocks of grain he had, carried over from preceding years, and only resort to borrowing from merchants or professional lenders when his stocks ran out before the following harvest in May. But to do so might turn out to be unwise if grain prices were to rise steeply as a result of shortages. Or, worse still, severe shortages might lead to a total dearth of supplies and he might consequently face starvation.

So it is fair to assume that in times of very bad yields, the farmer, to avoid being stigmatized as a foolish virgin, would, immediately following a poor harvest, try to borrow the full complement of grain he needs for sowing, consumption and fixed taxes/rent less whatever stocks he might have at hand.

Borrowing, it can thus be seen, will most likely be for periods of a full annual cycle, from early June to the following May harvest. Interest will thus accrue over 12 months and become due at the same time as the date of refund of the principal borrowed (i.e. immediately after harvesting).

The crunch comes when the farmer experiences a series of two or more years of very low grain yields. Without adequate stocks to tide him over, he will not be able to pay back his creditor at the due date. To overcome the problem, he will need to borrow more and 'capitalize' accrued interest at 'due' date. This may work—but only up to a point. At some stage, his indebtedness might reach a level where his further borrowing requirements could never be compensated, even by a long series of very high harvest yields. This is where he becomes insolvent and loses all creditworthiness. He has no option but to declare himself bankrupt and forfeit whatever assets he possesses to his creditor.

Table 2 below illustrates an example of such a situation assuming a seven-year spell of 0-level yields from year 8 to year 14. In the first few years, borrowing needs are low but these grow exponentially to the point where the borrower can no longer hope to reimburse his creditor, even were his yields to reach 1:50 levels indefinitely from year 15 onwards. This can be observed by the increasing debt level of year 16 over year 15. This might be an extreme case, however, and the chances of nil-level yields over seven years are very unlikely.

Table 2. Projected Borrowing Needs Assuming Seven Years of Nil Crop Yield Levels

All values represent months of consumption	*Year 8*	*Year 9*	*Year 10*	*Year 11*	*Year 12*	*Year 13*	*Year 14*	*Year 15*	*Year 16*
	Jun-May	*Jun-May*	*Jun-May*	*Jun-May*	*Jun-May*	*Jun-May*	*Jun-May*	*Jun-May*	*Jun-May*
A. Opening grain stock/ shortfall	13.04	0.04	-15.80	-35.12	-58.67	-87.40	-122.42	-165.13	-167.21
B. Grain borrowed at start of June	0.00	12.96	28.80	48.12	71.67	100.40	135.42	178.13	180.21
C. Grain sowed at start of December	-1.00	-1.00	-1.00	-1.00	-1.00	-1.00	-1.00	-1.00	-1.00
D. Household grain consumption	-12.00	-12.00	-12.00	-12.00	-12.00	-12.00	-12.00	-12.00	-12.00
E. Grain reaped at end of May (yield)	0.00	0.00	0.00	0.00	0.00	0.00	0.00	50.00	50.00
F. Borrowed grain due at end of May	0.00	-12.96	-28.80	-48.12	-71.67	-100.40	-135.42	-178.13	-180.21
G. Grain due as interest at end of May	0.00	-2.84	-6.32	-10.56	-15.72	-22.03	-29.71	-39.08	-39.54
H. Grain surplus/ shortfall (sum A:F)	0.04	-15.80	-35.12	-58.67	-87.40	-122.42	-165.13	-167.21	-169.75

Table 3. Projected Borrowing Needs Assuming Four Years of Very Poor Crop Yield Levels

All values represent months of consumption	*Year 8*	*Year 9*	*Year 10*	*Year 11*	*Year 12*	*Year 13*	*Year 14*	*Year 15*	*Year 16*
	Jun-May	*Jun-May*	*Jun-May*	*Jun-May*	*Jun-May*	*Jun-May*	*Jun-May*	*Jun-May*	*Jun-May*
A. Opening grain stock/ shortfall	13.04	1.04	-13.58	-31.41	-53.15	-52.67	-52.07	-51.35	-50.47
B. Grain borrowed at start of June	0.00	11.96	26.58	44.41	66.15	65.67	65.07	64.35	63.47
C. Grain sowed at start of December	-1.00	-1.00	-1.00	-1.00	-1.00	-1.00	-1.00	-1.00	-1.00
D. Household grain consumption	-12.00	-12.00	-12.00	-12.00	-12.00	-12.00	-12.00	-12.00	-12.00
E. Grain reaped at end of May	1.00	1.00	1.00	1.00	28.00	28.00	28.00	28.00	28.00
F. Borrowed grain due at end of May	0.00	-11.96	-26.58	-44.41	-66.15	-65.67	-65.07	-64.35	-63.47
G. Grain due as interest at end of May	0.00	-2.62	-5.83	-9.74	-14.51	-14.41	-14.28	-14.12	-13.92
H. Grain surplus/ shortfall (sum A:F)	1.04	-13.58	-31.41	-53.15	-52.67	-52.07	-51.35	-50.47	-49.39

Note: How debt starts to reduce as from year 13 (it would in fact be extinguished by year 29).

Table 3 above presents a more realistic scenario and shows how a farmer could survive a four-year spell of drought, say, that resulted in a yield of only 1:1 (one grain reaped for each grain sowed).

Table 4 below compares yield with debt over the 16-year period examined and shows how, in the first seven years, a farmer can cope with extreme swings in crop yields even though he has to resort to borrowing. But in the four calamitous years from year 8 to year 12, borrowings soar to unprecedented levels that can only be reduced through a long series

Table 4. Borrowing Limits at Given Yield Levels and Interest Rates

Yield	*Interest rate of 21.94% per annum*				*Interest rate of 60% per annum*				*Interest rate of 80% per annum*			
(months of con-sumption)	*Yrs to insolv'cy (a)*	*Subseq. yield (b)*	*Or min. yield of (c)*	*Over next no. of yrs (d)*	*Yrs to insolv'cy (a)*	*Subseq. yield (b)*	*Or min. yield of (c)*	*Over next no. of yrs (d)*	*Yrs to insolv'cy (a)*	*Subseq. yield (b)*	*Or min. yield of (c)*	*Over next no. of yrs (d)*
0	4	1:100	1:29	+/-17	3	1:121	1:55	7	2	1:79	1:43	6
1	4	1:94	1:28	+/-17	3	1:113	1:52	7	2	1:74	1:41	6
2	4	1:87	1:27	+/-17	3	1:105	1:49	7	2	1:69	1:39	6
3	4	1:81	1:26	+/-17	3	1:96	1:46	6	2	1:64	1:36	7
4	4	1:74	1:25	+/-17	3	1:88	1:42	7	3	1:111	1:58	6
5	4	1:67	1:23	+/-17	4	1:132	1:60	7	3	1:100	1:53	6
6	4	1:61	1:22	+/-17	4	1:117	1:54	7	3	1:89	1:48	6
7	4	1:54	1:21	+/-17	4	1:102	1:48	7	3	1:79	1:43	6
8	4	1:47	1:20	+/-17	4	1:87	1:42	7	3	1:68	1:38	6
9	5	1:51	1:20	+/-17	5	1:115	1:53	7	4	1:99	1:52	7
10	6	1:52	1:20	+/-17	5	1:89	1:43	7	4	1:78	1:42	7
11	8	1:57	1:21	+/-17	6	1:100	1:46	7	5	1:94	1:50	6
12	11	1:57	1:21	+/-17	8	1:125	1:57	7	6	1:88	1:47	7

Notes

(a) Number of years a farmer can withstand insolvency at given yield rate.
(b) Yield level required to absorb cumulative deficit, refund borrowings and pay accrued interest.
(c) Minimum yield levels required over number of years indicated in column (d) to refund borrowings and accrued interest.

of good years. With these observations in mind, Table 4 sets out the theoretical points at which a farmer could withstand very poor to poor crop yields before becoming insolvent. Here, we consider three separate rates of interest, ranging from 21.94% to 80%.

To take a few examples, a farmer could withstand a series of four consecutive crop yields equal to five months of grain consumption and still be solvent, when borrowing at 21.94% p.a., if his minimum subsequent yields over 17 years or so averaged out at 1:23. But with borrowings at 60% interest p.a., the minimal crop yields would have to reach 1:60. And at 80% interest p.a., he could only withstand three years. If, on the other hand, following his four bad years he were to borrow at 21.94% p.a. (i.e. one-sixtieth per month compounded over 12 months), he would be able to clear his debts completely with one bumper crop yielding 1:67.

Obviously, all the examples given and assumptions used are simplifications of possible events in actual practice. Variations or consistencies in crop yields would not follow such regular patterns as those given and market conditions may not actually have known quite such simple patterns (availability of grain, prices, rates of interest etc.). Care should be taken not to read more into these tables than they mean to demonstrate.

In the case of a farmer becoming insolvent, the creditor (lender) may choose to continue to assist his client, if he himself has the means to survive the hardships of the times, either through clemency (by not insisting on repayment of the principal or waving interest) or even charity (he provides food for the farmer and his household). He may, alternatively or in addition, take possession of the use of the land and require the farmer who is in his debt to work it in exchange for his upkeep until his arrears are settled—or until the following cancellation of debts (§7.4.7).

But a long series of lean years hits both debtor and creditor alike and might drive both to ruin and possibly starvation. Their interests merge very quickly at the first sign of a general famine. Mobility would be their first thought, initially to access immediate supplies from sources beyond their stricken territories; then, subsequently, resettlement in areas affording surer prospects of survival and eventual development.

In the examples illustrated in Table 4 above, for instance, using the same basic parameters (including an interest rate of 60%), it would take four consecutive years of extremely bad yields (i.e. 1:1) to reach the point where, theoretically, the farmer would never be able to service his debt (repay the lender both outstanding principal and accrued interest) even if yields were suddenly to swing to 1:100 levels. The debt will have spiralled beyond all possible return to solvency.

5.4.3 Note on Yield Levels, Assuming Interest Rates of 21.94% Per Annum

A 'passable' yield (1:13) is one that provides for the farmer's household consumption and leaves him enough grain for the next sowing.

A 'poor' yield (between 1:9 and 1:12) is one that is insufficient for his total annual needs (consumption plus next sowing) but for which recourse to borrowing will be limited to between one and four months' consumption, which would require a maximum yield of just under 1:51 in the following season to repay the creditor in full (principal and interest at 21.94% p.a.), assuming he has no outstanding debt from previous years. In theory, starting without debt and with a constant annual yield of 1:9, a farmer could sustain incremental indebtedness for five years before attaining insolvency.

A 'very poor' yield (1:0 to 1:8) would require borrowings (or additional borrowings) of between five and 13 months' consumption with the necessity of obtaining a yield of between 1:20 and 1:29 over 17 years to service the debt, assuming no outstanding debts from the previous year. In theory, starting without debt and with a constant annual yield of 1:1, a farmer could sustain incremental indebtedness during four years before attaining insolvency.

A 'good' yield (1:14 to 1:26) provides the farmer with between one and 13 months of carry-over (surplus) and would enable an indebted farmer to reimburse all or part of his debts and interest due (unless already in an irreversible debt spiral).

A 'very good' year (1:27 and above) provides a surplus of 17 or more months of consumption (i.e. an extra year or more) and increases a debtor's ability to repay past borrowings and accrued interest (unless already in an irreversible debt spiral).

When the problem is considered from the point of view of the grain merchant, low yields translate into lower surpluses collected, smaller quantities stored but the likelihood of their being sold abroad at a higher price or advanced locally against higher returns in forthcoming harvests. In years of lean cows, the expenses of the merchant are reduced since he has less produce to store and transport. Very low yield meant no collection and the need to import produce to keep the debtors alive. Hence, lenders did not grow fat from the hardships of farmers. However great or small his profits, the lender had to invest most of them into further credit to his producers to maintain his privileged access to future surplus. The result is that, through credit, trade and agriculture were integrated into a web of interdependence that belies notions of the parasitic lender. The lender-trader needed the farmer as much as the farmer needed the merchant. Neither party could afford to destroy the other.

5.4.4 Expected Credit Needs

The results of the simulation can now be integrated into scenarios built around different combinations of the consumption-smoothing measures mentioned in the Bible. We start with loans bearing interest and secured by a pledge on land.

(A) No sabbatical year (see §9.12) and no šemiṭṭah *(see §7.4.7).* Assuming a relatively low interest rate of 1/60 per 30-day month (i.e. 21.94% a year), to be paid at the end of 12 months together with the principal borrowed, on the strength of the projections tested using the model set up above, a farmer appears to withstand four years of very low crop yields (between 1:0 and 1:8) by borrowing the grain he needs from a merchant-lender. But to escape the debt spiral in the subsequent years, he would have to produce subsequent crop yields ranging from good to very good levels for one up to possibly 17 years. With higher interest rates, obviously the farmer's position becomes weaker and he can withstand fewer years of poor yields. In the event of foreclosure, the farmer cedes his rights to the land to his creditor and probably works for him until released by the creditor, if ever.

(B) Sabbatical year but no šemiṭṭah. As above, but the farmer's position worsens because he will have to rely on higher yields to bridge the missing harvest year.

(C) Sabbatical year and šemiṭṭah. As above, but the farmer's position is greatly secured: his chances of four very poor harvests out of six are slender, so the risk of his forfeiting land and independence is likewise small. But he will nevertheless remain reliant on good to very good crop yields in the year prior to the year the land must rest fallow. There is, however, the risk to the farmer that the lender, knowing that he will have to release his client from his debt in the year of *šemiṭṭah,* will not agree to provide further grain if the farmer is already in debt. However,

over the longer term, this might prove bad policy for the lender if the farmer were to starve (there would be no one then to cultivate the land) or switch his patronage to another merchant-lender. There are other possible combinations, but it is obvious that the *šemiṭṭah* provides the farmer with the most security by limiting substantially his risk of falling into a debt spiral leading to insolvency through a series of four or more very poor harvests.

The next configuration to consider is one with loans without interest but secured by a pledge on land:

(D) No sabbatical year, no šemiṭṭah. The farmer's position is much more secure than in case (a) above, but unless the lender is prepared to roll over the credit, that is, continue to provide the farmer further grain, the farmer runs the risk of the lender calling in his pledge and making him work the land on his behalf until the debt is paid off. The lender's interest is to continue to provide his client (at least the most reliable and productive farmers) with their needs because their interests are thus best provided for. A logical extension of the relationship between lender and farmer in the event of a ban on interest is for the two parties to form a partnership arrangement in which, in good harvest years, the profits from the merchant-lender's sale on the market of the farmer's excess grain is shared with the farmer. There are a variety of more structured arrangements that would also help to reduce further the risk to both the farmer and the merchant by smoothing out the good and bad harvest years, the one compensating for the other.

(E) Sabbatical year but no šemiṭṭah. As above (d), but as in (b), the farmer becomes reliant on higher crop yields to see him through the year the land lies fallow.

(F) Sabbatical year and šemiṭṭah. As in (e), but the farmer's position is greatly secured: his chances of six very poor harvests out of six are very slender, so the risk of his forfeiting land and independence is likewise small. But he will nevertheless remain reliant on good to very good crop yields in the year prior to the year the land must rest fallow. There is the risk to the farmer that the lender, knowing that he will have to release his client from his debt in the year of *šemiṭṭah*, will not agree to provide further grain if the farmer is already in debt. Over the longer term, however, this might prove bad policy for the lender if the farmer were to starve (there would be no one then to cultivate the land) or switch his

patronage to another merchant-lender. One might question whether the ban on interest compounded with the *šemiṭṭah* might not prove to be in some ways counter-productive. Debt release would have been instituted as a means of saving farmers from being caught up in a debt spiral that would lead to the loss of their land (i.e. the use of their land for their own subsistence and the accumulation of wealth) and their indenture to their creditors, some of whom might have abused their position of strength. But a ban on interest as well as the *šemiṭṭah* weakens the merchants' ability to fulfil their socio-economic role as intermediaries, both as traders and as lenders. Farmers would have been reliant on merchants to purchase their surplus grain just as they would also have relied on them for advances and facilities in times of need. On the other hand, the ban on interest compounded with the obligation to cancel debt obligations every seventh year might quite simply have wiped out the practice of lending altogether, substituting in its stead a new relationship between farmer and merchant, which would have taken the form of a partnership in which the farmer produced grain and the merchant provided working capital or operating needs (in the form of grain and any other supplies required) as well as his trading services to dispose profitably of surplus production. The parties would have shared the losses and profits or come to some other arrangement that secured the interests of each. It is in the framework of this new relationship that the notion of patronage (§6) takes all its meaning.

The size of loans, the amount of interest charged and whether loans were secured with a pledge or not reflected the creditworthiness of both parties. The situation described above, where unsecured loans at no interest are granted in exchange for all the surplus of the borrower, was the most advantageous position for *both* parties. In fact the loans are not loans anymore. The merchant shared the risk of production with the farmer by pledging to supply relief in the form of food and seed. The farmer participated in the commercial risk taken by the merchant by pledging to deliver his entire surplus to the merchant.

In the case of less creditworthy borrowers, the merchant hedged the risk he took by extending loans secured with pledges in work rather than land and at interest rates that could be modulated according to the risk or work involved. This is crucial to explain how farmers survived thanks to a continued source of credit provided by merchants who survived the *šemiṭṭah* without foreclosing land.

5.5 Loans to the Poor?

The very existence of loans implies that a lender has considered a borrower creditworthy. Determining the creditworthiness of a farmer involved a fair degree of confidence in his competence as well as expert knowledge of local conditions. This knowledge determined the success of a lender whose survival depended on weeding out rotten assets. Intimate knowledge of the 'reputation' (i.e. reliability and creditworthiness) of his debtors was crucial in preventing other lenders from becoming rivals. The necessity for any successful lender to identify the financial capacity of each farmer excluded and continues to exclude the poor from access to credit. In light of this basic principle, what should be made of common claims among biblical exegetes that the biblical prohibitions on loans with interests were designed to alleviate poverty?

> The purpose of the biblical prohibition against interest was to protect the poor. The Bible's logic may be understood as follows: (1) a person borrows because of economic hardship; (2) a loan is a righteous act performed to help relieve poverty; (3) to charge interest on a loan would be to take advantage of such poverty; (4) the law is written to ban this unfair practice. In Exodus and Leviticus the law specifically states that its concern is for the poor. In Deuteronomy, the economic status of the borrower is not mentioned. (Gamoran 1971: 130-31)

These lines were written to insist that the prohibition against interest was written with the poor in mind, against another study that suggested that the poor were not concerned by prohibitions of interest (Neufeld 1955: 398-99). Gamoran (1971: 130) argued that interest-bearing commercial loans were not explicitly banned because they were not considered to affect the poor. Yet, the notion that the poor have access to credit is as curious as the idea that the 'rich' can enrich themselves by exploiting the 'poor'. Someone may oblige a destitute person by providing food or seeds with hopes of return in the form of social esteem or such kinds of abstract rewards. In this case, however, one should talk about charity rather than credit. Loans relieve temporary shortages but they cannot relieve poverty. Taking advantage of poverty by lending is as fallacious as the notion of the rich who lend to the poor to get richer while leading a life of luxury *and* idleness (§4.5.7). The notions of 'soil without toil' and 'leisure plus luxury' reflect prophetic slur but not economic reality. A classical presentation of the fallacy runs as follows:

> As an indebted peasant or small tenant the poor man is the landlord's bondsman and sometimes a kind of serf or even slave—especially

> when he has to render regular or occasional services in addition to the payment of rent. 'The rich lord it over the poor; the borrower becomes the lender's slave (or, serf)'; says Proverbs 22:7. While the serf is working, the creditor or landlord draws an income without actually working for it, enjoying the pleasant life of the leisured class. (Lang 1982: 50)

In fact, Prov. 22:7 says nothing about the rich man's life. The stereotyped poor (רשים) over which the rich man (עשיר) rules are not necessarily destitute.

> עשיר ברשים ימשול ועבד לוה לאיש מלוה
>
> The rich rules over the poor and the borrower is the slave of the lender. (NRSV)
>
> The rich rules over the poor, and the servant of the borrower is for each lender. (literal)
>
> The rich will rule the poor, and servants will lend to their own masters. (LXX)
>
> As for the rich man, the poor man will rule over him and the slave will lend to him who lent to him. (Syriac as rendered in Fox 2009: 1029)

The NRSV clearly seeks to reinforce the modern notion that borrowing is slavery. Yet, ancient versions suggest the opposite. Instead of reading the second part of the verse as the corollary of the first part, the versions rendered it in antithetic parallelism with the servants lending to their own masters. The early translators may have thought in terms of the eschatological world turned upside down (Fox 2009: 1029), but the possibility remains that sudden reversals of fortunes were possible in both worlds and that financial difficulties did not always mean irreversible destitution. In fact, the Hebrew is a good illustration of antichresis. The borrower's servant works for the lender, which shows that the borrower is not destitute. In any case, the rich man's enjoyment of 'the pleasant life of the leisured class' is a modern addition to the text.

Idleness, even among the rich, led more quickly to misery than to wealth. Work was necessary for the rich as much as the poor. The focus now is the notion that interest-free loans were granted as expressions of concern for the poor. As Gamoran admits, the ban on interest in Deut. 23:20 does not mention the economic status of the borrower. The prohibition of interest-bearing loans is predicated on the simple fact that he is a brother, not that he is poor. Against Gamoran, however, the same can be said about Leviticus 25. Although he (wrongly) considers poverty and landlessness as the motives of the jubilee (§7.4), Houston (2008: 198) notes that 'None of the Hebrew nouns or adjectives meaning "poor" appears in the chapter.' Translating the *mwq* clauses as 'to become poor' (Lev. 25:35, 39, 47) is an interpretation. The primary idea is 'to sink, reduce, bow down' (HALOT 2:555). Temporary shortness of cash does not imply poverty, unless one considers every borrower as destitute. The matter here is default, not poverty.

This leaves Exod. 22:24 as the only connection between the poor and credit:

> אם כסף תלוה את עמי את העני עמך לא תהיה לו כנשה לא תשׂימון עליו נשך
>
> If you lend silver to my people, to the poor with you, do not be to him as a moneylender. Do not charge interest against him.

Focusing on the second clause, 'do not charge interest against him,' to explain the previous one, 'do not be as a moneylender,' exegetes read Exod. 22:24 as one of the three instances of the ban on interest. When, however, the change of pronoun from the singular תלוה and תהיה to the plural תשׂימון is seen as a secondary reinforcement (Levin 2003: 331), Exod. 22:24 becomes a straightforward statement of economic wisdom. Do not lend at all to the poor, with or without interest, since they will never be in a position to reimburse anything. The verse clearly excludes the poor (העני) from the ordinary members of 'my people' (עמי) to whom lending is common.

If the poor are excluded from credit and if interest-free loans to brothers express kinship relations rather than concern for the poor, new light is thrown upon other texts. For instance, the specific commendations for the judge in Ezekiel 18—return of the debtor's pledge and interest-free loans—are not related to the poor, contrary to Exod. 22:24 (Eng. 25) and Deut. 24:12, which delineate specific measures in dealing with the poor. It is only in verse 7b that Ezekiel 18 refers to the destitute:

> ואיש לא יונה חבלתו חוב ישיב גזלה לא יגזל לחמו לרעב יתן ועירם יכסה בגד (Ezek. 18:7)
>
> He does not oppress anyone, he returns to a debtor his pledge, he does not steal. His bread to a famished one he gives and the naked he covers (with) a garment.

The destitute is presented as the famished to whom the righteous man *gives* bread and the naked that he clothes (see Isa. 58:7). The pledge mentioned in the first half of the verse applies neither to the famished nor to the naked because lending to a poor man makes no sense whatsoever. That verses 7 and 8 cover the entire spectrum of society, not just the poor, is clear from actions that concern the rich as much as the poor. Abstention from oppression, from robbery and from inequity is mentioned along with the return of pledges and the charitable acts towards the destitute. The poor are *given* food and clothing while loans are granted to creditworthy people to whom the destitute do not belong. Fighting for social justice, exegetes consider every borrower as de facto a poor and destitute person, when in fact, economic realism, demonstrated by the very texts they use, shows that the poor belong to a separate category.

Much of the problem stems from the vagueness of economic descriptions and the vested interest ancient and modern writers have in keeping them vague. For instance, Aristotle's description of the Athenian situation before Solon's reforms shows that we are dealing more with a literary motif than with a precise analysis of the economic situation. Describing the oligarchy, Aristotle *AthConst* II.2 states,

> καὶ δὴ καὶ ἐδούλευον οἱ πέντες τοῖς πλουσίοις καὶ αὐτοὶ καὶ τὰ τέκνα καὶ γυναῖκες.
>
> the poor themselves and also their wives and children were actually in slavery to the rich.

Both the 'poor' and their 'slavery' would need qualification before meaningful conclusions could be drawn. Were the poor enslaved by the rich? Literally, the poor were servicing loans by providing work days with their entire families, exactly as Prov. 22:7 states (see above). Of course, they resented it, but that does not prove that the rich did nothing but get fat on the poor's back. Despite the vagueness of the literary descriptions of the rich and the poor, Ezekiel 18 clearly shows that the righteous man and his grandson are involved in two different activities directed to two separate categories of people. They grant loans to their clients and give bread to the poor. Their good deeds towards the poor may be motivated by pity or by consideration for other members of the family among which clients were present, but charity and loans remain separate activities.

The relatively stable rates of interest throughout the centuries reveal the absence of a credit market (Renger 1994: 203). Neither the Islamic and Ottoman strictures on interest rates nor the set up of a formal credit sector by the British Mandate had much influence on interest rates. The Ottoman laws limited interest at 9% (Nadan 2005: 6). In fact, it remained stable at c. 30% before and after the First World War despite the major economic upturn brought by the war after the Arab revolt (Nadan 2007: 59). Economic considerations overrode all others. Yet, there was no linkage between interest rates and inflation because merchants had a wider perspective than scholars who imagine them as merely exploitative and seeking maximum extraction of surplus. The broader perspective entails viewing 'money lending as an interlinked transaction, where a contract in the goods market was simultaneously a contract in the credit market' (Nadan 2007: 58).

5.6 Foreclosure?

The above claim that credit practices were not the primary cause of misery in the ancient world is contradicted by reports from European observers of transfers of land ownership resulting from debt. Gottlieb Schumacher, who spent most of his life in Palestine, reported that thanks to improved security conditions following the transfer of the seat of the Governor of the Hauran from Bosra to Sheikh Sa'ad, farmers risked further settlement and the Bedouin settled and built stone houses in which they stored their grain. Schumacher added, however, that unscrupulous speculation in the grain crops on the part of the Syrian merchants ruined all agricultural improvements in Syria and that the existing laws against usury should be quickly enforced to prohibit feudal tenure and prevent the property of the fellahin from passing into the hands of 'these unprincipled speculators' (Schumacher 1889: 22-3). In a similar tone, Claude Conder, who mapped out Palestine for the British army, painted another grim picture of the Hauran whose main object is the denunciation of French and Russian intrigues and of Islamic fanaticism. Conder mentioned having 'more than once been offered a village and its land for sale, the peasants being no longer able to pay the taxes or meet the demands of usurers, Jewish, Greek, or Armenian, into whose clutches they were falling, after paying 60 to 70 per cent for many years for money borrowed to pay the Government' (Conder 1883: 367). As a consequence, Conder explained that the population gradually died out because men are unable to marry and illicit relations are rare, or 'the elders of the village, with the consent of the rest of the men, sell themselves and their lands into the hands of some capitalist, or of the usurer who has lent the most money to the community' (Conder 1883: 367). What happened next is not told as Conder shifted his gaze towards a hypothetical capitalist willing to spend money on the rich soil of the Sharon plains. This would reap a good interest if, Conder advised, he might employ the native labour and 'better the physical and moral condition of his serfs by judicious liberality in bad seasons' (Conder 1883: 368).

Typical pages of Europeans quicker to give advice than to write a serious enquiry into the situation they reported! They cannot be blamed for being children of their times, but their claims cannot be taken at face value. Farmers were happy to feed the ajnabis (foreigner) with horror stories that may yield a little pity and money. And Conder duly noted that 'The cry of the people is the same throughout Syria, whatever their sect or stock: "Give us British rule, French rule, nay even a Russian, or a Greek, or a Jew to govern us, but save us from the Sultan and the Turk!"'[6] As Conder himself reported, missionaries were glad to indulge with funds to further the spread of the gospel (Conder 1883: 370). Under such conditions, which farmer was going to sing the praises of the merchants and of the government? Yet, it would be crucial to anyone trying to understand rural credit to discover the fate of the unfortunate village bought by the usurer. The most likely answer is that nothing happened. Life went on in that village as before, and for this reason Conder shifts to some new story. Did the usurer wait for the enlightened advice of the foreigner to better the condition of his 'serfs' by judicious liberality in bad seasons? Actually, Conder admitted that the peasant and the capitalist were in an equally grievous plight and that the Turkish Government was not better off (Conder 1883: 368-69). Despite the bias of the report, Conder did note that usurers were in no better shape than the farmers they exploited, which shows that the interpretation of usury as a way to make quick and easy money on the backs of poor farmers is simply wrong. The cause of the farmers' misery is to be found in a much more complicated combination of factors and Conder was probably more on target when he mentioned the war with Russia as well as the intrigues of the European powers as responsible for the hardship he saw. The usurer was as much a victim of the economic situation as the Sultan and the peasant were.

Denunciations of credit were not the apanage of European observers. Nineteenth-century Syrian jurist Muhammad bin 'Abidin also blamed moneylenders, but his better understanding of the context led him to identify salam as the cause of the ruin of villages (Rafeq 2002: 109). Similar to salam contracts, the Iranian taqavī was a form of advance whose main purpose was to tie farmers to the ground and ensure cultivation (Lambton 1991: 382-83). Traditional salam contracts were advance payment of crops at a price much lower than they would sell for after the harvest. In exchange, the buyer-investor provided for living expenses, covered urgent needs and paid the taxes. Yet, Ibn 'Abidin's observations do not reach much deeper into economic realities than the Europeans'. Noting the obvious poverty of the villages, he attributes it to the merchants, usual villains, thus merely repeating the villagers' complaint. The question that is never asked is whether villagers would have fared better without the merchants. Were usurious merchants and moneylenders the primary cause of the ruin of villages?

There are good reasons to doubt it since, during the Mandate, the British tried to lift the peasantry out of poverty by the elimination of 'exploitative' moneylenders considered, along with communal ownership of land, as 'traditional' structures that inhibited development (Nadan 2003; Metzer 2007; Al-Salim 2007). Agricultural banks were set up to offer low-interest loans to farmers in order to change the credit regime from the expensive informal system of lending on the black market to a cheaper, formal system of credit supplied by banks. Yet, despite official reports to the contrary, the fellahin continued to borrow at usurious rates from the grain merchants (Nadan 2005; 2007). The usury fallacy blinded the Mandate administration to the security net offered by the lender in case of harvest failures and other hardships.

Since all transactions took place at harvest time, the grain merchant came with his strong men to collect a share of the harvest which was not easily concealed. In worse cases of default, the land was 'taken' as well and the farmer became a tenant, working on his land as tenant or sharecropper for the merchant. As was the case in Bronze Age Nuzi, bad harvests and the consequent indebtedness of farmers did not cause loss of land for the indebted farmers (Domeris 2007: 145; Dosch 1987: 224-25). More by default than by design, moneylenders did accumulate land through debtors defaulting on loans. This, however, involved neither the transfer of the title of the land nor the transfer of the farmer for the aim of moneylending was to build a reliable network of suppliers of agricultural produce and to secure prices well below the market rate (Rogan 1999: 108-109). Given the low value of land in Palestine from the late Iron Age to the British Mandate, foreclosure of the land offered as security was only interesting as a way for the lender to secure a regular supply of produce, in that case because the lender owned the share of the crop that belonged to him as landlord (Nadan 2005: 32). It would have defeated the whole point of lending if the foreclosure of land pledged to secure the loan entailed the removal of the debtor from the land, since the lender was more interested in collecting grain at harvest time than in having to organize its production. At this point, it is worth recalling Woodhouse's argument concerning the Athenian hektemors. Woodhouse realized that the rent payable 'by the life tenant of a holding under the creditor-purchaser of a possessory right, bore no true economic relation to what had been advanced for that right' (Woodhouse 1938: 157). Contrary to modern loans for which repayment is planned in advance with a fixed amount to be paid at precise dates, repayments of ancient loans and rents by tenants were regulated by the actual yield of each year. Hence, the very notion of arrears and default hardly applies. After a bad harvest when the yield hardly sufficed to feed the tenant's family and to provide the seed for the next season, repayments were postponed until the next good harvest. Back in the Bronze Age, the Laws of Hammurabi (§48) state that cultivators were not obliged to pay their debts when the storm-god eroded or flooded their field or if the grain had not been produced through lack of water (Richardson 2000: 58-59). Such hardships were classified as 'acts of God' and automatically postponed the next repayment to the next harvest. Because the basic conditions of agriculture did not change much between Hammurabi's time and Iron Age Israel, it is safe to consider that 'acts of YHWH' did not cause the deprivation of farmers through foreclosure. Whether or not interest was charged for the delay becomes irrelevant when one realizes that both parties were interested in keeping credit alive.

5.7 Loans to Make Money?

The economic principles underlying much biblical exegetical writings are brilliantly presented in the following quote:

> The nobles and temple officials in a position to make loans to desperate peasants, however, were not members of village communities. Hence they had little incentive from regular interaction to observe such traditional customs [debt cancellations and interest-free loans]. Indeed, by taking interest on loans they could expand the wealth of their own households. (Horsley 2007: 25)

If the art of remaining rich certainly requires the ability to support the poor, it is surely not by granting loans to desperate peasants that the nobles expanded their wealth. Nor was Jerusalem an ivory tower that prevented its officials from knowing traditional customs and the socio-economical situation of villages within walking distance. The notion of the rich extending loans to the poor to despoil them of their meagre possessions is based on the modern notion of banks as institutions making money by lending money at higher interest rates than the rates at which they borrow. No such systems existed in the ancient world, where interest rates were determined by custom rather than by the market (Renger 1994: 191). The aim of agricultural credit was to obtain interest in the form of the debtor's labour rather than in his land (Van De Mieroop 2002b: 82; Wunsch 2002: 250; Faroqhi 2005: 208). Hence, however much he owed, a farmer remained in place and carried on farming the same land, servicing the loan with surpluses whenever there were any. This was still the case under the Ottomans, in spite of the rise of a land market following the registration of land. The ideal client for a merchant-moneylender remained the farmer who farmed the collateral because the property was less useful to the lender than was the produce of the land (Rogan 1999: 105).

The difficulty in breaking away from modern concepts of banking is compounded by the fact that the sale of labour power can be mediated in vastly different ways. Consider the following examples from papyrological evidence of the Byzantine era which reflects forms attested to in earlier eras. Labour is contracted through:

- A contract of employment which may or may not involve advance payment of wages.
- A type of lease in which the worker appears as a lessee who undertakes to 'lease' a series of operations, the tasks involved in them being the specific object of the lease.
- Advance payment of rent where the lessor is in fact a worker.
- A consumption loan, a form in which the advance payment of wages is mystified to strengthen the employer's control over the employee. The employer becomes creditor but his interest lies in the exaction of labour.
- The price paid in advance for the product of labour, that is, as a contract of advance sale where the owner of money appears to buy not labour itself but its product.
- Sharecropping, where the employee appears to pay his employer a rent in the form of a share of the crop, where actually his own share is a form of incentive wages and in the whole relationship is akin to piecework. (Banaji 2001: 198-99)

Contrary to modern practice, most arable land leases were concluded for the duration of a single year usually reduced to a number of months between sowing and harvest time. It is virtually impossible to determine whether the workers were landless, but they were not necessarily destitute. In fact, credit was the essential means by which employers gained some control over the supply of labour, fragmenting the solidarity of workers, establishing patronage relations which personalized relations between employers and employees. As in the Third World today, the main feature of all labour contracts was to treat wage advances as loans, which reflects a high instability of labour (Banaji 2001: 205). Selling tools and seeds and whatever farmers needed on credit was an essential part of ancient merchants' businesses, which during the first millennium BCE became much more independent from the temple and the palace than had been the case earlier (Dandamayev 1995). Operating with their own funds and at greater personal risk, these merchants foreclosed on their debtors' means of production only in extreme cases, to cover losses rather than to make a profit. The lenders' motives were to acquire a source of labour rather than to make money (Finley 1977: 180-81). Seizing the debtor and selling him abroad would have defeated the whole object of lending.

It is significant that wholesale grain merchants were the main if not the only moneylenders. Butchers and livestock dealers did not offer credit because the security they were interested in, animals, were movable property and could easily vanish (Nadan 2007: 59-60). Because grain and grain-growing land were the preferred securities, farmers who worked as tenants or labourers had no land to offer as security and were not offered loans (Nadan 2007: 58). This contradicts notions that the poor were exploited until they lost everything. But the credit requirement of such tenants and labourers were minimal since the responsibility for supplying seed and food in times of dearth fell on the landlord, not so much as in the form of loans as in the concrete expression of the solidarity arising from the mutual commitment that flowed from the integrated landlord-tenant relation. Both parties sought to retain as high as possible a level of prosperity for each other to make sure that the landlord would not be forced to sell the land and that the tenant would not seek employment elsewhere but remained healthy enough to work the land profitably (Nadan 2007: 64).

If exploitation is understood as the opposite of solidarity, exploitation of the land put a brake on the mutual exploitation of people. Besides moral or ethical considerations, it was in everyone's interest to keep interest rates and all other transactions such as sharecropping arrangements and wages at reasonable levels, since the economic systems integrated a number of checks and balances. Because lenders and borrowers had reliable information about each other, reliable borrowers were granted loans simply on the strength of their word, without signing a document. When the level of confidence was lower, a loan was granted after signing a document. A notoriously unreliable farmer received no loan. On the other side of the credit spectrum, a merchant who tried to impose exorbitant interest rates or became too harsh on the recovery of debts ran the risk of seeing another lender invade his territory and offer better terms. A potential new moneylender, however, would not intrude lightly onto another's turf since

> the entry price would be high, in the sense that the newcomer would lack the incumbent's detailed knowledge of the village. Naturally, imperfect information was a deterrent to lending. When a merchant-moneylender developed close connections with borrowers in a village, he could obtain better information. His risk was therefore reduced, and he could lend at a lower rate. (Nadan 2007: 60)

Therefore, in the long run, all parties benefited from conditions that were close to the best possible option available (Nadan 2005: 34). In the short run of course, merchants tried to squeeze as much resources as possible from their clients while farmers hid as much produce as possible from the tax collector, practising strategic default whenever possible and running away when things got too tight. Kings were under pressure either from their neighbouring enemies or from their overlords to 'lord it over' their own subjects and extract more revenues to defend the realm. Weak links, however, were constantly eliminated. Unreliable vassals were replaced or their kingdom was integrated. Oppressive merchants were replaced by more promising rivals. Unlucky, incompetent or unwise producers went bankrupt. Exploitation was at work at every level. Despite each actor feeling that the 'others' got a better deal than him, no one enjoyed *la dolce vita*.

Although the debt burden was less crushing than is usually claimed in literature, because 'usury' was not as terrible as pictured, creditors displayed little interest in recovering the entirety of loans and debtors were not eager to extinguish their loans. The reason for this behaviour is the link credit established between merchant and farmer, relations of patronage.

Notes

1. Hopkins (2002: 205) shows that imperial Rome took at least a century and a half to become what would appear as entirely parasitic if it had not housed the central administration. From 167 BCE, citizen landholders paid no taxes on Italian land. Citizens living in the city received a monthly dole of subsidized wheat from 122 BCE, an allowance that became totally free as from 58 BCE.

2. *Pecunia pecuniam parere non potest.* The doctrine of the sterility of money goes back to *Aristotle's Politika* I, iii, 16 (1257b; De Roover 1971; Zimmermann 1996: 170).
3. The Laws of Eshnunna 18a-21 (c. 1800 BCE); Hammurabi gap §t (c. 1700 BCE) establish interest rates of 20% on silver and 33 1/3% for barley, presumably per annum (Richardson 2000: 279).
4. Stein (1953: 169) mentions Elephantine Papyri Cowley 10 and 11 (456–55 BCE) and Tebtunis Papyri 817 and 818 (182 and 174 BCE) for loans by Jews to Jews. The demotic ostraka from Ayn Manawir (c. 407 BCE) record interest-free loans. They include a grace period (moratorium) of a month or two beyond the term (maturity date) after which the increase of 50% of the debts is applied. The lump sum of 50% is not presented as the remuneration of the loan, as was the case earlier, but as the sanction for the failure to reimburse the loan (Menu 1998: 399).
5. BM 33122 no. 73; Dar 345 no. 112; Dar 437 no. 122; Dar 453 no. 125; Dar 455 no. 126 (Abraham 2004: 336, 411, 428, 434-36).
6. 'Saved' from the Turks by the French, the Hauranis rebelled almost immediately afterwards. The Palestinians were saved by the British and are still dealing with the consequences (Conder 1883: 374).

Chapter 6

Debt and Patronage

In light of the regular legislation against patronage during the late Roman Empire, patronage was an excellent strategy to evade taxes and other burdens by both patrons and clients. Debt was not simply the patron's instrument to exploit clients. Debt was also the bond that sealed the solidarity of patrons and clients against the state while providing a form of subsistence insurance both to the clients and their patron (Grant 1976: 187; Scott 1976: 21-40; Finley 1983: 32; Seavoy 1986). The dog accepts the loss of liberty because it is the price of survival. As was the case already in ancient Mesopotamia, agricultural lending always resulted in long-standing debt, the repayment of the debt being 'a matter of wishful thinking rather than economic reality' (Wunsch 2002: 240). Interest rates were remarkably stable across the centuries because banking as a way to make money by lending money at higher interest than it was borrowed did not exist (Wunsch 2002: 247). Deposit banking existed only as a convenient way to avoid transporting silver (Jursa 2006). In such conditions, it is legitimate to ask why the rich lent money to small farmers at all.

The above discussion of interest rates has already provided the answer. Although returns from trade—moving surplus from where it is abundant to areas where it is less abundant—were higher, part of the overall profitability of such expensive and risky transfers depended upon the ability of the merchant to secure grain supplies directly from the producers at the lowest price. The next question is why did farmers accepted to tie themselves in such a way when they easily could get higher prices by storing their grain and selling it six months later when prices were at their highest level?

Merchants lend to farmers not to make money but to secure produce as part of a broader commercial strategy. Merchants accepted lending at little profit to help farmers keep afloat by paying their taxes and delaying repayments in exchange for produce to trade on the market. As farmers did not have the connections, expertise and means to trade their surplus beyond the small amounts they could barter on the local level with people who had the same produce at roughly the same time as they did, wholesale merchants specialized in turning surplus into assets and converting these assets into credit offered to the producers of the surplus they traded. The integration of production and trade through credit offered security to both. When climatic and social conditions left no surplus in the hands of the farmers, the creditor had every interest in keeping his debtor alive by extending further credit in the form of survival loans. In good years the creditor had direct access to the debtor's surplus at the lowest possible price. Debt sealed a bond between unequals similar to the bonds of solidarity between kin and equals within the village commune (Westbrook 2005; Finley 1981: 154-57). The bond established by credit complemented the bond of kinship and community. Most people were and still are enmeshed in complex ties of solidarity to kin, neighbour, patron and king or country. Risk fostered kinship and *musha*ʿ tenure (§2.1.2). Debt, as another type of insurance against common agricultural risks, forged patronage ties. Because kingship is a more distant reality, at the local level it is against kinship that patronage rubs shoulders. The tension between kin and patron surfaces in Prov. 18:24 and 27:10, which express scepticism about the value of kinship ties (Houston 2008: 46).

6.1 Patronage versus Kin?

In an article on patronage, Simkins (1999: 123-44) explains that patronage structured inequalities in Israelite society and at the same time patronage regulated and mitigated the effects of economic inequalities. According to Simkins, pre-monarchic Israel would have functioned principally along a patrimonial or domestic economy dominated by kin groups. The rise of the territorial kingdom saw the rise of a clientelist mode of production which placed kinsmen in competition with one another and gradually replaced extended kinship as the social relations of production and distribution (Simkins 1999: 139). Ethnography does not support the notion of patronage weakening kinship ties. Before chemical fertilizers, machinery, frozen and caned foods revolutionized production and storage and so led to the demise of open-field systems, changes in modes of production could hardly occur. The differences between Frühkapitalismus, Rentenkapitalismus, Tributarismus and other social sciences models retrojected onto the ancient world are intellectual constructions. In the absence of significant technical innovation, it is doubtful that the monarchy, the empires, monetization, urbanization or any other such factors induced major changes in economic systems (Kessler 1994; Houston 2008: 18-51). Economic relations remained basically the same, in spite of the slow rise of demography. Empires are said to have maximized the extraction of surpluses from the peasants, as if local sheikhs, kinglets and administrators were not already doing this within the limits of their possibilities before and after empires. Therefore, when it comes to defining ancient modes of production, Lenski's concept of the agrarian society seems broad enough to encompass the reality reflected in biblical texts, but its very broadness reduces its heuristic value since it applies to the economy of most human groups from the rise of agriculture to the industrial revolution (Lenski 1966: 189-296).

Since the concept of an agrarian society is too vague, scholars turn to archaeology for data supporting economic changes, as though precise enough economic data could be extracted from the ground plan of the few houses in a partially uncovered village hurriedly dug during salvage excavations. Walter Houston (2008: xi) entirely reworked his chapter on the ancient social context on the basis of publications by Avraham Faust. There is no denying the value of all archaeological excavations. The oft-quoted results of Tell el-Far'a north are indeed not unique any more (Houston 2008: 23). But have they been confirmed? On the basis of farmsteads in the vicinity of Jerusalem and in the northern valleys of the kingdom of Israel that were smaller in size and in shape than the norm, Faust and Houston deduce that their inhabitants had a lower standard of living because they were working the land for non-resident owners. Any larger building present is indentified as a public building serving the needs and representing the power of the state or of a private master (Houston 2008: 22). The argument is built on a series of inferences that reveal either a great naiveté or a wilful maximalism. First of all, it is extremely rare to find evidence of whether or not a house had an upper storey that would multiply the actual living space within a house by two. Then, it is never easy to distinguish between a courtyard, a garden, a paved stable, an outdoor kitchen and a 'living-room'. Some rooms were cellars rather than ground floors, which adds to the complexity of the identification of strata in multi-level settlements. Does the lack of burials combined with four-room houses, circumcision, the lack of decorated pottery, of imported pottery, and of temples indicate the presence of an egalitarian ideology in the Iron Age I highlands (Faust 2004; 2007:

94-95)? On the basis of the common self-aggrandizing propaganda found in the books of Samuel and Kings, Sparks (2008) doubts that the lack of royal inscriptions in the highlands is a distinctive ethnic marker revealing an egalitarian ethos, where such a direct display of royal power would not be looked upon favourably. Conclusions drawn from such approximate data must remain tentative and modest in spite of the ever more intricate academic castles built on very approximate data (Nurmi 2004: 230-51). What was an independent farmer? Did he enjoy a higher standard of living because his house was larger? Or was his house larger because he had to produce more to meet a heavier tax-burden? What is the correlation between tax burden and standard of living?

In the current state of biblical archaeology, *lmlk* impressions, *ostraca* from various tells, *bullae* of doubtful authenticity, partially excavated villages, very broad estimates of settlement sizes, approximate pottery sequences, microliths, pollens and bone analyses are unable to support the common claims that the economic situation of the peasants worsened, either in the eighth century or at any point afterwards (Houston 2004). The archaeological record as it stands can neither confirm nor disprove Domeris's claim that late Iron Age society had become an unequal society deprived of a sense of communal responsibility (Domeris 2007: 43-44; Houston 2008: 21). Such uncontrollable claims allow much leeway for personal fancy. If kingship and empire were the main causes for the impoverishment of peasants, one could expect that the so-called 'exilic' period, when population and imperial control were at a low ebb, would be hailed as a new Golden Age. To the contrary, the dark portrayal of this era in the Bible prevents such a logical conclusion, because Nehemiah 5 is read as the confirmation that the crisis worsened during the Persian era (Houston 2008: 25). Biblical exegesis is desperately awaiting fresh data and it tends to over-interpret archaeological finds that are used as proofs when they are in fact unable to sustain the great interpretative leap. Some such data is provided by the publication of Idumaean ostraca. Ian Stern concludes his analysis of onomastics in the ostraca by explaining that the drastic decrease in population that followed the Neo-Babylonian conquests and destructions in the Southern Levant created a non-competitive atmosphere (Stern 2007: 235). Less people meant less competition and more collaboration. Economically, however, the situation was less dynamic, which brings to the fore the question of the definition of a crisis. Can an economic crisis foster more harmonious relations between neighbours? Or are people happier when they have more to eat even though they have to work harder to pay more taxes?

Happiness of course is no economic notion, but it underlines the limits of social critique.

The interpretation of the archaeological record is further complicated by the interference of an on-going process of legitimation of the policies of the modern State of Israel towards the Palestinian population it controls. Faust seeks to prove the existence of a state of Israel in the Iron I, a state that was very different from its surroundings, a state that was democratic compared to its neighbours, a state that was really a nation (Faust 2006: 95-96). To identify the so-called four-room house as typically Judean, parallels outside the Palestinian central range are explained away as not of the four-room type and the many non-four-room houses in the central range are explained as mere variations on the model (Faust and Bunimowitz 2003). There is nothing like pseudo-history to supplement archaeology (Lemche 2010). The argument goes as follows. A primitive democracy must have existed in Israel during the period of the Judges, which Faust must be taking as a historical era or the argument would fail, and it was obviously never formally abolished since 'through the Bible it entered the fabric of western civilization' (Faust 2006: 96). These claims are a little too similar to modern political agendas to convince that their author's interpretation of the archaeological record 'are much less biased' than the claims of the old biblical archaeology (Faust 2006: 5). The political agenda is subsumed in what seems a neutral debate of experts over methodology. The convenient straw man is Mr Minimalist, but Faust is honest enough to state plainly his real concern in the last words of *Ethnogenesis*: 'This is not, of course, because the minimalists (most of them at least) have something against the Israelites. What they begrudge is modern Israel. Their political prejudice leads them to distort both history and method' (Faust 2006: 236).

It would be more correct to write that the minimalists begrudge maximalist interpretations of the archaeological record for methodological reasons. The heart of the matter is not the distortion of 'both history and method' but the political prejudice against the modern State of Israel that Faust presents as the minimalists' agenda. To brand critiques of the recycling of maximalist interpretations of the Bible and of archaeology as political prejudice is in itself a fair definition of political prejudice and shows how far Faust's argumentation is polluted by crucial political issues. For these ideological reasons as well as for reasons linked to the nature of archaeological processes, archaeology does not deserve the status of high court (Na'aman 2009a).

Since archaeology is no more neutral than biblical exegesis, patronage is recognized as a particularly helpful notion to understand ancient agrarian societies. Patronage remains a fundamental principle in modern Lebanon where it thrives side by side with kin. One turns first to one's own family for support, but because there is a limit to what kin can provide, everyone needs a *wasta*, a 'go-between or intermediary', a fundamental element of patronage. The *wasta* establishes the connection with a patron who is called upon to protect clients against the law, to get through administrative red tape, to provide contracts, employment and public services, to access education and medical treatment. In exchange, clients are expected to vote for their patron, to support him in demonstrations, and to accept the shortcomings and abuses of patronage: endemic corruption, nepotism, favouritism, the erosion of legislative and executive power, the reduction of politics to squabbles over patronage rights and boundaries, the sacrifice of broad national plans for short-run expediency. To retain the allegiance of clients and maintain their position, patrons block alternative supplies and substitute services and establish their own welfare associations, militia groups, sponsored labour unions, political parties. In this way, they preserve their positions while adapting and contributing to the modernization of society (Khalaf 1976: 202-204). This capacity to survive and adapt derives from two main factors: competition and individualism. Competition between patrons is fierce and highly selective. In the same way that charismatic leaders (*zu'ma*) lose their political clout when their power wanes, allegiance melts away when the patron loses the capacity to deliver or when the desired service becomes available through more advantageous channels. Individualism reflects the need to keep a tight supervision of clients through the agency of *qabaday* (toughies) who supervise the patron's network and work as his strong men (Johnson 1976).

The diachronic evolution from kin groups to patronage that Simkins and others use to plot changes in modes of production is thus unnecessary, except as a reflection of economic climates that have little to do with the rise of kingdoms and empires. In a stagnant economy, in the absence of trade, kinship is the main or the only provider of solidarity. This applies to the economic slump that characterized the transition between the Late Bronze and the Iron Age, but it is also true for Palestine between 586 and 450 BCE as well as later periods when the area found itself outside trade networks. As soon as trade and taxation create a demand for surpluses, merchants and tax collectors appear on the scene and patronage sets in.

Patronage opens new avenues for coping with new economic challenges without replacing kin, which remains the primary network of solidarity.

Between kin and patron, the village community is often forgotten as scholars often imagine 'pure' villages inhabited by a single lineage. Through communal tenure regimes such as the musha', the village commune managed local resources such as arable land, water, wood and pastures that were beyond the capabilities of kin. Kin is usually too small a unit to control an entire village and at the same time it spreads out geographically and covers an entire region through matrimonial alliances. Kin is liable to legal compensation in case of manslaughter while the village community is liable to taxation and functions as a tax-unit (§2.1.3). Next to kinship and village commune, religious institutions also play a specific role. An individual has to combine different functions to assume a position of leadership. In Lebanon for instance, a Maronite patriarch became a military and political leader. Today, a Shiite cleric combines these same attributes while a Sunni businessman became a patron for such a large section of the Lebanese population that his overlords took umbrage at his political clout and murdered him (Iskandar 2006; Blanford 2006).

The identification of specific modes of production should give way to the integration of kin and patronage as complementary social networks. Kingship, whether it is represented by a local king or by a distant emperor, constitutes the power of the state and cannot be ignored.

6.2 Compulsory versus Breakable Relations: King and Patron

Apart from particular moments when an individual may blur the distinction, patronage should be distinguished from the state. Considering its economic aspect, patronage is the sphere of the merchant rather than that of the monarch. The crown, directly or through the intermediary of a temple, absorbs tribute, taxes and conscripted services and redistributes some resources, a role curtailed by high operational costs and prestige spending. Through his role of dispenser of justice and order, the king regulates power. Military activities certainly have economic repercussions as the king brings wealth in the form of spoils, but it is a costly affair and there are setbacks, defeats and reprisals. Because economic development involves the ability to tap into remote resources through trade rather than war, the position of the sovereign appears far more parasitic than that of the much-decried merchants and moneylenders (Katz and Kemnitzer 1979: 53). The king produces little apart from order in the best of cases, but as holder of power, his relations with his subjects are compulsory and unbreakable. By contrast, the relations between patron and clients are voluntary, durable, mutual *and* breakable (Westbrook 2005: 211-15). Obviously, in a power vacuum, patrons soon start behaving like monarchs and enforce their own rule with the help of a militia. It then becomes dangerous to try breaking away from such a patron precisely because he is not functioning as a patron any more but as a local boss, thanks to the absence of a higher jurisdiction. Granted, the difference between a patron and a chief is not always obvious and the same person can play each role in turn, depending on changes in the balance of power. Yet, Deut. 17:20 names chariot forces besides marriage alliances and the accumulation of capital as one of the significant tools that enable a king to rule. Patrons can use marriage alliances and the accumulation of capital, but the moment they also acquire a force to impose their will, they are well on the way to turning into rulers.

It is thus the matter of breakableness that marks off a patron from a ruler, although the voluntary aspect of patronage relations is limited by the fact that it is almost impossible for clients to manage without patrons. A client will only terminate the relation to turn to another patron that seems to offer better returns or when the patron weakens and becomes unable to deliver. Hence, the solidarity between patrons should not be overemphasized (Lemche 1999: 92). While economic necessity entails elements of coercion and exploitation in relations of patronage, the voluntary aspect of the patron-client tie sets the farmers' relations to patrons on a fundamentally different plane from their status as subjects, which involved little or no element of choice. Kings could be and were indeed overthrown, but that was usually done by rivals within the ruling family, by grandees close to the ruler himself rather than from the grass-root level. Rivalry is indeed at work at every level. Clients also play the state against the patrons to pay less tax. The court (centre of the centre) regularly integrates members of peripheral aristocracies to play them off against its own elite (Parpola 2007).

The importance of the voluntary aspect and of the breakableness of the patron–client relation is emphasized in the story of Nabal's encounter with David at Carmel (1 Sam. 25). David's relation to Nabal involves force and criminal persuasion that eliminates the limited amount of choice and mutuality that characterizes patronage. Downplaying this element of force, M. Hamilton (2009: 521) presents David's request of a gift as an overture to create a reciprocal relationship. Since the text clearly shows that Nabal's mistake was the refusal to reciprocate, Hamilton rightly claims that David has given something valuable (2009: 516-17) and Hamilton adduces the testimony of Nabal's servant in 1 Sam. 25:15, that David's men caused no harm to Nabal's property, as support of David's goodwill (2009: 519). Hence, David anticipates some form of reciprocity (Hamilton 2009: 517). The problem is that the reciprocity is being forced upon Nabal. David does not leave any choice to Nabal and presents himself as the superior party that not only anticipates reciprocity but requires it immediately...or else! The sequel shows that David tolerates no delay and will not lower himself to bargaining. This is precisely why the story cannot be used as an illustration of patronage.

In this episode, David is not acting as a client asking for a favour from a patron. David pretends to come as an equal who requires his salary for past services, when in fact he clearly presents himself as the overlord exacting tribute. The difference between salary and favour is crucial. Had David abstained from mentioning the favours he supposedly did for Nabal by not molesting his shepherds, Nabal would have been granted the choice of giving food to David and his men as a gift, rather than as a salary. Whether or not David's protection of Nabal's flocks was real is irrelevant. Seeking to establish reciprocity by asking food as a favour, David would have then begun or continued protecting Nabal and Nabal would have continued feeding David, both carefully preserving the *fiction of equality*. Both parties would have preserved each other's freedom to present their action as liberalities rather than as contractual reimbursements of debts incurred previously. But the narrator has no interest in presenting his hero as bowing in front of Nabal to ask a favour. To the contrary, verses 5 and 6 play on the meanings of the word *šalom* (peace, compensation, retaliation) by which David insists that peace has a price. The price of peace is compensation, the settling of accounts. The first person in the expression 'we have not shamed/harmed/insulted them' (הכלמנום) in verse 7 (see also v. 15) underlines David's direct intervention in Nabal's affairs and holds a threat that David's men could have behaved otherwise, insisting that Nabal had better deliver food and do so quickly. David breaks the etiquette of patronage by inviting himself and asking for something due, instead of biding his time until Nabal is free to demonstrate his generosity and invite David, who would then have to pretend that what he received was a gift, not a salary. Worse, David sends low ranking men (נהרים) instead of presenting his request in person.

Nabal's reply to David's show of force is to return the insult. In his answer to David, it is the element of force to which Nabal objects. Nabal refuses to yield to the demands of the upstart strongman because David insists on establishing the relationship on unequal terms. Had Nabal previously agreed with David over the protection of his flocks, Nabal would have reciprocated with food supplied on that festive occasion. Had David asked for a favour, Nabal may have extended an invitation. But David couched his demand as wages rather than gifts when in fact it was clearly a case of tax exaction by an unauthorized agent. Hence, Nabal rejects David's fictitious reciprocity and unmasks it as a racket, underlining David's use of violent means to pressurize him, which would be unnecessary had the relation been as reciprocal as David claimed it was (Westbrook 2005). A patron is *not* a godfather, at least not a violent one. Nor is a patron a tax collector. Contrary to kin and king, both of which are involuntary and indissoluble, patronage is a volatile social reality based on a certain amount of freewill and reciprocity within a fiction of equality.

The difference between the ruler and the patron is made apparent in the source of their revenues and the way they use them. The king collects taxes, grants land and alms while the patron trades surplus and offers credit. Political and economic powers are quite distinct and often compete with each other. Everyone is an exploiter and is exploited, woe to those who are not exploited because they have nothing to contribute. They find themselves out of the direct economic network of exploitation. If raw military power makes the sovereign's relation to the subject compulsory and unbreakable, royal ideology legitimizes the powers of the sovereign.

6.3 The King: Patron of the Poor?

Despite the clear distinction between king and patron, regulator and transformer, their roles seem to blur in relation to the destitute as both compete again with each other, this time to be seen as protectors of the poor. Houston (2008: 46-47) adduces Job's self-description as a patron (father) to the poor (Job 29:16) and to the brother terminology in Deuteronomy 15 as expressions of patronage. Despite the etymological link between the words father and patron, despite the synonymy in common speech between a benefactor and a patron, Job's actions in favour of the poor are more properly defined as charity rather than patronage per se, the difference between the two being established by the fact that poor clients can contribute little to Job's position as a patron. The fact that Job uses attributes from royal ideology as in Job 29:25, in this case the protection of the poor, should not be used as a demonstration that the king functions as a patron to his subjects.

Houston (2008: 46) recognizes the difference which he locates in the focus of the benevolence. The king's benevolence is universal while the patron's is particularistic. Another difference is that patronage involves economically sound clients while charity benefits rotten assets such as the proverbial widows and orphans (Isa. 10:1-2). The alms-giver, whether he is a patron or a sovereign, certainly derives benefits in terms of reputation and honour from his benevolence. Although the king was not the sole alms-giver, charity is a crucial part of royal ideology that presents the ruler as protector of the poor (Weinfeld 1995: 45-56; Charpin 1996; Houston 1999). By contrast, 'Giving alms does not amount to being a patron' (Houston 2008: 46). The essence of patronage is not found in charity. Abusively termed 'royal patronage', the king's generosity is really charity granted in the name of justice while the patron grants favours in the name of good relations. Charity justified royal or stately power in the form of armed force and the right to extract taxes. Charity provided moral superiority to the ruler as well as preserving his rule. Hence, the longevity of the king (Ps. 72:5) is mentioned after general prosperity for the people and the special defence of the poor (Ps. 72:2-4), as if the king's survival depended directly upon these conditions. Justice and charity are not optional for the ruler. The gold of Sheba that he will receive (Ps. 72:15) is put on a parallel with the prayers addressed on his behalf. In verses 12-14, the poor and the needy that the king helped are the most fervent intercessors for his well-being and they are the direct or indirect source of his gold. Alms-giving is the *sine qua non* condition of the ruler's self-interest by which he recruits the support of the lowly against the great.

The rivalry between the ruler and the patrons at the top of the social scale places the prophetic fulminations against the rich in a different perspective. They are another expression of royal ideology rather than being motivated by abstract ethical principles. They that trample the needy (Amos 5:11; 8:4) are the same that use false balances (Amos 8:5) and plant vineyards (Amos 5:11) and the king presents himself as the redresser of the evils committed by the traders, investors and moneylenders, in a word, the patrons. The depiction of the patrons as threats to the poor (see also Isa. 10:1-2; 17:10) and the silencing of the patrons' essential role in financing agriculture through credit are prerequisites of royal ideology. Rather than free-lance Robin Hoods, the prophets (as texts at least) serve the king. When prophetic texts attack the king directly, the king in question is dressed up as a landlord (Naboth) or the prophet denies being a prophet (Amos 7:10-14).

Just as the ruler gains legitimacy as protector (rather than patron) of the poor, patrons also do charitable acts to gain honour and improve their position. Yet, patronage should not be confused with charity. As much as poverty bars them access to credit rather than forces the destitute to borrow, the primary aim of patronage is not the alleviation of poverty. The dangers of the double-confusion, 'borrower = poor' and 'patronage = charity', are illustrated by the following quote:

> To have to borrow because of poverty is always humiliating, but under the patronage-system debtor and creditor stand within a network of mutual obligation and solidarity—the client being cared for by his patron, at least being prevented from starving. Once this network is broken, the creditor no longer acknowledges any responsibility for his debtor and uses him as a source of income. The debtor, always in a precarious situation, is now even more estranged and becomes a depersonalized object to be exploited. (Lang 1982: 57)

The 'depersonalized object' remained a subject of the sovereign and as such an object of his solicitude, at least in theory. Hence, because the poor is insolvent, he has little to contribute concretely and he is left out by ordinary networks of exploitation either in tax for the king or in reimbursements of loans to the patron. But the poor are needed by the king to bolster his position against the most powerful patrons. Wrongly dubbed 'royal patronage', the ruler's beneficence to the poor is demarcated from patron-client networks since neither party has any choice in the matter. Besides the element of breakableness discussed above, the difference between the ruler and the patron is revealed in the difference between reciprocity and charity. The patron-trader grants no loans to the destitute because they are insolvent. The ruler has to be seen as provider of relief to the poor and through charity the poor exploit the king and the rich from whom he extracts taxes. To demarcate himself from the elite and to embody the reality of the 'state', the ruler justifies tax collection by distributing a portion to the destitute that have no means to reciprocate. The ruler's legitimacy is in danger the moment he stops doing that. It is quite wrong to imagine with Schäfer-Lichtenberger (1996: 105) that, once established, the monarchy is no longer in need of legitimation. Absalom challenges David's legitimacy by telling every Israelite seeking justice from the king that he would give them justice if only he was king. These acts of charity are presented as justice while patrons, when they decide to give alms to the poor, do it as an act of generosity or reciprocity. The ruler's justice is founded on an ideological use of charity while the patron's generosity is established by concrete acts to bolster transient networks of clients. The ruler grants tax exemptions while the merchant-patron extends the tenor of his credit. On the one hand, a due is written off; on the other hand, repayment is deffered. As much as the king derives his legitimacy from the protection of the unproductive elements of society—the poor, the widow and the orphan—the patron derives his legitimacy from his role of lending and trading surpluses for the producers. To survive politically, the king needs the poor as much as the poor need him. To survive economically, the patron needs the farmer's cheap supply of surplus as much as the farmer needs the valuable supply of seed and food in times of dearth.

This presentation is obviously too schematic to fully reflect reality, but it holds true for the biblical misrepresentation of social relations that criticizes the merchant and elevates the king, or at least some kings. The king may well present himself as the super patron while being in a client relation with another ruler (Lemche 1994: 127-29). Patrons may also take the ruler's place. For this reason, Assyrian kings regularly integrated members of peripheral elites into their entourage, giving them a chance to become patrons in order to undercut the monopoly of well-established courtiers and patrons whose influence became a threat (Parpola 2007). There is necessarily a tension between *the* ruler who can only be one, and the patrons who must be several. The king raises taxes that are uncompensated exactions and grants favours in the name of justice, which means that they require no compensation. By contrast, the patron grants favours in the name of good relations and always comes back knocking at the client's door. Another difference is that the ruler's relation to his subjects is marked by impersonality symbolized by the personification of justice as blind to personal considerations. Impersonality motivates the prohibition to show favour to the poor in Lev. 19:15. By contrast, the patron's relation to his clients is personal even if the distance is bridged by a *wasta* (intermediary).

Socio-political changes should be considered as oscillations of the balance of power between ruler and patrons rather than as a hypothetical continuum from tribal societies towards nation states and empires. The title of Lemche's article, 'From Patronage Society to Patronage Society', is right on target. The growing power of the state reduces without ever totally eliminating patrons. A ruler cannot be a patron to his subject, certainly not the head patron as Lemche (1996: 114) sees him. Being a ruler is fulfilling a very different function from that of a patron. Both are essential for the welfare of the general population, which depends on the competing interests between the ruler and the patrons and between the patrons themselves.

6.4 Biblical Prophets as Patrons?

While royal ideology is founded upon the notion of justice, the virulent denunciations of the rich in prophetic books are motivated more by chicanery between patrons vying with each other for the control of a thriving clientele than by some abstract notion of justice. Hence, Clines (1993: 146) asks whether Amos criticizes the rich because he is not one of them. Or prophetic writings denounce merchants in order to support royal ideology, either human or divine, that presents the ruler as the redresser of the merchants' abuses—usury and rapaciousness. In any case, biblical prophets are no patrons. They are *wastas*, intermediaries between human clients and the divine patron who find themselves in rivalry with other divine patrons (*ba'alim*) for human supporters (Westbrook 2005: 230). Westbrook's notion of intermediary patrons is a contradiction in terms. An intermediary is an essential link between patron and client. Gehazi's role in relation to Elisha constitutes a chain of *wasta* between the divine patron and the Shunamite. To build and retain an effective network of clients, patrons need intermediaries that are not patrons themselves. The patron is the one who holds what the clients seek, but the agency of intermediaries is essential for the system to function. Without such networks of *wasta*, the patron is condemned to remain a mere local sheikh. Prophetic texts are very clear that the patron is God, not the prophet. The Shunamite accepts Elisha's intervention as intermediary in an affair that her own connections could not solve: pregnancy. Hence, it is important to introduce the notion of intermediaries in patronage to avoid confusion. Between equals, there is solidarity expressed as brotherhood.

6.5 Patrons as Merchants

As the financial needs of the state grew, the state was less able to forgo rents or taxes. Hence, merchants played a crucial role between the producers and the state as they were the only ones able to capitalize surpluses in good years in order to invest them as loans to farmers in times of dearth, allowing the producers to continue paying their dues to the state.

The crucial role of trade and credit is obscured by the cliché of the usurious merchant (Wunsch 2002: 223). The confirmations of the cliché in the writings of the travellers of the eighteenth century CE and the absence of reliable econometric data keep the cliché alive. Yet, in ancient economy, as much as in its modern counterpart, production was not the main challenge. The main problem was and remains storage and distribution to even out the huge yearly and regional fluctuations of yields. Overproduction is only an effective buffer against a risky environment if normal surplus from good years can be 'banked' for use in bad years. Direct storage by producers absorbed the effects of low yields within a two- to three-year span. Conversion through feeding grain to animals is risky and wasteful (Halstead 1989: 79). Hence, conversion into inalterable values such as gold and silver was important. Debt was another option. It was not a proof of poverty but part of a strategy of conversion of surplus into the assurance of being supplied grain. Playing off regional differences, trade converted surpluses into precious metals or other assets which had to be 'ploughed' back in the form of credit to remain useful.

Because the crops of richer farmers were as much at risk as the crops of small farmers, the notion that rich farmers gradually improved their position as creditors is doubtful (Coote and Whitelam 1987: 136). The advantage gained by a larger profit in a good year was offset by greater losses during bad years. Hence, rich farmers were not in a position to lend much to their more modest colleagues, contrary to merchants whose success relied on their ability to serve as lenders because the returns from commercial ventures depended partly on their ability to secure access to cheap supplies directly from producers. Yet, commercial ventures involved greater risk than agricultural production. Neither merchants nor rich farmers were safe from misfortune and both categories had a vested interest in the economic well-being of small farmers.

Trade and credit are interrelated activities. Their imbrication is reflected in the impossibility to distinguish between debt-enslavement and ordinary pledging that the Egyptian language, like the Semitic languages, designates with the same words simply because slave and servants are occupational rather than social categories (Postgate 1987: 263; Hofman 2005). The borrower is indeed the slave of the lender (Prov. 22:7), but no more so than any one who has contracted a mortgage or a loan from a modern credit institution.

The semantic confusion between a slave and a debtor allows much leeway for modern readers to indulge in preconceptions that find much support in the Bible. The farmers are the victims of the merchants. Yet, the dichotomy between exploiters and exploited, rich and poor, haves and have-nots, landholders and tenants, should be replaced by a more differentiated mapping of economic actors: the state, patrons and clients, religious institutions and village communes. The state embodied by the ruler should be kept distinct from patrons who were primarily traders rather than owners of large estates.

Chapter 7

Debt in the Bible

7.1 The Sons of a Wife of a Son of the Prophets (2 Kgs 4:1-7)

Our understanding of Roman slavery remains precarious (McKeown 2007). Interpreting pre-Roman slavery is even more difficult since the term slavery covered a broad range of situations and social states. For instance, some slaves working on estates had their own households and owned slaves themselves (Uchitel 2005: 480). Despite this caveat, the anxious tone of the widow's plea to Elisha shows that misfortune was at hand. What was entailed by the lender's coming to take the two boys as servants or slaves (לעבדים הנשה בא לקחת את שני ילדי לו, 2 Kgs 4:1b) is left to the audience to imagine. There is no doubt that that ancient mothers were no more happy than modern mothers are seeing their sons leave home to work and this is enough for readers of all times to sympathize with the widow's plight. Because the story is set in a catalogue of miracles establishing the hero as a miracle worker, essential details are missing. Lack of specific details serves reader identification but it also prevents the recovery of the actual conditions reflected by the story. Yet, this passage is one of the few that seems to depict the economic situation prevailing in the kingdom of Israel.

The mother's statement that the sons are to be taken as servants or slaves (לעבדים) can mean two different conditions. Either her sons are about to become distrainees to speed up repayment or the boys are to be put to work by the creditor to pay back their father's debt. The main difference between the two is that distraint may imply a spell in prisons that functioned as workhouses run by the state, temples or individuals, where debtors worked off their debt (Dandamayev 1984: 160), while antichresis would involve working on the creditor's farm. In any case, that the creditor or moneylender (הנשה) is taking the sons for himself (לו) indicates that traffic in workdays is more likely than traffic in human bodies chained and sold like cattle on a slave market. This is about as far as one can go. It is inadequate to evaluate the economic situation of this family, and even more so to generalize it to the entire monarchic Israel. It would be necessary to know the age of the boys, whether they would be taken away from their mother and live on the creditor's farm. The distance between the mother's house and the creditor's farm would be determinant to judge the emotional impact of the separation. Would the mother also work to pay her dead husband's debt? If dislocation was the case, would the boys be taken away for good or would they return home when the creditor had no work for them? Emotionally, the harshness of the separation is relative to the age of the boys. Economically, however, the separation may be preferable for both the destitute mother and the children since the creditor was in a better position to feed them round the year. The same can be said about the various women and children taken as spoil, pledge, pawn or security (Exod. 21:7; Lev. 25:39-42; Isa. 10:2; 50:1; Amos 2:6; Job 24:9). Being taken by a rich family was one of the few viable options to secure the basic means of survival for destitute children. It was a charitable act out of which neither party made a fortune. If one insists on the term exploitation, the exploitation was mutual. In exchange for survival, the poor served the rich in menial tasks that contributed little to the immediate enrichment of the master. Who was going to make a fortune by exploiting such improbable sources of wealth? Another question would be whether pawning might constitute some kind of apprenticeship that would help secure a better future for the pawns.

Without disputing the dire situation of the widow and of her sons, one has to admit that 2 Kgs 4:1-7 contributes little to the understanding of debt bondage. That destitute parents delivered their children into the hands of their creditors demonstrates the existence of a system of social protection, whereas the creditor, who was in a better position than the parents, took over the needs of the children and relieved the parents of that burden, hence contributing to the survival of both generations. The same applies to the acquisition of slaves by raising exposed children. Using the example of the son of the widow in 2 Kgs 4:1-7, Premnath (2007: 176-77) admits that the creditor did not always benefit from the pawns because he had to provide housing, food, clothing, medical and religious expenses. But he also claims that 'Once the financial obligation was met, a pawn could be redeemed', a nonsense since upon the reimbursement of the loan redemption would be unnecessary! This system is similar to foster-parenting in modern societies. There is no denying the existence and the cruelty of slavery, but debt bondage entailed working after being paid, which, in principle, is not necessarily more exploitative than the status of salaried employees who work for a whole month *before* being paid or that of free-lance workers whose income is irregular and entirely dependant on quality and demand. As for working to pay back debts, it is no more degrading than receiving alms.

Despite the lack of details, this episode confirms the notion that credit is a proof of creditworthiness and that loans were not granted to destitute people (§5.4.1). The story does not tell how long the son of the prophet had been dead before the creditor came, but it is clear that the loan had been granted when he was alive. The death of the main breadwinner sounded the end of the creditworthy status of the family and set in the process of foreclosure. It is not so much a question of over-indebtedness as a matter of the loss of confidence of the creditor who considered that the woman and her sons were not in a position to reimburse the loan (Kessler 2006: 116). The mother's anxiety does not exclude that in the taking of the boys the 'loan shark' did a charitable act that transferred the costs of the upkeep of the boys from the mother to the creditor who may already have lost some money. A number of Mesopotamian texts record the sale of persons against food to remain alive in a time of distress (Hurowitz 1994).

The resolution of the crisis is also noteworthy. Instead of quoting oracles against Israel's fat capitalists (Amos 2:6-8) and threatening the loan shark that God would shake him out (Neh. 5:13) if he did not forgive the debt, the story has Elisha perform a miracle that enables the debt to be reimbursed through the market. This stress on maintaining creditworthiness says a lot about the social origins of those who penned the story. Instead of advising the widow to pick up her children and run away, Elisha suggests yet another loan. In verse 3, she is to borrow not a few (לא תמעיטי) empty vessels. In sound economic theory, the amount of money she would make is tied to the number of pots she could borrow. The story suggests that the neighbours had confidence in her ability to pay back, possibly because of her patronage connections through the prophet. The fact that in verse 6 only one son is present (בנה) to help fill the pots suggests that the other son was gone as guarantee for the loan of the pots.

If the overall contribution of 2 Kgs 4:1-7 to the discussion of debt bondage is very slim, it offers an unexpected illustration of the principle according to which the solution to debt is more debt, keeping the bond alive as long as possible rather than depending on charity.

7.2 Nehemiah 5: Freeing Debt Slaves?

Although the date of prophetic oracles is far too insecure to confirm the existence of a crisis in the eighth century BCE, Nehemiah 5 is used as confirmation for the eighth-century crisis that continued unabated into the Persian period. Rainer Albertz has written an impressive discussion of Nehemiah 5 which he takes as a historical report of a major economic crisis in the fifth century BCE brought about by the financial reform of Darius. Albertz (1994: 496) postulates that traditional smallholdings had aimed at self-sufficiency and were thus unable to shoulder the extra costs entailed by the obligation of paying a tribute in silver coins. The amount of the tribute was fixed in advance without heed to the actual yields of the harvest. A second cause for the crisis was the conscription for building the walls of Jerusalem.

Albertz's reading of Nehemiah 5 illustrates the academic view of the hapless peasant unable to adapt to new situations (§3), the victim of rulers blinded by greed that prevents them from realizing that their own welfare depends on that of their people. That greed motivates rulers and farmers and that people are not always very rational in their pursuit of their own interest is a valid generalization for all periods. It is also true that farmers, as with most other trades, consider themselves as victims of the 'system' and that no farmer in his right mind will admit to being comfortably prosperous. That rulers never have enough silver in their coffers is also correct. In these conditions, the crisis depicted in Nehemiah 5 is too congruent with common perceptions to be taken at face value. To test the notion that Nehemiah 5 reports an actual crisis, a number of problematic assumptions in Albertz's argument must be tested.

7.2.1 The Walls of Jerusalem Were Repaired during a Slack in Farming Activities

There was enough idle time between sowing and harvest to make sure that work gangs were conscripted outside these peaks of labour. Nehemiah 6:15 dates the completion of the wall on the 25th day of the month Elul, in the 52 days between 11 August and 2 October when the Sabbaths are excluded (Clines 1984: 176). This sets the work between the grain harvest and the next ploughing season. Although it is not certain that the crisis described in Nehemiah 5 is meant to be understood in temporal sequence, taking it as such places the crisis towards the end of July, halfway between the grain and the grape harvest (Blenkinsopp

1988: 255-56). If, as it stands in its present narrative context, the financial crisis is related to the extra burden involved by the restoration of the walls, the direct effects of the conscription would have been less serious than Albertz claims because it was carefully timed to avoid taking people away from their fields when they were most needed there. Apart from the case of an imminent attack, no ruler or governor would drag the farmers away from their fields during the harvest to work on the walls. Moreover, the restoration of Jerusalem would have boosted the economy of the province even if at first it meant extra costs to the local population.

7.2.2 Self-sufficiency Includes the Ability to Shoulder Extra Costs

Self-sufficiency implies more than the production of enough food to tide over one's dependants until the next harvest. At any period, smallholdings are geared to produce surplus, first because farmers are unable to know in advance the yield they will reap under the highly irregular Mediterranean rainfall. Hence, farmers, whatever the size of their holdings, plough and sow more than what would theoretically be necessary for the expected yield. Claiming with Albertz (1994: 496) that 'small farmers had to cut things down to the bone simply to get by, and it only took very slight additional difficulties like failures in the harvest or conscription for building the walls to upset their precarious situation over a broad front' is fine rhetoric. But it ignores the planning skills that ordinary farmers had as their survival across the millennia demonstrates. No doubt these farmers would have concurred with Professor Albertz that their situation was very precarious, but rhetoric only feeds the rhetor. Farmers survived by anticipating the harvest failures and the conscriptions they routinely encountered. Well before the Achaemenids arrived on the scene, self-sufficient farmers integrated the various taxes, rents, interests as well as unforeseeable expenses in the surface they ploughed and the amount of seeds they used each year, or they would not have been self-sufficient at all. If the obligation of paying taxes and dues in coin rather than in kind involved extra costs, these costs would have to be measured against the overall economic situation before the actual burden they represented to the farmer's budget could be evaluated. Were we ever in a position to evaluate these extra costs, the fresh economic opportunities resulting from Persian operations in Egypt may have offset the extra costs. Unfortunately, reliable quantitative studies will probably never be refined enough to allow any meaningful calculation of such costs. Nevertheless, several arguments in favour of an improvement of the overall economic situation in the second part of the Persian era can be advanced.

First, under peaceful conditions, it is not production but storage and transformation of surpluses into precious metals that pose the greatest challenge. The integration of Palestine into a large empire had positive effects on the rural economy, entailing a sharp reversal of the situation when the same area was a contested theatre of war (Crone 2007). As much as the economic buoyancy experienced in Syria-Palestine during the seventh century BCE was the direct consequence of their annexation into the Neo-Assyrian Empire, the integration of Egypt into the Persian Empire altered the strategic position of the southern Levant from a depleted Neo-Babylonian buffer zone to a vital route. The major campaigns Persian troops waged in Egypt further enhanced the economic position of Palestine by raising the demand for local surpluses. Even the damage done by armies in enemy territory was limited and without long-term consequences (Hanson 1998: 174-84). Grain-fields could only be torched within a short time before the harvest. The systematic destruction of crops and trees was beyond the ability of ravaging armies except in the vicinity of a besieged city where the besiegers had more time and needed to forage to feed themselves. Pests and wild animals caused much damage (Nollé 2005).

Second, the impact of the monetization of the economy is extremely hard to gauge (Briant, Henkelman and Stolper 2008). The requirement to pay taxes in silver reflects the generalization of trade and an increasing number of urbanites who did not grow the food they ate or an increasing amount of people drawing revenues besides the food they grew. In principle, this does not imply that the producers lost out when the state transferred upon them the responsibility of the realization of crops into silver. In fact, the contrary could be the case. Coinage encouraged lateral exchange among peers (Bresson 2008). The monetization of the economy saved on a heavy administration and developed mainly where the central state was weak, where taxation was not based mainly on corvée and the system of redistribution was lacking (Moreno García 2008: 147). Rathbone (1991: 327-28) shows that Egyptian rural estates extended monetization beyond the limit of the quantity of coin actually in circulation. Although they handled only a limited amount of cash and paid their workers in kind, they provided them with advance credit as part of their strategy to build up a reliable manpower. The temple of Jerusalem would have operated along similar lines. By contrast, in Ptolemaic and Roman Egypt the state continued to collect most taxes in kind in order to limit the rise of local markets and of urban networks specialized in non-agricultural activities that the state could not control as easily as agriculture (von Reden 2001; Rowlandson 2001; de Callataÿ 2005). Hence, one could argue that Darius' reform provided greater leeway to peripheral areas such as Yehud, a leeway that, if it did not immediately translate into greater prosperity, would have at least afforded more economic freedom and openings to the individual farmer there. Contrary to the claim that the 'crisis' in Nehemiah 5 was caused by the forced repopulation of Jerusalem (Neh. 11:1) that concentrated too many unproductive mouths into one place (Gross 1997: 270), the new commercial outlets had at least as many positive as negative repercussions for the local farmers. In light of the nature of ancient cities as essentially large villages populated by farmers and in which much space was devoted to gardens (Ussishkin 2006), the notion that urban mouths are unproductive can be dismissed. Even when monetization contributed to the rise of a non-agricultural sector in Jerusalem, these mouths were only unproductive from the point of view of grain production. Their feeding generated a local demand for agricultural surpluses as well as a local traffic of prebendary products in the form of leftovers of divine meals (Van Driel 2002).

7.2.3 A Fixed Tribute Is Adaptable at the Local Level

The idea that provinces had to pay a tribute fixed in advance without heed to the actual yields of the harvest is equally problematic. Was the treasury greedy enough to expect the fixed tribute when the harvest failed? The notion of a fixed tribute derives from Herodotus 3:89 who claimed that, as a result of a reform by Darius I, all the countries of the empire were obliged to pay taxes in silver.[1] Although Herodotus' figure for Babylonia—1,000 talents of silver annually—indicates a rounded figure that does not inspire any confidence in its reliability, the amount actually paid by each fiscal unit was carefully calculated according to the ability of each unit (see Plutarch *Mor.* 172-73; *Arist.* 24:1). Darius learnt from the rebellions he had crushed that setting the level of taxes on a fair basis was essential to the stability of the realm. He was thus the first ruler to publish an official tribute register (Briant 2002: 390-94). As far as we can see, it was realistic on the whole and nothing indicates that the level of taxation was more oppressive than during previous eras (Grabbe 2004: 195-97). We also note that the amount of tribute was fixed at the level of the larger fiscal units and allowed for adjustment of the amount paid by each sub-unit according to actual regional yields as long as the overall sum was delivered to the central treasury. The greater and more varied a fiscal unit, the greater flexibility it offered to the tax-collecting authority to adjust the amount of tribute collected according to yield variations year after year.

The aim of fixing an amount in advance for each fiscal unit was to guarantee a regular income to the royal treasury, and to limit the amount satraps could extract by shifting the responsibility for abuses upon their shoulders. Instead of protecting the satrap by allowing him to present himself to his tax-base as a mere underling carrying out orders, the satrap had to negotiate with the lower tax-collecting rungs. Flexibility was required since taxation is the result of a constant bargaining process between taxpayers and tax-users, each side presenting itself as the victim of the other. Abuses are more blatant when they are practised by the more powerful partner, but at every level there is resistance and dragging of feet. The amount finally collected had to reflect actual yield variations. Because greed is present at every level, some common sense is essential for survival. Common sense dictated that the taxation authority took into account the economic health of its tax base. Even when it was a punitive measure, a heavy tribute could only be a punctual measure that was bound to backfire if it was not followed by concrete demonstrations of clemency. Hence, the suppression of rebellions was routinely followed by temporary cancellation of taxes in spite of the fact that the rebels were defeated (Beaulieu 2000). The devastations incurred by the military operations that crushed the rebellion punished the treasury as much as the farmers of the region concerned. Following the example of Pasha Mehmet Ali, who ranged his Egyptian subjects in three categories—those who do not care except about themselves, the loyal and kind that are devoid of any sense of discretion and those that are in the same position as animals (Fahmy 1997: 282)—dominant powers may indeed treat their subordinates as milk cows but they still have to care for the cow to get milk (Grabbe 2004: 197).

The Romans could not facilitate the efforts of wealthy landowners to exact as great a surplus as possible without considering the well-being of the numerous small farmers. The sovereign used the law to establish a more even playing field to facilitate the type of investment and cooperation that could lead to economic growth (Kehoe 2007: 194). Although its ability to use the law to promote its interest in the form of fiscal revenues was subject to broad constraints, the Roman state consciously sought to promote a particular distribution of resources, not simply out of concern for justice but rather as a policy designed to promote fiscal goals (Kehoe 2007: 195). It is doubtful that the Persian

Empire could have lasted if the Achaemenids did not share a similar concern for the well-being of their tax base. If each year Darius actually received the amount fixed in advance, the regularity was the result of his subordinates' ability in steering constantly between the imperatives of drawing revenues while avoiding social disturbances. The sheer territorial size of a large empire afforded it the luxury of a regularity of revenues that smaller political entities could never enjoy because regional production failures could be compensated with the revenues from further afield.

At the local level, however, the bargaining process was a bitter game. Taxpayers systematically complained that they were fleeced and when times were hard, the satrap had to contribute from his own funds to make up for the missing revenues. This is exactly what is described in Neh. 5:2-5. The tone of subordinates' relations to their superiors was by definition lachrymose. On the receiving side of the tax flow, the burden was set at a higher level in order to compensate for the loss of revenues through swindling and resistance. The fact that Nehemiah 5 mentions no tax relief illustrates the bargaining process between local taxpayers and local administrators. Although the king's tax is mentioned at verse 4 as an aggravating factor that forced people to borrow in order to pay it, Nehemiah does not cancel it because his position did not afford him that kind of freedom. Instead, along with other measures discussed below, Nehemiah squeezes his own revenues to meet the expected amount of tribute by giving up collecting the governor's food allowance (Neh. 5:14-19). That Nehemiah claims that he did not collect his due for twelve years is also congruent with the ideology of the text, but one can expect that he had other sources of revenues or would he have continued serving as governor and supposedly feeding a hundred and fifty people daily (Neh. 5:17) if he did so twelve years in a row? In any case, the way Nehemiah tackled the problem gives the lie to the common notion that farmers bore alone the brunt of the fixed tribute. Stuck between a rock and a hard place, satraps, governors and other administrators had to steer an uneasy course between the exigencies of maximum tax extraction and social peace to preserve their positions and save their lives.

7.2.4 Reversing the Logic of the Crisis

Before mentioning Nehemiah's generous waiver of his food allowance (Neh. 5:14-19), the story relates how Nehemiah reacted to the crisis by forcing a group designated as *ḥorim* and *seganim* (Neh 5:7) to give up some of their dues. These measures are commonly read as taken to alleviate the crisis resulting from the repair of the walls. It is also possible to understand these measures as part of a package routinely taken to finance the restoration of city walls. In that case, the crisis was written as a backdrop for the portrayal of Nehemiah in a particularly favourable light. The crisis is a foil for the writer to render to Nehemiah what belonged to the Persian Caesar of the time.

In favour of this interpretation, Josephus' reports that the costs of a later restoration of the walls of Jerusalem was off-set by a temporary tax-exemption granted by Antiochus III (*Ant.* 12.3.3.138-44) suggest that the Persian administration could have decreed a similar tax-relief to enable the local population to shoulder the burden of reconstruction while saving on the transfer of funds from the central administration to the periphery. The question is whether the administration waited for the extra burden imposed on the province to turn into a crisis before acting to relieve it or whether it dealt preventively with problems that were easily foreseeable by taking some basic fiscal measures to finance the building project. The historicity of the crisis in Nehemiah 5 hinges upon this question. That the text shows Nehemiah acting on his own accord and from purely religious motives is congruent with the ideology of the text and cannot be adduced to counter the notion that Nehemiah's decisions were in fact standard administrative measures.

7.2.5 A Self-Serving Crisis

Much like Albertz, Levine (1996: 245) comments that Nehemiah 5 shows that the *aḥuzzah* system was not working well. 'Judeans were foreclosing on each other right and left, reducing one another to virtual serfdom, and probably charging usurious interest to boot. The commandments of Leviticus 25 and 27 were not kept and thus the rights of individual landowners were not preserved'. Another sweeping prophetic statement! If people foreclosed on each other and everyone became his neighbour's serf, society was definitely evolving towards a unique and highly interesting model. This is obviously not what catastrophic readings of Nehemiah 5 imply.

Nehemiah 5 opens with three verses, each one beginning with the words 'there are some who are saying' (יש אשר אמרים, Neh. 5:2, 3, 4) as though the narrator signalled that he reported rumours. Scholars like to see in the threefold rumour three successive phases of degradation that would be found in Lev. 25:25-55 (§7.4), but it requires reading 'slaves' (ערבים) for 'many (רבים) in verse 2, a reading devoid of textual support (Seeligman 2004: 327; Houston 2008: 29). Tellingly, Nehemiah's angry reaction is not followed by the thorough investigation of the matter that one would expect from a responsible administrator. Nehemiah masters his heartfelt emotions (וימלך לבי עלי) and, rather than 'thinking it over' (NRSV), he immediately brings charges against culprits. The identification of their wrongdoing, however, is a matter of interpretation since verse 7 reads משה with either *sin* or *shin*, opening a range of translations from 'charging interest', 'requiring pledges to secure loans', 'foreclosure and seizing of collaterals' to 'pressing for repayment'. The roots נשה and נשא do not necessarily imply interest or the interest charged could have been a mere one per cent per month (מאת; Gross 1997; Kessler 1989: 57-69). That Nehemiah states that he and his entourage were also involved in silver and grain loans (verse 10, נשים) hardly helps in identifying the sin of the *ḥorim* and *seganim*. It is not even clear whether Nehemiah is confessing any wrongdoing or exculpates himself and his family of the abuses he denounces (Gross 1997: 275). Although Nehemiah includes himself in the exhortation of verse 10b to give up (נעזבה נא) interest, pledges, foreclosure or immediate repayment (משא, this time with the final *aleph*), the abuses he denounces must be different from what he reproaches the *ḥorim* and *seganim* for. If the nature of their sin remains unclear, they are convenient scapegoats, taking the blame after which the narrator can present Nehemiah as the one who takes the lead in soothing the taxpayers.

The identification of these measures is not any clearer than the sin of the *ḥorim* and *seganim*. The matter is one of loans of silver and grain whose repayment is deferred, the interest abandoned or the collaterals returned, but there is no way to tell the duration of the relief, forever or for a month, until the forthcoming olive harvest or until the next grain harvest. Nehemiah either proposes that they stop the clock so that the burden would not accrue during the famine or he requires the end of 'inappropriate demands for repayment of loans in a time of financial stringency' (Gross 1997: 277).

The imposed measures are but loosely related to the problems reported in the first verses. Rather than writing off interest or reversing a process of concentration of land as it is commonly understood, fields, vineyards, olive groves, houses, silver, grain, must and oil are 'returned', like the houses, fields and vineyards of Jer. 32:15 (Reinmuth 2002: 132). The return of means of production concerns the collaterals used for the repayment of antichretic loans (fields, vineyards, olive groves, houses). Nehemiah forbids the creditors from collecting their percentage of produce from the forthcoming harvest. This measure would not alleviate the famine mentioned in verse 2, as it seems to have already forced people to borrow food. Instead, the returned product could have been used to pay the king's tax mentioned in verse 4. Tellingly, nothing is said about the 'enslaved' children of verse 5. The silence is all the more significant since, in his indictment, Nehemiah mentions Jews sold to *goyim* and contrasts 'our' buying (back) of these brothers (strangely, the word redemption is not used) to 'your' trading of brothers (verse 8). Gottwald (1999: 7) suggests that because they had been sold abroad, nothing could be done about the unfortunate daughters. But the *ketib* of verse 2 does not mention slavery. Nehemiah's silence over the return of slaves makes more sense in the context of the repair of the walls. The pressure exerted by the lenders took the form of a general rounding up of every able body, children included, among their debtors to carry baskets. Directly in charge of the project, Nehemiah had no interest in imposing the liberation of the debt 'slaves' and sending the workers back home. In spite of the famine that would have exacerbated the crisis, the impressment of workers and the payment of the king's tax remained in force. The amount of grain, oil, wine, rents and interest not collected was compensated by the conscription for the restoration of Jerusalem. The conversion of produce into workdays supplied during a period of low agricultural activity was beneficial to the debtors who found a way to increase the employment of idle bodies. In the long term, it also benefited the creditors who gained an exclusive stake in the city whose construction they had financed.

If delaying the collection of produce makes sense, doubts remain concerning the famine. Had it been as severe as verse 2 implies, the pawning of assets to pay taxes and reimburse loans in a time of food shortage probably went against common practice since farmers were not liable for acts of God (Hudson 2002: 29). Hammurabi's laws §48 state that cultivators were not obliged to pay their debts when the storm-god eroded or flooded their field or if the grain had not been produced through lack of water (Richardson 2000: 58-59). The same clause is found in the series *ana ittišu*, a scribal school-book preserved in the library of Ashurbanipal (Maloney 1974). The same postponement of dues is found in Roman and Byzantine texts (Krüger 1959: 189; Kaplan 1992: 162-63). There is no need to imply that Hammurabi's laws were binding to Persian Yehud to suggest that the measures taken by Nehemiah were the least a governor would take during a famine. Commentators are fooled by the ideology of the text when they understand Nehemiah's measures as expressions of deep piety rather than normal procedures. If pawning one's assets in order to buy grain was common practice, it does not entail, as Choon Leong Seow (2008: 209) suggests, that there was no let up of imperial taxes in time of famine and that mortgaged properties were foreclosed when borrowers defaulted for reasons beyond their control. Arguing the opposite requires postulating that lenders did not shoulder their share of the risk involved in production.

By lumping together food relief, pledges, the king's tax and debt 'slavery' in verses 2-5, Nehemiah 5 paints a paradigmatic catastrophe, a backdrop for the presentation of Nehemiah as an ideal governor. To this aim, the narrative is more effective when remaining on a general level. Anticipating the public reading of the law of Moses in Nehemiah 8–9, Nehemiah imposes measures that echo various legal texts of the Torah as long as one does not get too specific. Such a rhetorical aim invalidates interpretations of Nehemiah 5 as social reportage and as proof-text for an acute structural crisis during the Persian period (Miller 2010).

Even if it did report an actual crisis, the situation depicted is far less dramatic than exegetes would have us believe. Gottwald explains that 'The lethal combination of taxes and debts conspires to thrust many peasants into destitution' (Gottwald 1999: 2-3). There are, however, no clues for destitution in Nehemiah 5. That the fields and vineyards in verse 5 are said to be 'for others' (לאחרים) entails no expropriation and no destitution in the sense of the loss of one's assets or one would have to consider destitute every person who mortgages a property. The implication of the complaints is that portions of the produce of the debtors were being used by the creditors for servicing the debts. Keen to darken the picture and render Nehemiah even more righteous than the text does, Albertz (1994: 495) qualifies this portion as 'the lion's share of the harvest', but if the Athenian *hektemor*s are anything to go by, it would not exceed roughly a sixth or so within the next six months, or the creditor would have to extend more credit in the form of seed and food to keep his 'milk cows' alive. A similar proportion is mentioned in the story of Joseph's enslavement of the Egyptians (Gen. 47:13-26 and §5.2), as the landowner's share in pre-1958 Iraqi sharecropping contracts (Poyck 1962: 56; Steinkeller 1981: 128) and as the share of the crop (17%) due by the tribes that accepted to farm land in Raqqa at the end of the nineteenth century CE (Ababsa al-Husseini 2002: 464). It seems that for millennia, the produce dedicated to servicing loans and rents oscillated between a sixth and a fifth of any harvest. Above that proportion, it made no sense to lend since farmers would not be able to afford a greater burden.[2]

As they have houses, fields, vineyards, olive groves and stores of oil, must and grain (Neh. 5:11), the debtors in question are neither poor nor destitute and there is no question of injustice (against Bodi 2002: 201-202). The only hint of injustice may be found in the claim that 'our' flesh is like the flesh of our brothers (כבשׂר אחינו בשׂרנו) in verse 5a. The verse continues with the mention of the children of the complainers that are not treated as the children of others. The insistence on equality disproves the notion that the text is dealing with the care of the poor and destitute. Nehemiah 5 writes a dialogue between people who insist they are equals and who suffer from a temporary problem of liquidity. Then, the complainers state that they are forcing their children to serve (אנחנו כבשים את בנינו ואת בנתינו לעבדים). There are accusations of favouritism regarding the work of children who are not all treated the same. The progeny of influential families (including Nehemiah's?) supposedly managed to escape some tasks, possibly compulsory work. Such accusations would be preposterous if the people who filed the complaint did not consider themselves as part of the elite as much as Nehemiah.

The text demarcates several social circles rather than social classes. The core is Nehemiah with his brothers and his servants (נערי, v. 10). Then, the *ḥorim* and *seganim* (Neh. 5:7) are urged to go in the fear of the Lord away from the disgrace of the *goyim* that are qualified as 'our enemies' (verse 9). Although the *ḥorim* and *seganim* are accused of doing no good (לא טוב) in verse 9, their return of assets and goods and their repentance brings them back in the fold. By contrast, Nehemiah and his core group merely abandon this *masha* (הזה משא). A larger group is constituted by the people that filed the complaint. Do they represent the entire population of Yehud?

The great assembly (קהלה גדולה) Nehemiah convoked against the *ḥorim* and *seganim* may give the impression that the entire population of the province was there to denounce the abuse of loan sharks. The narrator may well have suggested as much, but despite their presentation as the people (העם) in verse 1, this is no *'am ha'aretz*. They addressed their grievances to their brothers the Jews (אחיהם היהודים) and insisted that they were their equals. Hence, contrary to Gottwald (1999: 4-6), the envisaged complainers are not marginal cultivators expropriated by larger landholders and merchants. As brothers they ask a favour on the basis of their equality and proximity with the lenders. This exclusive brotherhood was a close-knit group of affluent people to whom belonged the governor himself. Against Gottwald (1999: 3), Nehemiah's claim that his entourage lent money and grain is essential to his presentation as an active member of the corporation and it shows that he was *not* 'above the fray' of contending parties. Nehemiah, or the people who told his story and used him as their key figure, belonged to the group that decided to share the burden of the restoration of Jerusalem among itself because it expected a quick return on investment. Their brotherly love excluded the rabble of the province as well as other elite that did not qualify as 'Jews'. It is rather ironic that liberation theology has taken Nehemiah 5 as a paradigm of economic redress when in fact, it secures the exclusive control of the resources of a region by a small clique (Severino Croatto 1997; Williams 2002). At this point, the identity of the *goyim*, the enemies of Nehemiah and of the *ḥorim* and *seganim* should be discussed.

7.2.6 Nehemiah versus Mizpah and Samaria

Beyond the narrow brotherhood of Jerusalem entrepreneurs that identifies itself as *Yehudim* and *Yehudaye* in the books of Ezra and Nehemiah, the measures imposed by Nehemiah had repercussions at the regional level. Grabbe notes that Nehemiah may have bankrupted some of the creditors whose loans he forced them to turn into gifts (Grabbe 1998: 191). We have no way to measure the impact of the deferring of the collection of produce on the creditors, but Nehemiah's measures were not necessarily aimed against the *ḥorim* and *seganim* who, as brother Jews (Neh. 5:1 and 5:8), were offered the opportunity to invest in what would provide returns as soon as the new administrative centre functioned. Nehemiah's measures excluded the *goyim* who need not be sought overseas. In the context of the restoration of Jerusalem around the reign of Artaxerxes, they would have included the Benjaminite elite operating from Mizpah that administered the province for the Neo-Babylonians for over a century. The restoration of Jerusalem placed the Nehemiah group in direct competition with the Benjaminite elite. The rivalry between the two centres is discussed further in the next chapter.

To conclude the discussion of Nehemiah 5, there is too much rhetorical bias in Nehemiah 5 to justify the use of this text as the indicator of a structural crisis. Tellingly, the famine would be the most common hardship but in Nehemiah 5 it appears as a mere add-on. The famine enhances Nehemiah's position by darkening the backdrop. As for the waiving of produce imposed by Nehemiah, part of it was compensated by workdays provided by the entire families on the walls of the new Jerusalem. The rest of the burden was an investment from which benefits could reasonably be expected by the group who financed the reconstruction and thus secured a privileged position in the administration of the province. It is in every taxpayer's interest to claim economic difficulties. Even more so for the members of the imperial apparatus who were in charge of collecting the revenues and transferring them to the royal treasury. The higher the position they held in the apparatus, the greater the political ambition of these men who became the protagonists of the internal struggles that plagued the second half of Achaemenid rule. Nehemiah's position was much lower than that of the famous satraps, but it nevertheless gave him a slot in the Great King's fiscal extractions that 'strengthened the hands of his potential enemies before they reached his own treasuries' (Stolper 1985: 150). Without going as far as rebellion, Nehemiah had every interest in downplaying the prosperity of Yehud.

Nevertheless, the self-serving aspects of the crisis provide indirect support for Albertz's notion of a split in the upper class of Judah into two camps. Albertz envisages a group that used the social crisis 'shrewdly and unsentimentally to its own advantage and was not very bothered about the social damage that it caused, and one which showed solidarity with brothers who were becoming poorer and at a considerable financial sacrifice sought to protect them' (Albertz 1994: 499; 1997: 119-20). Albertz places Nehemiah among the sentimental elite that behaved like Job, using their high position to rescue the poor, generously supporting the distressed with alms and respecting the right of life of their slaves and leaseholders, 'the exact opposite of the wicked man' (Albertz 1994: 500). Such a division between good and bad rich is probably a little too Manichean. Albertz's good aristocrats, among whom he identifies Nehemiah, sought first and foremost, like every elite, to secure and preserve their position. The elite that somehow financed the production and the transmission of the Book of Nehemiah some centuries after the 'crisis' was not self-sacrificial even if they were so sentimental that they became the fathers of the poor (Job 29:16) and paid their taxes out of their own pockets. Their concern for the poor was no less interested than that of modern relief organizations. They were taking care of what they saw as their best interests when they waived their rightful share of produce. Neither these good rich nor Albertz's anti-social aristocrats could afford exploiting their social base to such an extent that the peasants had nothing to eat and lost their children and their land as well. Foolish administrations do exist but they do not last for centuries on end, as social-scientist exegesis want them to last, in order to bridge the gap of their own making from the eighth century BCE to Nehemiah's time. Domeris (2007: 149-50) now prolongs the crisis into the Hellenistic and

Roman eras. An entire millennium of continuous structural crisis negates the very notion of crisis, or it empties the notion of crisis of its gravity.

The notion of a structural crisis is also aberrant from the point of view of the meaning of the adjective 'structural'. Outside the artificial universe of theological writings, crises can only be linked to a particular *conjoncture* or set of economic circumstances, Braudel's intermediate category of historical change between ephemeral events and the *longue durée*. In the absence of a meaningful and energetic intervention to adapt to the situation, a crisis evolves into major upheavals that correct the problem or the combination of problems that caused the crisis in the first place. For instance, a power that exerts too great a pressure on its constituents caves in to internal forces or is overthrown by the external enemy that had forced it to overtax its own economy. The historical structure is inscribed in the *longue durée* precisely because it survives the effects of circumstantial crises. Wars and famines were the main causes of crises. Such crises were both violent and brief but the economy had the ability to recovery rapidly or the society in question simply disappeared (Chandezon 2000: 239). Yet, the use of the concept of crisis in Persian Yehud is not entirely unjustified as long as it is not deemed 'structural' and as long as it is limited to the political sphere. The restoration of Jerusalem (on its date see the next chapter) can be deemed a crisis in the sense of a turning point as it inaugurated a new era. Rather than an economic or social crisis, it was mainly a political crisis provoked by the change of local dynasties. The Benjaminite elite that had served the Neo-Babylonians was losing its privileges to a new group that successfully contested its position thanks to the backing of the Achaemenids. Most importantly, however, the biblical text and Nehemiah 5 in particular, was the voice of the winning elite, not that of the underdogs.

Albertz also used a number of texts from the Book of Job to support the notion of a crisis during the Persian era.

7.3 Job Who Must Have Sinned but Never Did

On the trail of *the* crisis, Albertz identified a precise historical context for an earlier crisis that would have prompted the composition of the so-called Babylonian Theodicy, one of the prototypes of the biblical Book of Job. According to Albertz, the composition of the Babylonian Theodicy reacted to particular events that took place in the year 1083 BCE. On the strength of this precise historical anchor, Albertz identifies a similar crisis in the Book of Job which he dates during the Persian period, as it expresses themes similar to those developed in Nehemiah 5 (Albertz 1981). Because the Babylonian Theodicy uses the *topos* of the hunger of the poor and attributes it to the rise of a new rich class, Albertz could claim that such an ongoing crisis that pitched the pious rich against the impious rich was indeed 'structural'. Yet, the similarity in motifs attests first and foremost to the stereotypical nature of the depiction of social relations. The 'history' in Albertz's reconstruction is found mostly in the title of the article unless one insists on designating as crisis the tensions that prevail in the ordinary relations between the various groups that constitute a society, any society. Our ancestors were likely to be just as dissatisfied with what they had as we are and were likely jealous of what others had. Yet, anachronism is lurking when the social struggles that arose from the industrial revolution are applied to rural societies of the first millennium BCE. Slave revolts and bread riots occurred before the seventeenth century CE, but it is no accident that trade-unions and Socialism appeared *after* the industrial revolution and the subsequent rise in the general level of wealth that, if it did not make the poor poorer, certainly increased the difference between the richest and poorest elements in any given society. In terms of health hazards and rhythms, the infernal working conditions in mines and factories were far worse than any farm work. The concentration of large numbers of workers under such working conditions was conducive to the rise of corporate solidarity and a kind of struggle that could never develop among farmers who were dispersed far and wide and who enjoyed long spells of low farming activity that blur the distinction between leisure class and working class. While the various accusations of the evil ones in the Bible resonate with Marxist denunciations of the exploitation of industrial masses, they are but stereotypes of real conditions in rural societies. Historically relevant information can certainly be wrung out of stereotypes, but at the price of careful analysis in light of comparative evidence. So far, this type of evidence is not forthcoming.

Although it springs from a context characterized by far more blatant social injustices, the treatment of Job by Gustavo Gutiérrez ends up being less ideological than Albertz's. Commenting on Job 24:2-14, Gutiérrez (1998: 34) explains that when Job found himself in the situation of the poor, he realized that God takes up the cause of the poor. To deconstruct the theology of retribution, Job counters his friends' accusation expressed by Zophar's description of how the rich man plunders the poor man's hut to satisfy his avarice (Job 20:15-21) and Eliphaz's accusations of Job's despoiling his needy brothers (Job 22:4-9). From a strictly economic point of view, spoils taken from the poor, if they really are poor, hardly enrich the plunderer.

In the argumentation developed by Eliphaz, the despoiling of the poor is an attempt to justify God and find an explanation for the magnitude of Job's suffering. In a major turn-about from his mild and encouraging stance in chapters 4–5, Eliphaz postulates that Job must have been oppressing the poor (Job 22:6-9; Clines 2006: 550-51). Job's own description of the misery of the poor in chapter 24 is, however, no guilty pleading. It is a charge against God who does nothing about it. The description of the condition of the poor is 'rhetoric rather than social reportage, for it is hardly in the interests of any landowner to starve his labourers so that they become too weak to carry out their physical work' (Clines 1998: 809). Eliphaz does not claim to have any direct evidence of Job's misbehaviour towards the poor. He merely infers that Job must have committed grave sins to deserve his fate. As Job rejects these accusations, there is nothing in the Book of Job that could be taken as proof of an actual crisis. Eliphaz's is a case of *argumentatio ad absurdum*, but in their eagerness to indict the rich, exegetes take it literally.

Taking a pledge for nothing (חנם, Job 22:6), whether it is taken from a brother or from a stranger, is not taking a pledge at all. It is straight theft since the garment does not secure any loan. Taking the orphan's donkey and the widow's ox for a pledge (Job 24:3) is mentioned because it is an obvious deviation from regular practice. Making people work without providing shelter, drink and food (Job 24:6-11) is stated because it is nonsensical from the point of view of both the workers and their employer. No doubt such things did happen sometimes but if they had represented regular practice their mention in this context would have defeated the rhetorical aim of the argument between Job and his friends. Glimpses of what is considered acceptable may nevertheless be found interspersed as counter-examples in the list of abuses. For instance, the 'man of arm' in Job 22:8 (איש זרוע) is rendered as a powerful man who steals all the land because he bought the favours of the authorities:

> ואיש זרוע לו הארץ ונשׂוא פנים ישב בה
>
> The powerful possess the land, and the favored live in it. (NRSV)
>
> as if the land belonged to the powerful, as if only the privileged should occupy it. (Clines)
>
> And you made favorites of some and settled them on the land. (NETS)

Job 22:8 seems out of place and interpreters have often emended it to tie it better with its immediate context and turn it into another accusation against Job (Clines 2006: 540-41). The idea of a 'powerful man' derives from the LXX that renders איש זרוע as ἐθαύμασας, 'you honoured'.[3] The translator was obviously baffled by נשׂוא פנים. He dropped 'the land' from the first part of the verse and replaced it with פנים from the second part of the verse, connecting πρόσωπον with τινων. The *New English Translation of the Septuagint* rendered both words as 'some', completing the erasure of the troubled 'raised faces' (Cox 2007: 683).

The expression 'man of arm' (איש זרוע) has proved equally troublesome. In Hebrew, it is never used to denote power. Only in English could a 'man of arm' be a *gendarme*. The Syriac remained much closer to the Hebrew than the LXX and read זרוע as זרע rendering it as a 'sower'.[4] This in turn suggests an agricultural sense for the 'lifted of faces' in the second part of verse 8. Commonly rendered as 'honoured ones' in light of 2 Kgs 5:1; Isa. 3:3 and 9:14, the faces in נשׂוא פנים could refer to surfaces of ploughed land, lifted up by the plough.[5] When the *waw* at the beginning of verse 8 is understood as adversative rather than consecutive, the verse is a reminder of the right of occupancy for anyone who sows uncultivated land, a right that Eliphaz suggests Job must have infringed upon. The same modification of the common translation of the word 'arms' can be applied to verse 9 where the 'arms of the orphan' (יתמים זרעות) may be understood as the *seedlings* of the orphans. The word 'seedling' is attested in Lev. 11:37 (זרוע) and in Isa. 61:11 (זרועיה). In the context of land in the previous verse, trampling young plants makes more sense than crushing orphans' arms. Together, Job 22:7-9 can be rendered as follows:

> 7 You must have given no water to the weary and you must have withheld bread from the hungry,
>
> 8 although the land should be for the man who sows and the one who ploughs its surface should reside in it,
>
> 9 you must have sent widows away empty-handed while the orphans' seedlings were trampled.

This translation does not solve all the problems presented in verses 8-9 but the sower in verse 8 recovers a possible biblical reference to the right of occupancy of waste (dead) land (*ihya al-mawāt*; Doumani 1995: 164) while the orphans' seedlings suggest the existence of orphan mortmain estates (*awqāf*; §1.4.7).

The very verses used in support of a structural crisis can be read as clues for the existence of the kind of latter practices that provided relief to the landless and to the orphans.

Were the above translation rejected and the traditional renderings maintained, Job 22:7-9 could not be adduced as clues for an economic crisis and social abuse since Job lists all the good he has done to the poor to disprove his friends' accusation and to cut short the notion of retribution (Job 29:12-17; 31:16-22, 38-40). In establishing his moral integrity, Job also annihilates the notion that his disaster has taught him the divine preferential love for the poor. If Job cared for the poor when he was a rich man, he is innocent and his losses did not teach him anything new. For the cause of the poor, it would be better to have Job repenting of his previous selfish life, but this is the friends' point of view, a point clearly rejected by Job and by God who vindicates unrepentant Job and accuses his accusers of having spoken wrongly (Job 42:7). The divine pedagogy is a figment of exegetical imagination (Krüger 2007; Guillaume 2007). Job had been on the side of the poor all along.

It is significant that the divine speeches steer clear of the moral and ethical concerns that drove much of the dialogues between Job and his friends. Therefore, Gutiérrez (1998: 87) abandons the language of prophecy (the title of part II) and he closes the study of Job with the notion of contemplation (the title of part III). Thanks to God's speeches, Job realizes that God's love operates beyond justice. Apart from a few theological niceties, such a lesson contributes little to the cause of the poor. In Marxian pharmacopoeia, such contemplative theology would belong to opiates since Gutiérrez (1998: 94) admits that when Job left the world of the rich to enter the world of the poor, he took the path of gratuitousness, not the path of justice. Gutiérrez is wise to say nothing about the epilogue where Job finds himself twice as rich as previously. Disturbed by this ending, many exegetes downplay its significance by stating that it is secondary. Yet, with or without the epilogue, the Book of Job negates the notion of a breakdown of social solidarity. The suffering of the poor is presented as an unlimited evil that is use by the friends to accuse Job and by Job to accuse God (Grenzer 2007). Self-righteousness is the name of the game, a game where the poor are but a foil.

Still, reproaches expressed in Job 3:14-15; 15:28 and 20:19 are sometimes presented by some scholars as aimed at the Judean population that was not exiled and lived in destroyed cities (Vermeylen 1994: 122-24). Although they are clearly not held responsible for the destruction, their occupation of the ruins is considered sinful because the destroyed places were under some special curse (see Josh. 6:17-24; Isa. 13:20; Jer. 51:26) or because the ruins were the dens of demons (Isa. 34:14; Vermeylen 1994: 119-21). A less esoteric explanation is possible when the 'ruins' (חרבות) are understood in light of the Palestinian Arabic *khirbe* that designates a satellite settlement. These settlements were temporary villages where people resided in shacks or in ancient ruins during ploughing and harvest times because they were too distant from their home base. The occupation of these 'ruins' indicated economic expansion and prosperity rather than decline. When people felt there was a new market for surpluses, the most enterprising expended their production by going further afield to put waste-land under the plough. As long as waste-land was plentiful and free, the best way to increase production was to increase the sown surface. In the first years, the new fields produced high yields that excited the jealousy of the people who remained in the village and predicted that the wealth of those who stayed in ruins to cultivate new fields would not endure (Job 15:29). Therefore, the occupancy of ruins indicates an expanding economy rather than a deep structural crisis. Other clues of a healthy economy can be found in the narrative framework of the Book of Job.

7.3.1 Job's Mother

The reference to Job's mother in Job 1:21, 'Naked I came out of my mother's womb and naked I return there', remains enigmatic unless one accepts that, in desperation, Job expresses the hope to return to his mother's womb. In light of Sir. 40:1d, 'Hard work was created for everyone, and a heavy yoke is laid on the children of Adam, from the day they come forth from their mother's womb until the day they return to the mother of all the living', the mother in question can be understood as a personification of the earth into which Job hopes to be interred soon (Vall 1995). The existence of a concept of a mother-earth elsewhere in the Hebrew Bible is, however, debated (Beentjes 2000; Reiterer 1994). A different suggestion derived from the world of ancient economics is possible.

The word *andarārum* related to the Hebrew *derōr*, 'release' (Lev. 25:10; Jer. 34:8; Ezek. 46:17), translates the Sumerian word *amargi* 'returning to mother'. In *amargi*, the element *ama*, 'mother', is metaphorical. It connotes the origin as it does in the Akkadian expression *tuppāt ummātim*, 'tablet of previous status' (Charpin 1986). *Amargi* signifies a return to the 'mother' situation, to the original economic status, usually through the return of pledged assets to their original owner following the waiving of debts or upon the retirement of an antichretic loan (Charpin 1987: 39). Hence, Job's oft-quoted words do not refer to his impending death or the womb of the mother-earth but to his financial situation at birth, stark naked and utterly destitute. This is how the translators of the LXX understood it. They rendered אשוב as ἀπελεύσομαι from ἀπολύω, a verb that conveys notions of 'release, relief, acquittal, freeing', in particular release from debt (Liddell and Scott 1996: 208). Hence, γυμνὸς καὶ ἀπελεύσομαι ἐκεῖ, literally 'naked I am released here', refers to Job's release from his obligations towards his debtors rather than his physical return to a hypothetical womb. Rendering 'naked also shall I return there' (Cox 2007: 691) translates the Hebrew rather than the Greek.

With this standard legal formula found in a modified form in Qoh. 5:14 (אמו ערום ישוב ללכת כשבא כאשר יצא מבטן), Job acknowledges the loss of his assets and declares himself bankrupt (Vogels 1994). To justify his insolvency, Job states that 'YHWH has given, YHWH has taken' (Job 1:21), which, as a case of *force majeure*, automatically releases him from financial liability, as bankruptcy does in modern economies. The ability to declare himself in a state of bankruptcy comes in addition to the fact that Mesopotamian farmers were not liable for acts of God and were not obliged to pay their debts when the storm-god eroded or flooded their field or if the grain had not been produced through lack of water (Richardson 2000: 58-59; Hudson 2002: 29; Kaplan 1992: 162-63). These measures give the lie to the common claim that two bad harvests in a row were enough to push farmers into an infernal spiral of destitution from which they had no chance to recover (§5.4.3).

Stating that YHWH has taken away what he had given, Job warns his business partners that due to an act of God he is broke and no longer able to honour his standing obligations. He also informs his dependants and clients that they should not rely on him for help any more. Therefore, the connection of nakedness with the maternal womb signifies destitution, not destination. In Qoh. 5:14 the naked return is not to the mother's womb but to the nakedness of his birth rendered by the expression 'as he came out' (כשבא). In Job 1:21, the place (שמה) towards which Job returns is not his mother's womb but the absolute poverty of the new born. Likewise, Deut. 28:48 connects nakedness (עירם) and destitution (חסר; Mathewson 2006: 55). Hence, Job's return to the mother's womb is a metaphor of Job's utter destitution. 'Naked I came out of my mother's womb and naked I return there' means 'I have become as destitute as when I came out of my mother's womb'. Contrary to the standard depiction of the infernal spiral of debt, Job's utter destitution did not turn him into a debt-slave nor did it enrich his creditors. The infernal cycle of destitution is yet another figment of the exegetical imagination.

7.3.2 *The Acquaintances'* qeśiṭah

Readers and commentators of the Book of Job focus upon the divine speeches and Job's final words (Job 42:1-6) and tend to dismiss the prose epilogue of the book as irrelevant (Hostetter 2005). Yet, a careful reading of Job's return to social life yields some interesting results. Having quenched divine folly by interceding for his friends, Job sees his brothers, sisters and acquaintances flocking back to his table (Job 42:11; Guillaume and Schunck 2007; Guillaume 2008). They bring comfort to the survivor and console him for the evil YHWH brought upon him (Greenberg 1983: 261). As Job had already found comfort when he saw God (Job 42:6), comfort other than spiritual must be meant here (Habel 1985: 585). Before his restoration, Job had cried out, 'my brothers are treacherous as a torrent…in the time of heat they disappear' (Job 6:15-17), and 'my relatives and my acquaintances have failed me, the guests of my house have forgotten me' (Job 19:14-15). Consolation comes with a price tag. To make up for having failed him during his darkest hour, those who abandoned him gather around Job's table with presents. Each guest gives Job a gold ring. Although the number of guests is not provided, the text twice states, 'each' and 'one', insisting that quantities are significant:

> ויתנו לו איש קשיטה אחת ואיש נזם זהב אשחד (Job 42:11b)

Besides the gold ring, each guest offers one *qeśiṭah* (קשיטה). Following ancient versions (LXX, 11QTarg. Job, Syriac), the *qeśiṭah* is translated as a 'lamb' or a 'ewe', although the attested meaning of the root קשט fits the context of the gold rings better than lambs. The root is well documented in the sense of 'dividing, splitting, apportioning, instalment' (HALOT III, 1150). The words *qesiṭah* and *taqsīṭ* are current in banking vocabulary to designate paying a debt in instalments (Barthélemy 1935: 663; Wehr 1979: 892). In light of the use of the word קשיטה in Gen. 33:19 (// Josh. 24:32), the *qeśiṭah* is a means of payment by which Jacob buys a pasturing share near Shechem:

> ויקן את חלקת השדה אשר נטה שם אהלו...במאה קשיטה
>
> He bought a share of the field where he had pitched his tent…for a hundred *qesiṭah*.

As a means of payment, the *qeśiṭah* refers to any asset, animal or currency. Besides a ewe, it is often understood as a coin (Guillaume 1968: 13, 140) or as a fraction of a shekel (Knauf 2008: 200). The shekel was indeed divided into a number of fractions from one half to one sixty-fourth.[6] Yet, none of these fractions had a name bearing any resemblance to a *qeśiṭah*. Moreover, it is rather uncommon to designate a large sum by an even larger number of smaller units. Were a *qeśiṭah* say a quarter of a shekel, one hundred *qeśiṭah* would have been expressed as 25 shekels rather than 100 *qeśiṭah*. Rather than a currency, the meaning of payment instalment makes more sense. Jacob could have agreed to pay for the field share in a hundred instalments of an unspecified amount. The amount is necessarily left open since it would be a fraction of the yield of the crop or of the flock. As a sharecropper, Jacob divides the yield between the sons of Hamor and himself. The translation of *qeśiṭah* as 'lamb' is not erroneous in itself since Jacob the shepherd would hand over to his landlord a number of animals in exchange for the use of land around Shechem, but 'lamb' is not the primary meaning of the word *qeśiṭah*. A *qeśiṭah* is an instalment for the repayment of a loan, a splitting of dues into smaller sums. Hence, Jacob's one-hundred *qeśiṭah*s relate either to the duration of the contract or to the number of instalments, not to a lump sum paid once for all. In a situation where land is not a commodity, what is sold is not the land but its usufruct paid yearly at the time of the harvest. One-hundred *qeśiṭot* are spread over one-hundred years, which corresponds to a very long sharecropping contract. In the case of Jacob, it signifies the willingness of Jacob and Shechem to establish long-term relations bound by matrimonial ties. It is not clear when a land market emerged (Jakobson 1971), but the proportional rates of the rental fees due for agricultural land display a great stability that indicates the absence of a supply-and-demand price pattern (Renger 1994: 189). In Persian Mesopotamia, land granted to soldiers (bow land) was underused (Stolper 1985: 149). It is during the Hellenistic and Roman eras that a land market of sorts arose. Hence, it is not surprising that the notion of lamb for *qeśiṭah* appears in the Greek translations (except for Symmachus).

In the case of Job, what each guest brought besides a golden ring did not necessarily take the form of hard cash, silver or sheep. It was not even a gift. Rather, family and acquaintances granted extensions of the duration on loans contracted by Job before his troubles. The rings helped Job forgive his acquaintances for letting him down at his darkest hour, while the *qeśiṭah* covered a number of credit operations. As the richest individual of the Orient, Job's wealth was mainly represented by and tied up in assets such as land, houses, slaves and herds (Job 1:3). Job would have lent assets to his business associates, his acquaintances and his clients. He would also have had recourse to borrowing, for instance to invest in joint ventures such as *ḫarranu* contracts (Lanz 1976; Radner 1999a).

The golden ring each guest gives to Job represents payments of sums owed to Job. Given Job's recent desperate situation, these rings could represent arrears. The death of Job's heirs had led his debtors to consider the payment of their debts towards Job less than urgent. When Job fell sick, they simply stopped paying altogether and waited to see whether he would survive at all since they knew that there would be no heir to claim the sums they owed to their father. Job's recovery forced his debtors to resume reimbursements of loans they had neither anticipated nor budgeted for. Hence, the gold rings soothed Job the creditor who found himself in urgent need of fresh funds to make up for his losses.

As a typical ancient businessman, Job was in the position of debtor as well as creditor. The *qeśiṭah* each guest gave to Job represented a credit moratorium granted by his acquaintances who agreed to delay repayment of sums he owed them and split them into several instalments. It is also possible to extend the notion of *qeśiṭah* as instalments to sums owed to Job that the guests paid back to Job besides the gold rings and which supplied Job with fresh funds to get started again.

Hence, behind the spiritual readings of the narrative framework of the Book of Job, understanding the mother in 1:21 and the *qeśiṭah* in 42:11 in concrete financial terms enhances the connexion and the coherence between the prologue and the epilogue. Continuing in this line, the *qeśiṭah* brought by Job's creditors also involved restitution of pledged assets they had, rashly as it turned out, seized outright when Job was struck with misfortune. Before the disastrous heavenly wager, Job would have pledged assets in their favour as security or collateral in the event of his defaulting on the repayment of any loan he had obtained from them. Goods pledged by a borrower in the ancient Near East were considered the temporary property of a lender until full repayment of the principal, when the lender would return the pledged goods to the borrower (Menu 1998a: 392). In Egypt, it is not before the reign of Pharaoh Apries (589–570 BCE) that evidence of real guarantees, that is, pledges on assets as shown in Aramaic contracts (rather than solemn or sacramental oaths that, if broken, entailed corporal punishment and a financial penalty) are found (Menu 1998a: 390). In the case of antichretic pledges, lenders retained for themselves in lieu of interest any yield that the pledged goods might render, for example, rent from a house, produce from a piece of land or the young of sheep, camels or cattle (Wunsch 2002: 238-44). These assets were not destroyed when Job's herds and servants were struck because they were in the hands of Job's creditors, who, on Job's declaration of insolvency (Job 1:21), would have seized them outright. Hence, the pledged goods, no longer being part of Job's assets, were safe from destruction by the satan. Once he was back in business, Job would need additional credit and more time to make up for the complete loss of his other, unencumbered (i.e. unpledged) assets before he could start paying off his arrears of debt. Only upon his full repayment of all outstanding debt would his creditors cancel the pledges that he had given them as collateral for the loans they had granted him. The return of divine favour gave confidence to his creditors who would have welcomed his reappearance and restored prominence within the business community with its consequent expectations of great returns for all of them. The inventory of Job's new assets in the next verse confirms that their patience and speculation were well rewarded.

Understanding the *qeśiṭah*, Job's mother and the orphans' seedlings as elaborate institutions and practices leaves little room for using the Book of Job to prove the existence of a crisis. In light of its continued use as a technical term to designate a credit instalment, the *qeśiṭah* confirms the principle also found in the story of the widow's oil (§7.1), that credit is an essential ingredient to a healthy economy and that only in extreme cases do debts lead to destitution. Elijah's advice to the widow was to borrow. Job's recovery involved renegotiating terms for the repayment of loans and the return of pledges. This view of credit challenges the common notion that economic recovery is only possible through cancelling debts. No study of credit in the Bible could be complete without considering Leviticus 25.

7.4 Yobel *and* šemiṭṭah

According to the sabbatical calendar, the *shofar* is sounded twice, on the first day of the seventh month, at every year for Teruah, and ten days later on the day of *Kippurim* every 49th year. The jubilee is not a year as suggested by the common designation of the 'year of the jubilee', but a particular day, the tenth day of the seventh month of every seven Sabbaths of year (Lev. 25:8-9).[7] Because the jubilee coincides with the day of *Kippurim* when the yearly load of sins of the children Israel is cleared thanks to the scapegoat that takes carries it away (Lev. 16:21-22), the jubilee is often understood as a release of debts.

7.4.1 No Debt Release on the Jubilee

The idea that the jubilee entails the cancellation of debts is reinforced by the fact that the word *derōr* in Lev. 25:10 derives from the same root as the term *andarāru* that designates Mesopotamian edicts of easements decreed at the beginning of a reign, after a war and following a famine (Villard 2007). Stated in almost every study relative to the jubilee (Bibb 2009: 31; Hamidović 2007: 16; Milgrom 2000: 2174; Habel 1995: 104; Wright 1990: 179; North 1954: 188), the view that the jubilee implied the release of debts was already held by Josephus who wrote that the jubilee released both slaves *and* debts (*Ant.* 3:282). Today, the jubilee inspires the Jubilee 2000 campaign that militates in favour of debt cancellation for severely indebted countries. Yet, halfway between Josephus and the Jubilee 2000 campaign, Maimonides (1979: 392) stated that 'The differences between the Sabbatical year and the jubilee year are as follows: the Sabbatical year cancels cash debts, while the jubilee year does not' (Jospe 1997: 96; Domeris 2007: 150; Fager 1993: 58; Ginsberg 1932: 389). A cursory look at Leviticus 25 shows Maimonides a better exegete than Josephus, at least on this particular point.

Contrary to the *šemiṭṭah* (שׁמטה) of Deuteronomy 15 that clearly cancels debts (§7.4.7), the biblical occurrences of the word *derōr* besides Leviticus 25 concern the release of slaves (Isa. 61:1; Jer. 34:8-20) or of land (Ezek. 46:17), never the waiving of debts. Nor does the 'release in the land for all its inhabitants' (דרור בארץ לכל ישביה) delineated as 'you will return each to his tenure and each to his family you will return' (ואישׁ אל בשׁפחתו תשׁבו ושׁבתם אישׁ אל אחזתו, Lev. 25:10b) imply any debt cancellation. The originality of the jubilee is that the release of all pledges is not the result of the cancellation of debts but of the fact that all loans reached their term together on the tenth day of the seven month of year 49. On that date, every loan granted since the previous jubilee has reached its maximum extension in time. Obviously, most loans granted during the previous 49 years had shorter terms and most pledges were returned before the jubilee, but the aim of the jubilee is to make sure that once every 49 years *all* running loans expired, not through cancellation but through the synchronization of their maximum term.

Naturally, the jubilee did not exclude periodical cancellations between jubilees, but it must be clear that debt cancellations are irrelevant to the jubilee. The jubilee cannot be explained in light of Mesopotamian *andurārum* edicts. In fact, these edicts did not cancel every type of debt. The 'fine print' of one such edict specified that only debts with dates of repayment that had not expired were cancelled, whereas on the day of the jubilee all dates of repayment were reached, every loan expired and so there were no debts to cancel. The same principle applies to the regulations concerning the release of Hebrew 'slaves' after seven years of service in Deut. 15:12-18 and after six years of self-leasing (ימכר *niph'al*) in Exodus 21:2-6 (Propp 2006: 190).

This type of self-bondage slavery is a work contract that may or may not result from destitution. The work serviced an antichretic loan which amount could not exceed the value of six or seven seasons. The amount of the loan was proportional to the amount of work required. It need not imply residence with the master or full-time employment. After the given number of years, the pledge was released, not because the creditor was particularly generous, but because the loan had been paid back in full through the work of the borrower. Exodus 21:3-11 and Deut. 15:12-18 underline the voluntary aspect of these work contracts with the possibility that some people may find a permanent tie to an employer preferable to self-employment and that the employer may provide a wife to a worker to consolidate or secure his services on a permanent basis.

Apparently, overdue debts were excluded from the release in *andurārum* edicts. Otherwise debtors would have been in the position of delaying repayments in view of an impending edict. The crucial difference between *andurārum* edicts and the jubilee is that the jubilee occurs on a date fixed in advance and known to everyone concerned. Had the jubilee entailed cancellation of debts, the risk of having debtors postpone repayment until the jubilee would have become institutionalized practice. Borrowers would have had every interest in delaying repayment of debts, with the obvious consequence of closing all access to credit, unless clauses against the jubilee were specified on the contract (Milgrom 2000: 2246; Villard 2007: 111-18). In Leviticus 25, there is neither *prosbol* nor a pious exhortation for lenders to be generous before the next debt cancellation as there is in Deut. 15:7-11 (see §7.4.7) because there are no debts to cancel on the jubilee. All pledges are released because all loans are fully reimbursed.

7.4.2 Maturity of Antichretic Loans

The return of all pledges on the day of the jubilee does *not* restore an equilibrium that was upset by insolvency. Leviticus 25 is often read in light of prophetic denunciations of the rich and described as ending the gradual destitution of indentured farmers who lost their land and ended up as slaves until their debts were waived, allowing their physical return onto the land from which they had been alienated (Milgrom

2000: 2191-98). Against Houston (2008: 189), the jubilee offers no 'fresh start for the wretched of the earth' for the simple reason that Leviticus 25 deals neither with the poor nor with the restoration of a purported original distribution of tribal land. What Milgrom (2000: 2193-98) presents as Stage One of the cycle of destitution (Lev. 25:25-28) does not involve the sale of part of the family land of an impoverished landowner because 'trading from his tenure' (מכר מאחזתו, Lev. 25:25) is not a transfer of real estate. The verb *mkr* is broader than the simple action of selling and the word 'tenure' (*'aḥuzzah*) does not refer to freehold property (§1.3.2), contrary to the particular case of urban property in verses 29-30. What is at stake in the rest of Leviticus 25 is the pledging of assets to secure loans with the produce of one's land tenure. The borrower is obviously *not* on the path towards irreversible destitution or the creditor would not grant him a loan. Claiming that the creditor wilfully grants the loan in order to increase his landholding defies the logic of credit. Grain merchants, the main source of credit, were interested in marketable produce, not in land (§6.5).

The principle of the jubilee is that after 49 years all antichretic loans have reached maturity. It is important at this stage to shed all notions of land sales. The jubilee does not set the price of land but the size of loans (Lemche 1976: 49; Skolnik 2007: 624). Having reached their term, all pledges—land as much as persons and animals—are released and returned to the possession of their previous possessor. The return accomplished on the jubilee is a stereotyped expression attested from the Sumerians to the Ptolemies for the release of pledges (Weinfeld 1995: 159; Radner 1999b: 269-71). It will be argued below that with its long cycle of 49 years, the jubilee does not concern farmers (§7.4.5). Imagining, for argument's sake, that the jubilee did concern farmers, at the jubilee indebted farmers would not move back to the farm they once owned and lost since in most cases farmers worked the land they pledged to secure loans since they had no other foreseeable resources. The borrower worked the pledged land while the creditor collected a portion of the harvest. The 'return' affected neither the ownership nor the possession of the land. The jubilee marked the term of the loan and the end of the creditor's hold on a portion of the debtor's produce because the loan was fully reimbursed. The same applies to the debt-slaves who usually went to work on the creditor's farm when they were needed and otherwise stayed at home. The jubilee marked the end of their duty towards the creditor. Unless they had actually moved to their creditor's farm, debtors did not physically return home. The return was not the consequence of a cancellation of debt but the result of the synchronization of loans which were granted at most until the date of the next jubilee.

7.4.3 No Stages of Gradual Destitution

The translation and interpretation of Leviticus 25 is daunting. Technical terms are vague and the argumentation is contorted. Hence, it has become the rule to explain the jubilee as halting a process of destitution in several stages each marked by the occurrence of the root *mwk* in verses 25, 35, 39 and 47. In fact, verse 25 refers to a brother who finds himself in need of credit. The need is not destitution but a temporary shortness of funds. The brother is considered creditworthy by another brother because he has valuable assets to pledge and he is likely to secure sufficient revenues in the foreseeable future. Were it not so, the whole notion of the self-redemption of the pledge in verses 26-27 and again in verse 49 would be a sham. The situation of the borrower envisaged as 'Stage One' is that of a man of means whose creditor considers creditworthy.

To support the notion of a downward spiral of debt, Milgrom adds the word 'further' in parenthesis in his translation of the next mentions of the root *mwk* in verses 35, 39 and 47 (Milgrom 2000: 2147). By this device, Stage Two (Lev. 25:35-38) receives the title 'Lost land' (Milgrom 2000: 2147, 2204). In fact, the passage deals with a brother whose hand fails his brother (מטה ידו עמך, Lev. 25:35), a case of default. Land is not mentioned except in the theological note of verse 38. The defaulter is not someone who 'incurred a crop failure on his reduced property (which, to begin with, probably supplied only a subsistence level) and he was forced to take out a new loan' (Milgrom 2000: 2204). To support the notion of an impoverished farmer, Milgrom has to add that through the default on the second loan the farmer 'lost his land, but the produce is still his' and that 'he rents the land from the creditor' (Milgrom 2000: 2204-2205). There is neither land loss nor a further loan here, only a problem in the reimbursement of loans, any loans. I argue below that there is no farmer either (§7.4.5).

In light of verses 44-46, Stage Three (Lev. 25:39-55) is read as debt-slavery. Yet, Milgrom notes the conspicuous absence of the provision for redemption attested for 'stages' One (and Four, see below). Milgrom's explanation is that the Israelite slave is not a slave and thus needs no redemption. He is a resident hireling whose work amortizes the principle (Milgrom 2000: 2216). This scenario is described in Lev. 25:39-40:

וכי ימוך אחיך עמך ונמכר לך לא תעבד בו עבדת עבד כשׂכיר כתושב יהיה עמך עד שנת היבל יעבד עמך

and when your brother is short (of cash) towards you and he pawns himself to you, you will not make him serve a servitude of slavery. As day-labourer, as resident he will be with you until the year of the jubilee he will serve with you.

Because he reads these verses as a consequence of worsening conditions experienced by the same brother as the one mentioned in stages one and two, Milgrom understands that the brother has now lost his land to his creditor and becomes a labourer on his own land, working for the new landlord. According to Milgrom, the impoverished brother 'no longer enjoys the usufruct of his forfeited land. Nonetheless, his status is not that of a slave, but of a resident hireling; he receives wages, all of which pay off the debt' (Milgrom 2000: 2212-13). Milgrom (2000: 2221) considers כשׂכיר כתושב a hendiadys and compounds the two words as a 'resident hireling,' which he claims is different from a simple hireling because he lives with his family on the landowner's property like a Californian migrant farm worker who receives room and board from his employer .

Schenker considers verses 47-54 as a fourth stage of destitution, this time that of a brother contracting loans from non-brothers, members of a rival elite (Schenker 2000b). Redemption of the pledged assets is advised and self-redemption is mentioned again, showing that destitution is not envisaged. The borrower retains the option of servicing the loan through the pledge until the jubilee. In all cases, the jubilee regulates credit between creditworthy people: 'When you pledge something or someone to your fellow do not cheat each other. The number of years until the jubilee will regulate the amount secured by the pledge. The amount will be proportional to the years until the jubilee since what you are pledging is only the produce' (Lev. 25:14-16). The jubilee regulated the size of loans that was determined by the number of harvests until the jubilee, both parties having thus the assurance that principal and interests would be paid in full. When entering into any capital loan arrangement, borrower and lender, knowing exactly when the next jubilee will be, fix the size of the loan accordingly. The 'count of years after the (previous) jubilee' (Lev. 25:15) determines the number of years until the next jubilee. The fewer years to run, the lesser the loan because there are fewer harvests ahead. The number of years left to run till the next jubilee determines the maximum amount of loans corresponding to a fair 'return' on that capital. The mathematics is extremely simple and the fact that every transaction is limited in time delineates each party's interest and obligations. The jubilee provides a yardstick for the term of the loan. The value of the loan is easily determined in number of years of average yield; borrowing and lending cannot exceed the remaining years before the next jubilee. In such a system, it would be a foolish lender indeed to lend over and above the value of the expected yield in number of harvests. There may be minimal shortfalls, if the yields have been poor, but that is the risk the lender is taking. The whole point and beauty of the jubilee is that it regulates credit and eliminates the need for debt cancellation because the size of loans is proportional to the number of harvests that can be realized on the land pledged to secure the loan before the full usufruct is returned to the tenure holder. With the jubilee-linked scale based on the residual value of the produce of the land, all leases come to an end at the jubilee when every debt has automatically been paid back in full. There are no outstanding debts left. By setting in advance a deadline by which all loans must have reached their maturity, Leviticus 25 renders debt cancellations irrelevant. The automatic release of all pledges purged the credit system and allowed fresh loans to be extended on the basis of unencumbered assets.

7.4.4 Utopian and Impractical?

In practice, 49 years is a very long time, far in excess of credit requirements of ancient farmers whose needs rarely exceeded a few years at most. Today, a farmer would indeed borrow over a longer period to finance the acquisition of expensive machinery, but in biblical times (as in developing countries today), the vast majority of farmers were smallholders whose main concern was to find the resources to cultivate the next season of crops. Smallholders needed finance to procure seed, to buy a draught animal and acquire a few basic implements to dig, hoe and harvest. Most costs could be written down within the growing season. Unless the jubilee was less than three years away, the whole notion of debt cancellation was irrelevant. When some unforeseen event occurred (drought, pests, natural catastrophe, raids and plundering) that might prevent repaying the loan, the *šemiṭṭah* of Deuteronomy 15 released arrears due on survival loans to small farmers, as was the case in Mesopotamia, but on a seven-year basis (§7.4.7).

Viewing the jubilee as cancelling debts, Houston (2008: 203) points out that the utopian character of the jubilee is no disqualification of its status as an icon of justice. In fact, the jubilee promotes justice because it is *not* utopian. Because credit did not lead to dispossession, lenders and borrowers kept debt-ties alive as long as possible by postponing reimbursement or by contracting new loans as soon as the previous ones were reimbursed (§5.4). If not, the jubilee would have been irrelevant. Had most borrowers been sucked into the spiral of debt and lost their patrimony through foreclosure, it would have been unnecessary to set a compulsory expiry date on all loans. The jubilee, however, did not break the cycle. On the morrow of the jubilee (day 11 of month 7), lenders could start lending again. The economic advantage of the jubilee was the clearance of pledges, a problem that becomes extremely complicated if loans do not expire regularly and the same assets become mortgaged 'to the last brick'. The jubilee purges the system of pledges by freeing all assets twice per century. The aim is not the protection of the inalienability of arable land or the fight for an ideal justice, but the sustaining of the viability of the credit system through the regular extinction of ties on assets. The failure to practice a general release regularly produces a type of tenure system, observed in Africa and in China, characterized by an extreme complexity of rights that enabled the use of land in credit operations without totally extinguishing residual claims (Macauley 2001). After a century or so of steady demographic growth, however, the number of individuals holding legitimate claims over any given asset becomes so large that residual claims stifle credit. Pledges cannot secure any further loan because in theory they still secure a number of previous loans. At the same time, the amounts of produce or land held by each claimant become meaningless.

7.4.5 A Brotherhood of Patrons

Once it is clear that the jubilee does not entail any release of debt, it is necessary to consider the implications of such long cycles of 49 years. The situation envisaged in Leviticus 25 is not relevant to farmers whose borrowing needs are limited to a few years at most. Besides the crucial difference between the release of debts during the seventh year (see §7.4.7; 9.2) and the release of pledges at the jubilee, the difference in duration is likely to reflect differences in the type of transactions and the amounts involved. Hence, I suggest that the jubilee concerns a brotherhood of patrons. Each patron had a clientele of farmers to whom he lent grain. Patrons, however, needed credit as much as their clients since credit is essential to commerce as much as to agriculture. Patrons could only maintain a significant network of clients if they could provide resources when clients experienced shortages. The notion of the rich automatically improving their position over the poor from the simple fact that they are rich is a fallacy because wealth does not eliminate risk (§4.5). Moreover, patrons were competing with other patrons for clients (§6.2), which in turn made it even more important for patrons to have access to sources of credit to supply grain to their clients in times of dearth.

Whereas the sabbatical year has the broadest possible scope, embracing the entire land and even the wild animals (Lev. 25:2-7), the jubilee-regulated system concerns a narrow circle. The words 'for you' (לכם) appear three times in verses 10-13. In verses 14-17, 'your fellow' (עמיתך) is followed by 'your brother' in verses 25, 35, 47-48 (אחיך). Regulations relative to urban property in Lev. 25:29-30 support the view that the brothers in question were no ordinary farmers. In the narrative framework of the desert fiction, the fellow is an Israelite (Milgrom 2000: 2177; Baker 2009: 87), but the brother is not. As the measures of Nehemiah 5, the jubilee regulations reflect competition between elites rather than the protection of the poor (Fitzpatrick-McKinley 2003: 28-32). The jubilee applies to transactions between a brotherhood of patrons. When dealing with farmers, brothers acted as patrons and practised the seventh-year debt release (§7.4.7). In their dealing with each other, the brothers practised the jubilee because the sums engaged were much larger than those granted to farmers.

Therefore, the presence of two different financial cycles, the seven years of the *šemiṭṭah* and the 49 years of the jubilee, indicates the existence of two main categories of credit. On the one hand, agricultural loans were granted by patrons to clients in the form of grain with a short cycle of debt cancellation. The aim of agricultural credit was the appropriation and the control of labour rather than making money through lending (§5.4.3). Therefore, keeping farmers alive was imperative. To this aim, arrears were cancelled after seven years (§7.4.7). On the other hand, commercial credit in the form of grain and silver took place between merchants and the elite, that is, between equals. Since the sums involved were much larger and the risk much greater than was the case with agricultural credit, commercial debts were not cancelled. For the same reason, the edict of Ammisaduqa excludes all assets engaged 'for business travel, for partnership' from the debt cancellations granted to farmers, shepherds and other producers (Hallo 2000: 363). Hence, to the social differentiation between patrons and clients corresponds the distinction between *šemiṭṭah*-regulated credit and jubilee-regulated credit. Rather than reading the jubilee in light of the *šemiṭṭah* and see it as but another round of debt cancellation in favour of the poor, the jubilee regulated commercial loans.

The sums engaged in commercial loans were much larger than those granted to farmers and they also offered the greatest opportunities for profit since they involved interregional trade that made the most of the price difference beyond the local level. Logically, commercial loans involved higher risk and higher interest rates than agricultural loans (§5.3.2). To 'beat the market' and pool their resources, merchants could organize themselves in corporations such as those associated with the biblical and extra-biblical *marzeaḥ* and the Greek *symposium* and *thiasos* (Carter 1997; Matthäus 1999; McLaughlin 2001). While research has focused mainly on the funereal context of these institutions, the *marzeaḥ* had broader functions (McLaughlin 2001: 66; Miralles Maciá 2007: 264). Upper-class men formed closed associations of brothers under the patronage of a deity. Membership was reserved for the elite and it was not all-inclusive. More than one *marzeaḥ* could function in any one city (McLaughlin 2001: 68). Each association owned buildings and land. The *bene-haggolah* mentioned in Ezra 9–10 are presented as members of such an exclusive association, the *qehal haggolah*. The members are called out to assemble in Jerusalem within three days to resolve a marriage issue. Absentees from the general assembly would be ostracized and their property confiscated by the group, revealing the economic implications of the affair. The Judeo-Babylonian *qehal* had great powers over its members and much autonomy to run its own commercial activities (Blenkinsopp 2001: 63-67). The members were called to celebrate the Passover together (Ezra 6:21). Drinking wine together was an important expression of the solidarity that united the members of a *marzeaḥ*. Besides drinking wine, the members of a *marzeaḥ* conducted transactions involving large amounts of money (McLaughlin 2001: 67), presumably joint business ventures such as caravan (*ḫarrānu*) and maritime partnerships among others.

Properly speaking, joint ventures involve no loans. A joint venture does not consist in one party extending a loan to another; it is a pooling of business interests through a joint investment in a one-off project and a sharing of the accompanying risks. If the joint venture meets with success, the profits are split between the parties but the investment of each is foregone should the venture fail.

Joint ventures, however, do not preclude loans granted between brothers. Such loans are mentioned in Lev. 25:35-38, which forbid interest on loans granted to 'your brother' (אחיך). The NRSV's translation of the word 'brother' as 'kin' is misleading. It points towards family solidarity and verses 35-38 are read as Stage Two in the debt spiral (§7.4.3). If the brother here is not a fellow farmer but a fellow patron, a member of the same commercial association, verses 35-38 set down the golden rule that secures the loyalty of the brothers and the cohesion of the brotherhood. Interest and penalty for delay in repayments are banned between brothers. Credit is extended free of charge entirely on confidence. Within the closed circle of the association, the 'brothers' grant interest-free loans to each other, stand together in legal solidarity, pawn the association's assets, and have a tacit agreement not to intrude on each other's networks of clients. Such commercial loans are granted to equals by equals who count on a justice based on calendrical mathematics rather than on a justice based on charity. Justice forbids cancelling debts since it would automatically break equality and endanger the creditworthiness of the entire brotherhood. Debts between brothers must be honoured at all cost. For this reason, Job cannot count on any forecoming *šemiṭṭah.* He warns his business associates of his losses immediately because his insolvency affects them directly (§7.3).

The suggestion that the jubilee applies to a brotherhood of patrons rather than to farmers throws a fresh light on the cryptic formula in Lev. 25:35b (עמך והחזקת בו גר ותושב וחי). The main problem is the understanding of the words 'resident and alien' (גר ותושב) that stand unconnected to the previous verb. The LXX adds ὡς in front of 'resident alien', which becomes the description of the status of the defaulting brother: 'Now, if your brother is needy and with you becomes weak in his hands, you shall help him *as* a guest and a resident alien, and your brother shall live with you' (NETS). The common understanding is that of a defaulting family member who is brought in to live physically with his brother. Yet, the text does not stipulate that the brother should live as a brother but (as) a resident alien.

What is the status of a resident alien? Ten verses earlier, in Lev. 25:23, the very same words are used in the plural (גרים ותושבים) to describe the status of the members of the intended audience, presumably every son of Israel to whom Moses' speech is addressed (Lev. 25:2). The implication is that every son of Israel living in Canaan is but a resident alien of YHWH to whom the land belongs (כי לי הארץ). Rendering גרים ותושבים in verse 23 as 'aliens and tenants', but גר ותושב in verses 35 and 47 as a 'resident alien', the translators of the NRSV resisted the notion that the defaulting brother residing with his creditor was reduced to the status of an ordinary fellow Israelite. Yet, if every son of Israel is a resident alien, the demotion described in verse 35 is not that of an Israelite that becomes a non-Israelite, but that of a brother in a commercial association who loses his membership and is treated as an ordinary Israelite. The brother patron is reduced to the status of a client. The brother becomes an obligee, a client to his former brother who is now his patron. For this reason, the end of the verse abstains from describing the resident alien as a brother: resident and alien he will live with you (גר ותושב וחי עמך). Two manuscripts of the LXX and of the Samaritan Pentateuch added the word 'brother' here, imitating the finale of verse 36. This, however, should not be followed precisely because verse 36 deals with the alternative that involves abstaining from charging interest and compensations so that brothers will be less likely to run into financial trouble. The argument is that abstaining from charging interest will ensure that your brother will continue living with you as a brother (וחי אחיך עמך) rather than as the defaulter of the preceding verse who lost his position as brother.

Instead of describing Stage Two of the destitution of a defaulting Israelite freeholder (§7.4.3), Lev. 25:35-38 prescribe interest-free loans to reduce the risk of default between members of a narrow circle of brothers. The same can be said about verses 39-43. Instead of describing an actual Stage Three of destitution of a freeholder, they depict the bleak consequences of a hypothetical defaulting brother as a warning. It is not a farmer who is in danger here but any member of a commercial association that would allow taking interest among its own members. Denying interest-free loans from each other could endanger the creditworthiness of the entire association. A defaulting brother would soon end up being taken care of by his creditor as a 'Californian migrant farm worker who receives room and board from his employer' (Milgrom 2000: 2221). Contrary to Milgrom's claim, the resident hireling (כשׂכיר כתושב) could not pay off the debt and receive wages as well (Milgrom 2000: 2221). Moreover, he would lose his equal status of brother and end up as a burden to rather than an associate of his creditor. The status of brother precludes charging interest while the brotherhood excludes ordinary Israelites. Fellow Israelites are clients to whom interest is charged but whose debts are cancelled on the seventh year. By contrast, the debts of brothers are never cancelled but nor are they charged interest.

The problem in considering all Israelites as resident aliens is that verses 45-46 consider the alien residing among you (התושבים הגרים) as the sole category of residents in Canaan from whom it is possible to buy servants or slaves (עבד ואמה) as perpetual tenure transmissible to one's heirs. At this point, it becomes extremely difficult to figure out the difference between a resident alien and an alien residing among you, if the slight modification of the phraseology is at all intended to convey any difference in status. Commentators do not accept to equate ordinary fellow Israelites with the alien residing among you and insist that they are not Israelite, since verse 46b states that slaves may be bought from the alien residing among you 'but as for your fellow Israelites, no one shall rule over the other with harshness' (NRSV). Milgrom insists that 'the *gēr* was not admitted into the peoplehood of Israel'. The *gēr* might become rich, achieve high social status, totally assimilate into Israelite society to the point of being a zealous worshipper of Israel's God, but 'he retained his ethnic label and was not reckoned an Israelite' (Milgrom 2000: 2231).

The problem with this distinction is the interplay between verses 44 and 45 concerning who it is allowed to buy chattel slaves from. Verse 44 states that they can be acquired from the *goyim* that are around you (הגוים אשר סביבתיכם). Verse 45, however, adds that chattel slaves may also be bought from the sons of the aliens residing among you (התושבים הגרים עמכם). As the Israelites are themselves YHWH's aliens and residents or resident aliens, the text comes dangerously close to arguing that slaves may be bought from the children of Israelite neighbours.

To preserve the distinction between the *gēr* and the real Israelite, Milgrom (2000: 2231) evokes Ruth, Ziba, Uriah, Doeg and Zelek as examples of prosperous *gērîm* who attained a high social status at the court and in the army. They were totally assimilated into Israelite society to the point of being zealous worshippers of YHWH, and yet, they retained their ethnic label and were not reckoned as Israelites. The problem is that none of those figures is designated as a *gēr*. Instead of evoking the books of Ruth and of Samuel, it seems preferable to argue that the solution is found in verse 46b: 'but among your brothers the sons of Israel, each among his brothers, you will not exploit him brutally'. Again, the NRSV clouds the issue and renders the brother as a fellow Israelite. Yet, the repetition of the brotherhood that immediately follows, 'each among his brothers' (איש באחיו), makes it clear that it is the status of brother that forbids enslavement, not the status of son of Israel. The difference between brother and fellow Israelite is maintained consistently throughout the chapter. Members belonging to the same commercial brotherhood are called to grant each other interest-free loans rather than foreclosing and turning their associates into slaves.

The failure to grant preferential credit conditions to brothers in need could lead to foreclosure because commercial loans are at stake. The social boundary runs between members and non-members of the same brotherhood, not between Israelites and foreigners.

In verse 35, the problem of a brother's self-sale is envisaged as a hypothesis to be avoided, not as a solution. The verb החזקת and the verb ἀντιλαμβάνω, by which the LXX renders חזק, here convey the sense of 'seizing' as well as the sense of 'rescuing'. Choosing the more aggressive option of seizure in the sense of foreclosure, Lev. 25:35-37 can be rendered as follows:

> 35 When your brother is short and his hand defaults towards you, you would have to seize him and as [LXX] any *gēr* and resident he would have to live with you. 36 (Therefore) do not take from him any interest and accrual for you must fear your God. Your brother among you he should remain (as long as possible). 37 (To this aim), do not advance your money to him against interest and against accrual do not advance his food.

Instead of stipulating that the brother should be taken as resident in the creditor's home, the phrase 'he would have to live with you' closes the description of the consequences of a hypothetical foreclosure of the debtor's assets in verse 35 before verses 36-37 stipulate interest-free loans to avoid the situation described in verse 35. That foreclosure would entail the loss of ownership of the defaulter's domicile clearly indicates that the brother is not a farmer living in a village hut. He lives in a house within a walled city. Hence, the discussion in verses 35-37 presupposes the distinction between urban and rural property in verses 29-31. Urban property is freely tradable and alienable but rural property can only be pawned and it has to be released at the jubilee. The foreclosure of a farmer's assets would not lead to his displacement and his loss of domicile. He would stay at home and work his land for the creditor as argued above (§4.5.3).

Verses 39-41 concern exclusively the brother and demonstrate how unpractical it would be to seize the defaulting brother's property given the general principle of the jubilee delineated in verses 10-13:

> וכי ימוך אחיך עמך ונמכר לך לא תעבד בו עבדת עבד (Lev. 25:39)
>
> If your brother, being (further) impoverished under your authority, is sold to you, do not make him work as a slave. (Milgrom 2000: 2147)
>
> When your brother defaults towards you, he would have to sell himself to you, you would not be allowed to make him work as a servant.

כשׂכיר כתושב יהיה עמך עד שנת היובלבו יעבד עמך (Lev. 25:40)

He shall remain under you as a resident hireling; he shall work under you until the jubilee year. (Milgrom 2000: 2147)

As a hireling, as a resident he would be with you until the year of the jubilee.

ויצא מעמך הוא ובניו עמו ושב אל משפחתו ואל אחזתו ישוב (Lev. 25:41)

Then he and his children with him shall be released from your authority; he shall return to his kin group and return to his ancestral holding. (Milgrom 2000: 2147)

And he would move away from you, him and his sons with him and he would return to his kin and to his tenure he would return.

Verses 39-41 pick up again the case of the defaulting brother evoked at verse 35. This time, the impossibility of making the defaulting brother work as a servant/slave underlines a second time how unprofitable foreclosure of a brother's asset would be and how much better it is to grant each other interest-free loans. Members of the same association should stand in unlimited solidarity. They stand and fall together. This type of solidarity, however, cannot extend to all fellow Israelites. The difference between the fellow (עמית) and the brother is clearly stated in verse 14:

וכי תמכרו ממכר לעמיתך או קנה מיד עמיתך אל תונו איש את אחיו (Lev. 25:14)

When you sell property to your fellow, or buy (any) from your fellow, you shall not cheat one another. (Milgrom 2000: 2146)

When you make a deal with your fellow or buy from your fellow do not be hard in business with your brother.

The 'fellow' and the 'brother' can be seen as parallel synonymous terms (Milgrom 2000: 2177), but doing so closes access to the intricacies of the entire jubilee pericope. Resisting the confusion of the brother with the fellow Israelite reveals that the request to grant special facilities applies specifically to the brother. The mention of the fellow in the first part of the verse indicates that it is not forbidden to grant facilities to fellow Israelites too, but the advice turns into a requirement when dealing with a member of the same trade guild. Because the sums invested by brothers in commercial ventures were much larger than the survival loans granted to farmers, the seizure of a brother's urban home or his indenture was to be avoided on two counts. First, his work as a servant or slave for his creditor would only cover his living expenses but would never be sufficient to make up for losses incurred during commercial operations. Milgrom (2000: 2223) claims that having no interest to pay, the debtor could apply all his wages to amortizing his debt. Rather than the absence of interest, it is the amount due that is significant here. Only trade operations could fetch the amounts of profit necessary to absorb losses incurred through commercial ventures. Hence, the only way to recoup debts was to tide the debtor over and hope that he would have more success in his next transactions. Second, foreclosure between brothers would send negative signals to clients and to rival guilds as to the creditworthiness of the brotherhood. Every brother of the guild would suffer. Again, it was better to cover up the difficulties encountered within the association. The demotion of a brother, his loss of equality within the guild, would negatively affect the entire group. Given the psychological factors involved in the perception of creditworthiness, the guild had to project a faultless image to the outside world.

Hence, it is crucial to maintain the distinction between the brother and the fellow in Leviticus 25. The survival of the inner circle of brothers is predicated upon the practice of a radically different type of social justice than the one imagined by standard interpretations of the jubilee. Nevertheless, the equation of the brother with the fellow Israelite occurred in the Diaspora where associate brothers and fellow Jews happened to be the same persons. Although it was not the situation envisaged by the text (see §10.4), the fusion of the fellow with the brother gave rise to the generalization of the ban on interest to fellow Jews, Christians and Moslems. The present development of Shariah banking based on the ban on interest supports the hard-core realism of the regulations transmitted in Leviticus 25.

7.4.6 No Land Reclamation

Another approach to the jubilee is the so-called 'land-reclamation' hypothesis. As the argument goes, Leviticus 25 was penned by returning Judean exiles or their descendants to legally justify the repossession of lands lost to the people who stayed in the land. Understanding the jubilee as stipulating that land must be returned to its original owners and 49 years as the time between deportation and return, the proponents of the land-reclamation hypothesis claimed that the jubilee provided the exiles in Babylonia with a legal basis for reclaiming ancestral lands in Canaan that had been lost during the years of their absence (Chaney 1991: 138; Ellickson and Thorland 1995: 403; Bergsma 2003: 226-30).

John Bergsma (2003) easily uncovered the problems underlying the land-reclamation hypothesis. There is no trace in Leviticus 25 of a land dispute pitting returning exiles and non-exiled Israelites. The jubilee supposedly benefited the priests and the small peasants at the beginning of the Persian era. Yet, there is no trace of a priestly grab for power in Leviticus 25 since the jubilee regulations work independently from priestly prerogatives. As for the independent small farmers, this category was not deported by the Babylonians. Hence, the jubilee had no particular relevance to reclaim land they had never lost.

Other scholars desperately searched for traces of jubilee-like practices before the destruction of Jerusalem to establish the antiquity of biblical laws, to little avail (Milgrom 2000: 2241-71).

Once the jubilee is seen as regulating credit among a small brotherhood of patrons rather than the return of land for destitute farmers, the search for the origin of the jubilee takes a new turn. The different groups identified by ethnic markers (Jews, Ammonite, Samarian, Moabite, Arab) were not fighting over land as such. The recovery of ancestral landholdings seized by those who remained in the land was *not* the main concern of the 'Jews' returning from Babylonia. The severe depopulation of the Southern Levant caused arable land to be lost primarily to thorns and brambles. The ban on sowing enforced every sabbatical year (Lev. 25:2-7) dealt with the brambles by forcing all the farmers to clear new land instead of working their fields. When so much land lies uncultivated, when so many villages are abandoned or almost empty, fighting over land makes no sense whatsoever. The idea of large waves of returnees scrambling for Palestinian land is a transparent projection of twenty-first century CE issues back to the fifth century BCE. The return from Babylonia during the Persian era left no archaeological traces (Lipschits 2005: 372). It was less numerous than suggested by the Bible and there are no clues in the Bible that the returnees were fighting for land. They are presented as settling back in their places of origin without any problem (Ezra 2:70; Neh. 7:73) and pressure was necessary to force a mere ten per cent to settle in Jerusalem because 'the city was wide and large, but the people in it were few and no houses had been built' (Neh. 7:4 and 11:1). There was no struggle over land between new settlers and the people that were not deported.

After 70 years (the minimal period of their absence), the claim of the children of the exiled elite over whatever land their parents held had long lapsed. After 70 years of continuous habitation and cultivation, the claim of any squatter would stand as good as ownership in front of a court anywhere in the world. Nevertheless, the land reclamation hypothesis remains popular (Meyer 2005: 288; Domeris 2007: 161; Lowery 2000: 69).

If some family members were left behind, the Babylonian cousins simply came back home without dislodging anyone. Or imperial policy dictated that newcomers settled in empty areas (Hoglund 1991: 57-60). Imagining as Pastor (1997: 14) does that people were sent from Babylon 'endowed with money, position, and royal support' to displace the local farmers and force them to 'move to marginal farming areas' would defeat all economic logic and would have been a sure recipe for disaster. It would have made more sense to leave them in Babylonia.

Land tenure never was an issue, neither in Leviticus 25 nor in any of the 25 centuries between the destruction of Jerusalem and the rise of Zionism. What the restoration of Jerusalem as a Persian administrative centre exacerbated was the rivalry over prebends and over the access to agricultural surpluses. Because over-abundant land had little value apart from the produce that could be grown on it, and because growing food required manpower that was in short supply, the obvious way to secure loans was through antichretic pledges. Land was inalienable, not because it was forbidden to sell it but because no one was interested in buying it. Neither the Neo-Babylonians nor the Persians had any interest in undercutting local elites. Absolute state ownership of the land is too expensive for most states to implement and is thus bound to remain vague (Moghadam 1990). Due to the practical limitations of maintaining central control over all land, co-opting the elite into the imperial apparatus of revenue extraction is more economical. This means sanctifying customary practice through the writing of divine law approved by the state (Macauley 2001: 340). Scholars tend to imagine ancient states in light of the full-blown modern states they know. Modern states achieved unprecedented levels of control over their territory thanks to the implementation of complex techniques of control, measure and registration which enable effective tax collection. Without these techniques, ancient states had to rely on the local elite with which it competed for revenues. Instead of being in collusion for the ruthless exploitation of the poor of the land, the king competed with the local elite that itself competed with other groups of local grandees for the control of the agricultural surplus. Every strong ruler achieved his position at the expense of the elite rather than at the expense of the farmers. As soon as the central state weakened, landlords interposed themselves between the ruler and the farmers. Ancient social relations were not so much class struggles as struggles between individual patrons who vied with each other for the control of clients (Horsley 2007: 58-62).

These thoughts are certainly not the final explanation of a text as complex as Leviticus 25. They should open new perspectives on the jubilee, a jubilee that entails no debt release, no land reform, and no land redistribution. Such a jubilee is not relevant to the poor. It regulates credit among a closed circle of patrons belonging to a particular elite that borrowed from each other amounts much larger than they lent to farmers. Hence, terms longer than the standard seven years of Deuteronomy 15 were necessary. Debt cancellations made sense for small amounts lent to farmers as they strengthened the patrons' hold over their networks of clients. Within the inner circle of patrons, however, debts had to be honoured at all costs in order to preserve the economic position of the corporation.

7.4.7 The šemiṭṭah *as Debt-Cancellation in the Context of Patronage*

Once the nature of the jubilee is clearly distinguished from debt cancellations, the *šemiṭṭah* (שְׁמטה) of Deuteronomy 15 appears as the sole biblical parallel to the Mesopotamian *andurārum* edicts. It cannot be presumed that the jubilee and the *šemiṭṭah* should be integrated together within the same economic vision since they belong to two separate legal collections. It is not even certain that these texts were ever meant to be applied as such. Yet, to get beyond the common recourse to utopia, the above credit simulation (§5.4) integrates the *šemiṭṭah* and the sabbatical year in the model as if they were both practised. The aim is to offer a simulation that could help exegetes realize that the purported utopian nature of these texts derives mostly from our failure to perceive ancient economics. Even if Deuteronomy 15 and Leviticus 25 were written by different scribes whose sole aim was to concoct intricate theological pies in the Jerusalem sky, the material they used derived directly from their daily practice. The writings of the handful of literati who penned those texts contain some reflections of actual life in Persian Yehud. For this reason, any attempt to reconstruct the history of this period should seek to retrieve these reflections. Obviously, it is necessary to sieve the theological embellishments and our model will hopefully contribute to show that the *šemiṭṭah*, the sabbatical year and the jubilee are not as utopian as they appear to modern readers.

The impact of the *šemiṭṭah* may be compared to the edict promulgated by Ammiṣaduqa (1646 BCE). J. P. J. Olivier claims that the 'fine print' of the edict limits the cancellation to debts with dates of repayment that had not expired. 'Otherwise debtors would have been in the position of delaying the repayments of their debts in view of an impending edict' (Olivier 1997: 20). Since there is no 'fine print' in Deuteronomy 15, it seems that the *šemiṭṭah* applied to every type of debt and was thus far more generous than Ammiṣaduqa. The *šemiṭṭah* could be considered utopian since it did not take into account economic exigencies. At this point, however, we are confronted with a problem of translation.

Although the Chicago Assyrian Dictionary (1999: 315, vol. R) indicates two different senses for *ribbātum*, 'arrears' and 'remainder, remnant', the translators of the edicts have settled for 'Rückstände, arrears' (Kraus 1958: 37; 1984: 155; Olivier 1997: 14; Hallo 2000: 362). This is problematic if Finkelstein (1969: 55) is correct when he claims that the edict cancelled only debts and obligations incurred *up to* the date of effectiveness of the edict or if Olivier is correct in his understanding that the cancellation concerned 'only those debts of which the date of refund had not expired' on the date the edict came into effect (Olivier 1988: 230; 1997: 15). In common speech, 'arrears' can designate any outstanding or owed quantities besides lateness in paying a debt or meeting an obligation (Collins 1994: 83), but specialists reserve the term arrears to 'amount of any past-due obligation', that is, that was not paid back on due-date so is now overdue (Dows and Goodman 1987: 19). In this case, arrears were excluded from Ammiṣaduqa's cancellations and the rendering of *ribbātum* as 'balance' is preferable (Lieberman 1989: 254). The presence in paragraph 5 of stipulations concerning the punishment of lenders who forcefully recovered debts prematurely, before the impending edict (Sweet 1986: 599) supports the notion that only the balance of amounts outstanding for loans that had not yet reached maturity were cancelled and that amounts overdue remained owing.

If the edict did not cancel arrears, it rewarded good payers and creditworthy borrowers, but in no way did it alleviate the situation of those who were behind in the repayment of their dues. Moreover, the edict sets up a precise date, 'the second day of the month of Addar' of year 37 of Ammiṣaduqa (Olivier 1997: 15), whereas the *šemiṭṭah* intervenes in the seventh year. Besides the absence of a precise day and of fine print to reduce the number of beneficiaries, the crucial difference is that the year of the *šemiṭṭah* is known in advance, contrary to the unpredictable Babylonian edicts. Olivier (1988: 230; 1997: 15) insists that if the date had been known in advance, borrowers would have had every interest in delaying repayment of debts, with the obvious consequence of closing all access to credit, unless clauses such as Hillel's *prosbol* were specified in the contract to protect the lender from the effects of a cancellation (Milgrom 2000: 2246). This is surely incorrect since it contradicts Olivier's own claim (1997: 20) that the edict did not cancel arrears. The opposite must be true. Debtors had to make sure to pay what they owed in time, if necessary by contracting another loan in order to benefit from the next cancellation. Therefore, the difference between the unexpectedness of the Akkadian edicts and the regularity of the *šemiṭṭah* becomes negligible. Neither institutionalized the risk of having debtors postpone repayment. Rather, the *šemiṭṭah* fostered patronage. Because they knew they would be expected to cancel the balance owed to them on the seventh year, lenders are exhorted to be generous before the *šemiṭṭah* (Deut. 15:7-11). There are reasons to think that the exhortation was hardly necessary and that the *šemiṭṭah* did not prevent lenders from lending grain during the sixth year and that the *šemiṭṭah* did not encourage farmers to delay reimbursing their loans until the seventh year.

Agricultural loans, even today, do not exceed one year's duration (they have a tenor of 12 months at most, except in cases where the loan is not to finance working capital needs but a long-term project such as land development with irrigation, buildings etc.). The farmer in antiquity would have borrowed grain as soon as possible after the harvest if his crop yield proved insufficient to meet all his needs for the coming 12 months (in modern financial terms, the credit he obtains would come under the heading of 'working capital finance'). His working capital needs consist in grain to feed his household, pay taxes, rent, and any overdue interest he has had to capitalize and any principal he has not been able to repay from previous years' borrowings.

Bearing in mind that, for practical reasons, a lender would make loans to a farmer in grain rather than in silver (you cannot plant silver, and what the farmer actually needs is seed for sowing and grain for feeding his family), it is always wise for a farmer to borrow seed/grain rather than silver with which to buy seed/grain from another source because by borrowing and then repaying in the same commodity as that which he produces, he does not expose himself to any risk of losing out on the transaction as a result of market price fluctuations that would affect the value of grain (e.g. a good harvest might result in over-supply, which would drive down grain prices; cheaper imports from abroad would also drive down prices, even in the case of a poor harvest). Today, gold-mining companies often prefer to borrow in gold rather than in dollars or another hard currency because this protects them from the vagaries of price fluctuations (Carew 1996: 159). Whatever the price of gold, they know in advance that if they borrow 100 kg of gold, they will have to pay back 100 kg of gold, which is the commodity they produce. Export companies that trade commodities priced in US dollars, for instance, tend to borrow in US dollars to avoid getting caught out if the US dollar were to rise sharply against other currencies.

The main problem farmers and lenders faced was the impossibility to foresee the forthcoming crop yield five months ahead of the time when borrowing would be necessary. A good level of early rains before sowing does not guarantee a good harvest. What both the farmer and the merchant know is that grain value rises sharply when supply is scarce and falls when there is an over-supply. The farmer's main concern is to ensure that he has sufficient grain to feed his household and dependants, sow his fields, pay his taxes and rent and purchase essential goods for his livelihood and basic comforts. The merchant's concern is to ensure he has access to a regular and reliable source of commodities that he can count on that will enable him to trade locally and possibly abroad at a profit, thus providing him with a livelihood. So he and the farmer might envisage one or other of the following schemes.

Scheme A: market price. In the event of a plentiful harvest, the farmer undertakes to sell his surplus grain (i.e. any grain that is in excess of his needs and local storage capacity) to the merchant at an agreed price. The question of price is a separate issue, which needs to be discussed. What matters here is that the farmer receives an immediate compensation for his surplus. The merchant then decides what he does with the grain: he might store some as a reserve for future loans to farmers or until market prices rise; he might export a portion abroad; and he might trade some against other commodities. In any event it is not the direct concern of the farmer. In the event of a poor harvest, the farmer borrows from the merchant the shortfall in grain needed over the next 12 months when the price of grain is low. Or, to pay less interest, the farmer may decide to borrow before sowing time, six months before the harvest, or at any other time up until the harvest. In any case, the rise of the market price of grain compensates the reduction of the amount paid as interest. At the end of the following harvest, assuming the yield is adequate, the farmer pays back the merchant the amount of grain borrowed plus interest. If the yield is inadequate, the farmer continues to borrow, his debt grows and the interest accrues at a compound rate. After a number of successive poor harvests (probably more than four; see §5.4), the farmer might find himself in a debt spiral unless the *šemiṭṭah* intervened.

Scheme B: insurance premium. The farmer and the merchant reach an agreement where the farmer hands over to the merchant all grain in excess of his needs and local storage capacity without necessarily receiving payment in return. Obviously this is an oversimplification. In practice, every case is different. Yet, the principle at work here is that the farmer agrees to convert his surplus into an insurance premium rather than asking for immediate payment. The farmer and the merchant save themselves a lot of expenses by exchanging the roles of creditor and debtor rather than assets. Instead of transporting grain backwards and forwards, the merchant credits the farmer's account after a good harvest and agrees to provide the farmer with grain to make up for any shortfall resulting from a poor harvest. The resulting advantage to each is as follows:

1. In good years, the merchant receives the farmer's excess grain at no cost to himself and disposes of it as he wishes. To make the most of his surplus, the farmer may decide to find a buyer for his grain, in which case he would undercut the local merchant, but he would have to take upon himself the cost of transport and transaction risks and he will find it hard to access grain at a decent price in times of dearth. Unless he has at his disposal the connections and the resources to do the work of the merchant himself, the farmer is unlikely to obtain better conditions than those offered by the local merchant. The farmer who has spare sons and beasts can more easily gain some extra revenues by offering transport facilities to the merchant whose capacities after the harvest are sure to be overloaded.
2. In bad years, the merchant lends the farmer the amount of grain that he needs over the next 12 months as a result of the harvest shortfall. The farmer thus has covered himself against the risk of an inadequate crop yield. The merchant, who has been acting as an insurance provider by compensating the farmer for his misfortunes, can rely on the farmer for future supplies of grain when harvests are plentiful. The farmer in effect pays the merchant an insurance premium when the harvests are plentiful and receives indemnities when they are poor.

Under scheme B, the farmer-merchant partnership ensures that (a) there is a safety-net for the farmer in times of misfortune and that he will not starve; (b) the land, which is in plentiful supply, will have a greater chance of continuing to provide grain by farmers who have the skills to produce grain but are themselves not in plentiful supply; (c) distribution of grain to the population, especially city-dwellers, will be better assured and the principle of food security is enhanced; (d) overall surpluses in excess of the needs of the country at large can be traded abroad and provide revenues or commodities that will benefit the country's economy. Under scheme B no interest is charged, no guarantees or pledges are given, peasants are not enslaved or taken into bondage other than having to give a commitment to pay their insurance premiums in the form of excess grain to their merchant-partners.

A third scheme can be added to the above schemes, a variation of scheme B, involving facilities rather than loans. In modern terminology, a 'facility' is the amount of credit that a lender agrees to extend to a borrower on stipulated terms and conditions. A 'loan' is the actual amount that the borrower draws down from the 'facility' that the lender has granted him and which is 'outstanding', that is, to be repaid to the lender at a due date. A 'facility' may be in place without the borrower having yet drawn down from it. For instance, a lender might grant a borrower a facility of a hundred units of commodity but the borrower may decide not to draw any of it down if he does not need it. Or he may draw down a portion of it only, corresponding with his needs. In the case of a farmer who knows he will need to borrow grain after a poor harvest, he may come to a standing arrangement with a lender (say a merchant who regularly purchases surpluses of harvested grain) to supply him with grain according to his needs. The lender would agree to grant the farmer a 'facility' upon which the farmer could draw in years of poor harvests, and which he would repay when the yields are adequate. A modern equivalent of such a facility is the bank overdraft.

In this sense, one could say that there is indeed a permanent arrangement between the lender and the farmer because the facility is 'rolled over', that is, automatically renewed each year. As long as a facility remains in place, the assets pledged to secure the loan also remain in place and would only be called if the farmer's debt spirals to the point of no return. The long-standing relationship that must have existed between merchants and farmers might well have rested on the assurance the farmer had of always being able to draw down credit when he needed it from a facility that the merchant-lender granted him. In exchange, the farmer would have given the merchant-lender an open, annually renewable pledge on his assets (land). There is no loss of tenure for the farmer as long as he remains solvent. The notion of security also persists. In time, the merchants and the farmers may have formed such a close bond, founded on mutual interest and dependency, that a strong partnership grew up, which eventually clouded the legal structure and contractual obligations between them. The merchant had little interest in taking over his client's land in the long run and may have preferred to cancel debts when times were hard.

Neither schemes guard against natural catastrophes, such as a long spell of drought that wipes out all food production, but maximizes chances of survival for the entire people. It is precisely against natural catastrophes as well as against war disasters that the *šemiṭṭah* acts. Standing in front of the heap of winnowed grain at the threshing floor, the owner, who, like Boaz of Bethlehem, spent the previous nights there to make sure no one stole the fruit of a whole year's labour, waits for the arrival of two important persons. In theory, the farmer is not allowed to transport the grain back home until the tax collector has assessed the amount to be paid as taxes. The grain merchant is also present to decide with the farmer how much he will collect as reimbursement of previous loans, unless the harvest is so poor that it is obvious that collecting anything will bite into the farmer's carry over. In that case, the lender has the choice of collecting some grain because he has a need for it elsewhere or leaving it all for the farmer's own needs and postponing the reimbursement of loans until the following harvest. In either case, the farmer might have to borrow grain for seeds in December, or at any later point before May, should his reserves dry out before the next harvest. Unless there was an immediate need nearby, such as a large army moving south towards Egypt, it was cheaper for both parties to save themselves transport costs by leaving the grain to the farmer.

Deuteronomy 15:1 states that the *šemiṭṭah* is to be made 'from the end of seven years' (מקץ שבע שנים). It is not crucial here to decide when the New Year is fixed. Suffice it to postulate that the taxes and reimbursements of loans are assessed at the threshing floor at the seventh harvest. Verses 2 and 3 oppose the debt owed by one's neighbour (רעהו) and one's brother (אחיו) that should not be collected while the foreigner (הנכרי) can be pressed for the payment of dues. At this point, I posit a different definition of the brother from the brother mentioned in relation to the jubilee (§7.4.5). Here, the brother is a fellow Israelite whereas in Lev. 25:35, the brother is a co-member in a commercial corporation. The seventh-year debt release concerns the survival of debts incurred as the result of harvest failures only. Because the providers of grain loans are mostly merchants, whether they work for a temple or by themselves, the *šemiṭṭah* cancels the debts of farmers owed to merchants. As seen above, commercial debts are excluded (§7.4.5).

Was the *šemiṭṭah* burdensome to the point of quenching credit and paralyzing the economy? We have hardly any way to estimate the actual burden of a general cancellation of debts every seventh year. Yet, the Neo-Assyrian evidence, the most relevant here, indicates that between 710 and 612 BCE the Assyrian rulers proclaimed five to seven *andurārum* edicts (710, 680, 676 expected, 668, 648?, 629, 612 BCE; Villard 2007: 121). The edicts were proclaimed at the beginning of the reign and at fairly regular intervals afterwards (Finkelstein 1965: 245). Compared with the seven years of the *šemiṭṭah*, debts seem to have been cancelled on average every 20 years. It is likely, however, that more edicts were proclaimed but that textual evidence for their proclamation has not yet been recovered. The number of *mīšarum* edicts was probably more than 15 for the last 150 years of the First Dynasty of Babylon (Sweet 1986: 582), at an average interval of five to seven years (Komoróczy 1982: 198; Olivier 1988: 228; Otto 1997: 41). Disputing the notion that they occurred regularly is playing on words. The edicts occurred often enough to render the regularity of the *šemiṭṭah* compared with the 'irregularity' of the *mīšarum* irrelevant. Both measures reflected economic realities. Hence Finkelstein (1965: 245) claimed that debt cancellations

> had to recur at fairly regular or predictable intervals. Were it not the case, and had the kings been free to announce the *misharum* without warning and at widely disparate intervals, there would have occurred a drying-up of the sources of credit and a virtual paralysis of economic activity every few years—after a reasonable lapse of time from the previous enactment. At worse, arbitrariness in such activity on the part of the crown would have served only to encourage subterfuges on the part of creditors and debtors, buyers and sellers, etc. to avoid being affected by the *misharum*, so that the very purpose of the act would have been frustrated.

Against this idea, Olivier (1988: 229) states that the 'regular recurrence of the *mēšarum*-acts would certainly have destroyed its very purpose... The system of *mēšarum*-acts could only function properly if the edicts were unexpectedly announced' (see also Otto 1997: 41). The truth probably lies in-between. It hardly mattered whether consumption debts were cancelled on a fixed six- to seven-year basis of one or twice per decade. Both reflected the average occurrence of drought and other disasters. Both correspond to the practical application of the ability of farmers to withstand the theoretical four years of successive harvest failures before sinking into the spiral of debts (§5.4). Since complete harvest failures hardly ever occur four years in a row, a decade corresponds to the natural rhythm required to protect producers from foreclosure.

The *šemiṭṭah,* however, also took care of the needs of the lenders. Canceling debts before they snowballed out of proportion helped lenders as much as merchants keep afloat since the financial health of merchants depended upon the ability of their clients to produce tradable surplus. Again, it is the fallacy of the seizure of land as the aim of agricultural credit that prevents exegetes from understanding that lenders and borrowers were in solidarity with each other rather than in competition (§5.6). Unless the crisis was so bad that everyone had to relocate, it was a question of survival for everyone, peasant, merchant and king or governor, to cancel debts in order to save the economic health of the entire society. Contrary to social-scientific claims to the contrary, the 'rich' did not enrich themselves in times of crisis (§5.7). Everyone lost. The crown or the provincial government had to forego tax revenues. Merchants had to abandon claims. Farmers had to manage with less to eat, starving the old and the young if necessary. It was crucial for everyone to find seeds for the next season.

Other considerations support the economic feasibility of a regular *šemiṭṭah,* the date of which was known to everyone concerned in advance. The credit simulation above suggests that under normal circumstances the amounts to be cancelled were small (§5.4). The amount cancelled represents the risk the merchant is taking. It is important at this point to insist that the *šemiṭṭah,* as much as in the Islamic banking system today, expects the lender to share the risk to a much greater extent than is the case in Western modern banking systems. Lenders, however, had ways to control their share of the risk as much as farmers had ways to reduce the risks of production (§2.1; §3).

A merchant would inevitably adjust the amount of future loans according to the amount cancelled at the last *šemiṭṭah.* Hence, honest, hard-working and astute farmers would have fewer problems than others getting grain when they needed it. The success of creditors is relative to their intimate knowledge of the creditworthiness of individual borrowers. A merchant may also decide to collect as much as possible of the seventh harvest, even biting into what he knows will be necessary for the farmer's family's yearly consumption and seed requirements, if he knew grain was in high demand elsewhere. Having made a profit, the merchant could offer a new loan some time between the next sowing season and the next harvest time, when the farmer's reserves were spent.

Here, the decision depends on supply and demand as well as on the relative bargaining power of each party. The merchant would be inclined to do a greater favour to his best clients who happened to be those who work better, who cheated him less by hiding some of the produce, and who contributed most to his position as patron over against the crown, the tax collectors and any other common enemies. Hence, a subtle mechanism of balance and checks is always at work.

The greater favours are done for the less risky borrowers who guarantee greater returns. The farmers also have a collective bargaining chip in the form of gossip that can have disastrous consequences to the renown of the lender and his position in a society where everyone knows everyone else's business. Deuteronomy 15:9-10 insists precisely on the risk that unhappy borrowers cry out to the Lord against a stingy lender and that divine blessing is conditional on generosity. This is more than a theological nicety. Conditional divine favour is an exact reflection of social regulation, whereas both a stingy lender and a cheating borrower will eventually pay for misdeeds that cannot remain secret for very long. Theology is used in internal politics for moralistically based social sanctioning. The rise of rich merchants, who have the financial ability to assume leadership roles at the village and the regional level, fosters political centralization and social stratification. The process, however, is not mathematical. It is not enough to be rich to be a leader any more than it is enough to get rich once to remain rich. Besides financial factors, political dynamics have to be taken into account. As 'a society becomes increasingly stratified and leadership becomes increasingly authoritative, there may be some systemic "break point" at which reverse dominance (as opposed to orthodox) hierarchy rather easily tends to turn itself upside down' (Boehm 1993: 239). In small-scale societies such as the villages of Persian Yehud, a leader can only consolidate his position of leadership by setting aside his individual tendencies to dominate and by submitting to the group even as he leads it (Boehm 1993: 238).

The mistake of the standard social-scientific notion of irresistible latifundialism is that it discusses the evolution of Israelite society in isolation from political factors that are known to undercut the rise of upstarts. Every society has levelling systems of reverse dominance.

7.4.8 The šemiṭṭah *and the Egalitarian Fiction*

No one can escape the effects of the various levelling mechanisms that operate against aggressive upstarts through public opinion: criticism, ridicule, gossip, shaming, ostracism, deposition, desertion and murder

(Boehm 1993: 230). Any amount a creditor wrote off was automatically ascribed to his credit *in illo tempore et ad aeternam*. Hence, in spite of the contrary claim in verse 11 ('there will never cease to be some poor among you'), the statement in Deut. 21:4 that 'there will be among you no poor because YHWH will certainly bless you in your land' can be taken as a fairly literal affirmation that credit protected farmers from destitution, an affirmation that flies in the face of social-scientist claims that the rich consolidated their position by extending credit to the poor (§5.4.3-5). While writing off arrears on survival loans every seventh year effectively protected most farmers from destitution, the *šemiṭṭah* positively affected the merchant. The *šemiṭṭah* provided a life insurance to the merchant as much as to the farmer. With the debts the merchant wrote off, the merchant bought a most effective protection against the leveling mechanisms that work in every society, especially in smaller ones. Any upstart, big man, chief, sheikh, any particularly charismatic or successful individual automatically attracts criticism from the rank and file who feels threatened. The preservation of a position of leadership as well as the physical survival of the leader requires treading a fine line. The leader must preserve some of the egalitarian fiction by downplaying his ambition and by concrete demonstrations of generosity. A would-be leader has to distribute food and gifts to show that he is altruistic and to prove that everyone stands to gain from his higher position (Boehm 1993: 235). The compulsory gifts redistribute wealth and put a price tag on the exercise of leadership.

The amount of food and gifts must, however, be carefully weighted so that it will not be interpreted as boastful, as an aggressive move to bribe and a clear attempt to break the egalitarian ethos of the group. The rank and file expects concrete rewards in exchange for their submission, but they also require respect. A successful leader is thus one who has enough tact to maintain the fiction of equality, one whose generosity is not showy. I suggest that it was in this delicate balance between superiority and equality that the *šemiṭṭah* was particularly useful.

The cancellation of the arrears of his clients was regular and significant enough to maintain a strong tie between merchants and farmers, patrons and their clientele. The insurance premium paid by the farmer to the merchant was a very valuable compensation of the economic risks incurred by every farmer who in turn could accept the loss of any surplus produced in good years. Yet, the amount actually cancelled for each client was unpublished. Farmers of the same village would certainly have a rough idea of the sum owed by each one of them, but the actual amount was a carefully guarded secret between the patron and his client, by which the patron continued to behave as a *primus inter pares* toward each of his clients. Merchant and client knew exactly how many measures were owed, but the patron had no interest in humiliating the most unfortunate farmers by divulging how much he wrote off. Moreover, the mathematics of the *šemiṭṭah* and its theological justification threw a discreet veil over the naked economic facts. The fact that the cancellation was a divine decree and that it took place automatically, without any human agency having to intervene or the debtor having to beg for it, did much to preserve the decency required to shield the honour of the debtor for which he felt even more thankful to his patron. Hence, whatever the amount of grain written off, the cancellation of debts in the name of God strengthened the position of the giver as much as that of the receiver.

Another merchant was unlikely to lend much to a farmer who has been denied a large loan by his habitual lender and who tried to elicit the generosity of a rival. The new merchant would try to get an idea of the creditworthiness of the potential client from the previous lender and would in any case avoid stepping on a colleague's turf unless the village farmers sent clear signals of their willingness to punish their present patron. Therefore, the amounts involved by the *šemiṭṭah* remained modest while their cancellation tightened rather than loosened the patron's hold over his clients. The exhortation to 'open your hand so that the poor will not curse you' (Deut. 15:7-8) transforms the debt into alms and credit into charity to enable farmers to remain afloat and patrons to maintain their network of clients by external demonstrations of justice. The same principle of generosity-induced inequality is at work today in Africa, flooded as it is with foreign aid that deepens rather than reduces the development differential between Third and First World countries (Moyo 2009).

Yet, wars, crickets, oppressive tax collectors, raids, mildew, droughts do occur, and more often than everyone likes. The various consumption-smoothing mechanisms discussed up to this point were not enough to prevent every case of debt from spiralling. In some cases, foreclosure had to take place to amputate the economic actor that had lost all creditworthiness so as to preserve the creditworthiness of the others. We are not concerned here whether the lender pays the farmer a wage or not, but the lender who would not ensure the farmer a minimal livelihood would do so at the peril of his own position as patron. The unequal relations between patron and clients (§6.2-5) paradoxically combined with the egalitarian fiction to sustain a level of solidarity between the rich and the poor that was high and real enough to belie the social-scientific notion that the rich got fat on the back of the poor (§4.5.6).

7.5 Chapter Summary

Discussing the Book of Proverbs, Domeris notes that the stereotypical lazy poor was a didactic warning for the young elite, although the stereotype indicates that poverty was no real threat to the elite. Then, under the pervasive influence of the spiritualization of poverty in the Bible, Domeris takes the 'oppressed poor' as a social reality, although he also terms it a stereotype (Domeris 2007: 124). The exegetical bias towards the poor commands to take passages teaching the elite to be kind to the needy (Prov. 14:31) as propaganda without any social repercussions. The poor are depicted as a defenceless group at the mercy of the rich and Domeris finds nothing to mitigate the collapse of the ethic of positive reciprocity that, in his opinion, prevailed throughout the Persian, Greek and Roman periods (Domeris 2007: 149-50). Jesus indeed pointed out to his disciples that the poor are always present, but this general fact does not establish the existence of a crisis understood as the breakdown of social relations. Even the great kings of the ancient Orient could not simply lord it over their subjects. Greed could never be given a free check, not even in the so-called Oriental despotism under which rulers, as elsewhere, presented themselves as guarantors of justice. That the *andarāru* edicts decreed across the centuries served royal propaganda does not negate the fact that they also reveal a certain concern of the crown for the well-being of its tax payers, even if the effects of such edicts were but temporary (Villard 2007). Besides the ruler's concerns for the lowly, patrons supplied farmers with credit and goods.

The spiritualization of the poor engenders the demonization of patrons and moneylenders. Admitting the economic role played by credit would turn ordinary farmers into regular players in the economy rather than poor victims of a structural crisis from the eighth century BCE through the Persian period and continuing unabated into the Roman era. If biblical texts construct a crisis rather than react against it, the representation of prophets as social critics and heroes of the cause of the poor collapses. It is time to move beyond the notion of Israelite prophets as the creators of ethical monotheism (Kuenen 1877: 549-93; Buss 2006). To do so, one should consider prophetic critiques as traces of the conflict between the ruler and patrons as well as the conflict between different elite groups.

As they accuse each other of misbehaviour towards the poor in the Book of Job, patrons vied with each other to be seen as the best protector of clients.

That the first millennium BCE witnessed a sustained demographic increase reaching unprecedented heights during the early Byzantine era is a problem for anyone arguing that reciprocity broke down and that the oppression of the poor increased, unless one admits that increased oppression goes hand in hand with a general improvement of living conditions that had positive effects on the health of the poor as much as the rich. Domeris and the exegetical tradition he follows postulate that the rich cannot become poor and that they need not work to remain rich while the poor are bound to become poorer, however hard they work. Sudden turns of fortunes, not necessarily as dramatic as Job's, are not considered, nor the various methods of relief and charity that existed in every society. If charity aims more at preserving social peace and preventing bread riots than at improving the conditions of the poor, there are enough mentions of the divine concern for the poor in the Hebrew Scriptures to assert that the exploitation of the poor by the rich never was an unchecked process. The recovery of ancient tenure systems in Part I ties up with the reconsideration of biblical texts relative to credit in this section to affirm that in Yehud, as in the modern world, loans were not for the poor. Nor was indebtedness an indicator of poverty, or the United States of America would rank among the poorest societies.

Notes

1. According to Herodotus III 89-97, Darius introduced a fixed standard between Babylonian silver and Euboian gold which resulted in the rise of white silver in contrast to silver with a *ginnu* mark (Bongenaar 1999: 173).
2. Through innovative institutions, the Ptolemies achieved greater revenue than their predecessors but only recaptured 12-14% of GDP (Manning 2010: 159)
3. ’Εθαύμασος δέ τινων πρόσωπον, ῴκισας δὲ τοὺς ἐπὶ τῆς γῆς, 'And you made favorites of some and settled them on the land' (Cox 2007; Hermisson 1998: 303; Clines 2006: 538).
4. *w'nš' ddr'n' 'lh 'rd' wrm' dpn' bt ytb gwwh* (and the man who is sowing to him the land, and the elevated of face inhabits inside it). Compare Targum: *wgbr nṣḥn lyh 'rd' wsbyr 'pyn yytyb bh* (and a victorious man—to him belongs the land, and the privileged dwell in it; Stec 1994: 150*; Mangan 1991: 56).
5. Compare פני אדמה in Gen. 2:6; Ps. 104:30.
6. Compare the Mesopotamian *zûzu* (half shekel), the *bitqu* (slice), the *mahat* (grain), the *girû* (carat), the *hallûru* (chickpea), the *uttetu* (barleycorn). The Hebrew shekel is divided into *nṣp, pym, bq‘* and *grḥ*. See Ezek. 45:12 (Powell 1992).

7. Lefèbvre (2003: 161-63) offers the most convincing explanation for the problem of the 49th year being the 50th year. The wilderness fiction imposes the vantage point of an audience about to enter the land for whom the first jubilee would occur in year 50 counted from the year of the arrival of the sons of Israel in Canaan. This elegant solution reveals the secondary nature of the question of how to survive three years without crops, a problem arising once the jubilee is considered as falling the year after the sabbatical year.

Part III

No Crisis in Yehud

There is no doubt that farmers did not like paying taxes and had to cope with all sorts of challenges. Yet, there is no reason to suppose that the fifth and fourth centuries BCE were particularly critical for Palestinian farmers. In light of the previous chapters, the helpless farmer crushed by absentee landlords belongs to the 'crisis' literary genre that provides a backdrop for the self-presentation of biblical exegetes as modern prophets. Without a good crisis, prophetic fulminations lose much of their bite. Therefore, catastrophic depictions of the situation of biblical farmers are crucial to the social-scientific approach. Clues to a continuing structural crisis are found in the Bible, even if the notion of a structural crisis is nonsense (§7.2.6). Albertz was particularly thorough in the compilation of crisis texts. The admission that 'Unfortunately, it is impossible to give an exact date to the texts mentioned'[1] helps to make the crisis endless. The financial difficulties mentioned in Nehemiah 5 (see §7.2) are a good prop for 'a far-reaching and long-lasting social crisis which shook post-exilic Judah to the core. The creeping decline of increasing numbers of population, which at times became acute, to a level below the minimum needs of existence, grew to an abuse which could no longer be overlooked by anyone who held a position of responsibility in the community' (Albertz 1994: 497). Narrating a crisis was indeed part of the negotiations that determined the tax-burden of each fiscal unit. Hence, a crisis narrative is meant to disguise the actual financial situation rather than reveal it. A decade *before* Albertz's work on Nehemiah 5, a specialist of the economy of the Persian era warned that the sweeping views of crushing taxation, silver shortage and general impoverishment before and after Darius' fiscal reform are flawed (Stolper 1985: 143-45). Nevertheless, the notion of crisis is too rewarding to be easily abandoned by biblical exegetes. Colleagues from emerging economies are now joining the game to keep the crisis alive.

In a recent volume on peasant poverty, Domeris (2007: 128-50) shifts the date of the most acute economic oppression of biblical peasants to the so-called 'post-exilic' period. While earlier studies considered the development of statehood in the kingdoms of Israel and Judah as the source of the economic oppression denounced by eighth-century BCE prophets (Lang 1982; Chaney 1983; Gottwald 1986; Coote and Whitelam 1986: 162; Coote 1991: 49-69; Premnath 1988; Hoppe 2004), Domeris identifies the rise of commercial empires and the subsequent development of a market economy and agricultural estates as causing deeper changes than ever in the traditional agrarian economy, changes considered entirely negative for the welfare of the peasants. A reminder of what we can know about the actual context may help recover a more realistic view of life in Persian Yehud.

Chapter 8

Life in Yehud

8.1 Demography in Yehud

The publication of the results of systematic surveys and of salvage excavations enabled quantitative studies with population estimates. There is an overall consensus that the destruction of Jerusalem had disastrous effects on the immediate periphery of the city. In Benjamin, the population gathered around the large tells of the area: Mizpah/Tell en-Nasbeh, Gibeon/el-Jîb, Gibeah/Tell el-Fûl. The case of Bethel/Beitin is disputed.

Finkelstein and Singer-Avitz (2009) claim that Bethel was probably uninhabited or almost deserted in the Babylonian and Persian periods. Given the difficulties in the interpretation of Kelso's excavations at Beitin, no firm conclusions can be drawn from its results (Knauf 2006). Then, there is enough leeway between 'probably uninhabited' and 'almost deserted' to leave open the possibility of some cultic and scribal activity, either at Bethel or at nearby Mizpah. If a sale contract from the antiquity market concerning a young bullock at an unidentified Jewish site in Babylonia is enough to support the existence of an academy that produced the Deuteronomistic History (Römer 2003),[2] the evidence in favour of Bethel remains overwhelming, despite Finkelstein's doubts. Maybe ancient Bethel was sited elsewhere, at el-Bireh rather than at Beitin, and Beitin was Beth-Aven (Wood 2008). Whether or not Bethel was inhabited, the Benjamin region was the most densely populated area in Yehud and Bethel is mentioned eleven times in the Torah, Jerusalem never.

Archaeological surveys suggest that only a third of Late Iron Age sites were occupied during the Persian period (216 sites out of 586). Moving from this rough estimate to the calculation of actual population levels is, however, fraught with difficulties as it hinges upon the size of each site and the density of its occupation (Faust 2007: 33). The 'packing' of population in any settlement can present variations of over 60% (Zevit 2007: 440-41). Surveyors estimated the surface of sites according to the area over which shards were scattered. Erosion, the spread of manure containing shards (Wilkinson 1982; Aldock, Cherry and Davis 1994), the extraction of soil from the sides of a deserted tell by local farmers, and the transport of soil to fill terraces increase the shard scatter and swell the estimated size of most sites (Gibson and Edelstein 1985: 150). Hence, the size of a settlement is a poor indicator of the size of its population. The identification of the course of the enclosure of a settlement could in theory provide fairly reliable estimates of its population. Such identification, however, is rare, and the results are extremely unreliable because the function of a wall encircling a city or a village extended beyond the protection of its inhabitants to include their gardens as well as empty spaces filled by the peasants living in the surrounding villages who came with their animals to seek protection during raids (Chandezon 2000: 238). The results for any single site can represent variations of 400%. There is a consensus that Persian sites were less densely populated than Late Iron Age ones. Carter (1999: 247) estimates the population of Persian Yehud at about one-third of what it was before the Babylonian conquest, but Faust (2007: 35) insists that Persian period estimates are exaggerated.

This inflationary trend is somewhat counterbalanced by the fact that not all existing sites were detected because the surveyors simply missed them or because the collection of shards was hindered. This was particularly the case in modern built-up areas, especially in Arab villages (Finkelstein 1997b: 13) where Israeli surveyors were not necessarily welcome, and in zones covered with thick vegetation as in the north of the Ayalon Valley, which surveyors deliberately ignored. Finkelstein and Magen (1993: 9*-11*) also warn that different teams used different methodologies and had different interests so that the collection of data faced very different challenges. Another factor to be taken into account is that the majority of Persian sites were small to very small settlements housing a hundred people at most (Carter 1999: 215-17; Faust 2007: 35). Being smaller than Late Iron Age sites, these Persian period farmsteads were more likely missed by the surveyors.

Finally, not all identified sites yielded datable pottery. For instance, 12% (67 out of 544) of the sites recorded by the Benjamin Hill Country Survey yielded no identifiable shards. Excluding sites recorded as tombs and those devoid of traces of walls, the settlement history of the remaining

47 sites (8% of the total) is totally unknown (#115, 121, 144, 149, 192, 209, 229, 252, 254, 275, 302, 275, 302, 324, 325, 326, 329, 336, 338, 356-58, 360-61, 368, 382, 384, 386, 400, 406, 408, 412-13, 415-17, 419, 421, 423, 426-28, 435, 456, 519, 537, 542). With its ten threshing floors and some terraces, site #498 must have been related to a nearby settlement. Therefore, missed and undated sites counterbalance inflated settlement sizes up to a point. Given these caveats, a rough two-thirds reduction of the total number of inhabited Iron Age sites seems acceptable for the centuries following the destruction of Jerusalem.

Faust (2007: 42) also points out that the figures for the Persian period represent the peak of the number of settlements rather than its nadir. Nevertheless, he agrees with Carter (1999: 247) and Lipschits (2004) that during the sixth century the highlands lost 80 to 90% of their population and that it took the two Persian centuries to achieve a modest recovery that merely doubled the Babylonian low. It is clear that the land was not empty after the destruction of Jerusalem and that the restoration of Jerusalem did not bring a return to the demographic and economic levels of the seventh century BCE. The *shivat Zion* had no demographic impact on Yehud (Lipschits 2005: 372). The return of waves of Jewish immigrants back to Zion after Cyrus' edict is as mythical as the empty land after the destruction of Jerusalem.

On the ground, very low demographic levels entail that much of the land cultivated before the destruction of Jerusalem was fallow. After half a century, two thirds of the previously cultivated fields were in advanced stages of reafforestation. The absence of pressure on land combined with low imperial involvement contributed to two opposite trends. On the one hand, the abundance of wild fauna and flora discouraged intensive agriculture and encouraged the mobility of a population living far apart in small temporary settlements, in shacks and tents that left few archaeological traces but spread them widely, further inflating population estimates. Rootedness was minimal. Fields were profitably abandoned after a few years of cultivation for others freshly cleared of the brambles that covered them. On the other hand, high mobility fostered insecurity for the rest of the population that concentrated in the central ridge clusters north and south of ruined Jerusalem. The dichotomy is not between the urban rich and the rural poor, as social-scientific studies suggest, but between official structures around Mizpah with little control over a thin and mobile population tapping abundant natural resources.

Cambyses' conquest of Egypt was the first of a series of events that would lead the Achaemenids to intervene directly in Yehud. Across the Achaemenid realm, the reigns from Cyrus to Darius I were otherwise characterized by continuity (Wiesehöfer 1999). A crucial turning-point took place under Xerxes in the aftermath of the defeats in Greece and the rebellions in Egypt and Babylon (Jursa 2007).

8.2 Xerxes' Temple Destructions and the Priestly Document

The Greek sources (Herodotus VII.1,5-8; Kuhrt 2007: 248) mention an Egyptian rebellion as the prelude to Xerxes' expedition in Greece. In 484 BCE, Xerxes led his first campaign against Egypt. The effort taxed Persian resources enough to require another four years before Xerxes could march against Greece, although Darius had already prepared the European campaign before his death (Briant 2002: 520). Xerxes appointed his brother Achaemenes rather than Pharandates, the previous satrap over Egypt who was in office in 486 BCE, possibly because the leader of the insurrection was Pharandates himself (Bresciani 1985: 509).

The official Persian sources on Xerxes' reign consist of 20 royal inscriptions. The longest is a trilingual text found in several copies in Persepolis and Parsagadae (Pritchard 1969: 316-17; Lecoq 1997: 256-58). After listing the countries belonging to his realm, Xerxes mentions a rebellious country, or several rebellious countries (Babylonian version), which he crushed and whose temple(s) he destroyed because they performed festivals to the *daeva*, evil gods of sorts. This information is about the only reference to any particular action in the bulk of Xerxes' highly repetitive and formulaic inscriptions.

Combined with persistent accusations of destructions of temples in Egypt by Cambyses and Artaxerxes III,[3] there is no reason to doubt that some temples were actively involved in rebellions and suffered retaliation from Persian kings. Cambyses' campaign set the tone for other campaigns to come. Xerxes does not specify in which country he destroyed temples, but Egypt and Greece were likely targets since they initiated the most significant rebellions Xerxes faced. The clergy of sanctuaries sited within the rebellious zones and nearby may have been asked to demonstrate their loyalty for the first time. Before Xerxes, local gods had simply been equated with Ahura Mazda (Bolin 1996: 138-39).

The idea of a Persian inquiry into local religious traditions in Yehud offers a downgraded version of the hypothesis of imperial authorization as the factor that spurred the production of the Torah (Frei 1996; Watts

2001). Instead of the entire Torah, it is the composition of the narrative ancestor of the Torah, the so-called Priestly Document, that makes sense in the context of Xerxes' investigation into the loyalty of local sanctuaries because it would explain the presence of some strikingly original traits (Guillaume 2009: 177-92).

The Priestly Document displays a radical policy of non-violence combined with a total black-out on temples and on sacrifices (Guillaume 2009: 169-73). Bethel and Mamre are mentioned but not Jerusalem, a thorn in the flesh to those who hold the common assumption that Jerusalem is the focus of the Torah's priestly layers (Guillaume 2009: 9, 49). It therefore seems reasonable to suggest that the document that provided the narrative frame of the Torah, from Creation to Canaan, was produced at a time when Jerusalem was non-existent or was secondary at a time when Benjamin eclipsed Jerusalem as the theological centre of Yehud. If Bethel was not settled during Xerxes' time, as Finkelstein and Singer-Avitz suggest (2009), Mizpah recognized Bethel's place as the locus of Benjaminite traditions.

Yet, there is a weighty argument in favour of Bethel's active role throughout the Neo-Babylonian rule over Yehud. Hurowitz (2006) demonstrates that the account of Jacob's dream (Gen. 28:10-22) bears striking parallels with the myth of Babylon's primeval foundation. If the Bethel legend appropriated traditions from Marduk's temple at Babylon, it is likely that Jacob's dream was composed at Bethel when the Babylonian empire dominated Yehud. The transfer of the literary motifs from Babylon to Bethel is the strongest available evidence of the centrality of Bethel at the time (Na'aman 2009b: 341). Such a close affiliation of Bethel to Babylon would have justified Xerxes' suspicions, considering that he had to quench several rebellions at Babylon in 481 BCE (led by Bel-šimanni) and in 479 BCE (led by Šamaš-eriba; Briant 1992; Horowitz 1995).

The 484 BCE Egyptian rebellion was the first sign that the Achaemenid Empire had reached its maximal extent. The military disasters that struck Xerxes confirmed that the Empire was badly overstretched and forced a redeployment of the imperial apparatus. The decision to increase production in Palestine was taken in the wake of the Persian defeats in Greece, when it became clear that the Persian hold over Egypt would not go uncontested. The strategic importance of the coast being greater than that of the highland, the Persians implemented concrete measures along the coastal stretch and it was not until the reign of Artaxerxes I that they set up a *birtā* in Yehud (Hoglund 1992: 202-205; Berquist

1995: 108; Carter 1999: 293; Betlyon 2004; Edelman 2005). The final chapter examines biblical economic texts in the context of the measures the Persians were likely to have taken to boost the economy and the production of Yehud between the military disasters of Xerxes in Greece and the building of Artaxerxes' *birtā* at Jerusalem.

Notes

1. The crisis proof-texts are Isa. 29:17-24; 35:1-2; 58:4-9; 59:1-21; Mal. 5:3; Ps. 37:7-33; 94:5-21; 109:2-3; Job 7:2-3; 14:6; 20:19; 22:6-7; 29:17; 31:16-20 (Albertz 1994: 636 n. 13).
2. See also Pearce (2006) who discusses the TAYN archive, a collection of one-hundred unpublished tablets from a private collection, hence from illegal excavations. A third of the corpus is said to originate from āl-Yāhūdu, an unidentified 'Judah-ville' in Babylonia.
3. Cambyses destroyed all temples but the Jewish one at Elephantine; Herodotus III,27–29.64; Plutarch, *De Iside et Osiride* 11.31; Aelian, *De natura animalium* X,28 (Porten and Yardeni 1986: A4.7, 13-14).

Chapter 9

Financing Production and Commerce

The present shift in the dating of the Persian revitalization of Jerusalem from Darius I to Artaxerxes I represents a time extention of a good 60 years. The erection of an administrative centre at Jerusalem around 450 BCE was but the culmination of a process that began soon after Xerxes' recovery of Egypt in 484 BCE. Considering the peripheral position of Yehud, the three decades between Xerxes' realization that Egypt was a weak link and the completion of the Jerusalem *birtā* correspond to the time it would take for new developments on the coast to make a significant enough impact on the economy of Yehud to justify the construction of an administrative structure at Jerusalem. I use these decades as the historical ground for the ban on sowing in the seventh year, the ban on interest-bearing loans, the seventh-year *šemiṭṭah* and the jubilee in an attempt to go beyond the common claim that these measures were utopian.

9.1 Seventh-year Debt Cancellation šemiṭṭah

The Wrigley and Schofield paradox (see §3) is based on the poor correlation between mortality among the medieval poor and famines. It implies the existence of relief systems and effective consumption-smoothing mechanisms that are invisible to the historian. I suggest that a similar paradox applies to first-millennium BCE farming in Canaan. Although the Bible mentions consumption-smoothing mechanisms, exegetes speculate that they did not work. Besides the fact that exegetes have a vested interest in downplaying the efficacy of these measures because without a crisis an unfavourable light is cast upon prophetic fulminations, the characterization of biblical financial texts as utopian is the result of misunderstanding. Although the ban on interest and the jubilee appear as obvious measures in favour of the poor, neither the jubilee (§7.4) nor the ban on interest-bearing loans (§9.3) were written for the benefit of ordinary farmers. They were not consumption-smoothing devices as such. The *šemiṭṭah* (§7.4.7) understood in the framework of patronage (§6.5) was by far the most efficient protection farmers had against financial disaster. The credit simulation above illustrates the impact of cancellations (§5.4.4) especially if they occurred regularly and fairly predictably (§7.4.7). The relation between the *šemiṭṭah* and the sabbatical year can now be considered.

9.2 Sabbatical Year

If the *šemiṭṭah* of Deuteronomy 15 was geared to relieve farmers by cleaning the slate every seventh year, the interdiction on sowing grain every seventh year of Lev. 25:3-7 seems to annihilate the benefits gained from the *šemiṭṭah.* Promises of abundant harvest in the sixth year (Lev. 25:18-22) are lame justifications of the ban and appear to support the notion that the entire chapter is utopian. Yet, the results of the credit simulation (§5.4) suggest that there is more truth than first meets the eye in the idea that farmers could survive the effects of a year without any harvest.

Since the *šemiṭṭah* and the sabbatical year are mentioned in different legal collections, nothing indicates that they were meant to be practised by the same people, at the same place, if they were meant to be practised at all. Admitting, for argument's sake, that the *šemiṭṭah* and the ban on sowing during the sabbatical year were practised in biblical Israel, it would make sense to have them coincide since the cancelling of debts would help farmers weather out the effects of the missing harvest.

We actually have a hint that the *šemiṭṭah* coincided with a ban on sowing in Exod. 23:10-11, which mention the relief of the poor:

> ושש שׁנים תזרע את ארצך ואספת את תבואתה
>
> והשׁביעי תשׁמטנה ונטשׁתה ואכלו אביני עמך ויתם תאכל חית השׂדה כן תעשׂה לכרמך לזירך
>
> 10 For six years you shall sow your land and gather in its yield; 11 but the seventh year you shall let it rest and lie fallow, so that the poor of your people may eat, and what they leave the wild animals may eat. You shall do the same with your vineyard, and with your olive orchard.

Contrary to most translations, verse 11 mentions neither rest nor fallow. The verbs שׁמט, from which *šemiṭṭah* is derived, and נטשׁ express actions of 'untying' and 'giving up', which makes a bit more sense in relation to the feeding of the poor than a fallow to feed the poor and the wild animals. Since the poor cannot wait until the seventh year to feed themselves, the idea is that the addressees are creditors who release the lien they placed over their debtors' assets, giving up their share of the produce from assets pawned to secure antichretic loans. Abstaining from collecting their share of the produce would provide for the needs of the 'poor' better than leaving the pawns uncultivated, but in this case, the poor in question are not destitute since they had assets to pawn (§5.5). Another reading is possible, however.

In light of verse 10, 'you shall sow' and 'you shall harvest' and in light of 'your vineyards' and 'your olive orchards' in the second part of verse 11, it is the assets of the creditors that should be left fallow and turned over to the poor who may graze their animals on them and pick whatever they found in the untended orchards. Asking creditors to abstain from collecting their share is an entirely different notion from allowing the poor to glean and graze on fallows, but they are clearly compounded in these two verses. If the combination of two such different strategies to alleviate the need of the poor obscures the practical implications of this passage to a modern audience, it nevertheless suggests that the two different strategies constituted two facets of the same economic approach. Therefore, Exod. 23:10-11 can be taken as an important clue to the coincidence of the ban on sowing (vv. 10 and 11b) with the *šemiṭṭah* (v. 10a). These verses combined the ban on sowing and the release of pawns because these two distinct operations occurred, or were supposed to occur, together every seventh year. That Neh. 10:31 and Leviticus 25, probably written at a different time by different people, also mention a ban on sowing and a release of pledges reinforces the connection between the two measures. It stands to reason to cancel outstanding debts when farmers were asked to forgo a harvest. Besides avoiding depleting stocks that had to tide farmers over to the next harvest, there was precious little for creditors to collect since loans were reimbursed by portions of the harvest rather than as amounts fixed in advance. If a ban on cultivation and harvest was imposed every seventh year, there was nothing to collect for creditors either.

A ban on sowing saved the seed that would have been wasted to drought or pests after a total harvest failure, but this does not provide a rationale for a counter-productive measure such as a total ban on cultivation every seventh year. If the ban would also have the positive effects of fallowing, it has long been shown that the ban is not equivalent to a fallow cycle because it is a general and realm-wide measure imposed on every field at the same time, whereas the logic of fallowing is rotation. Therefore, I suggested that freeing all farmers from labour-intensive ploughing and harvesting was intended as a means of redeploying farmers into work gangs for major land reclamation projects over an entire year, rather than for a few months at a time, as would be the case with ordinary corvée (Guillaume 2009: 103-105). The situation in Yehud following the Egyptian rebellions provides the context that is missing from the text because biblical scribes cancelled context to inscribe the texts in eternity. That the aim of the ban is elusive is no excuse for deeming the ban utopian.

Theologizing attempts to explain the ban in light of creation are popular (Kim 2010: 38-43), but they are far-fetched, and von Rad's claim (1961: 137) that there is no connection between creation and the ban remains valid. Another error is to spiritualize the ban and imagine that it provided farmers with a year-long sabbatical (Lefebvre 2003: 82-83; Kim 2010: 37). The text clarifies that the Sabbath of the seventh year is a Sabbath for the *land*, not for the farmers (Lev. 25:4). In the context of the steady demographic decline after the destruction of Jerusalem (§8), a total ban on sowing for the entire population of a province makes sense in anticipation of the passage of troops for a major campaign. Obviously, it seems paradoxical that a ban on sowing would contribute to stock-pile food. In fact, it would have been the most practical way to increase the surface of arable land to be sown in the following years.

Since we know that the Persians mounted several such major campaigns in Egypt, the passage of tens of thousands of troops and animals that had to be fed and equipped on the way required careful planning years in advance. According to Herodotus (VII.20), Xerxes' campaign against Greece was prepared four years in advance. The seventh-year ban on sowing would have been a most efficient measure, albeit a drastic one, to increase cultivated surface. In the absence of chemical fertilizers, the only way to increase surplus output is to put more land under the plough. Having lain fallow for a century, the land was very fertile, once cleared from the brush that naturally grows when ploughing and intensive grazing are discontinued.[1] Whereas farmers cleared land in their spare time when they felt the need to increase output, this process was by necessity a slow one since it was predicated upon the natural increase of population that was very slow. The corvée to which farmers were regularly submitted would have supplied some workdays towards the clearance of fresh land, but corvée duties had to be set during times of low agricultural activity (see §7.2.1). Hence, to multiply output within a few years in anticipation of the passage of armies towards Egypt required freeing the manpower available locally from the yearly routine of the most consuming activities, ploughing and harvesting, and apply it for an entire year to clear waste-land and multiply the arable surface.

Since the surface gained during the sabbatical year would have exceeded the capacity of the local population to cultivate it profitably the following years, the arrival of a wave of new settlers had to coincide with the end of the seventh year. The freshly cleared tracts of land could be attributed to the newcomers who settled in existing settlements to boost their capacity to cultivate greater surfaces (Ezra 2:70; Neh. 7:73). A complementary approach was to grant freshly cleared land to outsiders who had no relations with the local population.

While land was particularly plentiful in the Southern Levant after the Neo-Babylonian destructions, manpower was in chronic shortage (Grabbe 2004: 207) and remained so even during the high demographic levels reached during Roman times when lack of manpower continued to be the main cause for the abandonment of land (Jones 1964: 817). The available manpower had to be deployed to develop new estates while compensating the efforts of the farmers by preserving their land tenure. The worse possible scenario would have been to establish new estates by encroachment of the land tenure of existing Benjaminite settlements or to seize the land of indebted farmers and turn them into private estates (§4.2). As later documented in Ptolemaic Egypt, major land reclamation in the Fayyum involved the settlement of a majority of foreign *kleruchs* who were granted estates throughout the area in exchange for service to the crown (Manning 2003: 103-118). As always, estates were established on waste-land to be developed. As waste-land was particularly abundant around Jerusalem, it is hardly surprising that the Persians settled their personnel there to avoid encroaching upon the land of the existing population, in particular in Benjamin. Hence, most Persian-era medium-size settlements were set up in the immediate vicinity of Jerusalem where most of the waste-land was found (Carter 1999: 215-21) because new settlers were settled on uncultivated land (Warriner 1957: 8, 101). Estates were granted to individuals in the land-for-service system (Van Driel 2002: 226-73) in the same way that Arshama, the fifth-century BCE satrap of Egypt had an estate in Lahîru to feed his staff (Dandamayev 1993).

The question of how a population that missed a harvest could survive has to be answered in a more realistic way than is done in Lev. 25:21-22.

That YHWH would bless the sixth year so much that its surplus would be enough until the eighth year is a theological way to indicate that what Joseph did in Egypt could be done in Yehud (Gen. 41; §5.2). A year or two before the ban on sowing, a ban on exporting grain would ensure that all surpluses were stored locally. As the seventh-year ban only applies to the most labour-intensive activities (ploughing and harvesting grain and grapes, Lev. 25:4), products other than grain and wine were harvested as usual. Verses 6–7 explicitly state that the land provides the food during the sabbatical year. Aftergrowths as well as wild products (plentiful given the low human population levels) fed humans and animals. Contrary to Exod. 23:11, Lev. 25:4 does not include olive trees in the banned harvesting activities. Hence, olives, almonds, pomegranates, pistachios, figs, carobs, vegetables and honey were produced as usual (Schenker 2000a: 100). Today, olive trees are thoroughly trimmed every three to five years, with minor yearly pruning of dead wood and suckers. Therefore, the yields of olives and almonds would be little affected during the sabbatical year if the trees were tended the previous year in anticipation. People could easily survive the absence of grapes. While the stored grain surplus of previous years would make up for some of the missed harvest, additional supplies would be bought from neighbouring provinces in exchange for meat, leather, wool and dairy goods produced in greater quantities since the ban led farmers to rely even more on their livestock. Reduced culling in anticipation of the ban left larger herds that were pastured further away from the villages than was the case in normal years. A greater number of goats contributed actively to the clearance of fresh land for the years following the ban. Behind the flocks, the manpower freed from labour-intensive ploughing and harvesting cleared stones, repaired terraces, walls, wells and irrigation canals. Seen in this way, the ban on sowing in the seventh year was a highly pragmatic measure that is no less realistic than the way the books of Ezra and Nehemia present the return of thousands of exiles to Yehud. We know from administrative archives that the centre of the empire had the kind of bureaucracy that was necessary to implement such a vast operation (Briant 2002: 425-71). If Palestine is not Persepolis, it is nevertheless reasonable to imagine that the Achaemenid administrative apparatus along the crucial coastal roads to Egypt was able to organize to some extent the production of agricultural surplus in the highland. To be sure, it is impossible to know what actually happened since that kind of organization is not likely to be observable with the tools of present-day archaeology. But we have the biblical text, and the least we can do is to try to understand it better than dismissing it as utopian.

Farmers would certainly resent clearing fields for others instead of ploughing their own, but the clean slate of the *šemiṭṭah* constituted a trade-off. Renewed imperial involvement in the area also offered fresh economic opportunities to local farmers who would thus be less inclined to resist and escape to the fringes. The arrival of newcomers would have been resented, although some of the newcomers were relatives, while all shared the heavier tax burden. The description of the Persian era as a structural crisis (see §7.2) does not square up with the expected reality. If shortages were experienced, they were temporary and less severe than previously thought, since the more buoyant economy of this period better absorbed yield irregularities thanks to the greater number of producers and to the expansion of interregional trade. In theory, the ban on sowing in the seventh year was an extra burden farmers had to shoulder, but in practice, the *šemiṭṭah* lightened the burden, and the increase in the number of settlers and of the region's production contributed to the general improvement of living conditions.

9.3 The Ban on Interest against the Merchants of Benjamin

Contrary to the ban on sowing, the ban on interest-bearing loans appears as a straightforward measure in favour of the weaker economic actors. In fact, the ban on interest in Leviticus 25 concerned neither the poor nor the ordinary farmer. The modern understanding of interest as usury has been debunked in §5.3. Interest-free loans existed in the ancient world before the biblical ban. With and without interest, loans secured patronage relations and a safety net for borrowers *and* lenders alike, a safety net that rendered actual interest rates of secondary importance. Interest rates reflected the risk and the relation between lender and borrower, and the creditworthiness of the borrower. For this reason, the notion that the poor should be granted loans is economic nonsense (see §5.5). In this case, why does Exod. 22:24 present interest-free loans as a way to relieve the poor?

> אם כסף תלוה את עמי את העני עמך לא תהיה לו כנשה לא תשימון עליו נשך
>
> If you lend silver to my people, the needy with you, do not be to him as a moneylender, do not set interest against him/it.

The connection between interest-free loans and the poor here is ambiguous since the poor of your people (עני עמך) is side by side with 'my people' (עמי). The LXX rendered 'my people' as 'the brother', aligning the treatment of interest-free loans in Exodus with Lev. 25:36 and Deut. 23:20-21, where 'your brother' is the exclusive beneficiary of such preferential treatment. This led me to suggest that we are dealing here with rules applying to members of commercial brotherhoods (§7.4.5). Interest-free loans granted to farmers by merchants make little economic sense if the *šemiṭṭah* forces the same merchants to cancel rural debts every seventh year (§7.4.7). If the poor are really poor, lending them money at whatever interest rate makes even less sense than interest-free loans to peasants since the poor live from hand to mouth and consume whatever they get immediately with little prospect of being in a position to reimburse even the capital of the loan. Lending to the poor is like giving without any hope of recovery, but the poor themselves like to maintain the illusion of loans because it is less degrading. Instead of exhorting rich patrons to give generously to the poor, Exod. 22:24 insists on loans without interest and the condemnation of interest became a hallmark of biblical and Islamic practice (Rubin 2008), which shows that the scope of the ban was later broadened beyond the narrow confines of the Jerusalem commercial brotherhood.

Instead of brushing Exod. 22:24 aside as nonsensical, I take it as the first clue to the generalization of the ban on interest and the beginning of a process that led to the condemnation of interest as a sin in the wake of the foundation of a Persian *birtā* at Jerusalem. The integration of Yehud into the imperial structures marked the beginning of the end of the Benjaminite domination over Yehud as the administrative centre shifted from Mizpah to Jerusalem. The upper administrative echelons were held by newcomers from Babylonia unaffiliated to the local population. For this reason, the Bible insists that they were more 'Jewish' and therefore more legitimate than the Benjaminites who had been running the province for a century.[2]

If some of Mizpah's elite managed to retain a stake in the affairs of the province, the arrival of new actors on the scene challenged the monopoly of the small corporation of Benjaminite merchants that had extended credit to the farmers of Yehud. Chaney (1991) reads Leviticus 25 in this context of rivalry. Because it is read in light of Exodus 21 and Deuteronomy 15, the jubilee becomes a measure instituted by the Jerusalem returnees to gain the support of the populace through debt easements. In fact, the jubilee stipulates no debt release (§7.4.1). Therefore, the ban on interest of Lev. 25:36 is a more obvious way than the jubilee to gain the support of the local populace.

Benjaminite merchants lent against interest as was common in Elephantine and elsewhere (Seeligman 2004). Interest-free loans would be an obvious weapon in the hand of the Jerusalem elite in a commercial competition against Benjaminite, Ammonite and Ashdodite rivals. Hints at such a competition are found in Nehemiah 13 (Edelman 2006). How could Jerusalem offer interest-free loans?

In exchange for imperial support, the temple collected taxes and functioned as the treasury of the province (Schaper 1995; 1997; 2000: 145). To defray the costs and expenses linked to the administration of the temple, the priests had every interest in extending their activities beyond tax collection since, once the tribute due to the Imperial administration was paid, any extra profit would directly increase the revenues of the priestly families. Gradual monetarization optimized the redistribution of taxes to the military apparatus deployed along the Egyptian border and at the same time it rendered the services of moneylenders necessary since they were probably the only source of coins for the population. This was the case in Transjordan in the second part of the nineteenth century CE when the Ottomans integrated Southern Syria into the Imperial administration (Rogan 1999: 95-121). Loans were offered to the farmers in the form of foodstuffs. As had long been the case in Mesopotamia and in Egypt, the temple financed 'projects and transactions', to use modern financial terms, in particular the extensive raising of sheep (Briant 1979). The new developments in the province, however, met with the opposition of the local population that shouldered the financial costs of the construction of the Jerusalem and Garizim temples as well as providing the work gangs to do the work (Neh. 3). The books of Ezra and Nehemiah show that the restoration of Jerusalem did not merely involve the geographical transfer of Benjaminite structures from Mizpah to Jerusalem. Because the story was written much later, Benjaminites are not listed among Nehemiah's rivals. Yet, the restoration entailed the rise of a new elite that eventually prevailed over the old Benjaminite elite, thanks to Persian backing.

Under the fiscal pressure of the imperial administration, Jerusalem pressed the population of the province for surpluses. The merchant class of Benjamin and the *fellahin* of the entire province linked as they were by ancestral patronage relations, took the brunt of the pressure and closed ranks to resist the encroachments of Jerusalem, instead of producing a united front with Jerusalem. In exclusive partnership with the Jerusalem priests, the Judean merchants gained a dominating position in the trading activities in the province thanks to the interest-free loans they extended to farmers. Liquidities swelled temple revenues and ensured the growth of funds for further investment in projects and trade in addition to the necessary payments to keep the Persians content. But for the ban to be effective, it needed the charging of interest to be perceived as 'immoral'—that is, contrary to divine edicts. To this aim, the ban on interest emanates directly from YHWH's mouth (Lev. 25:35-38).

Persian fiscal pressure combined with a large demand created by the deployment of Persian forces in the area is the necessary condition for economic growth rather than the cause of a crisis. Paying more taxes is a proof of rising revenues rather than an indication of impoverishment. As every area on the periphery of major war theatres experiences an economic boom, resulting from the sudden demand created by the presence of armies nearby,[3] the province of Yehud now enjoyed a better position than had been the case when Xerxes descended upon Egypt. The development of the local economy, however, depended much upon the entrepreneurship of merchants. It is fair to assume that the priestly families of Jerusalem counted on merchants among their members to dent the monopoly of the old Benjaminite elite. To gain an edge over their better-established competitors, the Jerusalem merchants offered interest-free loans to farmers since their priestly brothers entrusted to them temple funds also at zero interest, thanks to extra revenues imposed under the guise of sacrifices:

> Leviticus and Numbers authorized the economic claims and religious authority of Aaronide priests, but they hid this reality by foregrounding the selfless ideal represented by the *'ōlāh*. They therefore pictured the regular priestly services as consisting mostly of *'ōlôt* offerings (Num 28–29), though their days must actually have been spent dealing mainly with the people's *šĕlāmîm*. (Watts 2007: 72)

Thanks to the financial security gained from the backing of the temple, the Jerusalem merchants could buy produce cash-down, stimulate production by advance supply of cash or inputs (seed, implements) and by advance buying of crops months before the harvest (Rogan 1999: 104; Menu 1982: 312-22). Having sold the products to the Persian administration with which they had privileged relations, the Jerusalem merchants could then reimburse their priestly brothers. Faithful to the ban on interest they had themselves proclaimed, the Jerusalem priests recovered the sums they had advanced to the members of their own families with a share of the net profit rather than with interest. If the hypothesis is correct, the temple priests found it strategically to their advantage to prefer a share of the merchants' trading profits to the interest. The reason is simple.

The ban on interest excluded the Benjaminite competitors who could not extend credit without taking interest and securing the loans with pledges because they did not have the backing of the temple treasury with which they had no direct connections. Intermarriage would have established connections, a solution denounced in Nehemiah 13.

The long-term benefit derived from interest-free loans by farmers may not have been as great as modern readers imagine since the temple had other ways to offset the comparative advantage of interest-free loans. The various tariffs recorded in the Torah would have been particularly onerous to farmers, had they been applied. One way to escape priestly taxation was the consecration of assets to the temple described in Leviticus 27, a system that prefigures the Islamic *waqf*. Strangely, the Bible and the modern champions of social justice focus their critique against the crown and against private merchants and leave the temple and the priesthood unscathed. Yet, interest rates are meaningless when considered in isolation from the overall economic context. The connection between the Jerusalem temple and the Persian *birtā* constituted a more weighty argument in favour of Jerusalem than interest-free loans. Palestinian farmers did not rush to British banks although they offered lower interest rates than moneylenders (§5.3.2; §5.6). It was the safety of Persian connections that attracted the farmers of Yehud away from the traditional moneylenders towards the new temple's bank. The lot of the ordinary farmer certainly improved, but as a consequence of the overall improvement of the economy rather than as a consequence of the elimination of interest-bearing loans.

Compared to the theological interpretation of the ban on interest as the affirmation of 'covenantal and divine compassion and deliverance that Israel was called to exhibit to the surrounding nations' (Williams 2009: 130), setting the ban in the context of a commercial war waged between patrons from Mizpah and from Jerusalem for the control of the economy of Yehud is prosaic. Yet, it avoids the obvious objection that Israel would have been a brighter light to the nations had it applied the ban on interests outside its narrow circle.

9.4 The Jubilee beyond Sentimental Piety

Having rejected the ban on interest as a consumption-smoothing device per se (§9.3), the jubilee is the last biblical measure to be considered. As discussed above (§7.4), the jubilee did not concern the farmers but regulated loans within a commercial brotherhood because the amounts involved far exceeded the credit requirements of cultivators. There is no need to repeat the discussion. Suffice it here to note that the jubilee was never meant to become the symbol of justice and the panacea for the economic troubles of today's poorer countries. Nevertheless, the jubilee may have contributed indirectly to the alleviation of economic hardship for the ordinary farmer. Excluding commercial debts from the seventh-year cancellations, the jubilee rendered the financial position of merchants more secure than that of Bronze Age Mesopotamian merchants who took the brunt of cancellations imposed by *andararum* edits. In turn, this improvement could have made merchants more willing to extend credit to farmers and cancel the balance of dues during the seventh year, thus improving the access of farmers to agricultural credit.

This understanding of the jubilee falls short of the vibrant calls for justice found in exegetical writings, but this is the price to be paid for the recovery of the hard and fast reality of the jubilee, away from utopia. The search for justice requires more than repeating prophetic fulminations. Justice requires understanding, understanding how the modern world functions as much as understanding how the ancient world functioned.

The religious criminalization of interest morphed into a criminalization of credit. Coupled with a misunderstanding of the biblical jubilee as a general cancellation of debts, the modern industry of international charity has convinced many that giving without strings is good and that lending is evil. As an outgrowth of the biblical sacralization of the poor, giving without expecting returns is deemed the only moral attitude. Colossal sums have been collected in rich countries and transferred to the Third World with little effect apart from supporting regimes that hide fortunes in tax-havens (Moyo 2009).

While the West develops marketing strategies to collect monies to 'help' the poor in developing countries that just will not develop, micro-loans give the lie to the notion that usurious lending is bad. Instead of giving generously, micro-credit requires full reimbursement before further loans may be extended. Instead of ruining the poor, usurious micro-credit systems succeeded where giving has failed, and the Pakistani Grameen Bank was awarded the Nobel Prize in 2002.

These developments should warn social-scientific exegetes. Today, the biblical sacralization of the poor serves the liberal paradigm that pushes for less state involvement in social action which in turn enables religious institutions to step in obligingly with their own charitable organizations. If the pauper is indeed God's client (Coulange 2007: 211-16), is he not also the client of his human patron who exchanges his liberalities against military and political support, fame and respectability? As patrons of the poor, religious organizations gain much social and political leverage by performing social tasks. The rich need the poor to remain rich and respectable as much as the poor need the rich to stay alive. An informal social contract has long existed between the political powers and religious institutions that are granted land with the expectation that they would maintain social order by guaranteeing sustenance to the poor (Bekar and Reed 2003: 353; Singer 2003; Bilici 2003). As transmitters of immaterial or spiritual rewards, religious institutions held and continue to hold a prime position in consumption smoothing since they convert charitable giving into reputation and honour. Working for a better world is crucial, but repeating slogans devoid of anchorage in ancient or present reality is not enough.

Nothing indicates that the Assyrian or Persian tax collectors were greedier than the tax collectors sent by Judean kings or Jerusalem priests. The wild imaginings of the literati about the poor and the destitute did not concern the ordinary farmer. In Job as in Isaiah 58, the mention of social abuses avoids blaming God for delays in the accomplishment of promises (Williamson 1999: 155). The mention of the hungry, the homeless and the naked in this context can hardly indicate that the presence of destitute people was a new phenomenon. Prophetic fulminations are a convenient outlet for the inevitable frustrations caused by the gap between ideal and reality, but they cannot be taken as social reportage. Instead of analysing social abuses with a view to developing strategies to alleviate them, prophetic texts hurl social abuses at the face of opponents in a strategy to denounce their position, to lay the blame upon the straw man of the 'nasty rich' and exculpate the writers and God.

Therefore, the notion of crises as spurring the production of biblical texts should be challenged. The number of destitute would have increased between the ninth century BCE and the turn of the era because the overall population increased. Apart from such 'natural' increase, there is no evidence, textual or archaeological, to support a long-term and worsening crisis in the Persian era. Economic pressure causes a rise in production levels and greater wealth for everyone, poor included, albeit in very different proportions. It is safe to apply to the period of the 'Second Temple' Houston's contention that 'before the end of the monarchic period there was no loss of independence or drastic deterioration in the standard of living of the rural population' (Houston 2008: 48). Crises certainly happened time and again but their incidence was too short to be visible in the archaeological record. Crises were mostly famines caused by the combination of natural disasters and war. Farmers knew how to cope with drought, war, crickets and mildew as long as they did not occur simultaneously or too close to one another. The combination of factors provoked famines that lasted a few years at most until the next normal harvest filled the stores. If one insists on calling 'crisis' the period of dearth that preceded the harvest, this kind of crisis was indeed recurrent, so much so that it belonged to the routine of yearly cycles. Severe famines were critical enough for the very young and the old who were the first ones to be famished to save the rest of the family (Brunt 1987: 131-55), but as a whole, families coped. The effects of less common crises were absorbed with varying degrees of success, depending on a web of factors that is too complex to recover.

Notes

1. Yields from virgin steppe land reach 20 to 30 per unit sown (compared to 3-5 in the Syrian western plains) without any fertilizers. Given good rain levels (three years out of ten in the Syrian Jazira, more in central Palestine), they can even reach the impressive figure of 60 or even 100 per unit (Métral 2000: 130 n. 14).
2. From the Assyrians to the Ottomans and later, colonial domination relied on outsiders. The Ottomans brought in Circassians in Akkar in the mid-seventeenth century CE, who functioned as de facto independent overlords in this fringe area and had a virtual monopoly over land and labour (Gilsenan 1984: 454-58).
3. The constant warfare in Northern Syria during the centuries preceding Islam depleted the Syrian economy and greatly favoured Arabia (Crone 2007). The same phenomenon was observed in Mandatory Palestine where the income of *fellahin* farms increased significantly during the Second World War. The rural economy of Palestine declined until the 1940s when the trend was reversed as a result of British military deployment to Palestine that began during the 1936–1939 Great Revolt and continued throughout the Second World War. Deployment boosted the demand for local goods, expanded job opportunities for urban migrants and created inflationary pressures that eased peasant debt (Nadan 2006: 145-71).

General Conclusion

The notion of social and economic crisis through which social-scientific exegesis reads key biblical texts and reconstitutes the conditions in ancient Israel has been found wanting. Tax pressure indeed forced farmers to produce more. Impressed work forced them to work when there was little to do in the fields. Loans had to be paid back with high interest rates. Yet, these extra burdens are not sufficient to provoke a crisis. It is the absence rather than the presence of taxes, corvée and credit that reveals a depressed economy. However exploitative economic relations are, they constitute a web of relations in which solidarity goes hand in hand with exploitation. In spite of high interest rates, farmers were better protected against climatic and political uncertainties when merchants and patrons were present to offer loans than when they had to rely only on kinship solidarity.

There was no structural crisis from the eighth century BCE onwards. The inhabitants of Yehud coped with the various circumstantial crises they faced but it is clear that they survived them or there would be no Bible today, at least not one produced long ago in the Palestinian central range. General conditions made life possible if not enviable; the iconic prophets disguised as heroes of social justice fade away into irrelevance. The error of social-scientific exegesis is to read the rivalry and the conflict of interest between the crown, the local elite and the farmers expressed in prophetic texts as the indication of a crisis when in fact they constitute the basis of healthy social interactions. Farmers never were hapless victims. The fact that prophetic texts only refer to the farmers' point of view on the extraction of surplus reveals the bargaining power of farmers. This does not mean that prophetic texts were produced by farmers. It reveals that anyone wanting to assume a position of leadership (patron or king) had to present himself as a champion of the farmers' cause. To that aim, farmers had to be depicted as poor and helpless rather than sanguinely coping with life's hazards. That the divine sphere was mobilized to play the role of the poor man's advocate is equally revealing of the power and resilience of small farmers who held the moral high ground. Prophetic denunciations of the rich should be read as evidence of the power struggle between different elite groups rather than as clues of the actual economic situation on the ground.

The ideological charge of prophetic texts does not exclude the regular recurrence of times of dearth, when famine led to the death of the youngest and the oldest. Yet, farmers were better equipped to face the harshness of famine during imperial times than under the sole rule of tribal 'egalitarianism' because larger political entities offer broader consumption-smoothing processes. Hence, the economic and social history of Persian Yehud cannot be subsumed under the vague category of crisis—although this does not imply a Gibbonian stance glorifying imperial eras, Roman or other, as most happy periods (Gibbon 1910: 78). The trendy post-colonial denigration of empires is, nevertheless, hardly more suitable. Happiness cannot be measured but, weighted against the little we know about the ancient world, the social-scientific slogans are deeply flawed.

The first mistake stems from the tyranny of the notion of land ownership (§1.3) and the failure to take into account the sufficient abundance of arable land and the importance of communal regimes (§2). Then, biblical exegetes reproduce the elite's condescension by depicting peasants as victims (§3) waiting for favours from above in order to survive. The realization that small farms retained an economic advantage over large estates and that estate holders had every interest in sharing risks with local farmers through sharecropping arrangements turns the social-scientific dogma into mere slogans (§4). Latifundia depriving small farmers and absentee landlords getting richer without raising a finger had no place in ancient Palestine. The idea that the rich made a fortune by lending to the poor bears no connection with the ancient world (§5). The positive effects of patronage and of debt must be recovered (§6) to reconstitute a more realistic picture of the conditions prevailing in Persian Yehud. A more realistic approach to the ancient economy yields some fresh exegetical insights, in particular in the books of Ruth (§4:4), Nehemiah (§7.2), Job (§7.3) and Leviticus (§7.4).

Social-scientific biblical exegesis accords too much credence to prophetic ranting and not enough credence to non-prophetic economic texts. Hence, consumption-smoothing mechanisms described in the Bible are deemed utopian. In light of ancient economics, they appear quite realistic, although only the *šemiṭṭah* had a direct impact on the finances of ordinary farmers (§9.1). The ban on interest-bearing loans sought to enlarge the clientele of the newly built temple at Jerusalem (§9.3). The sabbatical year was a burden rather than a holiday, but it would have dramatically increased the population-bearing capacity of the province of Yehud (§9.2). The jubilee did not concern farmers and the way it is presented by well-meaning biblical exegetes appears particularly misguided in light of economic developments in today's world (9.4).

Glossary

allodial: a type of possession that is free from obligations, such as rents or service due to an overlord. In common-law countries such as England and Wales, the crown is the sole holder of allodial titles.

anatocism: compound interest by which interest is charged both on principal and on interest earned during previous compounding periods.

antichresis, antichretic loan: a contract by which a creditor acquires the right of reaping the fruit or other revenues of the fixed assets, persons or animals given to him in pledge.

birtā: Aramaic (Ezra 6:2), Hebrew *birah*, loanword from Akkadian *birtu*, a fort or a citadel within a settlement with military personnel such as Artaxerxes I built in Jerusalem around 450 BCE.

cadastre: an official land register recording category, ownership and boundaries for taxation purposes.

champion or **champaign**: any expanse of common unenclosed land.

corvée: French, unpaid work.

dhukūr: Arabic, 'male', designate a type of *musha'* tenure by which lots are shared out according to the number of male adults.

emphyteutic lease: a type of real-estate contract specifying that the lessee must improve the property.

escheat: the reverting of the property of a person who dies intestate and without heir.

feddān: Arabic, 'yoke of oxen', a variable unit of surface of agricultural land.

fief: property granted by a medieval lord to a vassal for his maintenance in return for services.

furlongs: long furrows, strips of arable land allotted in open-field tenure systems.

hacienda: Spanish, large estate or plantation.

kleruch: Greek, 'lot-holder', a settler who received a plot of agricultural land in a colony against military service.

lien: a right to retain possession of another's assets (or of a portion of them) pending discharge of a debt.

tenure: holding or occupying of real estate.

latifundia: Latin, plural of *latifundium*, 'large estate'.

longue durée: French, 'long-term', the permanent or very slowly evolving structures, in particular of geography and climate, used by historian Ferdinand Braudel in contrast to political events and economic circumstances.

musha': Arabic, 'shared', term used by European observers to describe open-field tenure in the Levant.

prosbol: Rabbinic term designating a clause in a loan contract protecting the lender from the effect of future debt cancellations.

tanzimat: Turkish, 'reorganization', an era of reforms between 1839 and 1876 to modernize the Ottoman Empire.

tariff: Arabic, 'notification', list of dues to the priests according to the nature of the offering, such as found in the books of Leviticus and Numbers and in Punic inscriptions.

usufruct: from Latin *usus* and *fructus*, the right of use and enjoyment of a thing belonging to another provided the substance of the thing is preserved.

wasta: Arabic, 'intermediary' in networks of patronage and favouritism.

Bibliography

Ababsa al-Husseini, Myriam. 2002. 'Mise en valeur agricole et contrôle politique dans la vallée de l'Euphrate (1865–1946).' *Bulletin d'Etudes Orientales* 53-54: 459-88.

— 2007. 'Contre-réforme agraire et conflits fonciers en Jazîra syrienne (2000–2005).' *Revue d'Études des Mondes Musulmans et Méditerranéens* 115-116: 211-30.

'Abbas Hamid, Ra'uf. 2002. 'Why Study Ownership? An Approach to the Study of the Social History of Egypt.' In N. Hanna (ed.). *Money, Land and Trade*. London: L. B. Tauris: 37-49.

Abcarius, Michel Fred. 1946. *Palestine through the Fog of Propaganda*. London: Hutchinson & Co.

'Abd Al-Kader, A. 1959. 'Land, Property and Land Tenure in Islam.' *Islamic Quarterly* 5: 4-11.

Abraham, K. 2004. *Business and Politics under the Persian Empire*. Bethesda: CDL.

Al-Salim, F. 2007. 'Politics of Agriculture.' *Journal of Palestine Studies* 36: 107.

Adams, R. McC. 1982. 'Property Rights and Functional Tenure in Mesopotamian Rural Communities.' In *Studies and Languages of the Ancient Near East*. Warminster: Aris & Phillips: 1-14.

Ahlström, Gosta W. 1993. *The History of Ancient Palestine from the Paleolithic Period to Alexander's Conquest*. Ed. D. V. Edelman; Sheffield: Academic Press.

Albertz, Rainer. 1981. 'Der sozialgeschichtliche Hintergrund des Hiobbuches und der «Babylonischen Theodizee».' In J. Jeremias and L. Perlitt (eds). *Die Botschaft und die Boten*. Neukirchen–Vluyn: Neukirchener: 349-72; repr. in idem. 2003. *Geschichte und Theologie: Studien zur Exegese des Alten Testaments und zur Religionsgeschichte Israels*. Berlin: de Gruyter: 107-34.

— 1990. 'Der Kampf gegen die Schuldenkrise.' In R. Albertz (ed.). *Der Mensch als Hüter seiner Welt*. Stuttgart: Calwer: 40-60.

— 1994. *A History of Israelite Religion in the Old Testament Period*. London: SCM.

— 1997. 'Die Theologisierung des Rechts im Alten Israel.' In Rainer Albertz, *Religion und Gesellschaft 1*. Münster: Ugarit-Verlag: 115-32.

— 2003. 'Zur Wirtschaftspolitik des Perserreiches.' In R. Albertz (ed.). *Geschichte und Theologie*. Berlin: de Gruyter: 335-57.

— 2007. 'Social History of Ancient Israel.' In H. G. M. Williamson (ed.). *Understanding the History of Ancient Israel*. Oxford: University Press: 347-367.

Aldock, Susan E., John F. Cherry and Jack L. Davis. 1994. 'Intensive Survey, Agricultural Practice and the Classical Landscape of Greece.' In Ian Morris (ed.). *Classical Greece: Ancient Histories and Modern Archaeologies*. Cambridge: University Press: 137-70.

Allred, L. B. 2006. *Cooks and Kitchens: Centralized Food Production in Late IIIrd Millennium Mesopotamia*. PhD Dissertation; Johns Hopkins University, Baltimore.

Alt, Albrecht. 1955. 'Mica 2,1-5 GHS ANAGASMOS in Juda.' In N. A. Dahl and A. S. Kapelrud (eds). *Interpretationes ad vetus testamentum pertinentes Sigmundo Mowinkel septuagenario missae*. Oslo: Land og Kirche: 13-23.

— 1959. 'Der Anteil des Königtums an der sozialen Entwicklung in den Reichen Israel und Juda.' In *Kleine Schriften zur Geschichte des Volkes Israel 3*. München: Beck: 348-72.

Altorki, Soraya and Donald P. Cole. 2006. 'Land and Identity among Awlad 'Ali Bedouin: Egypt's Northwest Coast.' In Dawn Chatty (ed.). *Nomadic Societies in the Middle East and North Africa: Entering the 21st Century*. Leiden: Brill: 634-53.

Aperghis, Gerassimos G. 2000. 'War Captives and Economic Exploitation: Evidence from the Persepolis Fortification Tablets.' In Jean Andreau, Pierre Briant and René Descat (eds). *La guerre dans les économies antiques*. Saint-Bertrand-de-Comminges: Musée départemental: 127- 44.

Artus, Olivier. 2009. 'Les frontières de la communauté judéenne à la lumière du livre de *Ruth*.' *Transeuphratène* 37: 11-20.

Ashburner, W. 1912. 'The Farmer's Law.' *Journal of Hellenic Studies* 32: 68-95.

Aswad, B. C. 1971. *Property Control and Social Strategies in Settlers in a Middle Eastern Plain*. Ann Arbor: University of Michigan.

Atkinson, David. 1983. *The End of the Russian Land Commune 1905–1930*. Stanford: Stanford University Press.

Atran, Scott. 1986. '*Hamula* Organisation and Masha'a Tenure in Palestine.' *Man* 21: 271-95.

Ault, Warren O. 1973. *Open-field Farming in Medieval England: A Study of Village By-laws*. London: Georges Allen and Unwin.

Avioz, Michael. 2006. 'The Analogies between the David-Bathsheba Affair and the Naboth Narrative.' *Journal of Northwest Semitic Languages* 32: 115-28.

Baer, Gabriel. 1983. 'Landlord, Peasant and the Government in the Arab Provinces of the Ottoman Empire in the 19th and Early 20th Centuries.' In J.-L. Bacqué-Grammont and P. Dumont (eds). *Economies et sociétés dans l'Empire ottoman*. Paris: CNRS: 261-74.

Baker, David L. 2009. *Tight Fists or Open Hands? Wealth and Poverty in Old Testament Law*. Grand Rapids: Eerdmans.

Baker, John Hamilton. 1990. *An Introduction to English Legal History*. London: Butterworths.

Baldwin, Peter. 2004. 'Comparing and Generalizing: Why All History Is Comparative, yet No History Is Sociology.' In D. Cohen and M. O'Connor (eds). *Comparison and History*. New York: Routledge: 1-22.

Banaji, Jairus. 1997. 'Modernizing the Historiography of Rural Labour: An Unwritten Agenda.' In M. Bentley (ed.). *Companion to Historiography*. London: Routledge: 88-104.

— 2001. *Agrarian Change in Late Antiquity*. Oxford: University Press.

Bar, Doron. 2004. 'Frontier and Periphery in Late Antique Palestine.' *Roman and Byzantine Studies* 44: 69-92.

Bar Ilan, Meir. 1990. 'Infant Mortality in the Land of Israel in Late Antiquity.' In S. Fishbane and J. N. Lightstone (eds). *Judaism and Jewish Society.* Montreal: Concordia University: 3-25.

Barkai, Haim. 1996. 'Oppenheimer and the Zionist Resettlement of Palestine: The *Genossenschaft* versus the Collective Settlement.' In V. Caspari and B. Schefold (eds). *Franz Oppenheimer und Adolph Lowe: zwei Wirtschaftswissenschaftler der Frankfurter Universität.* Marburg: Metropolis: 17-63.

Barthélemy, A. 1935. *Dictionnaire Arabe-Français.* Paris: Geuthner.

Bartlett, R. 1990. *Land Commune and Peasant Community in Russia.* Basinstoke: Macmillan.

Bauks, Michaela. 2004. 'Die Begriffe *morašah* und *'aḥuzzah* in Pg. Überlegungen zur Landkonzeption der Priestergrundschrift.' *Zeitschrift für die alttestamentlische Wissenschaft* 116: 171-88.

Beattie, Derk Robert George. 1994. *The Targum of Ruth.* Collegeville, MN: Liturgical Press.

Beaulieu, Paul-Alain. 2000. 'A Land Grant on a Cylinder Seal and Assurbanipal's Babylonian Policy.' In S. Graziani (ed.). *Studi sul vicino oriente antico 1.* Napoli: Istituto Universitario Orientale: 25-46.

Beentjes, Pancratius C. 2000. 'Canon and Scripture in the Book of Ben Sira.' In Magne Sæbø (ed.). *Hebrew Bible/Old Testament 1/2.* Göttingen: Vandenhoeck & Ruprecht: 591-605.

Bekar, Cliff T. and Clyde G. Reed. 2003. 'Open Fields, Risk, and Land Divisibility.' *Explorations in Economic History* 40: 308-25.

Ben Zvi, Ehud. 1999. 'Wrongdoers, Wrongdoing and Righting Wrongs in Micah 2.' *Biblical Interpretation* 7: 87-100.

— 2007. 'The House of Omri/Ahab in Chronicles.' In L. L. Grabbe (ed.). *Ahab Agonistes.* London: T&T Clark: 41-53.

Ben-Barak, Zafrira. 1981. 'Meribaal and the System of Land Grants in Ancient Israel.' *Biblica* 62: 73-91.

Bendor, S. 1996. *The Social Structure of Ancient Israel.* Jerusalem: Simor.

Bergen, W. J. 1999. *Elisha and the End of Prophetism.* Sheffield: Sheffield Academic Press.

Berger, Yitzhak. 2009. 'Ruth and the David-Bathsheba Story.' *Journal for the Study of the Old Testament* 33: 433-52.

Bergheim, Samuel. 1895. 'Land Tenure in Palestine.' *Palestine Exploration Fund Quarterly*: 189-91.

Bergsma, John Sietze. 2003. 'The Jubilee: A Post-Exilic Priestly Attempt to Reclaim Lands.' *Biblica* 84: 225-46.

Berquist, Jon L. 1995. *Judaism in Persia's Shadow*. Minneapolis: Fortress.

Betlyon, John W. 2004. 'Egypt and Phoenicia in the Persian Period: Partners in Trade and Rebellion.' In G. N. Knoppers and A. Hirsch (eds). *Egypt, Israel, and the Ancient Mediterranean World.* Leiden: Brill: 455-77.

Bibb, Bryan D. 2009. *Ritual Words and Narrative Worlds in the Book of Leviticus.* New York: T. & T. Clark.

Bilici, Faruk. 2003. 'Les 'imâret ottomanes: un instrument de lutte contre la pauvreté.' In J.-P. Pascual (ed.). *Pauvreté et richesse dans le monde musulman*. Paris: Maisonneuve & Larose: 271-88.

Bingen, J. 1973. 'Présence grecque et milieu rural ptolémaïque.' In M. I. Finley (ed.). *Problèmes de la terre en Grèce ancienne*. Paris: Mouton & Co: 217-22.

Blanford, Nicholas. 2006. *Killing Mr Lebanon*. London: I. B. Tauris.

Blanton, Richard E. 2000. *Hellenistic, Roman and Byzantine Settlement Patterns of the Coast Lands of Western Rough Cilicia*. Oxford: Archeopress.

Blenkinsopp, Joseph. 1988. *Ezra–Nehemiah*. Philadelphia: Westminster.

— 1995. 'Deuteronomy and the Politics of Post-Mortem Existence.' *Vetus Testamentum* 45: 1-16.

— 2001. 'Did the Second Jerusalemite Temple Possess Land?' *Transeuphratène* 21: 61-68.

Bloch, Marc. 1961. *Feudal Society*. London: Routledge & Kegan Paul.

Bloch-Smith, Elisabeth, and B. Alpert Nakhai. 1999. 'A Landscape Comes to Life.' *Near Eastern Archaeology* 62: 62-92, 101-27.

Blum, Erhard. 2000. 'Der Nabotüberlieferung und die Kompositionsgeschichte der Vorderen Propheten.' In R. G. Kratz; T. Krüger and K. Schmid (eds). *Schriftauslegung in der Schrift*. Berlin: de Gruyter: 111-28.

Blum, Jerome. 1978. *The End of the Old Order in Rural Europe*. Princeton: Princeton University Press.

Boadt, L. 1982. *Jeremiah 26–52, Habakkuk, Zephaniah, Nahum*. Wilmington: Glazier.

Bodi, Daniel. 2002. *Jérusalem à l'époque perse*. Paris: Geuthner.

Boer, Roland. 2003. *Marxist Criticism of the Bible*. London: T. & T. Clark.

— 2007. 'The Sacred Economy of Ancient Israel.' *Scandinavian Journal of the Old Testament* 21: 29-48.

Bohlen, Reinhold. 1978. *Der Fall Nabot*. Trier: Paulinus.

Boehm, Christopher. 1993. 'Egalitarian Behavior and Reverse Dominance.' *Current Anthropology* 34: 227-54.

Bolens, Lucie. 1974. *Les méthodes culturales au Moyen Age d'après les traités d'agronomie andalous*. Genève: Médecine et Hygiène.

Bolin, Thomas M. 1996. 'The Temple of יהו at Elephantine and Persian Religious Policy.' In Diana V. Edelman (ed.). *The Triumph of Elohim*. Grand Rapids: Eerdmans: 127-44.

Bongenaar, A. C. V. M. 1999. 'Money in the Neo-Babylonian Institutions.' In J. G. Dercksen (ed.). *Trade and Finance in Ancient Mesopotamia*. Leiden: NINO: 159-74.

Bordreuil, Pierre Felice Israel and Dennis Pardee. 1998. 'King's Command and Widow's Plea.' *Near Eastern Archaeology* 61: 2-13.

Borowski, Oded. 1987. *Agriculture in Iron Age Israel*. Winona Lake, IN: Eisenbrauns.

— 2002. *Agriculture in Iron Age Israel*. Leiden: Brill.

— 2003. *Daily Life in Biblical Times*. Leiden: Brill.

Bosrup, Ester. 1970. *The Conditions of Agricultural Growth. The Economics of Agrarian Change under Population Pressure*. London: Allen & Unwin.

Botta, A. F. 2006. 'The Legal Function and Egyptian Background of the שליט Clause.' *Maarav* 13: 193-209.

— 2008. *Aramaic and Egyptian Legal Traditions at Elephantine.* London: T. & T. Clark.
Braudel, Fernand. 1972. *The Mediterranean.* London: Collins.
— 1973. *Capitalism and Material Life 1400–1800.* London: Weidenfeld & Nicholson.
Bresciani, Edda. 1985. 'The Persian Occupation of Egypt.' In Ilya Gershevitch (ed.). *Cambridge History of Iran.* II. Cambridge: Cambridge University Press.
Bresson, Alain. 2008. *L'économie de la Grèce des cités. Les espaces de l'échange.* Paris: A. Colin.
Briant, Pierre. 1978. 'Contrainte militaire, dépendance rurale et exploitation des territoires achéménides.' *Index* 8: 1-51; repr. in P. Briant. 1982. *Rois, tributs et paysans.* Besançon: Belles Lettres: 175-225.
— 1979. 'L'élevage ovin fans l'empire achéménide.' *Journal of the Economic and Social History of the Orient* 22: 136-61.
— 1992. 'La date des révoltes babyloniennes contre Xerxès.' *Studia Iranica* 21: 7-20.
— 2002. *From Cyrus to Alexander.* Winona Lake, IN: Eisenbrauns.
Briant, Pierre Wouter, F. M. Henkelman and Matthew W. Stolper (eds). 2008. *L'archive des Fortifications de Persépolis.* Paris: de Boccard.
Brown, P. C. 1985. 'Land Redistribution Schemes in Tokugawa Japan.' Paper presented at the Annual Meeting of the American Historical Association, New York, 28 December, 1985. Accessed 26 March 2009. http://dlc.dlib.indiana.edu/archive/00003585/01/Brownland_redistribution_in_tokugawa_japan.pdf.
Brueggemann, Walter. 1993. 'Trajectories in Old Testament Literature and the Sociology of Ancient Israel.' In N. K. Gottwald and R. A. Horsley (eds). *The Bible and Liberation.* New York/London: Orbis/SPCK: 201-26.
Brunt, P. A. 1987. *Italian Manpower: 225 B.C.– A.D. 14.* Oxford: Oxford University Press.
Buhl, Frants. 1899. *Die sozialen Verhältnisse der Israeliten.* Berlin: Reuther & Reichard.
Burckhardt, J. L. 1819. *Travels in Syria and the Holy Land.* Ed. W. M. Leake; London: Printed for Sir R. Phillips.
Burford, A. 1993. *Land and Labor in the Greek World.* Baltimore: John Hopkins University.
Bush, Frederic W. 1996. *Ruth/Esther.* Dallas: Word Books.
Buss, M. J. 2006. 'The Place of Israelite Prophecy in Human History.' In B. E. Kelle and M. Bishop Moore (eds). *Israel's Prophets and Israel's Past.* New York: T. & T. Clark.
Cahen, C. 1954. 'Fiscalité, propriété, antagonismes sociaux en Haute-Mésopotamie au temps des premiers 'Abbāsides d'après Denys de Tell-Mahré.' *Arabica* 1: 136-52.
Canaan, T. 1916. 'Die Wintersaat in Palaestina.' *Zeitschrift der deutschen morgenländischen Gesellschaft* 70: 164-78.
Capogrossi Colognesi, Luigi. 1979. 'Le régime de la terre à l'époque républicaine.' In *Terre et Paysans dépendants dans les sociétés antiques.* Paris: CNRS: 313-65.
Cardascia, G. 1959. 'Le concept babylonien de propriété.' *Revue internationale des droits de l'Antiquité* 6: 19-32.
Carew, Edna. 1996. *The Language of Money 3.* Crows Nests: Allen & Unwin.
Carroll, Robert P. 1986. *Jeremiah.* London: SCM Press.
Carter, Charles E. 1999. *The Emergence of Yehud in the Persian Period.* Sheffield: Sheffield Academic Press.

Carter, J. 1997. 'Thiasos and Marzeah.' In Susan Langdon (ed.). *New Light on a Dark Age*. Columbia: Missouri University: 72-112.

Causse, Antonin. 1937. *Du groupe ethnique à la communauté religieuse*. Paris: Alcan.

Chandezon, Christophe. 2000. 'Guerre, agriculture et crises d'après les inscriptions hellénistiques.' In J. Andreau, P. Briant and R. Descat (eds). *La guerre dans les économies antiques*. Saint-Bertrand-de-Comminges: Musée départemental: 231-52.

Chaney, Marvin L. 1983. 'Ancient Peasant Movements and the Formation of Premonarchic Israel.' In D. N. Freedman and D. F. Graf (eds). *Palestine in Transition: The Emergence of Ancient Israel*. Sheffield: Almond Press: 39-90.

— 1991. 'Debt Easement in Israelite History and Tradition.' In D. Jobling, P. L. Day and G. T. Sheppard (eds). *The Bible and the Politics of Exegesis*. Cleveland, OH: Pilgrim: 127-40.

— 1993. 'Bitter Bounty: The Dynamics of Political Economy Critiqued by the Eighth-Century Prophets.' In N. K. Gottwald and R. A. Horsley (eds). *The Bible and Liberation; Political and Social Hermeneutics*. Maryknoll, NY: Orbis: 250-63.

— 1999. 'Whose Sour Grapes? The Addressees of Isaiah 5:1-7 in the Light of Political Economy.' *Semeia* 87: 105-22.

Charpin, Daniel. 1986. 'Transmission des titres de propriété et constitution des archives privées en Babylonie ancienne.' In K. R. Veenhof (ed.). *Cuneiform Archives and Libraries*. Leiden: Brill: 121-40.

— 1987. 'Les décrets royaux à l'époque paléo-babylonienne, à propos d'un ouvrage récent.' *Archiv für Orientforschung* 34: 36-44.

— 1996. 'Le bon pasteur: idéologie et pratique de la justice royale à l'époque paléo-babylonienne.' In ARGO (ed.). *Les moyens d'expression du pouvoir dans les sociétés anciennes*. Leuven: Peeters: 101-14.

— 2000. 'Les prêteurs et le palais: les édits de *mīšarum* des rois de Babylone et leurs traces dans les archives privées.' In A. C. V. M. Bongenaar (ed.). *Interdependency of Institutions and Private Entrepreneurs*. Istanbul: NINO: 185-211.

Childe, V. G. 1954. *What Happened in History*. Harmondsworth: Penguin.

Clines, David J. A. 1984. *Ezra, Nehemiah, Esther*. Grand Rapids: Eerdmans.

— 1993. 'Metacommenting Amos.' In H. A. McKay and D. J. A. Clines (eds). *Of Prophets' Visions and the Wisdom and Sages*. Sheffield: JSOT Press: 142-60.

— 1998. 'Quarter Days Gone: Job 24 and the Absence of God.' In D. J. A. Clines, *On the Way to the Postmodern*. Sheffield: Sheffield Academic Press, 1998: II, 801-22.

— 2006. *Job*. Nashville: Thomas Nelson.

Coçgel, M. M. 2006. 'Agricultural Productivity in the Early Ottoman Empire.' *Research in Economic History* 24: 161-87.

Collins. 1994. *Collins English Dictionary*. Glasgow: HarperCollins Publishers.

Conder, Claude Reignier. 1883. *Heth and Moab*. London: R. Bentley & Sons.

Confino, Michael. 1969. *Systèmes agraires et progrès agricole*. Paris: Mouton.

Conte, E. 2003. 'Agnatic Illusions: The Element of Choice in Arab Kinship.' In F. A. Jabar and H. Dawod (eds). *Tribes and Power. Nationalism and Ethnicity in the Middle East*. London: Saqi: 15-49.

Cogan, Mordechai. 2001. *1 Kings*. New York: Doubleday.

Cogan, Mordechai, and Haim Tadmor. 1988. *II Kings*. New York: Doubleday.

Cook, S. L. 2004. *The Biblical Roots of Biblical Yahwism*. Atlanta: SBL.

Coote, Robert B. 1991. *In Defense of Revolution*. Minneapolis: Fortress Press.

Coote, Robert B., and Keith W. Whitelam. 1986. 'The Emergence of Israel: Social Transformation and State Formation following the Decline in Late Bronze Age Trade.' In N. K. Gottwald (ed.). *Social Scientific Criticism of the Hebrew Bible and its Social World: The Israelite Monarchy.* Chico: Scholars Press: 107-47; repr. in C. E. Carter and C. L. Meyers (eds). 1996. *Community, Identity, and Ideology.* Winona Lake, IN: Eisenbrauns: 335-76.

— 1987. *The Emergence of Early Israel in Historical Perspective.* Sheffield: Sheffield Academic Press.

Coulange, Pierre. 2007. *Dieu, ami des pauvres.* Fribourg: Academic Press.

Courby, F., and C. Picard. 1924. *Recherches archéologiques à Stratos d'Acarnanie.* Paris: E. de Boccard.

Cox, Claude E. 2007. 'Iob.' In *New English Translation of the Septuagint.* Oxford: Oxford University Press.

Cripps, Eric L. 2007. *Land Tenure and Social Stratification in Ancient Mesopotamia.* Oxford: Archaeopress.

Cronauer, Patrick T. 2005. *The Stories about Naboth the Jezreelite.* New York: T. & T. Clark.

Crone, Patricia. 2007. 'Quraysh and the Roman Army: Making Sense of the Meccan Leather Trade.' *Bulletin of the School of Oriental and African Studies* 70: 63-88.

— 2003. *Pre-Industrial Societies: Anatomy of the Pre-Modern World.* Oxford: Oneworld.

Cuno, Kenneth M. 1995. 'Was the Land of Syria Miri or Milk? An Examination of Juridical Differences within the Hanafi School.' *Studia Islamica* 81: 121-52.

Cussini, E. 1992. 'The Aramaic Law of Sale and the Cuneiform Legal Tradition.' PhD dissertation; John Hopkins University.

Dahlman, Carl. 1980. *The Open Fields and beyond: A Property Rights Analysis of an Economic Institution.* Cambridge: Cambridge University Press.

Dahood, Mitchell. 1981. *Psalms.* II. New York: Doubleday.

Dalman, Gustaf. 1964. *Arbeit und Sitte.* I/1. Hildesheim: Georg Olms.

Dandamayev, A. 1993. 'Achaemenid Estates in Lahîru.' *Iranica Antiqua* 27: 117-123.

Dandamayev, Muhammad A. 1984. *Slavery in Babylonia from Nabopolassar to Alexander the Great.* DeKalb: Northern Illinois University Press.

— 1987. 'Free Hired Labor in Babylonia during the Sixth through Fourth Centuries B.C.' In M. A. Powell (ed.). *Labor in the Ancient Near East.* New Haven: American Oriental Society: 271-79.

— 1995. 'The Neo-Babylonian tamkârû.' In Ziony Zevit, Seymour Gittin and Michael Sokoloff (eds). *Solving Riddles and Untying Knots.* Winona Lake, IN: Eisenbrauns: 523-30.

Davies, John K. 1977. 'Athenian Citizenship: The Descent Group and the Alternatives.' *Classical Journal* 73: 105-21.

Davis, Ellen F. 2009. *Scripture, Culture and Agriculture.* Cambridge: Cambridge University Press.

de Callataÿ, François. 2005. 'L'instauration par Ptolemée Ier Soter d'une économie monétaire fermée.' In F. Duyrat and O. Picard (eds). *L'exception égyptienne? Production et échanges monétaires en Egypte hellénistique et romaine.* Le Caire: IFAO: 117-133.

De Graf, K. 2008. 'Giving a Loan Is Like Making Love.' In K. Verboven, K. Vandorpe and V. Chankowski (eds). *Pistoi dia tèn technèn.* Leuven: Peeters: 3-16.

De Geus, Cornelis. H. J. 1983. 'Agrarian Communities in Biblical Times: 12th to 10th Centuries BCE.' In *Rural Communities, Second Part, Antiquity*. Paris: Dessain & Tolra: 207-37.

De Roover, R. 1971. *La pensée économique des scolastiques. Doctrines et méthodes*. Montréal: Institut d'Études Médiévales.

Dearman, J. Andrew. 1988. *Property Rights in the Eighth-Century Prophets*. Atlanta: Scholars Press.

Deist, Ferdinand E. 2002. *The Material Culture of the Bible*. Sheffield: Sheffield Academic Press.

Del Sarto, Raffaela A. 2006. *Contested State Identities and Regional Security in the Euro-Mediterranean Region*. New York: Palgrave.

Delcambre, Anne-Marie. 1993. 'Art. Milk.' In *Encyclopaedia of Islam*. VII. Leiden: Brill.

Denizeau, Claude. 1960. *Dictionnaire des parlers arabes de Syrie, Liban et Palestine*. Paris: Maisonneuve.

Dietrich, Walter. 2005. 'Gewalt in der israelitischen Gesellschaft.' In W. Dietrich and M. Mayordomo, *Gewalt und Gewaltüberwindung in der Bibel*. Zürich: TVZ.

Dölger, Franz (ed.). 1960. *Beiträge zur Geschichte der byzantinischen Finanzverwaltung besonders 10. und 11. Jahrhunderts*. Hildesheim: Georg Olms.

Domeris, William Robert. 2007. *Touching the Heart of God*. New York: T. & T. Clark.

Dosch, G. 1987. 'Non-Slave Labor in Nuzi.' In M.A. Powell (ed.). *Labor in the Ancient Near East*. New Haven: American Oriental Society: 223-36.

Doumani, Beshara. 1995. *Rediscovering Palestine*. Berkeley: University of California.

Dows, John, and Jordan John Goodman. 1987. *Dictionary of Finance and Investment Terms*. New York: Barron.

Dowson, Ernest MacLeod. 1930. *Progress in Land Reforms, 1923–1930*. Kent: Colonial Office.

Driver, G. R., and J. C. Miles. 1935. *The Assyrian Laws*. Oxford: Clarendon.

Du Boulay, J. 1994. *Portrait of a Greek Mountain Village*. Limni: Denise Harvey.

Duby, Georges. 1968. *Rural Economy and Country Life in the Medieval West*. Columbia: University of South Carolina.

Dumper, M. 1994. *Islam and Israel: Muslim Religious Endowments and the Jewish State*. Washington: Institute for Palestine Studies.

Duncan-Jones, Richard P. 1982. *The Economy of the Roman Empire*. Cambridge: Cambridge University Press.

Dušek, Jan. 2007. *Les manuscrits araméens du Wadi Daliyeh et la Samarie vers 450–332 av. J.-C.* Leiden: Brill.

Edelman, Diana. 1991. *King Saul in the Historiography of Judah*. Sheffield: Sheffield Academic Press.

— 2001. 'Did Saulide-Davidic Rivalry Resurface in Early Persian Yehud?' In J. A. Dearman and M. P. Graham (eds). *The Land That I Will Show You*. Sheffield: Sheffield Academic Press: 69-91.

— 2005. *The Origins of the 'Second' Temple*. London: Equinox.

— 2006. 'Tyrian Trade in Yehud under Artaxerxes I: Real or Fictional? Independent or Crown Endorsed?' In Oded Lipschits (ed.). *Judah and the Judeans in the Persian Period*. Winona Lake, IN: Eisenbrauns: 207-46.

— Forthcoming. 'Hidden Polemics.'

Ellickson, Robert C. 1993. 'Property in Land.' *The Yale Law Journal* 102: 1315-400.

Ellickson, Robert C., and Charles D. Thorland. 1995. 'Ancient Land Law: Mesopotamia, Egypt, Israel.' *Chicago-Kent Law Review* 71: 327-414.

Elliger, Karl. 1962. 'Allotment.' *The Interpreter's Dictionary of the Bible*. Nashville: Abingdon: 85-86.

Eskenazi, T. C. 1992. 'Out from the Shadows.' *Journal for the Study of the Old Testament* 54: 27-31.

Evans, D. J., R. J. Vos and K. P. Wright (eds). 2003. *Biblical Holism and Agriculture*. Pasadena: William Carey Library.

Eyre, Christoph J. 2000. 'The Agricultural Cycle, Farming, and Water Management in the Ancient Near East.' In J. M. Sasson (ed.). *Civilizations of the Ancient Near East*. I. Peabody: Hendrickson: 175-89.

— 2004. 'How Relevant was Personal Status to the Functioning of the Rural Economy in Pharaonic Egypt?' In B. Menu (ed.). *La dépendance rurale en Egypte ancienne dans l'Antiquité proche-orientale*. Cairo: IFAO: 157-86.

Fager, J. A. 1993. *Land Tenure and the Biblical Jubilee*. Sheffield: Sheffield Academic Press.

Fahmy, K. 1997. *All the Pasha's Men*. Cambridge: Cambridge University Press.

Fales, Mario. 1984. 'A Survey of Neo-Assyrian Land Sales.' In T. Khalidi (ed.). *Land Tenure and Social Transformation in the Middle East*. Beirut: AUB: 1-15.

Faroqhi, Suraiya. 2005. 'Indebtedness in the Bursa Area, 1730–1740.' In Mohammad Afifi *et al.* (eds). *Sociétés rurales ottomanes*. Cairo: IFAO: 197-213.

Faust, Avraham. 2004. 'Mortuary Practices, Society and Ideology.' *Israel Exploration Journal* 54: 174-90.

— 2006. *Israel's Ethnogenesis*. London: Equinox.

— 2007. 'Settlement Dynamics and Demographic Fluctuations in Judah.' In Y. Levin (ed.). *A Time of Change*. London: T. & T. Clark: 23-51.

— 2009. 'Cities, Villages, and Farmsteads: The Landscape of Leviticus 25:29-31.' In J. David Schloen (ed.). *Exploring the* Longue durée. Winona Lake: Eisenbrauns: 103-12.

Faust, Avraham, and Shlomo Bunimowitz. 2003. 'The Four Room House.' *Near Eastern Archaeology* 66: 22-31.

Feinberg, C. L. 1982. *Jeremiah*. Grand Rapids: Eerdmans.

Fick, Gary W. 2008. *Food, Farming, and Faith*. Albany: SUNY.

Finkelstein, Israel. 1989. 'The Emergence of the Monarchy in Israel: The Environmental and Socio-Economic Aspects.' *Journal for the Study of the Old Testament* 44: 43-74; repr. in C. E. Carter and C. L. Meyers (eds). 1996. *Community, Identity, and Ideology*. Winona Lake, IN: Eisenbrauns: 377-403.

— 1997a. 'Ethno-historical Background: Land Use and Demography in Recent Generations.' In Israel Finkelstein, Zvi Lederman and Shlomo Bunimovitz (eds). *Highlands of Many Cultures*. Tel Aviv: Tel Aviv University: 109-30.

— 1997b. 'Methods of Field Survey and Data Recording.' In Israel Finkelstein, Zvi Lederman and Shlomo Bunimovitz (eds). *Highlands of Many Cultures*. Tel Aviv: Tel Aviv University: 11-24.

— 2008. 'Archaeology and the List of Returnees in the Books of Ezra and Nehemiah.' *Palestine Exploration Quarterly* 140: 1-10.

Finkelstein, Israel, and Yitzhak Magen. 1993. *Archaeological Survey of the Hill Country of Benjamin*. Jerusalem: Israel Antiquities Authority.

Finkelstein, Israel, and Lily Singer-Avitz. 2009. 'Reevaluating Bethel.' *Zeitschrift des Deutschen Palästina-Vereins* 125: 33-48.
Finkelstein, J. J. 1965. 'Some New Misharum Material and Its Implication.' In H.G. Güterbock and T. Jacobsen (eds). *Studies in Honor of Benno Landsberger on His Seventy-Fifth Birthday.* Chicago: Oriental Institute: 233-46.
— 1969. 'The Edict of Ammiṣaduqa: A New Text.' *Revue d'Assyriologie et d'Archéologie Orientale* 63: 45-64.
Finley, Moses I. 1977. 'Die Schuldknechtschaft.' In H. G. Kippenborg (ed.). *Seminar: die Entstehung der antiken Klassengesellschaft.* Frankfurt: Suhrkamp: 173-204.
— 1981. *Economy and Society in Ancient Greece.* London: Chatto & Windus.
— 1983. *Politics in the Ancient World.* Cambridge: Cambridge University Press.
Firestone, Y. 1981. 'Land Equalization and Factor Scarcities: Holding Size and the Burden of Impositions in Imperial Central Russia and the Late Ottoman Levant.' *Journal of Economic History* 41: 813-33.
— 1990. 'The Land-equalizing Mushâ' Village.' In G. G. Gilbar (ed.). *Ottoman Palestine.* Leiden: Brill: 91-130.
Fisher, S. 1919. *Ottoman Land Laws.* Oxford: Clarendon.
Fitzpatrick-McKinley, A. 2003. 'Ezra, Nehemiah and Some Early Greek Lawgivers.' In C. Hezser (ed.). *Rabbinic Law in its Roman and in Near Eastern Context.* Tübingen: Mohr Siebeck: 17-49.
Forbes, H. A. 1976. 'We Have a Little of Everything.' In M. Dimen and E. Friedl (eds). *Regional Variation in Modern Greece and Cyprus* New York: Academy of Sciences: 236-50.
Foucault, Michel. 1972. *The Archaeology of Knowledge.* London: Tavistock.
Fox, Michael V. 2009. *Proverbs 10–31.* New Haven, CN: Yale University Press.
Foxhall, L. 1990. 'The Dependant Tenant: Land Leasing and Labour in Italy and Greece.' *Journal of Roman Studies* 80: 97-114.
— 2002. 'Access to Resources in Classical Greece.' In P. Cartledge, E. E. Cohen and L. Foxhall (eds). *Money, Labour and Land.* London: Routledge: 209-20.
Franklin, Norma. 2008. 'Jezreel: Before and after Jezebel.' In Lester L. Grabbe (ed.). *Israel in Transition.* New York: T. & T. Clark: 45-53.
Freedman, H. 1977. *Jeremiah.* London: Soncino.
Frederiksen, M. W. 1971. 'The Contribution of Archaeology to the Agrarian Problem of the Gracchan Period.' *Dialoghi di archeologia* 4-5: 330-67.
Frei, Peter. 1996. 'Zentralgewalt und Lokalautonomie im Achämenidenreich.' In P. Frei and K. Koch (eds). *Reichsidee und Reichorganisation im Perserreich.* Fribourg Göttingen: Universitätsverlag Vandenhoeck & Ruprecht: 5-131.
Frick, Frank S. 1999. 'Response: Reconstructing Ancient Israel's Social World.' *Semeia* 87: 233-54.
Fried, Lisbeth S., and D. N. Freedman. 2001. 'Was the Jubilee Year Observed in Preexilic Judah?' In J. Milgrom, *Leviticus 23–27.* New York: Doubleday: 2257-70.
Friedmann, K. J. 1984. 'Fencing, Herding, and Tethering in Denmark, from Open-field Agriculture to Enclosure.' *Agricultural History* 58: 586-87.
Frolov, Serge. 2004. *The Turn of the Cycle.* Berlin: de Gruyter.
Fuks, Alexander. 1984. 'Social-Economic Revolutions in Greece.' In idem, *Social Conflict in Ancient Greece.* Leiden: Brill: 9-39.
Gallant, Thomas W. 1991. *Risk and Survival in Ancient Greece.* Cambridge: Polity.

Gamble, Clive. 1982. 'Leadership and "Surplus" Production.' In Colin Renfrew and Steven Shennan (eds). *Ranking, Resource and Exchange*. Cambridge: Cambridge University Press: 100-105.

Gamoran, Hillel. 1971. 'The Biblical Law against Loans on Interest.' *Journal of Near Eastern Studies* 30: 127-34.

Garnsey, Peter. 1988. *Famine and Food Supply in the Graeco-roman World*. Cambridge: Cambridge University Press.

— 1998. 'Famine in History.' In idem, *Cities, Peasants and Food in Classical Antiquity*. Cambridge: Cambridge University Press: 272-92.

Gauthier, Philippe. 1973. 'A propos des clérouquies athéniennes du Ve siècle.' In M. I. Finley (ed.). *Problèmes de la terre en Grèce ancienne*. Paris: Mouton: 163-78.

Gayraud, Roland P. 2003. 'Pauvreté et richesse dans l'Egypte médiévale.' In J.-P. Pascual (ed.). *Pauvreté et richesse dans le monde musulman*. Paris: Maisonneuve & Larose: 173-81.

Gehrke, Hans-Joachim. 1985. *Stasis*. München: C. H. Beck.

Gelb, I. J. 1965. 'The Old Mesopotamian Ration System.' *Journal of Near Eastern Studies* 24: 230-43.

George, Henry. 2005. *Progress and Poverty. An Inquiry into the Cause of Industrial Depressions and of Increase of Want with Increase of Wealth: The Remedy*. Repr., New York: Cosimo.

Gerber, Haim. 1985. *Ottoman Rule in Jerusalem 1890–1914*. Berlin: Schwartz.

— 1987. *The Social Origins of the Modern Middle East*. London: Lynne Rienner.

Gere, Cathy. 2009. *Knossos and the Prophets of Modernism*. Chicago: University of Chicago Press.

Geremek, B. 1997. *Poverty: A History*. Oxford: Blackwell.

Gerleman, G. 1977. 'Nutzrecht und Wohnrecht: zur Bedeutung von *'ḥzh* und *nḥlh*.' *Zeitschrift für die alttestamentlische Wissenschaft* 89: 313-25.

Getzler, J. 1998. 'Roman Ideas of Landownership.' In S. Bright and J. Dewar (eds). *Land Law*. Oxford: Oxford University Press: 81-106.

Ghalwash, Maha. 1998. 'Land Acquisition by the Peasants of Mid-Nineteenth Century Egypt: The Ramya System.' *Studia Islamica* 88: 121-39.

Gibbon, Edward. 1910. *The Rise and Fall of the Roman Empire 1*. London: Everyman.

Gibson, Shimon, and Gershon Edelstein. 1985. 'Investigating Jerusalem's Rural Landscape.' *Levant* 17: 139-55.

Gilbert, M. 2007. 'Les conditions du pouvoir. Le regard des sages sur la classe dirigeante (Pr 28-29).' *Revue théologique de Louvain* 38: 313-35.

Gilsenan, Michael. 1984. 'A Modern Feudality? Land and Labour in North Lebanon, 1858–1950.' In T. Khalidi (ed.). *Land Tenure and Social Transformation*. Beirut: AUB: 449-63.

Ginsberg, E. 1932. 'Economics of the Bible.' *Jewish Quarterly Review* 22: 343-408.

Goldingay, John. 2006. *Psalms 1–41*. Grand Rapids: Baker Academic.

Gorni, Yosef. 1989. *From Rosh Pina and Degania to Dimona*. Tel-Aviv: MOD Books.

— 1998. 'Thoughts on Zionism as a Utopian Ideology.' *Modern Judaism* 18: 241-51.

Gossai, H. 1993. *Justice, Righteousness and the Social Critique of the Eighth Century Prophets*. New York: Lang.

Gottheil, Fred M. 1986. 'Money and Product Flows in Mid-19th Century Palestine: The Physiocratic Model Applied.' In D. Kushner (ed.). *Palestine in the Late Ottoman Period*. Jerusalem/Leiden: Yad Izhak Ben-Zvi/Brill: 211-30.

Gottwald, Norman Karol. 1986. 'The Participation of Free Agrarians in the Introduction of Monarchy to Ancient Israel: An Application of H. A. Landsberger's Framework for the Analysis of Peasant Movements.' *Semeia* 37: 77-106.

— 1993. 'Prolegomenon.' In N. K.Gottwald, *The Hebrew Bible and its Social World and Ours.* Atlanta: Scholars: i-xxx.

— 1999. 'The Expropriated and the Expropriators in Nehemiah 5.' In M. R. Sneed (ed.). *Concepts of Class in Ancient Israel.* Atlanta: Scholars: 1-20.

— 2003. 'The Puzzling Politics of Ancient Israel.' In J. C. Exum and H. G. M. Williamson (eds). *Reading from Left to Right.* Sheffield: Sheffield Academic Press: 196-204.

Grabbe, Lester L. 1998. *Ezra–Nehemiah.* London: Routledge.

— 2001. 'Sup-Urbs or Only Hyp-Urbs? Prophets and Populations in Ancient Israel and Socio-Historical Method.' In L. L. Grabbe and R. D. Haak (eds). *'Every City Shall Be Forsaken'.* Sheffield: Sheffield Academic Press: 95-123.

— 2004. *A History of the Jews and Judaism in the Second Temple Period 1.* London: T. & T. Clark.

— 2008. *A History of the Jews and Judaism in the Second Temple Period 2.* London: T. & T. Clark.

Granott, Abraham. 1952. *The Land System in Palestine.* London: Eyre & Spottiswoode.

Grant, Elihu. 1976. *The People of Palestine: An Enlarged Edition of 'The Peasantry of Palestine'.* Westport, CN: Hyperion.

Graupner, Axel. 1991. *Auftrag und Geschick des Propheten Jeremia: Literarische Eigenart, Herkunft und Intention vordeuteronomistischer Prosa im Jeremiabuch.* Neukirchen–Vluyn: Neukirchener Verlag.

Gray, John. 1967. *Joshua, Judges and Ruth.* London: Nelson.

Gray, Kevin, and Susan Francis Gray. 1998. 'The Idea of Property in Land.' In S. Bright and J. Dewar (eds). *Land Law.* Oxford: Oxford University Press: 15-51.

Grenzer, M. 2007. 'Die Armenthematik in Ijob 24.' In T. Seidl and S. Ernst (eds). *Das Buch Ijob. Gesamtdeutungen–Einzeltexte–Zentrale Themen.* Frankfurt am Main: Peter Lang: 229-78.

Greenberg, M. 1983. *Ezekiel 1–20.* Garden City, NY: Doubleday.

Greenfield, J. L. 1992. 'Two Notes on the Apocryphal Psalms.' In M. Fishbane and E. Tov (eds). *Sha'rei Talmon.* Winona Lake, IN: Eisenbrauns.

Gropp, D. M. 1993. 'The Origin and Development of the Aramaic Šallīṭ Clause.' *Journal of Near Eastern Studies* 52: 31-6.

Gross, Andrew D. 2008. *Continuity and Innovation in the Aramaic Legal Tradition.* Leiden: Brill.

Gross, Carl D. 1997. 'Is There Any Interest in Nehemiah 5?' *Scandinavian Journal of the Old Testament* 11: 270-78.

Guillaume, Alfred. 1968. *Studies in the Book of Job.* Leiden: Brill.

Guillaume, Philippe. 2007. 'Job's Intercession: Antidote to Divine Folly.' *Biblica* 88: 457-72.

— 2008. 'Dismantling the Deconstruction of Job.' *Journal of Biblical Literature* 127: 491-99.

— 2009. *Land and Calendar.* London: T. & T. Clark.

— 2010. 'The Hidden Benefits of Patronage: Debt.' In E. Pfoh (ed.). *Anthropology and the Bible: Critical Perspectives.* Piscataway, NJ: Gorgias Press: 105-24.

Guillaume, Philippe, and Michael Schunck. 2007. 'Job's Intercession: Antidote to Divine Folly.' *Biblica* 88: 457-72.

Gutiérrez, Gustavo. 1998. *On Job.* Maryknoll: Orbis.

Habel, Norman C. 1985. *The Book of Job.* London: SCM Press.

— 1995. *The Land is Mine.* Minneapolis: Fortress Press.

Habel, Norman C., and Peter Trudinger (eds). 2008. *Exploring Ecological Hermeneutics.* Atlanta: SBL.

Hallo, William W. 2000. 'The Edicts of Samsu-Iluna and His Successors.' *The Context of Scripture.* Leiden: Brill: II, 134.

HALOT. 1994–2000. *The Hebrew and Aramaic Lexicon of the Old Testament.* Leiden: Brill.

Halstead, Paul. 1989. 'The Economy Has a Normal Surplus.' In P. Halstead and J. O'Shea (eds). *Bad Years Economics: Responses to Risk and Uncertainty.* Cambridge: Cambridge University Press: 68-80.

— 2002. 'Traditional and Ancient Rural Economy in Mediterranean Europe: Plus ç'a change.' In W. Scheidel and S. von Reden (eds). *The Ancient Economy.* Edinburgh: Edinburgh University Press: 53-70.

Hamidović, David. 2007. *Les traditions du jubilé à Qumrân.* Paris: Geuthner.

Hamilton, Mark W. 2006. 'The Creation of Saul's Royal Body: Reflections on 1 Samuel 8–10.' In C. S. Ehrlich and M. C. White (eds). *Saul in Story and Tradition.* Tübingen: Mohr Siebeck: 139-55.

— 2009. 'At Whose Table? Stories of Elite and Social Climbers in 1–2 Samuel.' *Vetus Testamentum* 59: 513-32.

Hanioğlu, M. Şükrü. 2008. *A Brief History of the Late Ottoman Empire.* Princeton: Princeton University Press.

Hanson, V. D. 1998. *Warfare and Agriculture in Classical Greece.* Berkeley: California University Press: 174-84.

Haque, Ziaul. 1977. *Landlord and Peasant in Early Islam.* Islamabad: Islamic Research Institute.

Heller, Roy L. 2006. *Power, Politics and Prophecy.* New York: T. & T. Clark.

Heltzer, Michael. 1976. *The Rural Community in Ancient Ugarit.* Wiesbaden: L. Reichert.

— 1987. 'Labor in Ugarit.' In M. A. Powell (ed.). *Labor in the Ancient Near East.* New Haven: American Oriental Society: 237-50.

— 1996. 'The Symbiosis of Public and Private Sectors in Ugarit, Phoenicia and Palestine.' In M. Hudson and B.A. Levine (eds). *Privatization in the Ancient Near East and Classical World.* Cambridge, MA: Peabody Museum of Archaeology and Ethnology: 176-88.

Henrey, K. H. 1954. 'Land Tenure in the Old Testament.' *Palestine Exploration Quarterly* 86: 5-15.

Hens-Piazza, G. 2006. *1–2 Kings.* Nashville: Abingdon.

Hermisson, Hans-Jürgen. 1998. 'Von Gottes und Hiobs Nutzen. Zur Auslegung von Hi 22.' In J. Barthel, H. Jauss and K. Koenen (eds). *Studien zu Prophetie und Weisheit. Gesammelte Aufsätze.* Tübingen: Mohr Siebeck: 300-19.

Hickey, T. M. 2007. 'Aristocratic Landholding and the Economy of Byzantine Egypt.' In R. S. Bagnall (ed.). *Egypt in the Byzantine World 300–700.* Cambridge: Cambridge University Press: 288-308.

Hofmann, Tobias. 2005. *Zur sozialen Bedeutung zweir Begriffe für <Diener>: b3k und h.m.* Basel: Schwabe Verlag.

Hoglund, Kenneth G. 1991. 'The Achaemenid Context.' In P. R. Davies (ed.). *The Persian Period.* Sheffield: JSOT Press: 54-73.

— 1992. *Achaemenid Imperial Administration in Syria-Palestine and the Missions of Ezra and Nehemiah.* Atlanta: SBL.

Holladay, W. L. 1989. *Jeremiah 2.* Minneapolis: Fortress Press.

Home, Robert. 2003. 'An "Irreversible Conquest"? Colonial and Postcolonial Land Law in Israel/Palestine.' *Social Legal Studies* 12: 291-310.

Hopkins, David C. 1996. 'Bare Bones: Putting Flesh on the Economics of Ancient Israel.' In V. Fritz and P. R. Davies (eds). *The Origins of the Ancient Israelite States.* Sheffield: Sheffield Academic Press: 121-39.

Hopkins, K. 2002. 'Rome, Taxes, Rents and Trade.' In W. Scheidel and S. Von Reden (eds). *The Ancient Economy.* Edinburgh: Edinburgh University Press: 190-231.

Hoppe, Leslie J. 2004. *There Shall Be No Poor among You: Poverty in the Bible.* Nashville: Abingdon.

Horowitz, Wayne. 1995. 'An Astronomical Fragment from Columbia University and the Babylonian Revolts against Xerxes.' *Journal of the Ancient Near Eastern Society* 23: 61-67.

Horsley, Richard A. 2007. *Scribes, Visionaries and the Politics of Second Temple Judea.* Louisville, KY: Westminster John Knox.

Hossfeld, Frank-Lothar, and Erich Zenger. 2005. *Psalm 2.* Minneapolis: Augsburg Fortress.

Hostetter, E. C. 2005. 'The Antitheodicy of a Man in the Land of Uz.' *Expository Times* 116: 336-37.

Houston, Walter J. 1999. 'The King's Preferential Option for the Poor: Rhetoric, Ideology and Ethics in Psalm 72.' *Biblical Interpretation* 7: 341-67.

— 2003. 'The Role of the Poor in Proverbs.' In J. C. Exum and H. G. M. Williamson (eds). *Reading from Left to Right.* Sheffield: Sheffield Academic Press: 229-40.

— 2004. 'Was There a Social Crisis in the Eighth Century?' In J. Day (ed.). *In Search of Pre-Exilic Israel.* London: T. & T. Clark: 130-49.

— 2006. *Contending for Justice: Ideologies and Theologies of Social Justice in the Old Testament.* London: T. & T. Clark.

— 2008. *Contending for Justice. Ideologies and Theologies of Social Justice in the Old Testament.* London: T. & T. Clark, rev. edn.

— 2009. 'Exit the Oppressed Peasant? Rethinking the Background of Social Criticism in the Prophets.' In J. Day (ed.) *Prophecy and the Prophets in Ancient Israel.* London: T. & T. Clark.

Hubbard, Robert L., Jr. 1988. *The Book of Ruth.* Grand Rapids, MI: Eerdmans.

Hudson, Michael. 2002. 'Reconstructing the Origins of Interests-Bearing Debt and the Logic of Clean Slates.' In M. Hudson and M. van De Mieroop (eds). *Debt and Economic Renewal in the Ancient Near East.* Baltimore: CDL: 7-58.

Hurowitz, Victor A. 1992. *I have Built You an Exalted House.* Sheffield: Sheffield Academic Press: 73-74.

— 1994. 'Joseph's Enslavement of the Egyptians (Genesis 47.13-26) in Light of Famine Texts from Mesopotamia.' *Revue Biblique* 101: 355-62.

— 2006. 'Babylon in Bethel—New Light on Jacob's Dream.' In S. W. Holloway (ed.). *Orientalism, Assyriology and the Bible.* Sheffield: Phoenix: 436-48.

Inalcik, H. 1991. 'The Emergence of Big Farms, *Çiftliks*: State, Landlords, and Tenants.' In Ç. Keydar and F. Tabak (eds). *Landholding and Commercial Agriculture in the Middle East.* Albany: State University of New York: 17-34.

Isager, Signe, and Jens Erik Skydsgaard. 1992. *Ancient Greek Agriculture.* London: Routledge.

Iskandar, Marwan. 2006. *Rafiq Hariri and the Fate of Lebanon.* London: Saqi Books.

İslamoğlu, Huri. 2001. 'Modernities Compared: State Transformations and Constitutions of Property in the Qing and Ottoman Empires.' *Journal of Early Modern History* 5: 353-86.

İslamoğlu-İnan, Huri. 1994. *State and Peasant in the Ottoman Empire.* Leiden: Brill.

Issawi, Charles. 1982. *Economic History of the Middle East and North Africa.* London: Methuen & Co.

Jackson, B.S. 2006. *Wisdom-Laws: A Study of the Mishpatim of Exodus 21:1–22:16.* Oxford: Oxford University Press.

Jackson, Sherman. 1956. *Islamic Law and the State: The Constitutional Jurisprudence of Shihab al-Din al-Qarafi.* Leiden: Brill.

Jakobson, V. A. 1971. 'Some Problems Connected with the Rise of Landed Property.' In H. Klengel (ed.). *Beiträge zur socialen Struktur des alten Vorderasien.* Berlin: Akademie-Verlag: 33-37.

Jankowska, N. B. 1991. 'Asshur, Mitanni, and Arrapkhe.' In I. M. Diakonoff (ed.). *Early Antiquity.* Chicago: University of Chicago Press: 228-60.

Jaussen, Antonin. 1948. *Coutumes des Arabes au pays de Moab.* Paris: Gabalda.

Johansen, B. 1988. *The Islamic Law on Land Tax and Rent: The Peasant's Loss of Property Rights as Interpreted in the Hanefite Legal Literature of the Mamluk and Ottoman Periods.* London: Croom Helm.

Johnson, Michael. 1976. 'Political Bosses and their Gangs: Zu'ama and qabadayat in the Sunni Muslim Quarters of Beirut.' In E. Gellner and J. Waterbury (eds). *Patrons and Clients in Mediterranean Societies.* London: Duckworth: 207-24.

Jones, Arnold Hugh Martin. 1964. *The Later Roman Empire.* Oxford: Basil Blackwell.

Jones, D. R. 1992. *Jeremiah.* Grand Rapids: Eerdmans.

Jospe, R. 1997. 'Sabbath, Sabbatical and Jubilee: Jewish Ethical Perspectives.' In H. Ucko (ed.). *The Jubilee Challenge. Utopia or Possibility.* Geneva: WCC Publications: 77-98.

Jursa, Michael. 2005. *Neo-Babylonian Legal and Administrative Documents.* Münster: Ugarit-Verlag.

— 2006. 'Agricultural Management, Tax Farming and Banking.' In P. Briant and F. Joannès (eds). *Actes du colloque 'La transition entre l'Empire achéménide et les royaumes hellénistiques'.* Paris: De Boccard: 137-222.

— 2007. 'The Transition of Babylonia from the Neo-Babylonian Empire to Achaemenid Rule.' In H. Crawford (ed.). *Regime Change in the Ancient Near East and Egypt.* New York: Oxford University Press: 73-94.

— 2008. 'The Remuneration of Institutional Labourers in an Urban Context in Babylonia in the First Millennium BC.' In P. Briant, W. F. M. Henkelman and M. W. Stolper (eds). *L'archive des Fortifications de Persépolis.* Paris: de Boccard: 387-428.

Kamen, Charles Samuel. 1991. *Little Common Ground.* Pittsburg: University of Pittsburg Press: 136-43.

Kaplan, M. 1992. *Les hommes et la terre à Byzance.* Paris: Publications de la Sorbonne.

Katz, Naomi, and David Kemnitzer. 1979. 'Mode of Production and the Process of Domination: The Classical Kingdom of Dahomey.' In M. E. Léons and F. Rothstein (eds). *New Directions in Political Economy: An Approach from Anthropology.* Westport: Greenwood: 49-82.

Kaufman, Stephen A. 1984. 'A Reconstruction of the Social Welfare System of Ancient Israel.' In W. B. Barrick and J. R. Spencer (eds). *In the Shelter of Elyon.* Sheffield: JSOT Press.

Kedar, S. 2001. 'The Legal Transformation of Ethnic Geography: Israeli Law and the Palestinian Landholder 1948–1967.' *International Law and Politics Quarterly* 33: 923-1000.

Kehoe, Dennis P. 2007. *Law and the Rural Economy in the Roman Empire.* Ann Arbor: University of Michigan.

Kennedy, Hugh. 1985. 'From Polis to Medina: Urban Change in Late Antique and Early Islamic Syria.' *Past and Present* 106: 3-27; repr. in idem. 2006. *The Byzantine and Early Islamic Near East.* Aldershot: Ashgate: 3-27.

— 2004. 'Elite Incomes in the Early Islamic State.' In J. Haldon and L. I. Conrad (eds). *The Byzantine and Early Islamic Near East.* Princeton: Darwin: 13-28.

Kerény, Karl. 1972. 'The Trickster in Relation to Greek Mythology.' In P. Radin (ed.). *The Trickster.* New York: Schocken.

Kessler, Rainer. 1989. 'Das hebräische Schuldenwesen Terminologie und Metaphorik.' *Wort und Dienst* 20: 57-69; repr. in idem. 2009. *Studien zur Sozialgeschichte Israels.* Stuttgart: KBW: 31-45.

— 1994. 'Frühkapitalismus, Rentenkapitalismus, Tributarismus, antike Klassengesellschaft Theorien zur Gesellschaft des alten Israel.' *Evangelische Theologie* 54: 413-27; repr. in idem. 2009. *Studien zur Sozialgeschichte Israels.* Stuttgart: VKB: 57-71.

— 2006. *Sozialgeschichte des alten Israel.* Darmstadt: WBG.

Khalaf, Samir. 1976. 'Changing Forms of Political Patronage in Lebanon.' In E. Gellner and J. Waterbury (eds). *Patrons and Clients in Mediterranean Societies.* London: Duckworth: 185-205.

Kim, Sun-Jong. 2010. 'Les enjeux théologiques des bénéficiaires de l'année sabbatique (Lev 25,6-7).' *Zeitschrift für die Alttestamentliche Wissenschaft* 122: 33-43.

Kitz, Anne M. 2000. 'Undivided Inheritance and Lot Casting in the Book of Joshua.' *Journal of Biblical Literature* 119: 601-18.

Klat, Paul. 1958. 'Mushaa' Holdings and Land Fragmentation in Syria.' *Middle East Economic Papers* 4: 12-24.

Kloppenborg, J. S. 2006. *The Tenants in the Vineyard.* Tübingen: Mohr Siebeck.

— 2008. 'The Growth and Impact of Agricultural Tenancy in Jewish Palestine (III BCE–I CE).' *Journal of the Economic and Social History of the Orient* 51: 31-66.

Knauf, Ernst Axel. 2006. 'Bethel: The Israelite Impact on Judean Language and Literature.' In Oded Lipschits (ed.). *Judah and the Judeans in the Persian Period.* Winona Lake, IN: Eisenbrauns: 291-349.

— 2008. *Josua.* Zürich: TVZ.

— 2011. 'Inside the Walls of Nehemia's Jerusalem: Naboth's Vineyard.' In Israel Finkelstein and Nadav Na'aman (eds). *The Fire Signals of Lachish: Studies in the Archaeology and History of Israel in the Late Bronze Age, Iron Age, and Persian Period in Honor of David Ussishkin.* Winona Lake, IN: Eisenbrauns: 185-94.

Kohler, Josef. 1959. 'Gemeinderschaft und Familiengut im israelitischen Recht.' *Zeitschrift für Vergleichende Rechtswissenschaft* 17: 217-22.
Komoróczy, G. 1982. 'Zur Frage der Periodizität der altbabylonischen Mišarum-Erlässe.' In M. T. Larsen and J. N. Postgate (eds). *Studies and Languages of the Ancient Near East*. Warminster: Aris & Phillips: 196-204.
Kramer, Carol. 1982. *Village Ethnoarchaeology*. London: Academic Press.
Kraus, F. R. 1958. *Ein Edikt des Königs Ammi-ṣaduqa von Babylon*. Leiden: Brill.
— 1984. *Königliche Verfügungen in altbabylonischer Zeit*. Leiden: Brill.
Kron, J. G. 2008. 'The Much Maligned Peasant.' In L. de Ligt and S. Northwood (eds). *People, Land, and Politics*. Leiden: Brill: 71-120.
Krüger, Paul. 1959. *Corpus iuris civilis*. II. Berlin: Weidmann.
Krüger, Thomas. 2007. 'Did Job Repent?' In T. Krüger, M. Oeming, K. Schmid and C. Uehlinger (eds). *Das Buch Hiob und seine Interpretationen*. Zürich: TVZ: 217-30.
Kuenen, Abraham. 1877. *The Prophets and Prophecy in Israel*. London: Longmans, Green & Co.
Kuhrt, Amélie. 2007. *The Persian Empire*. I. London: Routledge.
Kyrtatas, Dimitris J. 2002. 'Domination and Exploitation.' In P. Cartledge, E. E. Cohen and L. Foxhall (eds). *Money, Labour and Land*. London: Routledge: 138-55.
Lacocque, André. 2004. *Le livre de Ruth*. Genève: Labor et Fides.
Lambton, Ann K. S. 1991. Landlord and Peasant in Persia. London: Tauris: 382-83.
Lancaster, W., and F. Lancaster. 1995. 'Land Use and Population in the Area North of Kerak.' *Levant* 27: 103-26.
Launderville, Dale. 2001. 'Anti-monarchical Ideology in Israel in Light of Mesopotamian Parallels.' In L. Boadt and M. S. Smith (eds). *Imagery and Imagination in Biblical Literature*. Washington: Catholic Biblical Association of America: 119-28.
Lang, Bernhard. 1982. 'The Social Organisation of Peasant Poverty in Biblical Israel.' *Journal for the Study of the Old Testament* 7: 47-63; repr. in idem. 2008. *Hebrew Life and Literature*. Farnham: Ashgate: 47-60.
— 1983. 'Prophetie und Ökonomie im alten Israel.' In G. Kehrer (ed.). *'Vor Gott sind alle gleich.'* Düsseldorf: Patmos: 53-73.
Latron, A. 1939. *La vie rurale en Syrie et au Liban*. Beyrouth: Institut français de Damas.
Lanz, Hugo. 1976. *Die neubabylonischen—arrânu-Geschäftsunternehmen*. Berlin: Schweitzer.
Lecoq, Pierre. 1997. *Les inscriptions de la Perse achéménide*. Paris: Gallimard.
Lefèbvre, Jean-François. 2003. *Le jubilé biblique*. Fribourg: Editions Universitaires.
Lefort, Jacques. 2002. 'The Rural Economy, Seventh-Twelfth Centuries.' In A. E. Laiou (ed.). *The Economic History of Byzantium*. Washington, DC: Dumbarton Oaks: 231-310.
Leibowitz, Yeshayahu. 1995. *Peuple. Terre. Etat*. Paris: Plon.
Lemche, Niels Peter. 1976. 'The Manumission of Slaves-the Fallow Year-the Sabbatical Year-the Jobel Year.' *Vetus Testamentum* 26: 38-59.
— 1985. *Early Israel*. Leiden: Brill.
— 1994. 'Kings and Clients: On Loyalty between the Ruler and the Ruled in Ancient Israel.' *Semeia* 66: 119-32.

— 1997. 'On Doing Sociology with "Solomon".' In Lowell K Handy (ed.). *The Age of Solomon*. Leiden: Brill: 312-35.
— 1999. 'The Relevance of Working with the Concept of Class in the Study of Israelite Society in the Iron Age.' In M. R. Sneed (ed.). *Concepts of Class in Ancient Israel*. Atlanta: Scholars: 89-98.
— 2010. 'Avraham Faust and Israelite Ethnicity.' In E. Pfoh (ed.). *Anthropology and the Bible: Critical Perspectives*. Piscataway: Gorgias Press: 93-104.
Lenski, Gerhard Emmanuel. 1966. *Power and Privilege*. New York: McGraw Hill.
Levin, Christoph. 2003. 'The Poor in the Old Testament: Some Observations.' In C. Levin (ed.). *Fortschreibungen*. Berlin: de Gruyter: 322-38.
Levine, Baruch A. 1996. 'Farewell to the Ancient Near East: Evaluating Biblical References to Ownership of Land in Comparative Perspective.' In M. Hudson and B. A. Levine (eds). *Privatization in the Ancient Near East and Classical World*. Cambridge, MA: Peabody Museum of Archaeology and Ethnology: 223-52.
Lewis, Bernard. 1979. 'Ottoman Land Tenure and Taxation in Syria.' *Studia Islamica* 50: 109-24.
Lewis, D. M. 1973. 'The Athenian *Rationes Centesimarum*.' In M. I. Finley (ed.). *Problèmes de la terre en Grèce ancienne*. Paris: Mouton & Co: 187-99.
Liddell, H. G., and R. Scott. 1996. *A Greek-English Lexicon*. Oxford: Oxford University Press.
Lieberman, Stephen J. 1989. 'Royal "Reforms" of the Amurrite Dynasty.' *Bibliotheca Orientalis* 46: 242-60.
Lipschits, Oded. 1999. 'The History of the Benjamin Region under Babylonian Rule.' *Tel Aviv* 26: 155-90.
— 2004. 'The Rural Settlement in Judah in the Sixth Century BCE: A Rejoinder.' *Palestine Exploration Quarterly* 136: 99-108.
— 2005. *The Fall and Rise of Jerusalem*. Winona Lake, IN: Eisenbrauns.
Lirb, H. J. 1993. 'Partners in Agriculture.' In F. J. A. M. Meijer and H. W. Pleket (eds). *De agricultura*. Amsterdam: Gieben: 263-95.
Liverani, Mario. 1965. 'Il fuoroscitismo in Siria nella tardo eta del Bronzo.' *Revista Storica Italiana* 77: 315-36.
— 1975. 'Communautés de village et palais royal dans la Syrie du IIème millénaire.' *Journal of the Economic and Social History of the Orient* 18: 146-64.
Lowery, R. H. 2000. *Sabbath and Jubilee*. St Louis: Chalice.
Lust, Johan Erik Eynikel, and Katrin Hauspie (eds). 2003. *Greek-English Lexicon of the Septuagint*. Stuttgart: Deutsche Bibelgesellschaft.
Macauley, Melissa. 2001. '*A World Made Simple*: Law and Property in the Ottoman and Qing Empires.' *Journal of Early Modern History* 5: 331-52.
Macfarlane, Alan. 1978. *The Origins of English Individualism*. Oxford: Basil Blackwell.
MacKenzie, J. A., and M. Phillips. 2006. *Textbook on Land Law*. Oxford: Oxford University Press.
Maimonides, Moses ben. 1979. *The Code of Maimonides*. VII. *The Code of Agriculture*. New Haven: Yale University Press.
Malina, Bruce J. 1982. 'The Social Sciences and Biblical Interpretation.' *Interpretation* 36: 229-42.
Malkin, Irad. 2005. 'Herakles and Melqart: Greeks and Phoenicians in the Middle Ground.' In E. S. Gruen (ed.). *Cultural Borrowings and Ethnic Appropriations in Antiquity*. Stuttgart: Franz Steiner: 238-58.

Maloney, R. P. 1974. 'Usury and Restrictions on Interest-Taking in the Ancient Near East.' *Catholic Biblical Quarterly* 36: 1-20.

Mandel, Ernest. 1971. 'The Asiatic Mode of Production and the Historical Preconditions for the Rise of Capitalism.' In *The Formation of the Economic Thought of Karl Marx*. London: NLB: 116-39.

Mangan, Céline. 1991. *The Targum of Job*. Collegeville: Liturgical Press.

Mankowski, Paul V. 2000. *Akkadian Loan Words in Biblical Hebrew*. Winona Lake: Eisenbrauns.

Manning, Joseph Gilbert. 2003. *Land and Power in Ptolemaic Egypt*. Cambridge: Cambridge University Press.

— 2010. *The Last Pharaohs: Egypt under the Ptolemies, 305–30* BC. Princeton/ Oxford: Princeton University Press.

Maon, P. 1972. 'Propriété.' *Supplément au Dictionaire de la Bible*. VIII. Paris: Letouzey et Ané.

Martin, R. 1971. *Recherches sur les agronomes latins*. Paris: Belles Lettres.

Martinez-Sève, L. 2007. 'L'expression de la fiscalité chez Flavius Josèphe.' In J. Andreau and V. Chankowski (eds). *Vocabulaire et expression de l'économie dans la monde antique*. Pessac: Ausonius: 399-421.

Marx, Karl. 1964. *Pre-Capitalist Economic Formations*. London: Lawrence & Wishart.

Matthäus, H. 1999. 'The Greek Symposion and the Near East.' In R. Docter and E. Moormann (eds). *Classical Archaeology towards the Third Millennium*. Amsterdam: Allard Pierson Museum: 256-60.

Matthews, Victor H. 2009. 'The Determination of Social Identity in the Story of Ruth.' In P. Dutcher-Walls (ed.). *The Family in Life and Death*. New York: T. & T. Clark: 16-27.

Mathewson, Dan. 2006. *Death and Survival in the Book of Job*. New York: T. & T. Clark.

McCloskey, Deidre N. 1975. 'The Persistence of English Common Fields.' In W. N. Parker and E. L. Jones (eds). *European Peasants and their Markets*. Princeton: Princeton University Press: 73-119.

— 1976. 'English Open Fields as Behavior towards Risk.' *Research in Economic History* 1: 124-70.

— 1991. 'The Prudent Peasant: New Findings on the Open Fields.' *Journal of Economic History* 51: 343-55.

McGinnis, J. 2003. 'A Corvée Gang from the Time of Cyrus.' *Zeitschrift für Assyriologie und vorderasiatische Archäologie* 93: 88-115.

McKeown, Niall. 2007. *The Invention of Ancient Slavery*. London: Duckworth.

McLaughlin, John L. 2001. *The Marzēah in the Prophetic Literature*. Leiden: Brill.

Menu, Bernadette. 1971. 'Le régime juridique des terres en Égypte pharaonique. Moyen Empire et Nouvel Empire.' *Revue historique de droit français et étranger* 49: 555-85.

— 1982. 'Vente de céréales sur pied.' In idem, *Recherches sur l'histoire juridique, économique et sociale de l'ancienne Egypte*. Paris: Geuthner: 312-22.

— 1998a. 'Modalités et réglementation du prêt en Egypte à l'époque de la première domination perse.' In idem (ed.). *Recherches sur l'histoire juridique, économique et sociale de l'ancienne Egypte 2*. Le Caire: IFAO: 385-400.

— 1998b. 'La détention des terres en Egypte au premier millénaire avant J.-C.' In idem (ed.). *Recherches sur l'histoire juridique, économique et sociale de l'Egypte ancienne 2.* Le Caire: IFAO: 173-82.

Métral, Françoise. 1984. 'Land Tenure and Irrigation Projects in Syria.' In T. Khalidi (ed.). *Land Tenure and Social Transformation in the Middle East.* Beirut: AUB: 465-81.

— 2000. 'Managing Risk: Sheep-rearing and Agriculture.' In M. Mundy and B. Musallam (eds). *The Transformation of Nomadic Society in the Arab East.* Cambridge: Cambridge University Press: 123-44.

Mette, Norbert. 2006. 'Naboth. 1 Könige.' In M. Keuchen, H. Kuhlmann and H. Schroeter-Wittke (eds). *Die besten Nebenrollen: 50 Porträts biblischer Randfiguren.* Leipzig: Evangelische Verlagsanstalt: 142-46.

Metzer, J. 2007. '*The Palestinian Peasant Economy Under the Mandate: A Story of Colonial Bungling* by Amos Nadan.' *The Economic History Review* 60.2: 432-34.

Meyer, E. E. 2005. *The Jubilee in Leviticus 25: A Theological Ethical Interpretation from a South African Perspective.* Münster: LIT.

Michel, Nicholas. 2001. 'Migrations de paysans dans le Delta du Nil au début de l'époque ottomane.' *Annales islamologiques* 35: 241-90.

— 2002. 'Villages désertés, terres en friche et reconstruction rurale en Egypte au début de l'époque ottomane.' *Annales islamologiques* 36: 197-251.

Migot-Adholla, Shem, Peter B. Hazell, Benoit Blarel and Frank Place. 1991. 'Indigenous Land Rights Systems in Sub-Saharan Africa: A Constraint on Productivity.' *World Bank Economic Review* 5: 155-75.

Milgrom, Jacob. 1997. 'Leviticus 25 and Some Postulates of the Jubilee.' In H. Ucko (ed.). *The Jubilee Challenge: Utopia or Possibility.* Geneva: WCC Publications: 28-32.

— 2000. *Leviticus.* New York: Doubleday.

Miller, Marvin Lloyd. 2010. 'Nehemiah 5: A Response to Philippe Guillaume.' *Journal of Hebrew Scriptures* 10: article 13.

Millett, Paul. 1991. *Lending and Borrowing in Ancient Athens.* Cambridge: Cambridge University Press.

Miralles Maciá, Lorena. 2007. *Marzeah y thíasos: Una institución convival en el Oriente Próximo Antiguo y el Mediterráneo.* Madrid: Universidad Complutense.

Moghadam, F. E. 1990. 'Property Rights and Islamic Revolution in Iran.' In H. Esfandiari and A. L. Udovitch (eds). *The Economic Dimensions of Middle Eastern History.* Princeton: Darwin: 147-78.

Moreno García, Juan Carlos. 2008. 'La dépendance rurale en Égypte ancienne.' *Journal of the Economic and Social History of the Orient* 51: 99-150.

Moyo, Dambisa. 2009. *Dead Aid.* London: Penguin.

Muffs, Yochanan. 1969. *Studies in the Aramaic Legal Papyri from Elephantine.* Leiden: Brill.

Muhs, B. P. 2005. *Tax Receipts, Taxpayers, and Taxes in Early Ptolemaic Thebes.* Chicago: University of Chicago Press: 29-30.

Müller, Reinhard. 2004. *Königtum und Gottesherrschaft. Untersuchungen zur alttestamentlichen Monarchiekritik.* Tübingen: Mohr Siebeck.

Mundy, Martha. 1986. 'Qada' 'Ajlun in the Late 19th Century.' *Levant* 28: 79-97.

— 1996. 'La propriété dite *musha'* en Syrie: une note analytique à propos des travaux de Ya'akov Firestone.' *Revue du monde musulman et de la Méditerranée* 79-80: 267-81.

Mundy, Martha, and Richard Saumarez Smith. 2007. *Governing Property, Making the Modern State*. London: I. B. Tauris.

Murphy, Roland E. 1998. *Proverbs*. Nashville: Thomas Nelson.

Na'aman, Nadav. 2008. 'Naboth's Vineyard and the Foundation of Jezreel.' *Journal for the Study of the Old Testament* 33: 197-218.

— 2009a. 'Does Archaeology Really Deserve the Status of a "High Court" in Biblical Historical Research?' Paper delivered at the SOTS/OTW meeting, Lincoln.

— 2009b. 'Saul, Benjamin and the Emergence of "Biblical Israel" (Continued, Part 2).' *Zeitschrift für die alttestamentlische Wissenschaft* 121: 335-49.

Nadan, Amos. 2003. 'Colonial Misunderstanding of an Efficient Peasant Institution.' *Journal of the Economic and Social History of the Orient* 46: 320-54.

— 2005. 'The Competitive Advantage of Moneylenders over Banks in Rural Palestine.' *Journal of the Economic and Social History of the Orient* 48: 1-39.

— 2006. *The Palestinian Peasant Economy under the Mandate: A Story of Colonial Bungling*. Cambridge, MA: Harvard University Press.

— 2007. 'Merchants and Peasants in the Nazareth Region, 1922–47.' *Journal of Peasant Studies* 34: 51-68.

Naveh, Joseph. 1960. 'A Hebrew Letter of the Seventh Century b.c.' *Israel Exploration Journal* 10: 130-36.

Nicholson, E. W. 1975. *The Book of the Prophet Jeremiah 26–52.* Cambridge: Cambridge University Press.

Near, Henry. 1992. *The Kibbutz Movement.* Oxford: Oxford University Press.

Neufeld, Edward. 1955. 'The Prohibition against Loans at Interest in Ancient Hebrew Laws.' *Hebrew Union College Annual* 26: 355-412.

— 1960. 'The Emergence of a Royal-Urban Society in Ancient Israel.' *Hebrew Union College Annual* 31: 31-53.

Nielsen, Kirsten. 1985. 'Le choix contre le droit dans le livre de Ruth.' *Vetus Testamentum* 35: 201-12.

— 1997. *Ruth.* Louisville: Westminster John Knox.

— 2007. 'Construction of Meaningful Contexts on War, Lions, Dogs, Birds and a Vineyard.' *Scandinavian Journal of the Old Testament* 21: 218-27.

Nollé, J. 2005. 'Boars, Bears, and Bugs: Farming in Asia Minor and the Protection of Men, Animals, and Crops.' In S. Mitchell and C. Katsari (eds). *Patterns in the Economy of Roman Asia Minor*. Swansea: Classical Press of Wales: 53-82.

North, Robert. 1954. *Sociology of the Biblical Jubilee.* Rome: Pontifical Biblical Institute.

Noth, Martin. 1958. *The History of Israel.* London: Black.

Nurmi, Janne J. 2004. *Die Ethik unter dem Druck des Alltags.* Åbo: Akademis Förlag.

O'Leary, Brendan. 1989. *The Asiatic Mode of Production.* Oxford: Basil Blackwell.

Ober, Josiah. 2006. 'Solon and the *Horoi*.' In J. H. Blok and A. P. M. H. Lardinois (eds). *Solon of Athens: New Historical and Philological Approaches.* Leiden: Brill: 441-56.

Olivier, Hannes. 1988. 'The Periodicity of the *Mēšarum* Again.' In W. Claassen (ed.). *Text and Context.* Sheffield: Sheffield Academic Press: 227-36.

Olivier, J. P. J. 1997. 'Restitution as Economic Redress.' *Zeitschrift fur altorientalische und biblische Rechtsgeschichte* 3: 12-25.

Osborne, R. 1992. 'Is It a Farm?' In B. Wells (ed.). *Agriculture in Ancient Greece.* Stockholm: Svenska Institutet i Athen: 21-27.

Otto, Eckart. 1997. 'Programme der sozialen Gerechtigkeit.' *Zeitschrift für Altorientalische und Biblische Rechtsgeschichte* 3: 26-63.

Parpola, Simo. 2007. 'The Neo-Assyrian Ruling Class.' In T. R. Kämmerer (ed.) *Studien zu Ritual und Sozialgeschichte im Alten Orient.* Berlin: de Gruyter: 257-74.

Pastor, Jack. 1997. *Land and Economy in Ancient Israel.* London: Routledge.

Patai, Raphael. 1949. 'Musha' Tenure and Cooperation in Palestine.' *American Anthropologist* 5.3: 436-45.

Paul, Shalom M. 1991. *Amos.* Ed. Frank M. Cross; Minneapolis: Fortress Press.

Paulus, S. 2009. 'Ein Beitrag zum mittelbabylonischen Immobilarkauf.' *Archiv für Orientforschung* 35: 318-25.

Payne, G. 2004. 'Land Tenure and Property Rights: An Introduction.' *Habitat International* 28: 167-79.

Pearce, Laurie. 2006. 'New Evidence for Judeans in Babylonia.' In Oded Lipschits and Manfred Oeming (eds). *Judah and the Judeans in the Persian Period.* Winona Lake, IN: Eisenbrauns: 399-412.

Pearson, H. W. 1957. 'The Economy Has No Surplus: Critique of a Theory of Development.' In K. Polanyi, C. M. Arensberg and H. W. Pearson (eds). *Trade and Markets in the Early Empires.* Glencoe: Free Press: 320-41.

Pečíka, J. 1973. 'Homestead Farms in Classical and Hellenistic Hellas.' In M. I. Finley (ed.). *Problèmes de la terre en Grèce ancienne.* Paris: Mouton: 111-47.

Pellat, C. 1993. 'Art. *Musha*'.' In C. E. Bosworth, E. van Donzel, W. P. Heinrichs and C. Pellat (eds). *The Encyclopaedia of Islam New Edition.* Leiden: Brill: VII, 667.

Petrusewicz, Marta. 1996. *Latifundium: Moral Economy and Material Life in a European Periphery.* Ann Harbor: University of Michigan.

Pleins, J. D. 2001. *The Social Visions of the Hebrew Bible.* Louisville: Westminster John Knox.

Porten, Bezalel, and Ada Yardeni. 1986. *Textbook of Aramaic Documents from Ancient Egypt.* I. *Letters.* Jerusalem: Hebrew University.

Postgate, J. Nicholas. 1982. 'Ownership and Exploitation of Land in Assyria in the First Millennium BC Ilku and Land Tenure in the Middle Assyrian Kingdom: A Second Attempt.' In idem, *Societies and Languages of the Ancient Near East.* Warminster: Aris & Phillips: 303-12.

— 1987. 'Employer, Employee and Employment in the Neo-Assyrian Empire.' In M. A. Powell (ed.). *Labor in the Ancient Near East.* New Haven, CN: American Oriental Society: 257-70.

Pottage, Alain. 1998. 'Evidencing Ownership.' In S. Bright and J. Dewar (eds). *Land Law.* Oxford: Oxford University Press: 129-50.

Powell, Marvin A. 1990. 'Masse und Gewicht.' In D. O. Edzard (ed.). *Reallexikon der Assyriologie.* Berlin: de Gruyter: VII, 457-517.

— 1992. 'Weights and Measures.' In D. N. Freedman (ed.) *Anchor Bible Dictionary.* Garden City: Doubleday: VI, 897-908.

— 1994. 'Elusive Eden: Private Property at the Dawn of History.' *Journal of Cuneiform Studies* 46: 99-104.

Powelson, J. P. 1994. *Centuries of Economic Endeavor.* Ann Arbor: University of Michigan.

Poyck, A. P. G. 1962. 'Farm Studies in Iraq.' *Mededeligen van de Landbouwhogeschool te Wageningen Nederland* 62: 1-99.

Premnath, D. N. 1988. 'Latifundialization and Isaiah 5.8-10.' *Journal for the Study of the Old Testament* 40: 49-60 ; repr. in D. J. Chalcraft (ed.). 1997. *Social-scientific Old Testament Criticism.* Sheffield: Sheffield Academic Press: 301-12.

— 2007. 'Loan Practices in the Hebrew Bible.' In R. B. Coote and N. K. Gottwald (eds). *To Break Every Yoke.* Sheffield: Phoenix : 173-85.

Pritchard, James B. 1969. *Ancient Near Eastern Texts Relating to the Old Testament.* Princeton: Princeton University Press.

Propp, William H. C. 2006. *Exodus 19–40.* New York: Doubleday.

Quass, F. 1993. *Die Honorationenschicht in den Städten des griechischen Ostens.* Stuttgart: Steiner.

Quataert, Donald. 1991. 'Rural Unrest in the Ottoman Empire, 1830–1914.' In F. Kazemi and J. Waterbury (eds). *Peasants and Politics in the Modern Middle East.* Miami: Florida International University Press: 38-49.

Radner, Karin. 1999a. 'Traders in the Neo-Assyrian Period.' In J. G. Dercksen (ed.). *Trade and Finance in Ancient Mesopotamia.* Leiden: Brill: 101-27.

— 1999b. 'The Neo-Assyrian Period.' In R. Westbrook and R. Jasnow (eds). *Security for Debt in Ancient Near Eastern Law.* Baltimore: The Johns Hopkins University Press: 265-88.

Rafeq, Abdul-Karim. 1984. 'Land Tenure Problems and their Social Aspects in Syria.' In T. Khalidi (ed.). *Land Tenure and Social Transformation in the Middle East.* Beirut: AUB: 371-96.

— 2002. 'Making a Living or Making a Fortune in Ottoman Syria.' In N. Hanna (ed.). *Money, Land and Trade.* London: L. B. Tauris: 101-23.

— 2003. 'The Poor in Ottoman Damascus.' In J.-P. Pascual (ed.). *Pauvreté et richesse dans le monde musulman.* Paris: Maisonneuve & Larose: 217-26.

Rathbone, Dominic. 1991. *Economic Rationalism and Rural Society in Third-Century A.D. Egypt.* Cambridge: Cambridge University Press.

Redditt, Paul L. 1995. *Haggai, Zechariah, Malachi.* Grand Rapids: Eerdmans.

Reed, Clyde G., and Cliff T. Bekar. 2003. 'Religious Prohibitions against Usury.' *Explorations in Economic History* 40: 347-68.

Reinmuth, Titus. 2002. *Der Bericht Nehemias.* Fribourg-Göttingen: Universitätsverlag-Vandenhoeck & Ruprecht.

Reiterer, F. V. 1994. 'Der Verhältnis Ijobs und Ben Sira.' In W. A. M. Beuken (ed.). *The Book of Job.* Leuven: Peeters: 405-29.

Renger, J. M. 1994. 'Comments on Economic Structures in Ancient Mesopotamia.' *Orientalia* 63: 157-208.

— 1995. 'Institutional, Communal, and Individual Ownership or Possession of Arable Land in Ancient Mesopotamia from the End of the Fourth to the End of the First Millennium B.C.' *Chicago-Kent Law Review* 71: 269-319.

Rhodes, P. J. 2006. 'The Reforms and Laws of Solon: An Optimistic View.' In J. H. Blok and A. P. M. H. Lardinois (eds). *Solon of Athens: New Historical and Philological Approaches.* Leiden: Brill: 248-60.

Richardson, Gary. 2003. 'What Protected Peasants Best? Markets, Risk, Efficiency, and Medieval English Agriculture.' *Research in Economic History* 21: 299-356.

Richardson, M. E. J. 2000. *Hammurabi's Laws*. Sheffield: Sheffield Academic Press.

Rofé, Alexander. 1988. 'The Vineyard of Naboth. The Origin and Message of the Story.' *Vetus Testamentum* 38: 89-104.

Rogan, Eugene L. 1999. *Frontiers of the State in the Late Ottoman Empire*. Cambridge: Cambridge University Press: 95-121.

Römer, Thomas. 2003. 'Réponse à l'étude critique de Philippe Guillaume.' *Revue de Théologie et de Philosophie* 135: 59-62.

Ron, Zvi. 1966. 'Agricultural Terraces in the Judean Mountains.' *Israel Exploration Journal* 16: 33-49, 111-22.

Rosafio, P. 1993. 'The Emergency of Tenancy and the *Precarium*.' In F. J. A. M. Meijer and H. W. Pleket (eds). *De agricultura*. Amsterdam: Gieben: 164-76.

Rose, E. J. 1968. *Henry George*. New York: Twayne.

Rosenberg, Avraham Yosef. 2001. *Proverbs: A New English Translation*. New York: Judaica Press.

Rostovtzeff, Michael Ivanovitch. 1941. *The Social and Economic History of the Hellenistic World*. Oxford: Clarendon.

Roubineau, Jean-Manuel. 2007. 'Les hektémores.' In J. Andreau and V. Chankowski (eds). *Vocabulaire et expression de l'économie dans le monde antique*. Pessac: Ausonius: 177-210.

Rowlandson, Jane. 1985. 'Freedom and Subordination in Ancient Agriculture. The Case of the *basilikoi georgoi* of Ptolemaic Egypt.' *History of Political Thought* 6: 327-47.

— 2001. 'Money Use among the Peasantry of Ptolemaic and Roman Egypt.' In A. Meadows and K. Shipton (eds). *Money and its Uses in the Greek World*. Oxford: Oxford University Press: 145-55.

Rubin, Jared. 2008. 'The Lender's Curse: A New Look at the Origin and Persistence of Interest Bans in Islam and Christianity [summary of a doctoral dissertation].' *Journal of Economic History* 68: 575-79.

Safrai, Z., and O. Sion. 2007. 'Nomad Settlement in Palestine during the Late Byzantine-Early Moslem Period.' In D. R. Edwards and C. T. McCollough (eds). *The Archaeology of Difference*. Boston: ASOR: 397-411.

Sait, Siraj, and Hilary Lim. 2006. *Human Rights in Islam: Law, Property and Access to Land*. London: Zed.

Sahlins, M. 1974. *Stone Age Economics*. London: Tavistock.

Sallares, Robert. 1991. *The Ecology of the Ancient Greek World*. Ithaca: Cornell University.

Sarpaki, A. 1992. 'The Mediterranean Triad or Is it a Quartet?' In B. Wells (ed.). *Agriculture in Ancient Greece*. Stockholm: Svenska Institutet i Athen: 61-76.

Sasson, Jack Murad. 1995. *Ruth*. Sheffield: Sheffield Academic Press.

Schaebler, Birgit. 2001. 'Practicing *musha*': Common Lands and the Common Good in Southern Syria under the Ottomans and the French.' In R. Owen (ed.). *New Perspectives on Property and Land in the Middle East*. Cambridge, MA: Harvard University Press: 241-311.

Schäfer-Lichtenberger, Christa. 1996. 'Sociological and Biblical Views of the Early State.' In V. Fritz and P. R. Davies (eds). *The Origins of the Ancient Israelite States*. Sheffield: Sheffield Academic Press: 78-105.

Schaper, Joachim. 1995. 'The Jerusalem Temple as an Instrument of the Achaemenid Fiscal Administration.' *Vetus Testamentum* 45: 428-39.

— 1997. 'The Temple Treasury Committee in the Times of Nehemiah and Ezra.' *Vetus Testamentum* 47: 200-206.
— 2000. *Priester und Leviten im achämenidischen Juda: Studien zur Kult- und Sozialgeschichte Israels in persischer Zeit.* Tübingen: Mohr Siebeck.
Schenker, Adrian. 2000a. 'Der Boden und seine Produktivitat im Sabbat und Jubeljahr.' In idem, *Recht und Kult im Alten Testament.* Fribourg/Göttingen: Academic Press/Vandenhoeck & Ruprecht: 123-33.
— 2000b. 'The Biblical Legislation on the Release of Slaves.' In idem, *Recht und Kult im Alten Testament.* Fribourg/Göttingen: Academic Press/Vandenhoeck & Ruprecht: 134-49.
— 2004. *Älteste Textgeschichteder Königsbücher.* Fribourg/Göttingen: Academic Press/Vandenhoeck & Ruprecht.
Schloen, J. David. 2001. *The House of the Father as Fact and Symbol: Patrimony in Ugarit and in the Ancient Near East.* Winona Lake, IN: Eisenbrauns.
Schottroff, Willi. 1999. 'Die Armut der Witwen.' In F. Crüsemann and R. Kessler (eds). *Gerechtigkeit lehrnen.* Gütersloh: Kaiser: 134-64.
Schroeder, O. 1920. *Keilschrifttexte aus Assur verschiedenen Inhalts.* Leipzig: Hinrichs.
Schulz, Theodore W. 1965. *Transforming Traditional Agriculture.* New Haven: Yale University Press.
Schumacher, Gottlieb. 1889. *Across the Jordan.* London: A. P. Watt.
Scott, R. B. Y. 1965. *Proverbs. Ecclesiates.* Garden City, NY: Doubleday.
Scott, James C. 1976. 'Patronage or exploitation.' In E. Gellner and J. Waterbury (eds). *Patrons and Clients in Mediterranean Societies.* London: Duckworth: 21-40.
— 1987. 'Resistance without Protest and without Organization.' *Contemporary Studies in Society and History* 29: 417-52.
Seavoy, R E. 1986. *Famine in Peasant Societies.* Westport: Greenwood.
Seeden, H., and M. Kaddour. 1984. 'Space, Structures and Land in Shams ed-Dīn Tannīra on the Euphrates: An Ethnoarchaeological Perspective.' In T. Khalidi (ed.). *Land Tenure and Social Transformation in the Middle East.* Beirut: AUB: 495-526.
Seeligman, Isac Leo. 2004. 'Darlehen, Bürgschaft und Zins in Recht und Gedankenwelt der Hebräischen Bibel.' In I. L. Seeligmann and E. Blum (eds). *Gesammelte Studien zur Hebräischen Bibel.* Tübingen: Mohr Siebeck: 319-48.
Seow, Choon Leong. 1997. *Ecclesiates.* Garden City: Doubleday.
— 2008. 'The Social World of Ecclesiastes.' In L. G. Perdue (ed.). *Scribes, Sages, and Seers.* Göttingen: Vandenhoeck & Ruprecht: 189-217.
Severino Croatto, José. 1997. 'The Debt in Nehemiah's Social Reform: A Study of Nehemiah 5:1-19.' In L. E. Vaage (ed.). *Subversive Scriptures. Revolutionary Readings of the Christian Bible in Latin America.* Valley Forge: Trinity Press: 39-59.
Shaw-Taylor, Leigh. 2001. 'Parliamentary Enclosure and the Emergence of an English Agricultural Proletariat.' *Journal of Economic History* 61: 640-62.
Sider, R. J. 1997. 'Evaluating the Triumph of the Market.' In H. Ucko (ed.). *The Jubilee Challenge: Utopia or Possibility.* Geneva: WCC Publications: 112-33.
Silver, Morris. 1983. *Prophets and Markets: The Political Economy of Ancient Israel.* Boston: Kluwer-Nijhoff.

Simkins, R A. 1999. 'Patronage and the Political Economy of Monarchic Israel.' *Semeia* 87: 123-44.

Singer, Amy. 1992. 'Peasant Migration: Law and Practice in Early Ottoman Palestine.' *New Perspectives on Turkey* 8: 49-65.

— 1994. *Palestinian Peasants and Ottoman Officials*. Cambridge: Cambridge University Press.

— 2003. 'The Privileged Poor in Ottoman Jerusalem.' In J.-P. Pascual (ed.). *Pauvreté et richesse dans le monde musulman*. Paris: Maisonneuve & Larose: 257-70.

Siquans, Agnethe. 2009. 'Foreignness and Poverty in the Book of Ruth.' *Journal of Biblical Literature* 128: 443-52.

Slanski, K. E. 2003. *The Babylonian Entitlement Narûs (kudurrus)*. Boston: ASOR.

Smith, Jonathan Z. 1982. 'A Pearl of Great Price and a Cargo of Yams. A Study in Situation Incongruity.' In J. Z. Smith (ed.). *Imagining Religion*. Chicago: University of Chicago Press: 90-101.

Smith, Ralph L. 1984. *Micah–Malachi*. Waco: Word Books.

Sneed, Mark. 1996. 'The Class Culture of Proverbs: Eliminating Stereotypes.' *Scandinavian Journal of the Old Testament* 10: 296-308.

Sommer, B. D. 2000. 'The Babylonian Akitu Festival: Rectifying the King or Renewing the Cosmos.' *Journal of the Ancient Near Eastern Society* 27: 81-95.

Sonnen, C. M. 1927. 'Landwirtschaftliches vom See Genesareth.' *Biblica* 8: 65-87.

Sparkes, P. 2007. *European Land Law*. Oxford: Hart.

Sparks, Kenton L. 2008a. 'Review of Avraham Faust, *Israel's Ethnogenesis: Settlement, Interaction, Expansion and Resistance*'. *Review of Biblical Literature*. http://www.bookreviews.org.

— 2008b. *Ethnicity and Identity in Ancient Israel*. Winona Lake, IN: Eisenbrauns.

Stec, D. M. 1994. *The Text of the Targum of Job*. Leiden: Brill.

Stein, Kenneth W. 1984. *The Land Question in Palestine, 1917–1939*. Chapel Hill: University of North Carolina.

Stein, S. 1953. 'The Laws of Interest in the Old Testament.' *Journal of Theological Studies* 4: 161-70.

Steinkeller, Piotr. 1981. 'The Renting of Fields in Early Mesopotamia and the Development of the Concept of "Interest" in Sumerian.' *Journal of the Economic and Social History of the Orient* 24: 113-45.

— 2002. 'Money-lending Practices in Ur III Babylonia: The Issue of Economic Motivation.' In M. Hudson and M. Van de Mieroop (eds). *Debt and Economic Renewal in the Ancient Near East*. Bethesda: CDL: 109-37.

— 2004. 'Towards a Definition of Private Economic Activity in Third Millenium Babylonia.' In R. Rollinger and C. Ulf (eds). *Commerce and Monetary Systems in the Ancient World: Means of Transmission and Cultural Interaction*. Wiesbaden: Franz Steiner: 91-111.

Stern, Ian. 2007. 'The Population of Persian Period Idumea according to the Ostraca.' In Y. Levin (ed.). *A Time of Change*. London: T. & T. Clark: 205-38.

Stoianovitch, Trian. 1976. *French Historical Method*. Ithaca: Cornell University Press.

Stolper, Matthew W. 1985. *Entrepreneurs and Empire*. Leiden: NINO.

— 2001. 'Fifth Century Nippur: Texts of the Murašûs and from their Surroundings.' *Journal of Cuneiform Studies* 53: 83-132.

Sweeney, Marvin. 2000. *The Twelve Prophets 2*. Collegeville: Liturgical Press.

— 2007. *I and II Kings: A Commentary*. Louisville: Westminster.

— 2008. *Reading the Hebrew Bible after the Shoah: Engaging Holocaust Theology.* Minneapolis: Fortress.

Sweet, R. F. G. 1986. 'Some Observations on the Edict of Ammiṣaduqa Prompted by Text C.' In Lawrence T. Geraty and Larry G. Herr (eds). *The Archaeology of Jordan and Other Studies.* Berrien Springs, MI: Andrews University: 579-600.

Tabuteau, Emily Zack. 1988. *Transfers of Property in Eleventh-Century Norman Law.* Chapel Hill: University of North Carolina: 95-112.

Tavares, Ricardo. 2007. *Eine königliche Weisheitslehre? Exegetische Analyse von Sprüche 28-29 und Vergleich mit den ägyptischen Lehren Merikaras und Amenemhats.* Fribourg: Academic Press.

Terzibaşoğlu, Y. 2005. 'Stuggles over Land and Population Movements in North-Western Anatolia, 1877–1914.' In M. Afifi *et al.* (eds). *Sociétés rurales ottomanes.* Cairo: IFAO: 297-308.

Thirsk, Joan and J. P. Cooper (eds). 1972. *Seventeenth Century Economic Documents.* Oxford: Clarendon.

Thompson, E. P. 1978. 'The Grid of Inheritance.' In J. Goody, J. Thirsk and E. P. Thompson (eds). *Family and Inheritance.* Cambridge: Cambridge University Press: 328-60.

Thompson, J. A. 1980. *The Book of Jeremiah.* Grand Rapids: Eerdmans.

Thompson, Kenneth. 1963. *Farm Fragmentation in Greece.* Athens: Serbinis.

Thür, G. 1997. 'Art. Daneion.' In Hubert Cancik, Helmuth Schneider und Manfred Landfester (eds). *Der Neue Pauly.* Stuttgart: Metzler: III, 309-10.

Turkanik, Andrzej S. 2008. *Of Kings and Reigns.* Tübingen: Mohr Siebeck.

Tute, R. C. 1927. *The Ottoman Land Laws, with a Commentary on the Ottoman Land Code of 7th Ramadan 1274.* Jerusalem: Greek Convent Press.

Uchitel, Alexander. 2005. 'Land-Tenure in Mycenaean Greece and the Hittite Empire: Linear B Land-Surveys from Pylos and Middle Hittite Land-Donations.' *Journal of the Economic and Social History of the Orient* 48: 473-86.

United Nations. 2005. 'Islam, Land and Property, Islamic Land Tenures and Reform.' In *United Nations Human Settlements Programme.* Nairobi: UN-HABITAT: paper 2.

Ussishkin, David. 2006. 'The Borders and "de facto" Size of Jerusalem in the Persian Period.' In O. Lipschits and M. Oeming (eds). *Judah and the Judeans in the Persian Period.* Winona Lake, IN: Eisenbrauns: 147-66.

Vall, Gregory. 1995. 'The Enigma of Job 1,21a.' *Biblica* 76: 325-42.

Van De Mieroop, Marc. 2002a. 'Credit as a Facilitator of Exchange in Old Babylonian Mesopotamia.' In M. Hudson and M. Van De Mieroop (eds). *Debt and Economic Renewal in the Ancient Near East.* Bethesda: CDL: 163-72.

— 2002b. 'A History of Near Eastern Debt.' In M. Hudson and M. Van De Mieroop (eds). *Debt and Economic Renewal in the Ancient Near East.* Bethesda: CDL: 59-94.

Van den Berghe, Pierre L. 1981. *The Ethnic Phenomenon.* New York: Elsevier.

Van der Spek, Robartus J. 1993. 'New Evidence on Seleucid Land Policy.' In F. J. A. M. Meijer and H. W. Pleket (eds). *De agricultura.* Amsterdam: Gieben: 61-77.

— 1995. 'Land Ownership in Babylonian Cuneiform Documents.' In M. J. Geller and H. Maehler (eds). *Legal Documents of the Hellenistic World.* London: Warburg Institute: 173-245.

Van Driel, G. 1998. 'Land in Ancient Mesopotamia.' In B. Haring and R. de Maaijer (eds). *Landless and Hungry.* Leiden: Research School CNWS: 19-49.

— 2002. *Elusive Silver.* Leiden: Nederlands Instituut voor het Nabije Oosten.

Van Leewen, M. 2000. *The Logic of Charity.* New York: St Martin's Press.

Van Wees, Hans. 2006. 'Mass and Elite in Solon's Athens.' In J. H. Blok and A. P. M. H. Lardinois (eds). *Solon of Athens: New Historical and Philological Approaches.* Leiden: Brill: 351-89.

Vargyas, Péter. 2000. 'Babylonian Interest Rates: Weren't they Annual?' In S. Graziani (ed.). *Studi sul Vicino Oriente Antico.* Napoli: Istituto Universitario Orientale: 1095-1105.

Vaughan, C. E. 1915. *The Political Writings of Jean Jacques Rousseau.* I. Cambridge: Cambridge University Press.

Veblen, Thorstein. 1899. *The Theory of the Leisure Class: an Economic Study of Institutions.* New York: Macmillan.

Velud, C. 2000. 'French Mandate Policy in the Syrian Steppe.' In M. Mundy and B. Musallam (eds). *The Transformation of Nomadic Society in the Arab East.* Cambridge: Cambridge University Press: 63-80.

Vesco, Jean-Luc. 2006. *Le Psautier de David.* Paris: Cerf.

Vermeylen, Jacques. 1994. 'Le méchant dans les discours des amis.' In W. A. M. Beuken (ed.). *The Book of Job.* Leuven: Leuven University Press: 101-28.

Villard, Pierre. 2007. 'L'*(an)durāru* à l'époque néo-assyrienne.' *Revue d'Assyriologie et d'Archéologie Orientale* 101: 107-23.

Vogels, W. 1994. 'Job's Empty Pious Slogans (Job 1,20-22; 2,8-10).' In W. A. Beuken (ed.). *The Book of Job.* Leuven: Leuven University Press: 369-76.

Von Rad, Gerhard. 1943. 'Verheissenes Land und Jahwes Land im Hexateuch.' *Zeitschrift des deutschen Palästina-Vereins* 66: 191-204.

— 1961. 'Das theologische Problem des alttestamentlichen Schöpfungsglaubens.' In idem (ed.). *Gesammelte Studien zum Alten Testament.* München: Kaiser: 136-47.

Von Reden, Sitta. 2001. 'The Politics of Monetization in Third-Century BC Egypt.' In A. Meadows and K. Shipton (eds). *Money and its Uses in the Greek World.* Oxford: Oxford University Press: 70-73.

Wagenaar, J. A. 2001. *Judgement and Salvation. The Composition and Redaction of Micah 2–5.* Leiden: Brill.

Wåhlin, Lars. 1988. 'Occurence of *musha'* in Transjordan.' *Geografiska Annaler* 70 B3: 375-79.

— 1994. 'Inheritance of Land in the Jordanian Hill Country. *British Journal of Middle Eastern Studies* 21: 57-84.

Warriner, Doreen. 1957. *Land Reform and Development in the Middle East.* London: Royal Institute of International Affairs.

— 1975. 'Land Tenure in the Fertile Crescent in the Nineteenth and Twentieth Centuries.' In Charles Issawi (ed.). *The Economic History of the Middle East 1800–1914.* Chicago: University of Chicago Press: 71-78.

Watts, James W. (ed.). 2001. *Persia and Torah: The Theory of Imperial Authorization of the Pentateuch.* Atlanta: SBL.

Watts, James W. 2007. *Ritual and Rhetoric in Leviticus.* Cambridge: Cambridge University Press.

Weber, Max. 1976. *The Agrarian Sociology of Ancient Civilization.* London: New Left.

Wehr, Hans. 1979. *A Dictionary of Modern Written Arabic.* Wiesbaden: Otto Harrassowitz.

Weinfeld, Moshe. 1995. *Social Justice in Ancient Israel and in the Ancient Near East.* Jerusalem: Magnes.

Weiser, Arthur. 1962. *The Psalms.* London: SCM Press.

Wenham, Gordon J. 1994. *Genesis 16–50.* Waco: Word Books.

Westbrook, Raymond. 1989. 'Cuneiform Law Codes and the Origin of Legislation.' *Zeitschrift für Assyriologie* 79: 201–22.

— 2005. 'Patronage in the Ancient Near East.' *Journal of the Economic and Social History of the Orient* 48: 210-33.

Westermann, Claus. 1985. *Genesis 12–36.* London: SPCK.

Weulersse, Jacques. 1946. *Paysans de Syrie et du Proche Orient.* Paris: Gallimard.

White, K. D. 1970. *Roman Farming.* London: Thames and Hudson.

Whitelam, Keith W. 1979. *Just King: Monarchical Judicial Authority in Ancient Israel.* Sheffield: JSOT Press.

Whittaker, Charles R. 1976. 'Agri Deserti.' In M. I. Finley (ed.). *Studies in Roman Property.* Cambridge: Cambridge University Press: 137-65.

— 1983. 'Late Roman Trade and Traders.' In P. Garnsey, K. Hopkins and C. R. Whittaker (eds). *Trade in the Ancient Economy.* London: Chatto & Windus: 163-80.

Whittaker, Charles R., and Peter Garnsey. 1998. 'Rural Life in the Later Roman Empire.' In A. Cameron and P. Garnsey (eds). *Cambridge Ancient History.* Cambridge: Cambridge University Press: XIII, 277-311.

Wiesehöfer, Josef. 1999. 'Kontinuität oder Zäsur? Babylon unter den Achämeniden.' In J. Renger (ed.). *Babylon: Focus mesopotamischer Geschichte, Wiege früher Gelehrsamkeit, Mythos in der Moderne.* Saarbrücken: SDV: 167-88.

Williams, Gary R. 2002. 'Contextual Influences in Readings of Nehemiah 5.' *Tyndale Bulletin* 53: 57-74.

Williams, Michael J. 2009. 'Taking Interest in Taking Interest (Deuteronomy 23:20-21).' In N. Sacher Fox, D. A. Glatt-Gilad and M. J. Williams (eds). *Mishneh Todah.* Winona Lake, IN: Eisenbrauns: 113-32.

Williamson, Hugh G. M. 1991. 'Jezreel in the Biblical Texts.' *Tel Aviv* 18: 72-92.

— 1999. 'Promises, Promises! Some Exegetical Reflections on Isaiah 58.' *Word and World* 19: 153-60.

Williamson, K. 1996. *The Poetical Works of Christopher Smart.* VI. Oxford: Clarendon.

Wilkinson, T. J. 1982. 'The Definition of Ancient Manuring Zones by Means of Extensive Sherd Sampling Techniques.' *Journal of Field Archaeology* 9: 323-33.

Wood, Bryant G. 2008. 'The Search for Joshua's Ai.' In R. S. Hess, G. A. Klingbeil and P. J. Ray, Jr (eds). *Critical Issues in Early Israelite History.* Winona Lake, IN: Eisenbrauns: 205-40.

Woodhouse, William John. 1938. *Solon the Liberator.* Oxford: Oxford University Press.

Wrigley, E. Anthony, and Roger S. Schofield. 1981. *The Population History of England.* London: Harvard University Press.

Wright, C. J. H. 1990. *God's People in God's Land.* Grand Rapids: Eerdmans.

Wunsch, Cornelia. 1999. 'The Egibi Family's Real Estate in Babylon (6th Century BC).' In M. Hudson and B.A. Levine (eds). *Urbanization and Land Ownership in the Ancient Near East*. Cambridge, MA: Peabody Museum of Archaeology and Ethnology: 391-420.

— 2002. 'Debt, Interest, Pledge and Forfeiture in the Neo-Babylonian and Early Achaemenid Period.' In M. Hudson and M. Van De Mieroop (eds). *Debt and Economic Renewal in the Ancient Near East*. Bethesda: CDL: 221-55.

— 2005. 'Women's Property and the Law of Inheritance in the Neo-Babylonian Period.' In R. Westbrook and D. Lyons (eds). *Women Property in Ancient Near Eastern and Mediteranean Societies*. Washington, DC: Center for Hellenic Studies. Electronic publication: www.chs.harvard.edu/publications.sec.

Yon, Marguerite. 2006. *The City of Ugarit at Tell Ras Shamra*. Winona Lake, IN: Eisenbrauns.

Zevit, Ziony. 2005. 'Dating Ruth.' *Zeitschrift für die alttestamentlische Wissenschaft* 117: 574-600.

— 2007. 'Text Traditions, Archaeology, and Anthropology: Uncertainties in Determining the Populations of Judah and Yehud from ca. 734 to ca. 400 BCE.' In S. White Crawford (ed.). *'Up to the Gates of Ekron.'* Jerusalem: Israel Exploration Society: 436-43.

Zimmermann, R. 1996. *The Law of Obligations Mutuum*. Oxford: Clarendon.

Zwickel, Wolfgang. 1999. 'Die Wirtschaftsreform des Hiskia und die Sozialkritik der Propheten des 8. Jahrhunderts.' *Evangelische Theologie* 59: 356-77.

Index of Biblical References

Index of Authors

Index of Subjects

For Product Safety Concerns and Information please contact our EU
representative GPSR@taylorandfrancis.com
Taylor & Francis Verlag GmbH, Kaufingerstraße 24, 80331 München, Germany

www.ingramcontent.com/pod-product-compliance
Lightning Source LLC
LaVergne TN
LVHW011116300926
849160LV00008B/407
9781845539283